The Art, Humor, and Humanity
of Mark Twain

Underwood and Underwood

Samuel L. Clemens (Mark Twain) about 1907.

THE ART
HUMOR
AND HUMANITY OF

MARK TWAIN

Edited, with Commentary and Notes, by
MINNIE M. BRASHEAR
and ROBERT M. RODNEY

With an Introduction by
EDWARD WAGENKNECHT

NORMAN : UNIVERSITY OF OKLAHOMA PRESS

ACKNOWLEDGMENT is hereby made for permission most generously given by Harper and Brothers, publishers, to quote from the following published works by Mark Twain:

The uniform edition of Mark Twain's works, which comprises twenty-five volumes (1899–1910) and includes the following: *The American Claimant and Other Stories* (© 1892 by C. L. Webster and Company); *Personal Recollections of Joan of Arc* (© 1896 by Harper and Brothers); *The $30,000 Bequest and Other Stories* (© 1906 by Harper and Brothers); *Tom Sawyer Abroad* (© 1894 by C. S. Webster and Company); *Tom Sawyer, Detective, and Other Stories* (© 1896 by Harper and Brothers).

Also *Europe and Elsewhere* (© 1923 by Harper and Brothers); *Mark Twain's Autobiography* (© 1924 by Harper and Brothers); *Mark Twain in Eruption* (© 1940 by Harper and Brothers); *Mark Twain's Letters* (© 1917 by Harper and Brothers); *Mark Twain's Notebook* (© 1935 by Harper and Brothers); *Mark Twain's Speeches* (© 1929 by Harper and Brothers); *The Mysterious Stranger and Other Stories* (© 1922 by Harper and Brothers); *What Is Man? and Other Essays* (© 1917 by Harper and Brothers); and from Albert Bigelow Paine's *Mark Twain: A Biography* (© 1912 by Harper and Brothers), 3 vols.

Library of Congress Catalog Card Number 59–7962

ISBN 978-0-8061-4331-6 (paper)

Copyright 1959 by the University of Oklahoma Press, Publishing Division of the University. Composed and printed at Norman, Oklahoma, U.S.A., by the University of Oklahoma Press. First edition. Paperback published 2012.

All rights reserved. No part of this publication may be reproduced, stored in a retrieval system, or transmitted, in any form or by any means, electronic, mechanical, photocopying, recording, or otherwise—except as permitted under Section 107 or 108 of the United States Copyright Act—without the prior permission of the University of Oklahoma Press.

To the wise
and the young at heart—of all ages

Introduction

By EDWARD WAGENKNECHT

"A POET," said Keats, "is the most unpoetical of anything in existence, because he has no identity—he is continually in, for, and filling some other body." But Walt Whitman scribbled his dissent in the margin: "The great poet absorbs the identity of and the experience of others, and they are definite in him or from him; but he perceives them all through the powerful press of himself."

It would be impossible to indicate more clearly the difference between the kind of writer who projects himself into persons and experiences outside of himself and the kind of writer who creates by dramatizing his own personality. The one loses himself in his creation; the other keeps himself in the foreground of his picture and insists upon being personally important to his readers. In reading *Leaves of Grass*, one is always, as it were, in Whitman's own presence; this makes for a wonderful vividness but it also means that the reader's response to the writer's art will be powerfully conditioned by whether or not he happens to like his personality.

There is, of course, no absolute line of demarcation to be drawn in such matters, nor can one always be sure that the man and the artist and his purpose will be all of a piece. Shakespeare seems to have written with no sense of mission urging him on; one might, therefore, expect the personal elements to be larger in his world than in that of Milton, who wrote *Paradise Lost* "to justify the ways of God to men," or in that of Dante, who expounded in *The Divine Comedy* the conditions under which men must lose or find their souls. Yet as a matter of fact Shakespeare loses himself in his world, almost selflessly, while both Dante and Milton cannot or will not do anything of the kind. The Ultimate Beatitude and the

Scheme of Salvation reach us only as they are filtered through these particular personalities.

Other things being equal, one would suppose the Shakespeare type of imagination to be the higher and the more powerful, but with such giants as Dante and Milton in the other camp, it is not wise to dogmatize. We all know the self-dramatizing young artist who is able to write a novel or two based upon his own experience but who, once his memories have been exhausted, must either subside into silence or go on tying new ribbons on his old puppets to the end of his life. That is why, among other things, the autobiographical writer is often quite contemptuous toward the historical novelist, for instance; he could not vitalize materials foreign to himself; how, then, can he believe that anybody else could do so?

Whatever one's personal preferences in the matter may be, there will probably be general agreement that unless the self-dramatizing personality is a large personality and an attractive one, it will always be a deadly bore. Whitman himself said *Leaves of Grass* was "an attempt . . . to put a *Person,* a human being (myself, in the latter half of the Nineteenth Century, in America), freely, fully, and truly on record." In himself he intended to show humanity; in his own experiences he planned to reveal the life of his time. His success, though not absolute, was large; had he been a lesser man, his work would have been forgotten along with the weight of a great accumulation of vaporings and maunderings under which the world groans.

For all that, there are many of us who find a larger grandeur in the personality of another nineteenth-century writer of the Whitman (not Keats) type; I mean, of course, Mark Twain. What great writer has ever been more emphatically personally present in the reader's imagination than he? He wrote one of the greatest half-dozen books ever written in this country, yet we all tend to think of him as greater personally than anything he wrote. He also (let us be frank) wrote a great deal that was obviously second- or third-rate. But even this rarely fails to hold our interest because of the strong solution of himself that he has done up in the broth.

It seems very odd, then, that the book he himself called his autobiography should have recently been described as the most exasperating book in American literature. One might have supposed that he was foreordained from before the foundation of the world to write the greatest autobiography that has ever been written. He did not do so. In composing the shapeless monster he called his autobiography, he dedicated himself to literary chaos. Rejecting both a chronological and a topical method of organization, he dictated as the spirit moved him on any phase or aspect of his life that came into his head, imposing upon his literary executor the duty of printing his dictations in the order in which he made them. In the two volumes of extracts he printed in 1924, Albert Bigelow Paine was faithful to the master's wishes. In 1940, Bernard De Voto added a third volume of materials arranged topically. The year 1959 has seen the publication of a new edition edited by Charles Neider in which all the material included is rearranged chronologically so as to give, so far as possible, a systematic account of Mark Twain's life.

The results of Mr. Neider's labors, though far from perfect, do give us a much better idea of the sequence and relationship of Mark Twain's life experiences than the *Autobiography* has ever communicated before. But in the book you hold in your hands Miss Brashear and Mr. Rodney have remembered a very important fact which Mr. Neider did not remember, or which (it would be fairer to say) the particular task to which he dedicated himself did not permit him to remember. They have remembered that the whole vast body of Mark Twain's writings are autobiographical; they have chosen their contents accordingly from a vaster and aesthetically more impressive array of materials than Mr. Neider could command.

This is the kind of book that could only have been edited by people who really knew Mark Twain and his work. Our editors did not conceive the idea that a volume of selections from Mark Twain might be commercially profitable, after which they set to work to find the necessary material to fill it up. That, dear reader, in case you do not know it, is the way a good many anthologies are put together; this is not one of them. Miss Brashear is the author of perhaps the earliest really scholarly book about Mark Twain—*Mark Twain, Son of Missouri* (University of North Carolina Press, 1934). It is still one of the best; I am glad to avow my own debt to it. She and Mr. Rodney had no need to search for materials; they knew where they were. It was only a question of how much they could get in and what would be the best way to arrange them so as to share with others, perhaps the Mark Twain scholars of the future among them, their own knowledge of and love for this remarkable man whom his country needs so much as it seems to drift farther and farther away from his ideals.

Fascinating as Mark Twain the man is, our editors have never permitted themselves to forget that he was also a writer, or, as I have already indicated, that he wrote his life as well as lived it. Even those who have worked with Mark Twain's autobiography in the narrower sense have realized this. It has been said that Mark Twain had a bad memory. He did not. He had the very best kind of memory, a creative memory, and it operated very impressively upon the stuff of his own experience. That kind of a memory makes for great literature but it does not make for accuracy in factual writing, and Mark himself observed that as he grew older he tended to remember only the things that had never happened. It should not surprise anybody, for example, that Brashear and Rodney have drawn upon *The Prince and the Pauper* as well as upon Mark's factual writings to tell us what he thought about England and more particularly how he felt about her. "An imaginative experience," says Walter de la Mare, "is not only as real but far realer than an unimaginative one."

The extracts from *The Prince and the Pauper* are in what I may call the autobiographical part of this book, though I am not sure that the editors have thought about their divisions in quite this way. At any rate there is a shift of emphasis in the second half, where the reader is asked to center his attention upon Mark Twain's works rather than upon Mark Twain. Only, for the very reasons which I have already somewhat tiresomely adumbrated, no hard-and-fast line can be drawn between the two, and this is right, for there was no such line in his life.

I hope the readers who first meet Mark Twain in this expertly guided tour will know how lucky they are. Speaking for myself, I envy them.

Boston University
February 10, 1959

Contents

Introduction, by Edward Wagenknecht   vii
Preface   xvii
Tributes and Estimates   xxi

PART I. MARK TWAIN, MASTER STORYTELLER AND DESCRIPTIVE ARTIST   3

1. Missouri Boyhood   7
    Life in Rural Missouri   8
    Spring Fever   17
    Pandemonium in Church   18
    The Cat and the Pain-Killer   24
    The Circus   27
    River Valley Culture   30
    The Ice-Storm   35
    The Camp Meeting   37
    Nicodemus Dodge from Old Shelby   38
    The Minstrel Show   42

2. The River   46
    Steamboat A-Comin'!   47
    Just Solid Lonesomeness   49
    The Corpse-Maker and the Child of Calamity   52
    The River Palace   56
    Disillusionment   58
    A Lightning Pilot   60
    The Lesson   64
    An Arkansas Plantation   68

River Town	69
Colonel Sherburn and the Mob	71

3. **The West** — 78

Overland Stage	79
The Jack Rabbit	82
The Coyote	83
Pony Express	86
The Desert—A Harsh Reality	88
South Pass	90
Lake Tahoe	92
The Genuine Mexican Plug	93
Portrait of a Desperado	97
Buck Fanshaw's Funeral	99
Jim Baker's Bluejay Yarn	105

4. **The Magic Land** — 110

"Incomparable" England	111
An English Journey	111
A Naval Salute	113
A Dover Spectacle	115
Dreams of Splendor	117
A Prince in a Palace	119
The River Pageant	121
At Guildhall	122
The Royal Bedchamber	125
A State Dinner	127
The Recognition Procession	130
Coronation Day	131

5. **The World Outside** — 136

Lake Como	138
Milan—A Poem in Marble	140
Naples	143
Mount Vesuvius	146
Athens by Moonlight	149
Funchal	150
Jeypore	151

CONTENTS

Recipes	153
Woman's Work on the Continent	154
Civita Vecchia	154
The Arno	155
The Arabs of Jezreel	156
Mark Twain at the Opera	157
The Great French Duel	159
Aix-les-Bains	169
The Syrian Camel's Appetite	171
Ants' Antics	172
The Chameleon	177

PART II. MARK TWAIN, MISSOURI HUMORIST — 179

  1. Early Humor in Missouri — 181

  2. Mark Twain's Development as a Humorist — 186

The Dandy Frightening the Squatter	194
The Celebrated Jumping Frog of Calaveras County	197
To Raise Poultry	204
Speech on the Babies	207
The Private History of a Campaign That Failed	211
The Recent Carnival of Crime in Connecticut	230
A Scrap of Curious History	246
The Man That Corrupted Hadleyburg	254
A Connecticut Yankee in King Arthur's Court	304
The Mysterious Stranger	365

  3. The American Prometheus — 387

PART III. MARK TWAIN, EPIGRAMMATIST — 393

Chronology of Mark Twain's Life and Literary Career — 404
Selected Bibliography — 411
Index — 419

Illustrations

Samuel L. Clemens about 1907	*frontispiece*
Tom Sawyer and Huck Finn	*facing page* 40
Mark Twain as a young man	41
"Wooding up" on the Mississippi	72
Sam Clemens' pilot's license	73
The Jumping Frog	264
The cottage at Tuxedo Park	265
Doctor of Literature from Oxford	296
Working in bed	297

Preface

Who was Mark Twain? If asked this question,, the average teen-ager today would probably recall a Missouri writer who authored a boy's book about Tom Sawyer and another about Huckleberry Finn. He might also remember something about a jumping frog ("I haven't read it, but I understand it is a funny story"). In response to the same question the average adult who has had the advantage of a college education and possibly a course in American literature might conjure up (such is the magic of names) an image of river-boat piloting or a few other random scenes of early life on the Mississippi. Probably he would also think of an anachronistic Yankee modernizing King Arthur's England (the movies and a musical comedy might help him to this recall). And if his literary curiosity has led him to explore a little further, he might even recount something of a story he once read about a stranger who corrupted Hadleyburg—or was it that peculiar story called "The Mysterious Stranger" ("something supernatural, and rather pessimistic, not at all like Mark Twain, who was supposed to be a humorist, as I remember").

What was Mark Twain? If one consults the literary historians, the biographers, and the critics of the last half-century, one can find interpretations enough to satisfy almost any reader's predilection. Depending upon one's authority or source of information, Mark Twain was a professional humorist, a satirist, a social historian, a literary artist, a divine amateur, a frustrated genius, a great personality, a national celebrity, a legend, a spokesman of western democracy, a champion of the common man, the American prototype, a great cosmopolitan, a humanitarian, a philosopher, an incurable romantic, a dejected realist, or (today) simply the forgotten man. Such epithets afford the reader a necessary perspective and certain valuable perceptions, but singly and even collectively they characterize Mark Twain with only partial truth. The question still remains: What, essentially, was Mark Twain? The present editors believe that a close examination of the man's life and the reading of a representative cross section of his work will reveal that Mark Twain was essentially a fine literary artist, within the limitations of certain literary media; that he was a great humorist, in the profoundest sense of that word; and that he was a shrewd observer of life and human nature and a provocative commentator on what Balzac called "the human comedy," but which Mark Twain, with greater compassion, chose to call "the damned human race." Above all, the editors feel that Mark Twain and his writings are a vital part of the American experience, an experience that the present generation cannot afford to overlook if we are to preserve our sense of the American past. Putting aside the biographers, the critics, and the interpreters after giving them due consideration, the average reader must, as a final resort, decide for himself the meaning of that experience. This he can always do by going directly to Mark Twain himself and sharing that experience with him.

The primary purpose of this book is to introduce Mark Twain to a new generation of readers, and to renew the acquaintance of older readers with much that they may have enjoyed but forgotten from their reading of earlier days. To the critics and other editors is left the satisfaction of speculating about what Mark Twain might have been and what he might have accomplished if he had had a more conventional education, or if he had enjoyed a different *milieu*.

In the first part of the book the general reader is offered selections from all of Mark Twain's better-known works, together with extracts and short pieces from many of his less-well-known writings. The editors believe that these selections will persuade the reader to accept the Missouri writer as something more than a mere humorist. The second part is a brief survey of Mark Twain's contribution to the field of humor and an attempt to account for the Missouri origins of his humor. Following the shorter selections that exemplify Mark Twain's early humor, the editors offer "The Man That Corrupted Hadleyburg" and portions of *A Connecticut Yankee in King Arthur's Court* to demonstrate the transition from his earlier, more optimistic view of life to his later pessimism. Finally, selections from *The Mysterious Stranger* are intended to show the sardonic vein, the full expression of the humorist's despair over the plight of the human race. Underlying all of these writings, it is hoped, the reader will discern Mark Twain's essential humanity. If these pages enable the reader to enter Mark Twain's world and discover that its creator contributed something significant not only to Americana but to world literature itself, this book will have served its purpose.

    The editors wish to take this opportunity to express their appreciation to Harper and Brothers for permission, elsewhere acknowledged, to print the many selections from Mark Twain which have made this presentation possible.

Minnie M. Brashear
Robert M. Rodney

February 16, 1959

Tributes and Estimates

If BOOK SALES FIGURES and library withdrawal slips are any evidence, no American writer has been read more widely, both at home and abroad, than Mark Twain. With the exception of Benjamin Franklin, no American has been quoted more often by his fellow countrymen. And what is perhaps most significant from a purely literary point of view, no American writer has earned more enthusiastic tributes from both the critics and his fellow writers of the English-speaking world than Mark Twain. His acceptance has not been unanimous, of course, especially among the intellectuals; and as a personality he has been the subject of widely divergent interpretations. Whatever the disagreements among his critics, Mark Twain has lasted and has worn well for the general reader during a whole century of changing outlooks and literary tastes. Even the "humor" which pervades all his writings has proved its staying power, because his readers have discovered it to be of an exceptionally integrated kind, closely interwoven with his whole view of life, and loaded with serious implications. Whatever his many commentators have discovered in Mark Twain, most of them have been in agreement on one vital fact: everything about Mark Twain was grounded in his essential humanity. A perception of this "human" quality underlies the appraisals of all the outstanding writers and critics who have paid tribute to him. As early as 1883, Thomas Hardy, so utterly different from Mark Twain in background and temperament, remarked to William Dean Howells: "Mark Twain is not merely a great humorist. He is a very remarkable fellow in a very different way."[1] George Bernard Shaw pronounced

[1] Albert Bigelow Paine, *Mark Twain: A Biography*, II, 747.

him "by far the greatest American writer,"[2] while G. K. Chesterton saw in him "a great [Yankee] rustic."[3] To Arnold Bennett, Mark Twain was "always a divine amateur."[4] Even George M. Trevelyan, who had a much greater respect for historical truth than Mark Twain, asserted that "Mark Twain did more than any other man to make plain people in England understand plain people in America."[5] These professional opinions have been reflected by the British press consistently since 1910. The London *Times* had already entitled Mark Twain "Ambassador at large of the U.S.A." in 1899.[6] The London *Spectator* in 1912 characterized Mark Twain as a "flashing, generous, blasphemous, dejected, buoyant, and humorous genius."[7] Eight years later the *London Mercury* gave him this tribute: "Lincoln, Mark Twain, Walt Whitman! We should be hard put to find such a three in that granite grain."[8] During the half-century since his death, Mark Twain has won increasing recognition as a major literary figure. This recognition has come from a great variety of critics:

Archibald Henderson: "If one would lay his finger on the secret of Mark Twain's world-wide popularity as a humorist, he must find that secret primarily in the universality and the humanity of his humor .... Mark Twain ... is America's greatest cosmopolitan."[9]

Rudyard Kipling: "To my mind Mark Twain was beyond question the largest man of his time, both in the direct outcome of his work, and more important still, if possible, in his influence as a protesting force in an age of iron philistinism."[10]

Carl Van Doren: "He spoke in the American idiom as regards the usurping despots of the earth, the rights of the natural man, the superiority of republics to monarchies, the advantages of material

[2] *Harper's Weekly,* July 20, 1907.
[3] *The Bookman* (London), June, 1910.
[4] *Overland Monthly,* April, 1929.
[5] *Ibid.*
[6] May 23, 1899.
[7] October 12, 1912.
[8] December, 1920.
[9] *Harper's Monthly Magazine,* May, 1909.
[10] *Literary Digest,* April 20, 1935.

well-being, the hope that through individual freedom and public education the human mass might be advanced to a plane never yet reached."[11]

Fred Lewis Pattee: "He will live. Already has he become an American myth, already is he one of the most compelling of all our American characters, a man to class, so far as popular judgment is concerned, with Washington and Lincoln. He made the common people laugh. Who in all the history of literature has done more?"[12]

Ernest Hemingway: "All modern American Literature comes from one book by Mark Twain called *Huckleberry Finn.* . . . It's the best book we've had. All American writing comes from that. There was nothing before. There has been nothing as good since."[13]

Bernard De Voto: "More widely and deeply than any one else who ever wrote books, he shared the life of America. Printer, pilot, soldier, silver miner, gold-washer, the child of two emigrations, a pilgrim in another, a sharer in the flush times, a shaper of the gilded age—he, more completely than any other writer, took part in the American experience. . . . Whatever else this frontier humorist did, whatever he failed to do, this much he did. He wrote books that have in them something eternally true to the core of his nation's life. They are at the center; all other books whatsoever are farther away."[14]

Stephen Leacock: "I have always looked upon Mark Twain as the greatest literary figure America has seen, and the most truly American . . . . More than that, Mark Twain, by the spirit that animates all his books—his hatred of tyranny and injustice, his sympathy with the oppressed individual—did more than any other writer toward making the idea of liberty a part of the American heritage."[15]

Lionel Trilling: "Out of his knowledge of the actual speech of Amer-

[11] *The American Novel*, 184.
[12] *Mark Twain: Representative Selections*, lii.
[13] *The Green Hills of Africa* (New York, Charles Scribner's Sons, 1935), 22.
[14] *Mark Twain's America*, 321.
[15] Letter to George Ade, June 2, 1941, on the occasion of the founding of the Mark Twain Association of America, published in *The Twainian*, April, 1945.

ica Mark Twain forged a classic prose .... Forget the misspellings and the faults of grammar [of *Huckleberry Finn*], and the prose will be seen to move with the greatest simplicity, directness, lucidity, and grace .... Indeed, it may be said that almost every contemporary American writer who deals conscientiously with the problems and possibility of prose must feel, directly or indirectly, the influence of Mark Twain. He is the master of the style that escapes the fixity of the printed page, that sounds in our ears with the immediacy of the heard voice, the very voice of unpretentious youth."[16]

T. S. Eliot: "There is no more solitary character in fiction [than Mark Twain's Huckleberry Finn] .... We come to see Huck himself in the end as one of the permanent symbolic figures of fiction; not unworthy to take a place with Ulysses, Faust, Don Quixote, Don Juan, Hamlet and other great discoveries that man has made of himself."[17]

[16] *The Liberal Imagination: Essays on Literature and Society*, 117.
[17] Introduction to *The Adventures of Huckleberry Finn*, x.

The Art, Humor, and Humanity
of Mark Twain

I was the champion of hard unsentimental common sense and reason. I was entering the lists to either destroy knight errantry or be its victim.—Mark Twain, *A Connecticut Yankee*

For your race, in its poverty, has unquestionably one really effective weapon—laughter. . . . Against the assault of laughter nothing can stand.—Mark Twain, *The Mysterious Stranger*

PART I

Mark Twain, Master Storyteller and Descriptive Artist

MARK TWAIN, MASTER STORYTELLER AND DESCRIPTIVE ARTIST

MARK TWAIN was many things during his long life: journeyman printer, river-boat pilot, silver miner, newspaper reporter, editor, author, lecturer, traveler, publisher, and businessman. None of these vocations sufficiently describes him, nor do all of them put together give us a true understanding of the writer. Even the term "humorist," popularly applied to him by his own and succeeding generations, fails to identify him, because it does not reveal to the average reader the other more serious facets of Mark Twain's personality, and especially the underlying sensitivities of his nature that made him so much more than a mere humorist in the popular sense of that word. Looking beneath the surface geniality of the man, one discovers in Mark Twain a remarkable memory, a strong imagination, keen powers of observation, shrewd judgment of human nature, a strict and often tormenting conscience, and—what is perhaps most important for literary purposes —a hypersensitivity to the whole world around him. It was this hypersensitivity that, probably more than anything else, turned Mark Twain's literary talents in the direction of much fine descriptive and narrative prose. Many of his stories achieve a pathos, and many of his descriptions a reality, that humor by itself cannot reach. And his writing often rose to such an emotional intensity and crystallized into such vivid images that much of it must be called poetic.

As an author, Mark Twain lived largely in the past. The indelible impressions of his boyhood and young manhood were the materials from which he created his most poignant passages. In the opinion of many critics, books like *Life on the Mississippi* and *Huckleberry Finn* evoke a nostalgia for the American past unsurpassed by that of any other American writing.[1] Even when in later life he was busiest recording his travels and contemporary events, Mark Twain could never resist digressing from his immediate theme to describe a scene or relate an incident recalled from his years in the Mississippi Valley or in the Far West of America. The experiences of those earlier years, etched so sharply in the mind of the middle-aged and elderly Mark Twain, shaped the mind of young Samuel Clemens. The boy's responses to the sensuous world of the village streets, the farm, and the countryside; the young man's sensitive appreciation of the great river in all of its moods, his absorption of the Great West, his exhilaration from the color and movement of humanity in the great cities—all went into his stories and heightened both his descriptive and narrative art.[2] Keen as were his powers of observation, Mark Twain never took a mere bystander's view of life and the world: he felt such a strong affinity with all of humanity that he was receptive of all experience, and absorbed into his mind a multitude of impressions that later found emotional release through his writing. Those early experiences and impressions formed his attitudes and his general outlook on life, and they provided the matrix for all of Mark Twain's literary work.[3]

[1] In his incisive critique of *Huckleberry Finn,* Lionel Trilling appraises Mark Twain's Mississippi novel as "one of the world's great books and one of the central documents of American culture" because of its formative influence on all subsequent American prose writing (*The Liberal Imagination: Essays on Literature and Society,* 105). "There is no greater book in American literature," says Bernard De Voto of *Huckleberry Finn.* De Voto impressively argues the thesis that " 'Old Times on the Mississippi' is a study in pure ecstasy," and that *Tom Sawyer* "is wrought out of beauty and nostalgia" (Introduction to *The Portable Mark Twain,* 10ff.). Fred Lewis Pattee, who is not ready by any means to accept all of Mark Twain's work, testifies to the enduring appeal of the books with the Mississippi background: "As the years go by his masterpieces can be reduced to those half dozen volumes dealing with what may be called the great American romance, those volumes poured out of himself without thought that they were literature, those volumes spontaneously done without model or predecessor, the richest of them *Huckleberry Finn, Life on the Mississippi,* and the first eleven chapters of *The Gilded Age*" (Introduction to *Mark Twain: Representative Selections,* lii). T. S. Eliot, himself a native of the great river valley, acknowledges the evocative power of *Huckleberry Finn* (Introduction to *Huckleberry Finn*).

[2] The evolution of Samuel Clemens into Mark Twain the professional writer is ably set forth in two recent studies: Gladys C. Bellamy, *Mark Twain as a Literary Artist,* and Edgar M. Branch, *The Literary Apprenticeship of Mark Twain.* For the many earlier studies of Mark Twain's development of his literary craftsmanship, the reader is referred to the bibliography at the end of this book.

[3] For a graphic presentation of the world of Mark Twain's youth and its psychological impact on the mature writer, the reader should see Bernard De Voto, *Mark Twain's America.*

This matrix can best be understood and appreciated by a look into the several worlds of Mark Twain: the world of rural and small-town Missouri during the 1830's and 1840's; the world of the great Mississippi Valley during the 1850's; the world of the far western frontier during the 1860's; and finally two realms of the world outside America: England, his land of enchantment,[4] and Europe and the Near and Far East, his realms of disillusionment. No one has left a more vivid and authentic picture of these various worlds of Mark Twain than that writer himself, so that the reader can explore them through the eyes of a great descriptive artist and humorous narrator.

1. Missouri Boyhood

By MODERN STANDARDS, the village of Florida, Missouri, where Samuel Clemens was born, was hardly more than a crossroads settlement—without the crossroads. Its population totaled about 100 people in 1835. Even Hannibal, Missouri, where Sam's father took his wife and five children four years later, was a river-front village of only 450 people in 1839. But unlike Florida, whose expectations of becoming a great trading center and port at the head of the Salt River, were never fulfilled, Hannibal was growing rapidly with its small industries and its river trade. It took real civic pride not only in its rising commercial importance, but also in its cultural aspirations in the form of churches, schools, newspapers, libraries, and societies of all kinds.[1] Its location on the Mississippi River, the greatest highway in the country at that time, kept Hannibal in contact with the outside world; and there was a feeling of

[4] Mark Twain's response to England is the subject of a special study by Robert M. Rodney, "Mark Twain in England . . . ."
[1] Full and authentic accounts of pre–Civil War Hannibal have become available through the painstaking investigations of M. M. Brashear, *Mark Twain, Son of Missouri*, and Dixon Wecter, *Sam Clemens of Hannibal*. The larger matrix of the Mississippi Valley of the 1840's and 1850's is described in De Voto's *Mark Twain's America*.

expectancy in the air during those three decades before the Civil War, the era of Manifest Destiny and the great Westward Movement, that was felt by the folk of Hannibal as well as the people of the larger cities to the east. If the men and boys of Hannibal could not participate as directly as they would like in the great adventure taking place in other parts of America, they could at least always look up or down the river from their doorstep and tell themselves that the doorway into that glorious world was somewhere around the river's bend—St. Louis, St. Joseph, Independence, New Orleans, Memphis, Cincinnati, and a hundred other possible points of departure.

In this small-town atmosphere of growth and expectation Sam Clemens lived for fourteen years of his boyhood before he set out to explore the world and seek his fortune. These fourteen years were also spent very close to nature, for with the river and the bluffs and the woods and prairies only a few minutes' walk from the village, no normal boy could resist the lure of the open country or fail to find many opportunities to throw off the constraints of the home, the schoolroom, and the church. A boy's life in Mark Twain's Hannibal could be just as sensuous as that of a farm boy.

In fact, a farm played a very large part in Sam Clemens' life. Like most nineteenth-century children, young Sam had relatives living in the country. His Uncle John Quarles brought up a large family on a farm near Florida, and it was on this farm, with his many cousins and his kindly uncle and aunt, that Sam spent some of the happiest weeks of each year. The boy found temporary escapes and diversion enough in Hannibal, but on the Quarles farm he enjoyed complete liberation. His impressions of this farm life are his most poignant because they were probably his earliest and most sensuous. Almost half a century after he had left Hannibal, Mark Twain wrote a delectable description of some of those rural experiences:

LIFE IN RURAL MISSOURI (from *Mark Twain's Autobiography*[2])

« « « It was a heavenly place for a boy, that farm of my Uncle

[2] *Mark Twain's Autobiography* should not be confused with the amorphous and

John's. The house was a double log one, with a spacious floor (roofed in) connecting it with the kitchen. In the summer the table was set in the middle of that shady and breezy floor, and the sumptuous meals—well, it makes me cry to think of them. Fried chicken, roast pig; wild and tame turkeys, ducks, and geese; venison just killed; squirrels, rabbits, pheasants, partridges, prairie-chickens; biscuits, hot batter cakes, hot buckwheat cakes, hot "wheat bread," hot rolls, hot corn pone; fresh corn boiled on the ear, succotash, butter-beans, string-beans, tomatoes, peas, Irish potatoes, sweet potatoes; butter milk, sweet milk, "clabber;" watermelons, muskmelons, cantaloupes —all fresh from the garden; apple pie, peach pie, pumpkin pie, apple dumplings, peach cobbler—I can't remember the rest. The way that the things were cooked was perhaps the main splendor—particularly a certain few of the dishes. For instance, the corn bread, the hot biscuits and wheat bread, and the fried chicken. . . .[3]

The farmhouse stood in the middle of a very large yard; and the yard was fenced on three sides with rails and on the rear side

purely burlesque sketch that he published in 1871 entitled *Autobiography and First Romance*. Nor should the reader expect to find Mark Twain writing his true account of himself with any conformity to conventional "autobiography." He began in 1870 to record random notes, reminiscences, and sketches of his earlier years, to which he added sporadically for over three decades. Most of the real *Autobiography* was written from recollection rather than notes. After the death of Mrs. Clemens and his return from Italy in 1904, Mark Twain permitted certain portions of his autobiography to be published in *Harper's Weekly* and *The North American Review* in 1904 and again in 1906-1907. The remainder of his reminiscences he dictated to Albert Bigelow Paine during the years 1906-1908. The *Autobiography* was not published in its final form until 1924, fourteen years after Mark Twain's death. Although Mark Twain himself admitted that his account of his life followed an "apparently systemless system," one which is "a complete and purposed jumble" (*Autobiography*, II, 246), much of this book achieves a literary level equal to his best writing in his Mississippi stories. The passage on life in rural Missouri, written in 1897 when Mark Twain was past sixty, is infused with the same exhilaration and nostalgia that animate *Tom Sawyer, Life on the Mississippi,* and *Huckleberry Finn*, written when Mark Twain was ten to twenty years younger. The reader is urged to explore further into the *Autobiography*, not so much for a factual account of its author's life as for the psychological reality that informs all of his reminiscences.

[3] This description of the Quarles family dinner table has many precedents in American literature, notably Washington Irving's description of the bountiful Van Tassel farmhouse and Ichabod Crane's gastronomic visions in "The Legend of Sleepy Hollow." The reader will recall parallel descriptions in such other earlier writers as Joel Barlow, James Fenimore Cooper, and Charles Dickens. An interesting example of Mark Twain's ability to describe a sharply contrasting scene can be found in his account of Colonel Sellers' turnip dinner in *The Gilded Age*, I, Chap. 11.

with high palings; against these stood the smoke-house; beyond the palings was the orchard; beyond the orchard were the negro quarters and the tobacco fields. The front yard was entered over a stile made of sawed-off logs of graduated heights; I do not remember any gate. In a corner of the front yard were a dozen lofty hickory trees and a dozen black walnuts, and in the nutting season riches were to be gathered there.

Down a piece, abreast the house, stood a little log cabin against the rail fence; and there the woody hill fell sharply away, past the barns, the corn-crib, the stables, and the tobacco-curing house, to a limpid brook which sang along over its gravelly bed and curved and frisked in and out and here and there and yonder in the deep shade of overhanging foliage and vines—a divine place for wading, and it had swimming pools, too, which were forbidden to us and therefore much frequented by us. For we were little Christian children and had early been taught the value of forbidden fruit.[4]

In the little log cabin lived a bedridden white-headed slave woman whom we visited daily and looked upon with awe, for we believed she was upward of a thousand years old and had talked with Moses. The younger negroes credited these statistics and had furnished them to us in good faith. We accommodated all the details which came to us about her; and so we believed that she had lost her health in the long desert trip coming out of Egypt, and had never been able to get it back again. She had a round bald place on the crown of her head, and we used to creep around and gaze at it in reverent silence, and reflect that it was caused by fright through seeing Pharaoh drowned. We called her "Aunt" Hannah, Southern fashion. She was superstitious, like the other negroes; also, like them, she was deeply religious. Like them, she had great faith in prayer and employed it in all ordinary exigencies, but not in cases where a dead certainty of result was urgent. Whenever witches were around she tied up the remnant of her wool in little tufts, with white thread, and this promptly made the witches impotent. . . .[5]

---

[4] Mark Twain's picture of his Uncle John Quarles' Missouri farm in the *Autobiography* is almost identical in its details with Huck Finn's description of the Phelps's "one-horse cotton plantation" in Arkansas as Huck comes to the last episode of his adventures (see Section 2, "The River," in this book).

[5] For other Mark Twain portrayals of Negro women the reader is referred to

LIFE IN RURAL MISSOURI

I can see the farm yet, with perfect clearness. I can see all its belongings, all its details; the family room of the house, with a "trundle" bed in one corner and a spinning-wheel in another—a wheel whose rising and falling wail, heard from a distance, was the mournfulest of all sounds to me, and made me homesick and low spirited, and filled my atmosphere with the wandering spirits of the dead; the vast fireplace, piled high, on winter nights, with flaming hickory logs from whose ends a sugary sap bubbled out, but did not go to waste, for we scraped it off and ate it; the lazy cat spread out on the rough hearthstones; the drowsy dogs braced against the jambs and blinking; my aunt in one chimney corner, knitting; my uncle in the other, smoking his corn-cob pipe; the slick and carpetless oak floor faintly mirroring the dancing flame tongues and freckled with black indentations where fire coals had popped out and died a leisurely death; half a dozen children romping in the background twilight; "split"-bottomed chairs here and there, some with rockers; a cradle—out of service, but waiting, with confidence; in the early cold mornings a snuggle of children, in shirts and chemises, occupying the hearthstone and procrastinating—they could not bear to leave that comfortable place and go out on the wind-swept floor space between the house and the kitchen where the general tin basin stood, and wash.[6]

Along outside of the front fence ran the country road, dusty in the summertime, and a good place for snakes—they liked to lie in it and sun themselves; when they were rattlesnakes or puff adders, we killed them; when they were black snakes, or racers, or belonged to the fabled "hoop" breed, we fled without shame; when they were "house snakes," or "garters," we carried them home and put them in Aunt Patsy's work basket for a surprise; for she was prejudiced against snakes, and always when she took the basket in her lap and they began to climb out of it it disordered her mind.

Roxanna in *Pudd'nhead Wilson* and Aunt Rachel in "A True Story" in *Sketches New and Old*.

[6] This scene of the farm family gathered at the winter fireside is obviously one of the most nostalgic themes in American art and literature. Mark Twain's description is unquestionably inspired by his own poignant memories, but interesting parallels can be found in the works of many American writers, the most celebrated being John Greenleaf Whittier's *Snow-Bound* and Hamlin Garland's *A Son of the Middle Border*.

She never could seem to get used to them; her opportunities went for nothing. . . .[7]

Beyond the road where the snakes sunned themselves was a dense young thicket, and through it a dim-lighted path led a quarter of a mile; then out of the dimness one emerged abruptly upon a level great prairie which was covered with wild strawberry plants, vividly starred with prairie pinks, and walled in on all sides by forests. The strawberries were fragrant and fine, and in the season we were generally there in the crisp freshness of the early morning, while the dew beads still sparkled upon the grass and the woods were ringing with the first songs of the birds.

Down the forest slopes to the left were the swings. They were made of bark stripped from hickory saplings. When they became dry they were dangerous. They usually broke when a child was forty feet in the air, and this was why so many bones had to be mended every year. I had no ill luck myself, but none of my cousins escaped. There were eight of them, and at one time and another they broke fourteen arms among them. . . .

The country schoolhouse was three miles from my uncle's farm. It stood in a clearing in the woods and would hold about twenty-five boys and girls. We attended the school with more or less regularity once or twice a week, in summer, walking to it in the cool of the morning by the forest paths, and back in the gloaming at the end of the day. All the pupils brought their dinners in baskets—corn dodger, buttermilk, and other good things—and sat in the shade of the trees at noon and ate them. It is the part of my education which I look back upon with the most satisfaction. My first visit to the school was when I was seven. A strapping girl of fifteen, in the customary sunbonnet and calico dress, asked me if I "used tobacco"—meaning did I chew it. I said no. It roused her scorn. She reported me to all the crowd, and said:

"Here is a boy seven years old who can't chew tobacco."

By the looks and comments which this produced I realized that I was a degraded object, and was cruelly ashamed of myself. I determined to reform. But I only made myself sick; I was not able

---

[7] Jane Clemens, Mark Twain's own mother, was the prototype for Tom Sawyer's "Aunt Sally," but the domestic life of Sam Clemens' Uncle John and Aunt Patsy Quarles suggested many of the incidents for *The Adventures of Tom Sawyer*.

to learn to chew tobacco. I learned to smoke fairly well, but that did not conciliate anybody and I remained a poor thing, and characterless.[8] I longed to be respected, but I never was able to rise. Children have but little charity for one another's defects.

As I have said, I spent some part of every year at the farm until I was twelve or thirteen years old. The life which I led there with my cousins was full of charm, and so is the memory of it yet. I can call back the solemn twilight and mystery of the deep woods, the earthy smells, the faint odors of the wild flowers, the sheen of rain-washed foliage, the rattling clatter of drops when the wind shook the trees, the far-off hammering of woodpeckers and the muffled drumming of wood pheasants in the remoteness of the forest, the snapshot glimpses of disturbed wild creatures scurrying through the grass—I can call it all back and make it as real as it ever was, and as blessed. I can call back the prairie, and its loneliness and peace, and a vast hawk hanging motionless in the sky, with his wings spread wide and the blue of the vault showing through the fringe of their end feathers. I can see the woods in their autumn dress, the oaks purple, the hickories washed with gold, the maples and the sumachs luminous with crimson fires, and I can hear the rustle made by the fallen leaves as we plowed through them. I can see the blue clusters of wild grapes hanging among the foliage of the saplings, and I remember the taste of them and the smell. I know how the wild blackberries looked, and how they tasted, and the same with the pawpaws, the hazel-nuts, and the persimmons; and I can feel the thumping rain, upon my head, of hickory nuts and walnuts when we were out in the frosty dawn to scramble for them with the pigs, and the gusts of wind loosed them and sent them down. I know the stain of blackberries, and how pretty it is, and I know the stain of walnut hulls, and how little it minds soap and water, also what grudged experience it had of either of them. I know the taste of maple sap, and when to gather it, and how to arrange the troughs and the delivery tubes, and how to boil down the juice, and how to hook the sugar after it is made, also how much better hooked sugar tastes than any that is honestly come by, let bigots say what they will. I know how a prize water-

[8] It is said that later in life Mark Twain acquired the art (or habit) of smoking an average of twenty-five cigars a day.

melon looks when it is sunning its fat rotundity among pumpkin vines and "simblins"; I know how to tell when it is ripe without "plugging" it; I know how inviting it looks when it is cooling itself in a tub of water under the bed, waiting; I know how it looks when it lies on the table in the sheltered great floor space between house and kitchen, and the children gathered for the sacrifice and their mouths watering; I know the crackling sound it makes when the carving knife enters its end, and I can see the split fly along in front of the blade as the knife cleaves its way to the other end; I can see its halves fall apart and display the rich red meat and the black seeds, and the heart standing up, a luxury fit for the elect; I know how a boy looks behind a yard-long slice of that melon, and I know how he feels; for I have been there. I know the taste of the watermelon which has been honestly come by, and I know the taste of the watermelon which has been acquired by art. Both taste good, but the experienced know which tastes best. I know the look of green apples and peaches and pears on the trees, and I know how entertaining they are when they are inside of a person. I know how ripe ones look when they are piled in pyramids under the trees, and how pretty they are and how vivid their colors. I know how a frozen apple looks, in a barrel down cellar in the wintertime, and how hard it is to bite, and how the frost makes the teeth ache, and yet how good it is, notwithstanding. I know the disposition of elderly people to select the speckled apples for the children, and I once knew ways to beat the game. I know the look of an apple that is roasting and sizzling on a hearth on a winter's evening, and I know the comfort that comes of eating it hot, along with some sugar and a drench of cream. I know the delicate art and mystery of so cracking hickory nuts and walnuts on a flatiron with a hammer that the kernels will be delivered whole, and I know how the nuts, taken in conjunction with winter apples, cider, and doughnuts, make old people's old tales and old jokes sound fresh and crisp and enchanting, and juggle an evening away before you know what went with the time. I know the look of Uncle Dan'l's kitchen as it was on the privileged nights, when I was a child, and I can see the white and black children grouped on the hearth, with the firelight playing on their faces and the shadows flickering upon the walls, clear back toward the cavernous gloom of the rear, and I can hear Uncle Dan'l telling the immortal tales which Uncle Remus Harris was to gather into his book and charm the world with, by and by;[9] and I can feel again the creepy joy which quivered through me when the time for the ghost story was reached—and the sense of regret, too, which came over me, for it was always the last story of the evening and there was nothing between it and the unwelcome bed.

I can remember the bare wooden stairway in my uncle's house, and the turn to the left above the landing, and the rafters and the slanting roof over my bed, and the squares of moonlight on the floor, and the white cold world of snow outside, seen through the curtainless window. I can remember the howling of the wind and the quaking of the house on stormy nights, and how snug and cozy one felt, under the blankets, listening; and how the powdery snow used to sift in, around the sashes, and lie in little ridges on the floor and make the place look chilly in the morning and curb the wild desire to get up—in case there was any. I can remember how very dark that room was, in the dark of the moon, and how packed it was with ghostly stillness when one woke up by accident away in the night, and forgotten sins came flocking out of the secret chambers of the memory and wanted a hearing; and how ill chosen the time seemed for this kind of business; and how dismal was the hoo-hooing of the owl and the wailing of the wolf, sent mourning by on the night wind.

I remember the raging of the rain on that roof, summer nights, and how pleasant it was to lie and listen to it, and enjoy the white splendor of the lightning and the majestic booming and crashing of the thunder. It was a very satisfactory room, and there was a lightning rod which was reachable from the window, an adorable

---

[9] Mark Twain met Joel Chandler Harris in New Orleans in the spring of 1882. Together with George Washington Cable they toured the old southern city. Harris had just begun the publication of his long series of classic American Negro folk stories known as the *Uncle Remus* tales, and Cable's *Old Creole Days* had started that writer on his successful career only two years before. It is more than coincidence that Mark Twain, Cable, and Harris became friends: all three of these writers had their origins in the great Mississippi Valley, wrote their best books about the life of the valley, and contributed largely to the local-color vogue that strongly shaped American literature during the last two decades of the century. Mark Twain's love of the Negro's tales, his dialect, his superstitions, and his customs is reflected everywhere in the Missouri writer's work.

and skittish thing to climb up and down, summer nights, when there were duties on hand of a sort to make privacy desirable.

I remember the 'coon and 'possum hunts, nights, with the negroes, and the long marches through the black gloom of the woods, and the excitement which fired everybody when the distant bay of an experienced dog announced that the game was treed; then the wild scramblings and stumblings through briers and bushes and over roots to get to the spot; then the lighting of a fire and the felling of the tree, the joyful frenzy of the dogs and the negroes, and the weird picture it all made in the red glare—I remember it all well, and the delight that everyone got out of it, except the 'coon.

I remember the pigeon seasons, when the birds would come in millions and cover the trees and by their weight break down the branches. They were clubbed to death with sticks; guns were not necessary and were not used.[10] I remember the squirrel hunts, and prairie-chicken hunts, and wild-turkey hunts, and all that; and how we turned out, mornings, while it was still dark, to go on these expeditions, and how chilly and dismal it was, and how often I regretted that I was well enough to go. A toot on a tin horn brought twice as many dogs as were needed, and in their happiness they raced and scampered about, and knocked small people down, and made no end of unnecessary noise. At the word, they vanished away toward the woods, and we drifted silently after them in the melancholy gloom. But presently the gray dawn stole over the world, the birds piped up, then the sun rose and poured light and comfort all around, everything was fresh and dewy and fragrant, and life was a boon again. After three hours of trampling we arrived back wholesomely tired, overladen with game, very hungry, and just in time for breakfast.[11] » » »

Every year about March or April a strange malady descends

[10] The slaughter of wild pigeons, as Mark Twain describes it, was a common occurrence in early America. James Fenimore Cooper wrote perhaps the most graphic description of this "sport" in *The Pioneers.*

[11] This projection of the elderly Mark Twain into the morning realm of childhood is in sharp contrast to the darker mood of his *The Mysterious Stranger, The Man That Corrupted Hadleyburg,* and *What Is Man?,* all of which were written about the same time as these autobiographical passages (1898). For this contrast, see Part II of this book.

upon the land and afflicts almost all Americans of all generations. Even urban America is susceptible to it, but it is especially virulent among people of small towns, especially village boys between the ages of eight and eighteen. If such boys cannot escape their environment, the disease reaches almost epidemic proportions among them, and there is no cure for it but to let it run its course. History records this malady at all times and in all places within the temperate zone, but nowhere apparently has its onslaught been more irresistible than in the great Mississippi Valley of America. The boy from early Missouri who, in many respects, never quite grew up all during his life and who later called himself "Mark Twain" when he turned to writing as a profession, describes this sickness as it affected himself and his generation in the valley a century ago:

SPRING FEVER (from *Tom Sawyer Detective*[12])

« « « The frost was working out of the ground, and out of the air, too, and it was getting closer and closer onto barefoot time every day; and next it would be marble-time, and next mumblety-peg, and next tops and hoops, and next kites, and then right away it would be summer and going in a-swimming. It just makes a boy homesick to look ahead like that and see how far off summer is. Yes, and it sets him to sighing and saddening around, and there's something the matter with him, he don't know what. But, any way, he gets out by himself and mopes and thinks; and mostly he hunts for a lonesome place high up on the hill in the edge of the woods, and sets there and looks away off on the big Mississippi down there a-reaching miles and miles around the points where the timber looks smoky and dim, it's so far off and still, and everything's so

---

[12] Although two decades separated *Tom Sawyer Abroad* (1894) and its companion *Tom Sawyer, Detective* (1896) from the original *Adventures of Tom Sawyer* (1875) and the sequels are usually considered to be only pale reflections of the first adventure, Bernard De Voto observed that the merits of *Tom Sawyer Abroad* have been badly underestimated: "It is among the very best of Mark's work, frequently on a level with *Huckleberry Finn* itself, and must eventually be recognized as what it is" (Introduction to *The Portable Mark Twain*, 32). *Tom Sawyer, Detective* is unquestionably a pedestrian piece of work in comparison even with the secondary story of the series, but the reader is rewarded with a few evocative descriptions and occasional characterizations and touches of humor reminiscent of Mark Twain's earlier creative genius.

solemn it seems like everybody you've loved is dead and gone, and you 'most wish you was dead and gone too, and done with it all.

Don't you know what that is? It's spring fever. That is what the name of it is. And when you've got it, you want—oh, you don't quite know what it is you *do* want, but it just fairly makes your heart ache, you want it so! It seems to you that mainly what you want is to get away; get away from the same old tedious things you're so used to seeing and so tired of, and see something new. That is the idea; you want to go and be a wanderer; you want to go wandering far away to strange countries where everything is mysterious and wonderful and romantic. And if you can't do that, you'll put up with considerable less; you'll go anywhere you *can* go, just so as to get away, and be thankful of the chance, too. » » »

Unfortunately, only one boy in a thousand can wander or travel into faraway places. The other boys simply have to stay home and help their families carry on the world's work—spring fever or no spring fever. The average boy, in the days of young Sam Clemens of Hannibal, Missouri, in the winter went to school and did chores; in the summer he went to church and did chores. In between he escaped the burden of life as best he could. His desperate desire for something to give animation, color, and sparkle to life often taxed his resourcefulness to the utmost. What, for instance, could a boy do to relieve the tedium of a long and droning church sermon on a drowsy summer morning? Sam Clemens, alias Tom Sawyer, once found the solution in a pinch bug and a poodle dog as accompaniment for the minister. The following is Mark Twain's account of that particular Sunday service (it is believed that Mark Twain, along with the copyright of his book, patented this particular method of relieving boredom, so the reader is warned against imitation):

PANDEMONIUM IN CHURCH (from *The Adventures of Tom Sawyer*[13])

« « « About half past ten the cracked bell of the small church

[13] For illuminating studies of *The Adventures of Tom Sawyer* and its sequels,

began to ring, and presently the people began to gather for the morning sermon. The Sunday-school children distributed themselves about the house and occupied pews with their parents, so as to be under supervision. Aunt Polly came, and Tom and Sid and Mary sat with her—Tom being placed next the aisle, in order that he might be as far away from the open window and the seductive outside summer scenes as possible. The crowd filed up the aisles: the aged and needy postmaster, who had seen better days; the mayor and his wife—for they had a mayor there, among other unnecessaries; the justice of the peace; the widow Douglas, fair, smart, and forty, a generous, good-hearted soul and well-to-do, her hill mansion the only palace in the town, and the most hospitable and much the most lavish in the matter of festivities that St. Petersburg could boast; the bent and venerable Major and Mrs. Ward; lawyer Riverson, the new notable from a distance; next the belle of the village, followed by a troop of lawn-clad and ribbon-decked young heart-breakers; then all the young clerks in town in a body—for they had stood in the vestibule sucking their cane-heads, a circling wall of oiled and simpering admirers, till the last girl had run their gantlet; and last of all came the Model Boy, Willie Mufferson, taking as heedful care of his mother as if she were cut glass. He always brought his mother to church, and was the pride of all the matrons. The boys all hated him, he was so good. And besides, he had been "thrown up to them" so much. His white handkerchief was hanging out of his pocket behind, as usual on Sundays—accidentally. Tom had no handkerchief, and he looked upon boys who had, as snobs.

The congregation being fully assembled, now, the bell rang once more, to warn laggards and stragglers, and then a solemn hush fell upon the church which was only broken by the tittering and whispering of the choir in the gallery. The choir always tittered and whispered all through the service. There was once a church choir that was not ill-bred, but I have forgotten where it was, now.

Tom Sawyer Abroad and *Tom Sawyer, Detective*, the reader is referred to J. Christian Bay, "Tom Sawyer, Detective; the Origin of the Plot," in *Essays Offered to Herbert Putnam* (ed. by W. W. Bishop and Andrew Keogh) (New Haven, Yale University Press, 1929), 80-88; Walter Blair, "On the Structure of *Tom Sawyer*," *Modern Philology*, Vol. XXXVII (1939), 75-88; and *Mark Twain's Letters to Will Bowen* (ed. by Theodore Hornberger) (Austin, 1941).

It was a great many years ago, and I can scarcely remember anything about it, but I think it was in some foreign country.

The minister gave out the hymn, and read it through with a relish, in a peculiar style which was much admired in that part of the country. His voice began on a medium key and climbed steadily up till it reached a certain point, where it bore with strong emphasis upon the topmost word and then plunged down as if from a springboard:

```
                              beds
                    on flow'ry
              the skies,
         toe                              of ease,
    car-ri-ed
   be
Shall I                               thro' blood-
                       and sail
                 the prize,
            to win                            -y seas!
      fight
   others
Whilst
```

He was regarded as a wonderful reader. At church "sociables" he was always called upon to read poetry; and when he was through, the ladies would lift up their hands and let them fall helplessly in their laps, and "wall" their eyes, and shake their heads, as much as to say, "Words cannot express it; it is too beautiful, *too* beautiful for this mortal earth."

After the hymn had been sung, the Rev. Mr. Sprague turned himself into a bulletin-board, and read off "notices" of meetings and societies and things till it seemed that the list would stretch out to the crack of doom. . . .

And now the minister prayed. A good, generous prayer it was, and went into details: it pleaded for the church, and the little children of the church; for the other churches of the village; for the village itself; for the county; for the state; for the state officers; for the United States; for the churches of the United States; for Congress; for the President; for the officers of the government; for poor sailors, tossed by stormy seas; for the oppressed millions groaning under the heel of European monarchies and Oriental despotisms; for such as have the light and the good tidings, and yet have not eyes to see nor ears to hear withal; for the heathen in the far islands of the sea; and closed with a supplication that the words he was about to speak might find grace and favor, and be as seed sown in fertile ground, yielding in time a grateful harvest of good. Amen.

There was a rustling of dresses, and the standing congregation sat down. The boy whose history this book relates did not enjoy the prayer, he only endured it—if he even did that much. He was restive all through it; he kept tally of the details of the prayer, unconsciously—for he was not listening, but he knew the ground of old, and the clergyman's regular route over it—and when a little trifle of new matter was interlarded, his ear detected it and his whole nature resented it; he considered additions unfair, and scoundrelly. In the midst of the prayer a fly had lit on the back of the pew in front of him and tortured his spirit by calmly rubbing its hands together, embracing its head with its arms, and polishing it so vigorously that it seemed to almost part company with the body, and the slender thread of a neck was exposed to view; scraping its wings with its hind legs and smoothing them to its body as if they had been coattails; going through its whole toilet as tranquilly as if it knew it was perfectly safe. As indeed it was; for as sorely as Tom's hands itched to grab for it they did not dare—he believed his soul would be instantly destroyed if he did such a thing while the prayer was going on. But with the closing sentence his hand began to curve and steal forward; and the instant the "Amen" was out the fly was a prisoner of war. His aunt detected the act and made him let it go.

The minister gave out his text and droned along monotonously through an argument that was so prosy that many a head by and by began to nod—and yet it was an argument that dealt in limitless fire and brimstone and thinned the predestined elect down to a company so small as to be hardly worth the saving. Tom counted the pages of the sermon; after church he always knew how many pages there had been, but he seldom knew any thing else about the discourse. However, this time he was really interested for a little while. The minister made a grand and moving picture of the assembling together of the world's hosts at the millennium when the lion and the lamb should lie down together and a little child should lead them. But the pathos, the lesson, the moral of the great spectacle were lost upon the boy; he only thought of the conspicuousness of the principal character before the onlooking nations; his face lit with the thought, and he said to himself that he wished he could be that child, if it was a tame lion.

Now he lapsed into suffering again, as the dry argument was resumed. Presently he bethought him of a treasure he had and got it out. It was a large black beetle with formidable jaws—a "pinchbug," he called it. It was in a percussion-cap box. The first thing the beetle did was to take him by the finger. A natural fillip followed, the beetle went floundering into the aisle and lit on its back, and the hurt finger went into the boy's mouth. The beetle lay there working its helpless legs, unable to turn over. Tom eyed it, and longed for it; but it was safe out of his reach. Other people uninterested in the sermon, found relief in the beetle, and they eyed it too. Presently a vagrant poodle-dog came idling along, sad at heart, lazy with the summer softness and the quiet, weary of captivity, sighing for change. He spied the beetle; the drooping tail lifted and wagged. He surveyed the prize; walked around it; smelt at it from a safe distance; walked around it again; grew bolder, and took a closer smell; then lifted his lip and made a gingerly snatch at it, just missing it; made another, and another; began to enjoy the diversion; subsided to his stomach with the beetle between his paws, and continued his experiments; grew weary at last, and then indifferent and absent-minded. His head nodded, and little by little his chin descended and touched the enemy, who seized it. There was a sharp yelp, a flirt of the poodle's head, and the beetle fell a couple of yards away, and lit on its back once more. The neighboring spectators shook with a gentle inward joy, several faces went behind fans and handkerchiefs, and Tom was entirely happy. The dog looked foolish, and probably felt so; but there was resentment in his heart, too, and a craving for revenge. So he went to the beetle and began a wary attack on it again; jumping at it from every point of a circle, lighting with his fore paws within an inch of the creature, making even closer snatches at it with his teeth, and jerking his head till his ears flapped again. But he grew tired once more, after a while; tried to amuse himself with a fly but found no relief; followed an ant around, with his nose close to the floor, and quickly wearied of that; yawned, sighed, forgot the beetle entirely, and sat down on it. Then there was a wild yelp of agony and the poodle went sailing up the aisle; the yelps continued, and so did the dog; he crossed the house in front of the altar; he flew down the other aisle; he crossed before the doors; he clamored up the home-stretch; his anguish grew with his progress, till presently he was but a woolly comet moving in its orbit with the gleam and the speed of light. At last the frantic sufferer sheered from its course, and sprang into its master's lap; he flung it out of the window, and the voice of distress quickly thinned away and died in the distance.

By this time the whole church was red-faced and suffocating with suppressed laughter, and the sermon had come to a dead standstill. The discourse was resumed presently, but it went lame and halting, all possibility of impressiveness being at an end; for even the gravest sentiments were constantly being received with a smothered burst of unholy mirth, under cover of some remote pew-back, as if the poor parson had said a rarely facetious thing. It was a genuine relief to the whole congregation when the ordeal was over and the benediction pronounced.

Tom Sawyer went home quite cheerful, thinking to himself that there was some satisfaction about divine service when there was a bit of variety in it. He had but one marring thought; he was willing that the dog should play with his pinchbug, but he did not think it was upright in him to carry it off. » » »

Dogs and ministers were not the only sufferers in Sam Clemens' world. Cats also came in for their share of affliction, especially if they were handy at a time when benighted aunts were trying to cure small boys of melancholia. One of the most animated episodes in Mark Twain's many accounts of his boyhood is also told in *Tom Sawyer*:

THE CAT AND THE PAIN-KILLER (from *The Adventures of Tom Sawyer*)

« « « One of the reasons why Tom's mind had drifted away from its secret troubles was, that it had found a new and weighty matter to interest itself about. Becky Thatcher had stopped coming to school. Tom had struggled with his pride a few days, and tried to "whistle her down the wind," but failed. He began to find himself hanging around her father's house, nights, and feeling very miserable. She was ill. What if she should die! There was distraction in the thought. He no longer took an interest in war, nor even in piracy. The charm of life was gone; there was nothing but dreariness left. He put his hoop away, and his bat; there was no joy in them any more. His aunt was concerned. She began to try all manner of remedies on him. She was one of those people who are infatuated with patent medicines and all new-fangled methods of producing health or mending it. She was an inveterate experimenter in these things. When something fresh in this line came out she was in a a fever, right away, to try it; not on herself, for she was never ailing, but on anybody else that came handy. She was a subscriber for all the "Health" periodicals and phrenological frauds; and the solemn ignorance they were inflated with was breath to her nostrils. All the "rot" they contained about ventilation, and how to go to bed, and how to get up, and what to eat, and what to drink, and how much exercise to take, and what frame of mind to keep one's self in, and what sort of clothing to wear, was all gospel to her, and she never observed that her health-journals of the current month customarily upset everything they had recommended the month before. She was as simplehearted and honest as the day was long, and so she was an easy victim. She gathered together her quack periodicals and her quack medicines, and thus armed with death, went about on her pale horse, metaphorically speaking, with "hell following after." But she never suspected that she was not an angel of healing and the balm of Gilead in disguise, to the suffering neighbors.

The water treatment was new, now, and Tom's low condition was a windfall to her. She had him out at daylight every morning, stood him up in the woodshed and drowned him with a deluge of cold water; then she scrubbed him down with a towel like a file, and so brought him to; then she rolled him up in a wet sheet and put him away under blankets till she sweated his soul clean and "the yellow stains of it came through his pores"—as Tom said.

Yet notwithstanding all this, the boy grew more and more melancholy and pale and dejected. She added hot baths, sitz baths, shower baths, and plunges. The boy remained as dismal as a hearse. She began to assist the water with a slim oatmeal diet and blister-plasters. She calculated his capacity as she would a jug's, and filled him up every day with quack cure-alls.

Tom had become indifferent to persecution by this time. This phase filled the old lady's heart with consternation. This indifference must be broken up at any cost. Now she heard of Pain-killer for the first time. She ordered a lot at once. She tasted it and was filled with gratitude. It was simply fire in a liquid form. She dropped the water treatment and everything else, and pinned her faith to Pain-killer. She gave Tom a teaspoonful and watched with the deepest anxiety for the result. Her troubles were instantly at rest, her soul at peace again; for the "indifference" was broken up. The boy could not have shown a wilder, heartier interest if she had built a fire under him.

Tom felt that it was time to wake up; this sort of life might be romantic enough, in his blighted condition, but it was getting to have too little sentiment and too much distracting variety about it. So he thought over various plans for relief, and finally hit upon that of professing to be fond of Pain-killer. He asked for it so often that he became a nuisance, and his aunt ended by telling him to help himself and quit bothering her. If it had been Sid, she would have had no misgivings to alloy her delight; but since it was Tom, she watched the bottle clandestinely. She found that the medicine did really diminish, but it did not occur to her that the boy was mending the health of a crack in the sitting-room floor with it.

One day Tom was in the act of dosing the crack when his aunt's yellow cat came along, purring, eyeing the teaspoon avariciously, and begging for a taste. Tom said:

"Don't ask for it unless you want it, Peter."

But Peter signified that he did want it.

"You better make sure."

Peter was sure.

"Now you've asked for it, and I'll give it to you, because there ain't anything mean about *me;* but if you find you don't like it, you mustn't blame anybody but your own self."

Peter was agreeable. So Tom pried his mouth open and poured down the Pain-killer. Peter sprang a couple of yards in the air, and then delivered a war-whoop and set off round and round the room, banging against furniture, upsetting flower-pots, and making general havoc. Next he rose on his hind feet and pranced around, in a frenzy of enjoyment, with his head over his shoulder and his voice proclaiming his unappeasable happiness. Then he went tearing around the house again spreading chaos and destruction in his path. Aunt Polly entered in time to see him throw a few double somersets, deliver a final mighty hurrah, and sail through the open window, carrying the rest of the flower-pots with him. The old lady stood petrified with astonishment, peering over her glasses; Tom lay on the floor expiring with laughter.

"Tom, what on earth ails that cat?"

"*I* don't know, aunt," gasped the boy.

"Why, I never see anything like it. What *did* make him act so?"

" 'Deed I don't know, Aunt Polly; cats always act so when they're having a good time."

"They do, do they?" There was something in the tone that made Tom apprehensive.

"Yes'm. That is, I believe they do."

"You *do?*"

"Yes'm."

The old lady was bending down, Tom watching, with interest emphasized by anxiety. Too late he divined her "drift." The handle of the telltale teaspoon was visible under the bed-valance. Aunt Polly took it, held it up. Tom winced, and dropped his eyes. Aunt Polly raised him by the usual handle—his ear—and cracked his head soundly with her thimble.

"Now, sir, what did you want to treat that poor dumb beast so for?"

"I done it out of pity for him—because he hadn't any aunt."

"Hadn't any aunt!—you numbskull. What has that got to do with it?"

"Heaps. Because of he'd a'had one she'd a'burnt him out herself. She'd a'roasted his bowels out of him 'thout any more feeling than if he was a human!"

Aunt Polly felt a sudden pang of remorse. This was putting the thing in a new light; what was cruelty to a cat *might* be cruelty to a boy, too. She began to soften; she felt sorry. Her eyes watered a little, and she put her hand on Tom's head and said gently:

"I was meaning for the best, Tom. And, Tom, it *did* do you good."

Tom looked up in her face with just a perceptible twinkle peeping through his gravity:

"I know you was meaning for the best, auntie, and so was I with Peter. It done *him* good, too. I never see him get around so since—"

"Oh, go 'long with you, Tom, before you aggravate me again. And you try and see if you can't be a good boy for once, and you needn't take any more medicine."[14] » » »

Just as in every other American town of older times, the highlight of the year in St. Petersburg (later Hannibal, Missouri)—for the boys and girls, at least—was the perennial circus. The circus of the 1840's was not the mammoth show that it has become today, but to the younger eyes of a Missouri river town, starved for the sight of daring action and colorful spectacle, the small traveling circus provided everything that we today expect of our movies and television and radio. The one-ring circus of Mark Twain's boyhood packed comedy, glamour, suspense, action—thrills that were "soul-satisfying" to its audience, as he would have expressed it. In *Huckleberry Finn*, through the eyes and tongue of an uneducated but sensitive and keenly observing boy, Mark Twain describes the main attraction of a typical circus of the middle nineteenth-century:

THE CIRCUS (from *The Adventures of Huckleberry Finn*)

« « « It was a real bully circus. It was the splendidest sight that ever was when they all come riding in, two and two, and gentleman

---

[14] For the genesis of Tom Sawyer's "Aunt Polly," see Howard S. Mott, Jr., "The Origin of Aunt Polly," *Publishers' Weekly*, Vol. CXXXIV (1938), 1821-23.

and lady, side by side, the men just in their drawers and undershirts, and no shoes nor stirrups, and resting their hands on their thighs easy and comfortable—there must 'a' been twenty of them—and every lady with a lovely complexion, and perfectly beautiful, and looking just like a gang of real sure-enough queens, and dressed in clothes that cost millions of dollars, and just littered with diamonds. It was a powerful fine sight; I never see anything so lovely. And then one by one they got up and stood, and went a-weaving around the ring so gentle and wavy and graceful, the men looking ever so tall and airy and straight, with their heads bobbing and skimming along, away up there under the tent-roof, and every lady's rose-leafy dress flapping soft and silky around her hips, and she looking like the most loveliest parasol.

And then faster and faster they went, all of them dancing, first one foot out in the air, and then the other, the horses leaning more and more, and the ringmaster going round and round the center pole, cracking his whip and shouting "Hi!-hi!" and the clown cracking jokes behind him; and by and by all hands dropped the reins, and every lady put her knuckles on her hips and every gentleman folded his arms, and then how the horses did lean over and hump themselves! And so one after the other they all skipped off into the ring, and made the sweetest bow I ever see, and then scampered out, and everybody clapped their hands and went just about wild.

Well, all through the circus they done the most astonishing things; and all the time that clown carried on so it most killed the people. The ringmaster couldn't ever say a word to him but he was back at him quick as a wink with the funniest things a body ever said; and how he ever *could* think of so many of them, and so sudden and so pat, was what I couldn't no way understand. Why, I couldn't 'a' thought of them in a year. And by and by a drunken man tried to get into the ring—said he wanted to ride; said he could ride as well as anybody that ever was. They argued and tried to keep him out, but he wouldn't listen, and the whole show come to a standstill. Then the people begun to holler at him and make fun of him, and that made him mad, and he begun to rip and tear; so that stirred up the people, and a lot of men begun to pile down off of the benches and swarm toward the ring, saying,

THE CIRCUS

"Knock him down! throw him out!" and one or two women begun to scream. So, then, the ringmaster he made a little speech, and said he hoped there wouldn't be no disturbance, and if the man would promise he wouldn't make no more trouble he would let him ride if he thought he could stay on the horse. So everybody laughed and said all right, and the man got on. The minute he was on, the horse begun to rip and tear and jump and cavort around, with two circus men hanging on to his bridle trying to hold him, and the drunken man hanging on to his neck, and his heels flying in the air every jump, and the whole crowd of people standing up shouting and laughing till tears rolled down. And at last, sure enough, all the circus men could do, the horse broke loose, and away he went like the very nation, round and round the ring, with that sot laying down on him and hanging to his neck, with first one leg hanging most to the ground on one side, and then t'other one on t'other side, and the people just crazy. It warn't funny to me, though; I was all of a tremble to see his danger. But pretty soon he struggled up astraddle and grabbed the bridle, a-reeling this way and that; and the next minute he sprung up and dropped the bridle and stood! and the horse a-going like a house afire, too. He just stood up there, a-sailing around as easy and comfortable as if he warn't ever drunk in his life—and then he begun to pull off his clothes and sling them. He shed them so thick they kind of clogged up the air, and altogether he shed seventeen suits. And, then, there he was, slim and handsome, and dressed the gaudiest and prettiest you ever saw, and he lit into that horse with his whip and made him fairly hum—and finally skipped off, and made his bow and danced off to the dressing-room, and everybody just a-howling with pleasure and astonishment. » » »

In his travels up and down the great Mississippi River valley, Mark Twain entered many homes and took as much interest in the domestic details of the people's daily lives as he did in circuses and steamboating and other more glamorous activities. The average home of any socially ambitious citizen of that time was almost a museum of oddities and Victorian fads, and to the observing eye and the shrewd mind of the young Missourian the most insignificant gimcrack told a story about the owner of the house or his wife and family. The more pretentious the house and its furnishings, the more they revealed. Through the eyes of Huckleberry Finn, who was inclined to be overly impressed by any display of culture, Mark Twain describes for us a typical middle-class home as we would find it in the 1840's and 1850's, although the description might apply to many American homes for many years after the Civil War:

RIVER VALLEY CULTURE (from *The Adventures of Huckleberry Finn*[15])

« « « It was a mighty nice family, and a mighty nice house, too. I hadn't seen no house out in the country before that was so nice and had so much style. It didn't have an iron latch on the front door, nor a wooden one with a buckskin string, but a brass knob to turn, the same as houses in town. There warn't no bed in the parlor, nor a sign of a bed; but heaps of parlors in towns has beds in them. There was a big fireplace that was bricked on the bottom, and the bricks was kept clean and red by pouring water on them and scrubbing them with another brick; sometimes they wash them over with red waterpaint that they call Spanish-brown, same as they do in town. They had big brass dog-irons that could hold up a saw-log. There was a clock on the middle of the mantelpiece, with a picture of a town painted on the bottom half of the glass front, and a round place in the middle of it for the sun, and you could see the pendulum swinging behind it. It was beautiful to hear that clock tick; and sometimes when one of these peddlers had been along and scoured her up and got her in good shape, she would start in and strike a hundred and fifty before she got tuckered out. They wouldn't took any money for her.

Well, there was a big outlandish parrot on each side of the clock,

[15] *Huckleberry Finn* was published in 1884, twenty-three years after Mark Twain left the Mississippi Valley. During the intervening years he lived largely in New York State and New England, where he worked sporadically at this novel and his *Life on the Mississippi* for about ten years before their publication. His many lecture trips into other parts of the country and his visits to Hannibal and other valley scenes of his early years in 1883 might very well have provided material for these domestic descriptions to add to his early recollections. Much of the river valley culture that emerges from *Huckleberry Finn* could describe the Midwestern home of the postwar period as well as that of the 1850's.

made out of something like chalk, and painted up gaudy. By one of the parrots was a cat made of crockery, and a crockery dog by the other; and when you pressed down on them they squeaked, but didn't open their mouths nor look different nor interested. They squeaked through underneath. There was a couple of big wild-turkey-wing fans spread out behind those things. On the table in the middle of the room was a kind of a lovely crockery basket that had apples and oranges and peaches and grapes piled up in it, which was much redder and yellower and prettier than real ones is, but they warn't real because you could see where pieces had got chipped off and showed the white chalk, or whatever it was, underneath.

This table had a cover made out of beautiful oilcloth, with a red and blue spread-eagle painted on it, and a painted border all around. It come all the way from Philadelphia, they said. There was some books, too, piled up perfectly exact, on each corner of the table. One was a big family Bible full of pictures. One was *Pilgrim's Progress*, about a man that left his family, it didn't say why. I read considerable in it now and then. The statements was interesting, but tough. Another was *Friendship's Offering*, full of beautiful stuff and poetry; but I didn't read the poetry. Another was Henry Clay's Speeches, and another was Dr. Gunn's *Family Medicine*, which told you all about what to do if a body was sick or dead. There was a hymn-book, and a lot of other books. And there was nice split-bottom chairs, and perfectly sound, too—not bagged down in the middle and busted, like an old basket. . . .

Well, as I was saying about the parlor, there was beautiful curtains on the windows: white, with pictures painted on them of castles with vines all down the walls, and cattle coming down to drink. There was a little old piano, too, that had tin pans in it, I reckon, and nothing was ever so lovely as to hear the young ladies sing "The Last Link Is Broken" and play "The Battle of Prague" on it. The walls of all the rooms was plastered, and most had carpets on the floors, and the whole house was whitewashed on the outside.

It was a double house, and the big open place betwixt them was roofed and floored, and sometimes the table was set there in the middle of the day, and it was a cool, comfortable place. Nothing couldn't be better. And warn't the cooking good, and just bushels of it too! ...

They had pictures hung on the walls—mainly Washingtons and Lafayettes, and battles, and Highland Marys, and one called "Signing the Declaration." There was some that they called crayons, which one of the daughters which was dead made her own self when she was only fifteen years old. They was different from any pictures I ever see before—blacker, mostly, than is common. One was a woman in a slim black dress, belted small under the armpits, with bulges like a cabbage in the middle of the sleeves, and a large black scoop-shovel bonnet with a black veil, and white slim ankles crossed about with black tape, and very wee black slippers, like a chisel, and she was leaning pensive on a tombstone on her right elbow, under a weeping willow, and her other hand hanging down her side holding a white handkerchief and a reticule, and underneath the picture it said "Shall I Never See Thee More Alas." Another one was a young lady with her hair all combed up straight to the top of her head, and knotted there in front of a comb like a chair-back, and she was crying into a handkerchief and had a dead bird laying on its back in her other hand with its heels up, and underneath the picture it said "I Shall Never Hear Thy Sweet Chirrup More Alas." There was one where a young lady was at a window looking up at the moon, and tears running down her cheeks; and she had on open letter in one hand with black sealing-wax showing on one edge of it, and she was mashing a locket with a chain to it against her mouth, and underneath the picture it said "And Art Thou Gone Yes Thou Art Gone Alas." These was all nice pictures, I reckon, but I didn't somehow seem to take to them, because if ever I was down a little they always give me the fan-tods. Everybody was sorry she died, because she had laid out a lot more of these pictures to do, and a body could see by what she had done what they had lost. But I reckon that with her disposition she was having a better time in the graveyard. She was at work on what they said was her greatest picture when she took sick, and every day and every night it was her prayer to be allowed to live till she got it done, but she never got the chance. It was a picture of a young woman in a long white gown, standing on the rail of a bridge all ready to jump off, with her hair all down her back, and looking up to the moon, with the tears running down her face, and she had two arms folded across her breast, and two arms stretched out in front, and two more reaching up toward the moon—and the idea was to see which pair would look best, and then scratch out all the other arms; but, as I was saying, she died before she got her mind made up, and now they kept this picture over the head of the bed in her room, and every time her birthday come they hung flowers on it. Other times it was hid with a little curtain. The young woman in the picture had a kind of a nice sweet face, but there was so many arms it made her look too spidery, seemed to me.

This young girl kept a scrap-book when she was alive, and used to paste obituaries and accidents and cases of patient suffering in it out of the *Presbyterian Observer*, and write poetry after them out of her own head. It was very good poetry. This is what she wrote about a boy by the name of Stephen Dowling Bots that fell down a well and was drownded:

ODE TO STEPHEN DOWLING BOTS, DEC'D

And did young Stephen sicken,
And did young Stephen die?
And did the sad hearts thicken,
And did the mourners cry?

No; such was not the fate of
Young Stephen Dowling Bots;
Though sad hearts round him thickened,
'Twas not from sickness' shots.

No whooping-cough did rack his frame,
Nor measles drear with spots;
Not these impaired the sacred name
Of Stephen Dowling Bots.

Despised love struck not with woe
That head of curly knots,
Nor stomach troubles laid him low,
Young Stephen Dowling Bots.

O no. Then list with tearful eye,
Whilst I his fate do tell.

> *His soul did from this cold world fly*
> *By falling down a well.*
>
> *They got him out and emptied him;*
> *Alas it was too late;*
> *His spirit was gone for to sport aloft*
> *In the realms of the good and great.*

If Emmeline Grangerford could make poetry like that before she was fourteen, there ain't no telling what she could 'a' done by and by. Buck said she could rattle off poetry like nothing. She didn't ever have to stop to think. He said she would slap down a line, and if she couldn't find anything to rhyme with it would just scratch it out and slap down another one, and go ahead. She warn't particular; she could write about anything you choose to give her to write about just so it was sadful. Every time a man died, or a woman died, or a child died, she would be on hand with her "tribute" before he was cold. She called them tributes. The neighbors said it was the doctor first, then Emmeline, then the undertaker—the undertaker never got in ahead of Emmeline but once, and then she hung fire on a rhyme for the dead person's name, which was Whistler. She warn't ever the same after that; she never complained, but she kinder pined away and did not live long. Poor thing, many's the time I made myself go up to the little room that used to be hers and get out her poor old scrap-book and read in it when her pictures had been aggravating me and I had soured on her a little. I liked all that family, dead ones and all, and warn't going to let anything come between us. Poor Emmeline made poetry about all the dead people when she was alive, and it didn't seem right that there warn't nobody to make some about her now she was gone; so I tried to sweat out a verse or two myself, but I couldn't seem to make it go somehow. 》 》 》

Mark Twain may have had his doubts about the true quality of domestic art in Mississippi homes such as the Grangerfords', and the gusto with which a Colonel Sellers could attack a turnip dinner in *The Gilded Age* was only a pathetic mockery of the kind of hospitality that had become a tradition in the Old South. Even the glamour of the Mississippi River boats could be dispelled by a closer look at the sham gilt and glitter of these works of man. But the Missouri boy who later wrote so profusely about his early days in the river valley never lost his admiration of the works of nature. Whether it was a lazy, sunny day at the boat landing, or a tumultuous night storm on the river, or the fresh dawn over the Illinois shore, Mark Twain always found in nature a genuine beauty that he sometimes thought lacking in human society. He retained, all of his life, a love of scenic grandeur and a delight in all the shades and colors of sky and woodland and water. One of the most ecstatic experiences of his boyhood was the periodic ice storm that transformed his region of the valley into a fantasia that he could vividly describe over half a century later:

THE ICE-STORM (from *Following the Equator*)

« « « In America the ice-storm is an event. And it is not an event which one is careless about. When it comes, the news flies from room to room in the house, there are bangings on the doors, and shoutings, "The ice-storm! the ice-storm!" and even the laziest sleepers throw off the covers and join the rush for the windows. The ice-storm occurs in midwinter, and usually its enchantments are wrought in the silence and the darkness of the night. A fine drizzling rain falls hour after hour upon the naked twigs and branches of the trees, and as it falls it freezes. In time the trunk and every branch and twig are incased in hard pure ice; so that the tree looks like a skeleton tree made all of glass—glass that is crystal-clear. All along the under side of every branch and twig is a comb of little icicles—the frozen drip. Sometimes these pendants do not quite amount to icicles, but are round beads—frozen tears.

The weather clears, toward dawn, and leaves a brisk, pure atmosphere and a sky without a shred of cloud in it—and everything is still, there is not a breath of wind. The dawn breaks and spreads, the news of the storm goes about the house, and the little and the big, in wraps and blankets, flock to the window and press together there, and gaze intently out upon the great white ghost in the grounds, and nobody says a word, nobody stirs. All are waiting; they know what is coming, and they are waiting—waiting for the miracle. The minutes drift on and on and on, with not a sound but the ticking of the clock; at last the sun fires a sudden sheaf of rays into the ghostly tree and turns it into a white splendor of glittering diamonds. Everybody catches his breath, and feels a swelling in his throat and a moisture in his eyes—but waits again; for he knows what is coming; there is more yet. The sun climbs higher, and still higher, flooding the tree from its loftiest spread of branches to its lowest, turning it to a glory of white fire; then in a moment, without warning, comes the great miracle, the supreme miracle, the miracle without its fellow in the earth; a gust of wind sets every branch and twig to swaying, and in an instant turns the whole white tree into a spouting and spraying explosion of flashing gems of every conceivable color; and there it stands and sways this way and that, flash! flash! flash! a dancing and glancing world of rubies, emeralds, diamonds, sapphires, the most radiant spectacle, the most blinding spectacle, the divinest, the most exquisite, the most intoxicating vision of fire and color and intolerable and unimaginable splendor that ever any eye has rested upon in this world, or will ever rest upon outside of the gates of heaven. 》 》 》

School pranks, circuses, ice storms, steamboat arrivals, and "poultry-raising" were not the only diversions of Mark Twain's boyhood. One of the perennial entertainments of the river valley communities was the revival, or "camp meeting" as it was more commonly known in those days. Religious fervor and mass conversions swept America in recurrent waves all through the nineteenth century, and nowhere were they more chronic than in the semifrontier and backwoods sections of Missouri and Arkansas during the twenty to thirty years preceding the Civil War. Like any normal youngster of his day, the young Sam Clemens was fascinated by the carryings-on of his elders at these religious gatherings. If he was too young to gather spiritual comfort from the revivalist preacher, he at least gained a great deal of entertainment from him. Later in life Mark Twain described a typical camp meeting as seen through the eyes of Huckleberry Finn:

THE CAMP MEETING
(from *The Adventures of Huckleberry Finn*)

« « « We got there [to the camp meeting] in about a half an hour fairly dripping, for it was a most awful hot day. There was as much as a thousand people there from twenty mile around. The woods was full of teams and wagons, hitched everywheres, feeding out of the wagontroughs and stomping to keep off the flies. There was sheds made out of poles and roofed over with branches, where they had lemonade and gingerbread to sell, and piles of watermelons and green corn and such-like truck.

The preaching was going on under the same kinds of sheds, only they was bigger and held crowds of people. The benches was made out of outside slabs of logs, with holes bored in the round side to drive sticks into for legs. They didn't have no backs. The preachers had high platforms to stand on at one end of the sheds. The women had on sun-bonnets; and some had linsey-woolsey frocks, some gingham ones, and a few of the young ones had on calico. Some of the young men was barefooted, and some of the children didn't have on any clothes but just a tow-linen shirt. Some of the old women was knitting, and some of the young folks was courting on the sly.

The first shed we come to the preacher was lining out a hymn. He lined out two lines, everybody sung it, and it was kind of grand to hear it, there was so many of them and they done it in such a rousing way; then he lined out two more for them to sing—and so on. The people woke up more and more, and sung louder and louder; and towards the end some begun to groan, and some begun to shout. Then the preacher begun to preach, and begun in earnest, too; and went weaving first to one side of the platform and then the other, and then a-leaning down over the front of it, with his arms and his body going all the time, and shouting his words out with all his might; and every now and then he would hold up his Bible and spread it open, and kind of pass it around this way and that, shouting, "It's the brazen serpent in the wilderness! Look upon it and live!" And people would shout out, "Glory!—A-a-*men!*" And so he went on, and the people groaning and crying and saying amen:

"Oh, come to the mourners' bench! come, black with sin! (*amen!*) come sick and sore! (*amen!*) come, lame and halt and blind! (*amen!*) come, pore and needy, sunk in shame! (*a-a-men!*) come, all that's worn and soiled and suffering!—come with a broken spirit! come with a contrite heart! come in your rags and sin and dirt! The waters that cleanse is free, the door of heaven stands open— oh, enter in and be at rest!" (*a-a-men! glory, glory hallelujah!*)

And so on. You couldn't make out what the preacher said any more, on account of the shouting and crying. Folks got up everywheres in the crowd, and worked their way just by main strength to the mourners' bench, with the tears running down their faces; and when all the mourners had got up there to the front benches in a crowd, they sung and shouted and flung themselves down on the straw, just crazy and wild. » » »

A perennial favorite with American readers and audiences of every generation since the Revolutionary "Yankee Doodle" is the ignorant rustic, or country bumpkin, who comes to the city and exposes his ignorance to the laughter and ridicule of the sophisticated. Occasionally this rustic turns out to have a sly sense of humor and an ingenuity that turn the hoaxes and the laughter of his persecutors back upon themselves. If he is this latter type, this fellow delights his audience even more. Americans have traditionally taken the part of the underdog, especially where cruelty or injustice are involved. Mark Twain was a strong champion of the underdog. One of his fondest recollections was that of the ignorant country boy who wanted to become a printer and came to Hannibal while Sam Clemens was an apprentice working on his brother's newspaper. How Nicodemus Dodge confounded the practical jokesters of Hannibal is recounted with Mark Twain's inimitable sense of character and skill in dialect:

NICODEMUS DODGE FROM OLD SHELBY (from *A Tramp Abroad*)

« « « When I was a boy in a printing-office in Missouri, a loose-jointed, long-legged, tow-headed, jeans-clad, countrified cub of about sixteen lounged in one day, and without removing his hands from the depths of his trousers pockets or taking off his faded ruin of a slouch hat, whose broken rim hung limp and ragged about his eyes and ears like a bug-eaten cabbage leaf, stared indifferently around, then leaned his hip against the editor's table, crossed his mighty brogans, aimed at a distant fly from a crevice in his upper teeth, laid him low, and said with composure:

"Whar's the boss?"

"I am the boss," said the editor, following this curious bit of architecture wonderingly along up to its clock-face with his eye.

"Don't want anybody fur to learn the business, 'taint likely?"

"Well, I don't know. Would you like to learn it?"

"Pap's so po' he cain't run me no mo', so I want to git a show somers if I kin, 'taint no diffunce what—I'm strong and hearty, and I don't turn my back on no kind of work, hard nur soft."

"Do you think you would like to learn the printing business?"

"Well, I don't re'ly k'yer a durn what I *do* learn, so's I git a chance fur to make my way. I'd just as soon learn print'n's anything."

"Can you read?"

"Yes—middlin'."

"Write?"

"Well, I've seed people could lay over me thar."

"Cipher?"

"Not good enough to keep store, I don't reckon, but up as fur as twelve-times-twelve I ain't no slouch. 'Tother side of that is what gits me."

"Where is your home?"

"I'm f'm old Shelby."

"What's your father's religious denomination?"

"Him? Oh, he's a blacksmith."

"No, no—I don't mean his trade. What's his *religious* denomination?"

"*Oh*—I didn't understand you befo'. He's a Freemason."

"No, no, you don't get my meaning yet. What I mean is, does he belong to any *church*?"

"*Now* you're talkin'! Couldn't make out what you was a-tryin' to git through yo' head no way. B'long to a *church*! Why, boss, he's ben the pizenest kind of a Free-will Babtis' for forty year. There ain't no pizener ones 'n what *he* is. Mighty good man, pap is. Everybody says that. If they said any diffrunt they wouldn't say it whar *I* wuz—not *much* they wouldn't."

"What is your own religion?"

"Well, boss, you've kind o' got me, thar—and yit you hain't got me so mighty much, nuther. I think 't if a feller he'ps another feller when he's in trouble, and don't cuss, and don't do no mean things, nur noth'n' he ain' no business to do, and don't spell the Saviour's name with a little g, he ain't runnin' no resks—he's about as saift as if he b'longed to a church."

"But suppose he did spell it with a little g—what then?"

"Well, if he done it a-purpose, I reckon he wouldn't stand no chance—he *oughtn't* to have no chance, anyway, I'm most rotten certain 'bout that."

"What is your name?"

"Nicodemus Dodge."

"I think maybe you'll do, Nicodemus. We'll give you a trial, anyway."

"All right."

"When would you like to begin?"

"Now."

So within ten minutes after we had first glimpsed this nondescript he was one of us, and with his coat off and hard at it.

Beyond that end of our establishment which was furthest from the street, was a deserted garden, pathless, and thickly grown with the bloomy and villainous "jimpson" weed and its common friend the stately sunflower. In the midst of this mournful spot was a decayed and aged little "frame" house with but one room, one window, and no ceiling—it had been a smoke-house a generation before. Nicodemus was given this lonely and ghostly den as a bedchamber.

The village smarties recognized a treasure in Nicodemus, right away—a butt to play jokes on. It was easy to see that he was inconceivably green and confiding. George Jones had the glory of perpetrating the first joke on him; he gave him a cigar with a firecracker in it and winked to the crowd to come; the thing exploded presently and swept away the bulk of Nicodemus' eyebrows and eyelashes. He simply said:

Underwood and Underwood

Tom Sawyer and Huck Finn have entertained three generations of readers. Here is a model of the statue of them erected at Hannibal, Missouri.

Culver Service

"He had . . . an eye so eagle-like that a second lid would not have been a surprise to me" (Bret Harte, on meeting Mark Twain for the first time). Mark Twain as a young man, from a photograph by Gurney.

"I consider them kind of seeg'yars dangersome,"—and seemed to suspect nothing. The next evening Nicodemus waylaid George and poured a bucket of ice-water over him.

One day, while Nicodemus was in swimming, Tom McElroy "tied" his clothes. Nicodemus made a bonfire of Tom's by way of retaliation.

A third joke was played upon Nicodemus a day or two later— he walked up the middle aisle of the village church, Sunday night, with a staring handbill pinned between his shoulders. The joker spent the remainder of the night, after church, in the cellar of a deserted house, and Nicodemus sat on the cellar door till toward breakfast-time to make sure that the prisoner remembered that if any noise was made, some rough treatment would be the consequence. The cellar had two feet of stagnant water in it, and was bottomed with six inches of soft mud.

But I wander from the point. It was the subject of skeletons that brought this boy back to my recollection. Before a very long time had elapsed, the village smarties began to feel an uncomfortable consciousness of not having made a very shining success out of their attempts on the simpleton from "old Shelby." Experimenters grew scarce and chary. Now the young doctor came to the rescue. There was delight and applause when he proposed to scare Nicodemus to death and explained how he was going to do it. He had a noble new skeleton—the skeleton of the late and only local celebrity, Jimmy Finn, the village drunkard—a grisly piece of property which he had bought of Jimmy Finn himself, at auction, for fifty dollars, under great competition, when Jimmy lay very sick in the tanyard a fortnight before his death. The fifty dollars had gone promptly for whiskey and had considerably hurried up the change of ownership in the skeleton. The doctor would put Jimmy Finn's skeleton in Nicodemus's bed!

This was done—about half past ten in the evening. About Nicodemus's usual bedtime—midnight—the village jokers came creeping stealthily through the jimpson weeds and sunflowers toward the lonely frame den. They reached the window and peeped in. There sat the long-legged pauper, on his bed, in a very short shirt, and nothing more; he was dangling his legs contentedly back and forth, and wheezing the music of "Camptown Races" out of a paper-overlaid comb which he was pressing against his mouth; by him lay a new jewsharp, a new top, a solid india-rubber ball, a handful of painted marbles, five pounds of "store" candy, and a well-gnawed slab of gingerbread as big and as thick as a volume of sheet-music. He had sold the skeleton to a traveling quack for three dollars and was enjoying the result! » » »

During his boyhood Mark Twain enjoyed many kinds of entertainment in Hannibal. Much of it was homemade, to be sure, and those healthy forms of amusement provide most of the pages of a book like *Tom Sawyer*: picnics, storytelling, candy pulling, singing bees, berrypicking, swimming, and the many other sports native to rural communities such as those in Marion County, Missouri. However, the cultural matrix of the boy Sam Clemens had its admixture of entertainment from the outside world. Occasionally spice would be added to the village life with the arrival of a lecturer, a politician of oratorical powers, a "hell-fire" revivalist, a medicine show, a mesmerist,[16] a troupe of actors, and once a year that event of events, the circus. The entertainment that made the most indelible impression, though, was none of these, not even the circus. It was the traveling minstrel show. One of the most truly American art forms of the nineteenth century, along with the Negro spiritual and the tall tale, the minstrel show came upon the American scene almost with the arrival of Sam Clemens and evolved its patter and rhythms and costume during his youth. From the retrospect of over sixty years, Mark Twain describes the "minstrel" in all its glory as graphically as if he had seen it only yesterday:

THE MINSTREL SHOW (from *Mark Twain in Eruption*)

« « « I remember the first negro musical show I ever saw. It must have been in the early forties. It was a new institution. In our village of Hannibal we had not heard of it before, and it burst upon us as a glad and stunning surprise.

---

[16] One of the most entertaining accounts of Mark Twain's many youthful hoaxes is his reminiscence of his principal role in a mesmerist's demonstration during the Hannibal days, in *Mark Twain in Eruption* (ed. by Bernard De Voto).

The show remained a week and gave a performance every night. Church members did not attend these performances, but all the worldlings flocked to them and were enchanted. Church members did not attend shows out there in those days. The minstrels appeared with coal-black hands and faces and their clothing was a loud and extravagant burlesque of the clothing worn by the plantation slave of the time; not that the rags of the poor slave were burlesqued, for that would not have been possible; burlesque could have added nothing in the way of extravagance to the sorrowful accumulation of rags and patches which constituted his costume; it was the form and color of his dress that was burlesqued. Standing collars were in fashion in that day, and the minstrel appeared in a collar which engulfed and hid the half of his head and projected so far forward that he could hardly see sideways over its points. His coat was sometimes made of curtain calico with a swallowtail that hung nearly to his heels and had buttons as big as a blacking box. His shoes were rusty and clumsy and cumbersome, and five or six sizes too large for him. There were many variations upon this costume and they were all extravagant, and were by many believed to be funny.

The minstrel used a very broad negro dialect; he used it competently and with easy facility, and it was funny—delightfully and satisfyingly funny. However, there was one member of the minstrel troupe of those early days who was not extravagantly dressed and did not use the negro dialect. He was clothed in the faultless evening costume of the white society gentleman and used a stilted, courtly, artificial, and painfully grammatical form of speech, which the innocent villagers took for the real thing as exhibited in high and citified society, and they vastly admired it and envied the man who could frame it on the spot without reflection and deliver it in this easy and fluent and artistic fashion. "Bones" sat at one end of the row of minstrels, "Banjo" sat at the other end, and the dainty gentleman just described sat in the middle. This middleman was the spokesman of the show. The neatness and elegance of his dress, the studied courtliness of his manners and speech, and the shapeliness of his undoctored features made him a contrast to the rest of the troupe and particularly to "Bones" and "Banjo." "Bones" and "Banjo" were the prime jokers and whatever funniness was to be gotten out of paint and exaggerated clothing they utilized to the limit. Their lips were thickened and lengthened with bright red paint to such a degree that their mouths resembled slices cut in a ripe watermelon.

The original ground plan of the minstrel show was maintained without change for a good many years. There was no curtain to the stage in the beginning; while the audience waited they had nothing to look at except the row of empty chairs back of the footlights; presently the minstrels filed in and were received with a wholehearted welcome; they took their seats, each with his musical instrument in his hand; then the aristocrat in the middle began with a remark like this:

"I hope, gentlemen, I have the pleasure of seeing you in your accustomed excellent health, and that everything has proceeded prosperously with you since last we had the good fortune to meet."

"Bones" would reply for himself and go on and tell about something in the nature of peculiarly good fortune that had lately fallen to his share; but in the midst of it he would be interrupted by "Banjo," who would throw doubt upon his statement of the matter; then a delightful jangle of assertion and contradiction would break out between the two; the quarrel would gather emphasis, the voices would grow louder and louder and more and more energetic and vindictive, and the two would rise and approach each other, shaking fists and instruments and threatening bloodshed, the courtly middleman meantime imploring them to preserve the peace and observe the proprieties—but all in vain, of course. Sometimes the quarrel would last five minutes, the two contestants shouting deadly threats in each other's faces with their noses not six inches apart, the house shrieking with laughter all the while at this happy and accurate imitation of the usual and familiar negro quarrel, then finally the pair of malignants would gradually back away from each other, each making impressive threats as to what was going to happen the "next time" each should have the misfortune to cross the other's path; then they would sink into their chairs and growl back and forth at each other across the front of the line until the house had had time to recover from its convulsions and hysterics and quiet down.

The aristocrat in the middle of the row would now make a remark which was surreptitiously intended to remind one of the end men of an experience of his of a humorous nature and fetch it out of him—which it always did. It was usually an experience of a stale and moldy sort and as old as America. One of these things, which always delighted the audience of those days until the minstrels wore it threadbare, was "Bones's" account of the perils which he had once endured during a storm at sea. The storm lasted so long that in the course of time all the provisions were consumed. Then the middleman would inquire anxiously how the people managed to survive.

"Bones" would reply, "We lived on eggs."

"You lived on eggs! Where did you get eggs?"

"Every day, when the storm was so bad, the Captain laid *to*."

During the first five years that joke convulsed the house, but after that the population of the United States had heard it so many times that they respected it no longer and always received it in a deep and reproachful and indignant silence, along with others of its caliber which had achieved disfavor by long service.

The minstrel troupes had good voices and both their solos and their choruses were a delight to me as long as the negro show continued in existence. In the beginning the songs were rudely comic, such as "Buffalo Gals," "Camptown Races," "Old Dan Tucker," and so on; but a little later sentimental songs were introduced, such as "The Blue Juniata," "Sweet Ellen Bayne," "Nelly Bly," "A Life on the Ocean Wave," "The Larboard Watch," etc.

The minstrel show was born in the early forties and it had a prosperous career for about thirty-five years; then it degenerated into a variety show and was nearly all variety show with a negro act or two thrown in incidentally. The real negro show has been stone dead for thirty years. To my mind it was a thoroughly delightful thing, and a most competent laughter-compeller and I am sorry it is gone. » » »

At the age of eighteen, Sam Clemens left Hannibal to follow his printer's trade in places with more opportunity for a young fellow with ambitions. For over three years he wandered about through the eastern cities, rubbing against the sharper angles of life, meeting with all kinds of people, listening to their experiences, so strange and new to a Missouri boy, and talking, always talking. But the idyl of his Hannibal days was not over. A decision to go from Cincinnati to New Orleans and a chance encounter with one of the finest river pilots of the time turned him from printing to piloting and brought him back to the Mississippi Valley. His four years on the river boats in the late 1850's were an episode almost as idyllic as his Missouri boyhood and, when added to the Hannibal experience, went into the forming of the later Mark Twain, American humorist, world traveler, and commentator on life.

2. The River

ALL THROUGH his life Mark Twain's most vivid memory was of the great Mississippi. The river was his playground when he was a young boy and liked nothing better than to go fishing or swimming or boating or picnicking along its banks. The river fascinated the teen-age boy with its ever changing traffic of rafts and barges and flatboats and magnificent steamers constantly sliding around the river bend, gliding past the town, and then melting away into the hazy, distant reaches of the river and those faraway places that all boys dream about. And as he grew into young manhood and set off down the river to see the world, before he reached New Orleans, Sam Clemens gave in to his lifelong ambition to become a river pilot. He apprenticed himself to a crack pilot in order to learn the trade. Although this piloting career was cut short by the Civil War, the young Missourian learned every channel, every twist, and every turn of the great river between St. Louis and New Orleans so well that he qualified as a licensed pilot. This experience won him the highest esteem of his fellows and satisfied his craving for the worldly experience, prosperity, and prestige which all young men sought in those flush times of the 1850's. Just as important, this piloting experience stored up in Sam Clemens's mind a wealth of impressions—impressions of people, of places, of high adventure, of plain everyday life, and of natural beauty—which enriched his writing for years to come.

Two of Mark Twain's finest books were created from his memory of those halcyon river days. *Life on the Mississippi* gives us an authentic account of the history and the grandeur and the great economic importance of the "Father of Waters" as it impressed an American one hundred years ago. In *Huckleberry Finn* the river sustains a pageant of life, portraying the many and various types of people who traveled and lived in the long river valley and made those semifrontier days so colorful: rogues and murderers, gamblers and showmen, raftsmen and runaway slaves, lynching mobs and revivalist preachers, plantation owners and homespun families, lovers, heroes, and everyday villains and gangsters. In both of these books the river itself becomes alive and takes on a personality of its own, playing an active part by transporting the valuable commerce of the region and carrying its people from one life into another. Occasionally it aids the escape of a runaway slave, traps a steamboat in its shifting channels or destroys lives in its more violent moods of storm and flood. Then again it solaces those who have entrusted themselves to its waters. Always the river is the foreground or background of human drama.[1]

In the following description Mark Twain recalls from his earliest days the part that the river played in the daily lives of a river-front town during the 1840's:

"STEAMBOAT A-COMIN'!" (from *Life on the Mississippi*[2])

« « « Once a day a cheap, gaudy packet arrived upward from St. Louis, and another downward from Keokuk. Before these events, the day was glorious with expectancy; after them, the day was a

---

[1] For a less idealized but probably more accurate description of life on the Mississippi River in pre–Civil War days, see Bernard De Voto's vivid account in his *Mark Twain's America*, Chap. V.

[2] *Life on the Mississippi* was written in two parts: "Old Times on the Mississippi" (Chaps. I–XXI of the final version of the book) was published serially in the January–June numbers of the *Atlantic Monthly* in 1875. The remainder of the book Mark Twain wrote over eight years later after he had revisited the river in April of 1882. He published the combined material under its present title in May of 1883.

dead and empty thing. Not only the boys, but the whole village, felt this. After all these years I can picture that old time to myself now, just as it was then: the white town drowsing in the sunshine of a summer's morning; the streets empty, or pretty nearly so; one or two clerks sitting in front of the Water Street stores, with their splint-bottomed chairs tilted back against the walls, chins on breasts, hats slouched over their faces, asleep—with shingle-shavings enough around to show what broke them down; a sow and a litter of pigs loafing along the sidewalk, doing a good business in watermelon rinds and seeds; two or three lonely little freight piles scattered about the "levee"; a pile of "skids" on the slope of the stone-paved wharf, and the fragrant town drunkard asleep in the shadow of them; two or three wood flats at the head of the wharf, but nobody to listen to the peaceful lapping of the wavelets against them; the great Mississippi, the majestic, the magnificent Mississippi, rolling its mile-wide tide along, shining in the sun; the dense forest away on the other side; the "point" above the town, and the "point" below, bounding the river-glimpse and turning it into a sort of sea, and withal a very still and brilliant and lonely one. Presently a film of dark smoke appears above one of those remote "points"; instantly a negro drayman, famous for his quick eye and prodigious voice, lifts up the cry, "S-t-e-a-m-boat a-comin'!" and the scene changes! The town drunkard stirs, the clerks wake up, a furious clatter of drays follows, every house and store pours out a human contribution, and all in a twinkling the dead town is alive and moving. Drays, carts, men, boys, all go hurrying from many quarters to a common center, the wharf. Assembled there, the people fasten their eyes upon the coming boat as upon a wonder they are seeing for the first time. And the boat *is* rather a handsome sight, too. She is long and sharp and trim and pretty; she has two tall, fancy-topped chimneys, with a gilded device of some kind swung between them; a fanciful pilot-house, all glass and "gingerbread," perched on top of the "texas" deck behind them; the paddle-boxes are gorgeous with a picture or with gilded rays above the boat's name; the boiler-deck, the hurricane-deck, and the texas deck are fenced and ornamented with clean white railings; there is a flag gallantly flying from the jack-staff; the furnace doors are open and the fires glaring bravely; the upper decks are black with passengers; the captain stands by the big bell, calm, imposing, the envy of all; great volumes of the blackest smoke are rolling and tumbling out of the chimneys—a husbanded grandeur created with a bit of pitch-pine just before arriving at a town; the crew are grouped on the forecastle; the broad stage is run far out over the port bow, and an envied deck-hand stands picturesquely on the end of it with a coil of rope in his hand; the pent steam is screaming through the gauge-cocks; the captain lifts his hand, a bell rings, the wheels stop; then they turn back, churning the water to foam, and the steamer is at rest. Then such a scramble as there is to get aboard, and to get ashore, and to take in freight and to discharge freight, all at one and the same time; and such a yelling and cursing as the mates facilitate it all with! Ten minutes later the steamer is under way again, with no flag on the jack-staff and no black smoke issuing from the chimneys. Aften ten more minutes the town is dead again, and the town drunkard asleep by the skids once more. » » »

On other occasions young Sam Clemens felt the spell of the river on some lonely island away from the settlements of men. Some of his finest descriptions were evoked by his experiences of the fresh and fleeting beauty of the river at dawn and the vastness and stillness of the mighty stream as it swept on from day into night.

JUST SOLID LONESOMENESS (from *The Adventures of Huckleberry Finn*)

« « « Two or three days and nights went by; I reckon I might say they swum by, they slid along so quiet and smooth and lovely. Here is the way we put in the time. It was a monstrous big river down there—sometimes a mile and a half wide; we run nights, and laid up and hid daytimes; soon as night was most gone we stopped navigating and tied up—nearly always in the dead water under a towhead; and then cut young cottonwoods and willows, and hid the raft with them. Then we set out the lines. Next we slid into the river and had a swim, so as to freshen up and cool off; then we set down on the sandy bottom where the water was about knee-deep, and watched the daylight come. Not a sound anywheres—perfectly still—just like the whole world was asleep, only sometimes the bullfrogs a-cluttering, maybe. The first thing to see, looking away over the water, was a kind of dull line—that was the woods on t'other side; you couldn't make nothing else out; then a pale place in the sky; then more paleness spreading around; then the river softened up away off, and warn't black any more, but gray; you could see little dark spots drifting along ever so far away—trading-scows, and such things; and long black streaks—rafts; sometimes you could hear a sweep screaking; or jumbled-up voices, it was so still, and sounds come so far; and by and by you could see a streak on the water which you know by the look of the streak that there's a snag there in a swift current which breaks on it and makes that streak look that way; and you see the mist curl up off of the water, and the east reddens up, and the river, and you make out a log cabin in the edge of the woods, away on the bank on t'other side of the river, being a wood-yard, likely, and piled by them cheats so you can throw a dog through it anywheres; then the nice breeze springs up, and comes fanning you from over there, so cool and fresh and sweet to smell on account of the woods and the flowers; but sometimes not that way, because they've left dead fish laying around, gars and such, and they do get pretty rank; and next you've got the full day, and everything smiling in the sun, and the songbirds just going it!

... And afterwards we would watch the lonesomeness of the river, and kind of lazy along, and by and by lazy off to sleep. Wake up by and by, and look to see what done it, and maybe see a steamboat coughing along up-stream, so far off towards the other side you couldn't tell nothing about her only whether she was a stern-wheel or side-wheel; then for about an hour there wouldn't be nothing to hear nor nothing to see—just solid lonesomeness. Next you'd see a raft sliding by, away off yonder, and maybe a galoot on it chopping, because they're most always doing it on a raft; you'd see the ax flash and come down—you don't hear nothing; you see that ax go up again, and by the time it's above the man's head then you hear the *k'chunk!*—it had took all that time to come over the water. So we would put in the day, lazying around, listening to the stillness. Once there was a thick fog, and the rafts and things that went by was beating tin pans so the steamboats wouldn't run over them. A scow or a raft went by so close we could hear them talking and cussing and laughing—heard them plain; but we couldn't see no sign of them; it made you feel crawly; it was like spirits carrying on that way in the air. . . .

Sometimes we'd have that whole river all to ourselves for the longest time. Yonder was the banks and the islands, across the water; and maybe a spark—which was a candle in a cabin window; and sometimes on the water you could see a spark or two—on a raft or a scow, you know; and maybe you could hear a fiddle or a song coming from one of them crafts. It's lovely to live on a raft. We had the sky up there, all speckled with stars, and we used to lay on our backs and look up at them, and discuss about whether they was made or only just happened. . . .

Once or twice of a night we would see a steamboat slipping along in the dark, and now and then she would belch a whole world of sparks up out of her chimbleys, and they would rain down in the river and look awful pretty; then she would turn a corner and her lights would wink out and her powwow shut off and leave the river still again; and by and by her waves would get to us, a long time after she was gone, and joggle the raft a bit, and after that you wouldn't hear nothing for you couldn't tell how long, except maybe frogs or something.

After midnight the people on shore went to bed, and then for two or three hours the shores was black—no more sparks in the cabin windows. These sparks was our clock—the first one that showed again meant morning was coming, so we hunted a place to hide and tie up right away. . . .

We got away as soon as it was good and dark. . . . We come in sight of the little bunch of lights by and by—that was the town, you know—and slid by, about a half a mile out, all right. When we was three-quarters of a mile below we hoisted up our signal lantern; and about ten o'clock it come on to rain and blow and thunder and lighten like everything. . . . My souls, how the wind did scream along! And every second or two there'd come a glare that lit up the white-caps for a half a mile around, and you'd see the islands looking dusty through the rain, and the trees thrashing around in the wind; then comes a *h-whack!*—bum! bum! bumbleumble-um-bum-bum-bum-bum—and the thunder would go rumbling and grumbling away, and quit—and then *rip* comes another flash and another sockdolager. The waves most washed me off the raft sometimes, but I hadn't any clothes on, and didn't mind. We didn't have no trouble about snags; the lightning was glaring and flittering around so constant that we could see them plenty soon enough to throw her head this way or that and miss them. » » »

Out of those early boyhood days on the river emerge, in Mark Twain's memory, the last remnants of the frontier days—the raftsmen. In his *Old Times on the Mississippi*, Mark Twain describes how he and his friends used to swim out to the great lumber rafts as they swept down past Hannibal from the north woods on their way to the Gulf. For a half-hour or so the boys would ride the raft down river in order to watch the burly raftsmen manning the sweeps. Occasionally these men would simply be sitting in a group on the raft swapping yarns and singing. If their drinking had been too heavy and tempers rose too hot, a brief but furious fight might break out—or, more often, several of the raftmen would simply threaten each other. Their threatening attitudes and boasts of prowess provided many "screamers" of American frontier folklore.[3] Mark Twain's account of these characters is one of the most vivid, seemingly fantastic, yet authentic pictures of river life in American literature:

THE CORPSE-MAKER AND THE CHILD OF CALAMITY[4]
(from *Old Times on the Mississippi*)

« « « . . . There was thirteen men there—they was the watch

---

[3] The evolution of these frontier boasters, known originally among their fellows as "ring-tailed roarers" and later as "screamers," is traced by E. A. Botkin in his *Treasury of American Folklore* (New York, Crown Publishers, 1944). As Botkin points out, "the 'screamer' is the ring-tailed roarer grown maudlin, who boasts out of his weakness rather than his strength" (p. 51). In spite of their weakness, Mark Twain's "Corpse-Maker" and his "Child of Calamity" epitomize the tall talk and the colorful dialect that were inherent in the humor of the whole breed of American backwoodsmen and river men for many generations. Botkin provides many fine samples of this literary tradition.

[4] Mark Twain originally intended this raftsman episode for *Huckleberry Finn*, whose river escapades provide the proper context. The author inserted the sketch

on deck of course. And a mighty rough-looking lot, too. They had a jug, and tin cups, and they kept the jug moving. One man was singing—roaring, you may say; and it wasn't a nice song—for a parlor, anyway. He roared through his nose, and strung out the last word of every line very long. When he was done they all fetched a kind of Injun war-whoop, and then another was sung. It begun:

> There was a woman in our towdn,
> In our town did dwed'l [dwell],
> She loved her husband dear-i-lee,
> But another man twyste as wed'l.
>
> Singing too, riloo, riloo, riloo,
> Ri-too, riloo, rilay —— e,
> She loved her husband dear-i-lee,
> But another man twyste as wed'l.

And so on—fourteen verses. It was kind of poor, and when he was going to start on the next verse one of them said it was the tune the old cow died on; and another one said: "Oh, give us a rest!" And another one told him to take a walk. They made fun of him till he got mad and jumped up and begun to cuss the crowd, and said he could lam any thief in the lot.

They was all about to make a break for him, but the biggest man there jumped up and says:

"Set whar you are, gentlemen. Leave him to me; he's my meat."

Then he jumped up in the air three times, and cracked his heels together every time. He flung off a buckskin coat that was all hung with fringes, and says, "You lay thar tell the chawin-up's done"; and flung his hat down, which was all over ribbons, and says, "You lay thar tell his sufferin's is over."

Then he jumped up in the air and cracked his heels together again, and shouted out:

"Whoo-oop! I'm the old original iron-jawed, brass-mounted,

in his earlier *Old Times on the Mississippi*, with the following comment: "By way of illustrating keelboat talk and manners, and that now departed and hardly remembered raft life, I will throw in, in this place, a chapter from a book which I have been working at, by fits and starts, during the past five or six years, and may possibly finish in the course of five or six more" (*Life on the Mississippi*, Author's National Edition, 19).

copper-bellied corpse-maker from the wilds of Arkansaw! Look at me! I'm the man they call Sudden Death and General Desolation! Sired by a hurricane, dam'd by an earthquake, half-brother to the cholera, nearly related to the smallpox on the mother's side. Look at me! I take nineteen alligators and a bar'l of whiskey for breakfast when I'm in robust health, and a bushel of rattlesnakes and a dead body when I'm ailing. I split the ever-lasting rocks with my glance, and I squench the thunder when I speak! Whoo-oop! Stand back and give me room according to my strength! Blood's my natural drink, and the wails of the dying is music to my ear. Cast your eye on me, gentlemen! and lay low and hold your breath, for I'm 'bout to turn myself loose!"

All the time he was getting this off, he was shaking his head and looking fierce, and kind of swelling around in a little circle, tucking up his wristbands, and now and then straightening up and beating his breast with his fist, saying, "Look at me, gentlemen!" When he got through, he jumped up and cracked his heels together three times, and let off a roaring "Whoo-oop! I'm the bloodiest son of a wildcat that lives!"

Then the man that had started the row tilted his old slouch hat down over his right eye; then he bent stooping forward, with his back sagged and his south end sticking out far, and his fists a-shoving out and drawing in in front of him, and so went around in a little circle about three times, swelling himself up and breathing hard. Then he straightened, and jumped up and cracked his heels together three times before he lit again (that made them cheer), and he began to shout like this:

"Whoo-oop! bow your neck and spread, for the kingdom of sorrow's a-coming! Hold me down to the earth, for I feel my powers a-working; Whoo-oop! I'm a child of sin, *don't* let me get a start! Smoked glass, here, for all! Don't attempt to look at me with the naked eye, gentlemen! When I'm playful I use the meridians of longitude and parallels of latitude for a seine, and drag the Atlantic Ocean for whales! I scratch my head with the lightning and purr myself to sleep with the thunder! When I'm cold I bile the Gulf of Mexico and bathe in it; when I'm hot I fan myself with an equinoctial storm; when I'm thirsty I reach up and suck a cloud dry like a sponge; when I range the earth hungry, famine follows in my tracks! Whoo-oop! Bow your neck and spread! I put my hand on the sun's face and make it night in the earth; I bite a piece out of the moon and hurry the seasons; I shake myself and crumble the mountains! Contemplate me through leather—*don't* use the naked eye! I'm the man with a petrified heart and biler-iron bowels! The massacre of isolated communities is the pastime of my idle moments, the destruction of nationalities the serious business of my life! The boundless vastness of the great American desert is my enclosed property, and I bury my dead on my own premises!" He jumped up and cracked his heels together three times before he lit (they cheered him again), and as he come down he shouted out: "Whoo-oop! bow your neck and spread, for the pet child of Calamity's a-coming!"

Then the other one went to swelling around and blowing again—the first one—the one they called Bob; next, the Child of Calamity chipped in again, bigger than ever; then they both got at it at the same time, swelling round and round each other and punching their fists most into each other's faces, and whooping and jawing like Injuns; then Bob called the Child names, and the Child called him names back again; next, Bob called him a heap rougher names, and the Child come back at him with the very worst kind of language; next, Bob knocked the Child's hat off, and the Child picked it up and kicked Bob's ribbony hat about six foot; Bob went and got it and said never mind, this warn't going to be the last of this thing, because he was a man that never forgot and never forgive, and so the Child better look out, for there was a time a-coming, just as sure as he was a living man, that he would have to answer to him with the best blood in his body. The Child said no man was willinger than he for that time to come, and he would give Bob fair warning, *now*, never to cross his path again, for he could never rest till he had waded in his blood, for such was his nature, though he was sparing him now on account of his family, if he had one.

Both of them was edging away in different directions, growling and shaking their heads and going on about what they was going to do; but a little black-whiskered chap skipped up and says:

"Come back here, you couple of chicken-livered cowards, and I'll thrash the two of ye!"

And he done it, too. He snatched them, he jerked them this way and that, he booted them around, he knocked them sprawling faster than they could get up. Why, it warn't two minutes till they begged like dogs—and how the other lot did yell and laugh and clap their hands all the way through, and shout, "Sail in, Corpse-Maker!" "Hi! at him again, Child of Calamity!" "Bully for you, little Davy!" Well, it was a perfect pow-wow for a while. Bob and the Child had red noses and black eyes when they got through. Little Davy made them own up that they was sneaks and cowards and not fit to eat with a dog or drink with a nigger; then Bob and the Child shook hands with each other, very solemn, and said that they had always respected each other and was willing to let by-gones be bygones. So then they washed their faces in the river; and just then there was a loud order to stand by for a crossing, and some of them went forward to man the sweeps there, and the rest went aft to handle the after sweeps. » » »

Mark Twain could never completely separate the river from the gaudy floating palaces that were the true splendor of the age to the eyes of the Mississippi Valley people. The small boys of that time might dream of circuses and minstrel shows, the young men and ladies might dream of knights and castles and charging steeds, but young Sam Clemens dreamt only of steamboats. To see a proud stern-wheeler gliding majestically by was the high light of the week. To step aboard one was to enter heaven for the young Missourian. And to take passage on one or to mount to the pilot house and take over the wheel was—well, indescribable, except for Mark Twain's pen. A boy's vision of a steamboat's exterior has already been described. Here is how Mark Twain describes the interior of one of the finer packet boats of old times on the Mississippi as an observant passenger would see it:

THE RIVER PALACE (from *Life on the Mississippi*)

« « « When he stepped aboard a big fine steamboat, he entered a new and marvelous world: chimney-tops cut to counterfeit a spraying crown of plumes—and maybe painted red; pilot-house,

THE RIVER PALACE

hurricane-deck, boiler-deck guards, all garnished with white wooden filigree-work of fanciful patterns; gilt acorns topping the derricks; gilt deerhorns over the big bell; gaudy symbolical picture on the paddle-box, possibly; big roomy boiler-deck, painted blue, and furnished with Windsor armchairs; inside, a far-receding snow-white "cabin"; porcelain knob and oil-picture on every stateroom door; curving patterns of filigree-work touched up with gilding, stretching overhead all down the converging vista; big chandeliers every little way, each an April shower of glittering glass-drops; lovely rainbow-light falling everywhere from the colored glazing of the skylights; the whole a long-drawn, resplendent tunnel, a bewildering and soul-satisfying spectacle! in the ladies' cabin a pink and white Wilton carpet, as soft as mush, and glorified with a ravishing pattern of gigantic flowers. » » »

The luxury and splendor of the Mississippi boats may have overawed the younger Sam Clemens, but as he grew up and became a pilot-apprentice, the boats and the river took on a different and more absorbing meaning for him—navigation. For four years he studied and practiced the craft of piloting.[5] Although he never lost his sense of the river's beauty, its shape and color and movement became technical problems on the solution of which his job, the safety of his boat, and the lives of his passengers depended. This new point of view comes out most strikingly in his contrast between

[5] How Mark Twain turned to piloting from journeyman printer is told in a few matter-of-fact sentences in his autobiography: "I had been reading Lieutenant Herndon's account of his explorations of the Amazon and had been mightily attracted by what he said of coca. I made up my mind that I would go to the headwaters of the Amazon and collect coca and trade in it and make a fortune. I left [Cincinnati] for New Orleans in the steamer *Paul Jones* with this great idea filling my mind. One of the pilots of that boat was Horace Bixby. Little by little I got acquainted with him, and pretty soon I was doing a lot of steering for him in his daylight watches. When I got to New Orleans I inquired about ships leaving for Para and discovered that there weren't any, and learned that there probably wouldn't be any during that century. It had not occurred to me to inquire about these particulars before leaving Cincinnati, so there I was. I couldn't get to the Amazon. I had no friends in New Orleans and no money to speak of. I went to Horace Bixby and asked him to make a pilot out of me. He said he would do it for five hundred dollars, one hundred dollars cash in advance. So I steered for him up to St. Louis, borrowed the money from my brother-in-law, and closed the bargain" (*Mark Twain's Autobiography*, II, 289).

the popular romantic view of the river and the pilot's professional view:

DISILLUSIONMENT (from *Life on the Mississippi*)

« « « The face of the water, in time, became a wonderful book— a book that was a dead language to the uneducated passenger, but which told its mind to me without reserve, delivering its most cherished secrets as clearly as if it uttered them with a voice. And it was not a book to be read once and thrown aside, for it had a new story to tell every day. Throughout the long twelve hundred miles there was never a page that was void of interest, never one that you could leave unread without loss, never one that you would want to skip, thinking you could find higher enjoyment in some other thing. There never was so wonderful a book written by man; never one whose interest was so absorbing, so unflagging, so sparklingly renewed with every reperusal. The passenger who could not read it was charmed with a peculiar sort of faint dimple on its surface (on the rare occasions when he did not overlook it altogether); but to the pilot that was an *italicized* passage; indeed, it was more than that, it was a legend of the largest capitals, with a string of shouting exclamation-points at the end of it, for it meant that a wreck or a rock was buried there that could tear the life out of the strongest vessel that ever floated. It is the faintest and simplest expression the water ever makes, and the most hideous to a pilot's eye. In truth, the passenger who could not read this book saw nothing but all manner of pretty pictures in it, painted by the sun and shaded by the clouds, whereas to the trained eye these were not pictures at all, but the grimmest and most dead-earnest of reading-matter.

Now when I had mastered the language of this water, and had come to know every trifling feature that bordered the great river as familiarly as I knew the letters of the alphabet, I had made a valuable acquisition. But I had lost something, too. I had lost something which could never be restored to me while I lived. All the grace, the beauty, the poetry, had gone out of the majestic river! I still kept in mind a certain wonderful sunset which I witnessed when steamboating was new to me. A broad expanse of the river was turned to blood; in the middle distance the red hue brightened into gold, through which a solitary log came floating, black and conspicuous; in one place a long, slanting mark lay sparkling upon the water; in another the surface was broken by boiling, tumbling rings, that were as many-tinted as an opal; where the ruddy flush was faintest, was a smooth spot that was covered with graceful circles and radiating lines, ever so delicately traced; the shore on our left was densely wooded, and the somber shadow that fell from this forest was broken in one place by a long, ruffled trail that shone like silver; and high above the forest wall a clean-stemmed dead tree waved a single leafy bough that glowed like a flame in the unobstructed splendor that was flowing from the sun. There were graceful curves, reflected images, woody heights, soft distances; and over the whole scene, far and near, the dissolving lights drifted steadily, enriching it every passing moment with new marvels of coloring.

I stood like one bewitched. I drank it in, in a speechless rapture. The world was new to me, and I had never seen anything like this at home. But as I have said, a day came when I began to cease from noting the glories and the charms which the moon and the sun and the twilight wrought upon the river's face; another day came when I ceased altogether to note them. Then, if that sunset scene had been repeated, I should have looked upon it without rapture, and should have commented upon it, inwardly, after this fashion: "This sun means that we are going to have wind to-morrow; that floating log means that the river is rising, small thanks to it; that slanting mark on the water refers to a bluff reef which is going to kill somebody's steamboat one of these nights, if it keeps on stretching out like that; those tumbling 'boils' show a dissolving bar and a changing channel there; the lines and circles in the slick water over yonder are a warning that that troublesome place is shoaling up dangerously; that silver streak in the shadow of the forest is the 'break' from a new snag, and he has located himself in the very best place he could have found to fish for steamboats; that tall dead tree, with a single living branch, is not going to last long, and then how is a body ever going to get through this blind place at night without the friendly old landmark?"

No, the romance and beauty were all gone from the river. All the value any feature of it had for me now was the amount of usefulness it could furnish toward compassing the safe piloting of a steamboat. » » »

Mr. Bixby, who taught his cub pilot many a useful lesson, was one of the finest river pilots of his time. His reputation came not only from his steadiness and reliability, but also from his ability to take occasional chances and come through safely. That masterly and unshakable knowledge of the river that the older pilot insisted on in apprentices was only one part of his skill; the other indispensables were his cool-headedness and his nerve. No one admired these qualities in others more than Mark Twain, and nowhere are they better dramatized than in his account of an exciting incident in Bixby's piloting career:

A LIGHTNING PILOT (from *Life on the Mississippi*)

« « « The pilot-house was full of pilots, going down to "look at the river." What is called the "upper river" (the two hundred miles between St. Louis and Cairo, where the Ohio comes in) was low; and the Mississippi changes its channel so constantly that the pilots used to always find it necessary to run down to Cairo to take a fresh look, when their boats were to lie in port a week; that is, when the water was at a low stage. A deal of this "looking at the river" was done by poor fellows who seldom had a berth, and whose only hope of getting one lay in their being always freshly posted and therefore ready to drop into the shoes of some reputable pilot, for a single trip, on account of such pilot's sudden illness, or some other necessity. And a good many of them constantly ran up and down inspecting the river, not because they ever really hoped to get a berth, but because (they being guests of the boat) it was cheaper to "look at the river" than stay ashore and pay board. In time these fellows grew dainty in their tastes, and only infested boats that had an established reputation for setting good tables. All visiting pilots were useful, for they were always ready and willing, winter or summer, night or day, to go out in the yawl and help buoy the channel or assist the boat's pilots in any way they could. They were likewise welcome because all pilots are tireless talkers, when gathered together, and as they talk only about the river they are always understood and are always interesting. Your true pilot cares nothing about anything on earth but the river, and his pride in his occupation surpasses the pride of kings. . . .

Next morning I felt pretty rusty and low-spirited. We went booming along, taking a good many chances, for we were anxious to "get out of the river" (as getting out to Cairo was called) before night should overtake us. But Mr. Bixby's partner, the other pilot, presently grounded the boat, and we lost so much time getting her off that it was plain the darkness would overtake us a good long way above the mouth. This was a great misfortune, especially to certain of our visiting pilots, whose boats would have to wait for their return, no matter how long that might be. It sobered the pilothouse talk a good deal. Coming up-stream, pilots did not mind low water or any kind of darkness; nothing stopped them but fog. But down-stream work was different; a boat was too nearly helpless, with a stiff current pushing behind her; so it was not customary to run down-stream at night in low water.

There seemed to be one small hope, however: if we could get through the intricate and dangerous Hat Island crossing before night, we could venture the rest, for we would have plainer sailing and better water. But it would be insanity to attempt Hat Island at night. So there was a deal of looking at watches all the rest of the day, and a constant ciphering upon the speed we were making; Hat Island was the eternal subject; sometimes hope was high and sometimes we were delayed in a bad crossing, and down it went again. For hours all hands lay under the burden of this suppressed excitement; it was even communicated to me, and I got to feeling so solicitous about Hat Island, and under such an awful pressure of responsibility, that I wished I might have five minutes on shore to draw a good, full, relieving breath, and start over again. We were standing no regular watches. Each of our pilots ran such portions of the river as he had run when coming up-stream, because of his greater familiarity with it; but both remained in the pilothouse constantly.

An hour before sunset Mr. Bixby took the wheel, and Mr. W. stepped aside. For the next thirty minutes every man held his watch in his hand and was restless, silent, and uneasy. At last somebody said, with a doomful sigh:

"Well, yonder's Hat Island—and we can't make it."

All the watches closed with a snap, everybody sighed and muttered something about its being "too bad, too bad—ah, if we could *only* have got here half an hour sooner!" and the place was thick with the atmosphere of disappointment. Some started to go out, but loitered, hearing no bell-tap to land. The sun dipped behind the horizon, the boat went on. Inquiring looks passed from one guest to another; and one who had his hand on the door-knob and had turned it, waited, then presently took away his hand and let the knob turn back again. We bore steadily down the bend. More looks were exchanged, and nods of surprised admiration—but no words. Insensibly the men drew together behind Mr. Bixby, as the sky darkened and one or two dim stars came out. The dead silence and sense of waiting became oppressive. Mr. Bixby pulled the cord, and two deep, mellow notes from the big bell floated off on the night. Then a pause, and one more note was struck. The watchman's voice followed, from the hurricane-deck:

"Labboard lead, there! Stabbord lead!"

The cries of the leadsmen began to rise out of the distance, and were gruffly repeated by the word-passers on the hurricane-deck.

"M-a-r-k three! M-a-r-k three! Quarter-less-three! Half twain! Quarter twain! M-a-r-k twain! Quarter-less-"

Mr. Bixby pulled two bell-ropes, and was answered by faint jinglings far below in the engine-room, and our speed slackened. The steam began to whistle through the guage-cocks. The cries of the leadsmen went on—and it is a weird sound, always, in the night. Every pilot in the lot was watching now, with fixed eyes, and talking under his breath. Nobody was calm and easy but Mr. Bixby. He would put his wheel down and stand on a spoke, and as the steamer swung into her (to me) utterly invisible marks—for we seemed to be in the midst of a wide and gloomy sea—he would meet and fasten her there. Out of the murmur of half-audible talk, one caught a coherent sentence now and then—such as:

"There; she's over the first reef all right!"

After a pause, another subdued voice:

"Her stern's coming down just *exactly* right, by *George!*"

"Now she's in the marks; over she goes!"

Somebody else muttered:

"Oh, it was done beautiful—*beautiful!*"

Now the engines were stopped altogether, and we drifted with the current. Not that I could see the boat drift, for I could not, the stars being all gone by this time. This drifting was the dismalest work; it held one's heart still. Presently I discovered a blacker gloom than that which surrounded us. It was the head of the island. We were closing right down upon it. We entered its deeper shadow, and so imminent seemed the peril that I was likely to suffocate; and I had the strongest impulse to do *something*, anything, to save the vessel. But still Mr. Bixby stood by his wheel, silent, intent as a cat, and all the pilots stood shoulder to shoulder at his back."

"She'll not make it!" somebody whispered.

The water grew shoaler and shoaler, by the leadsmen's cries, till it was down to:

"Eight-and-a-half! E-i-g-h-t feet! E-i-g-h-t feet! Seven-and-"

Mr. Bixby said warningly through his speaking-tube to the engineer:

"Stand by, now!"

"Ay, ay, sir!"

"Seven-and-a-half! Seven feet! *Six*—and-"

We touched bottom! Instantly Mr. Bixby set a lot of bells ringing, shouted through the tube, "*Now*, let her have it—every ounce you've got!" then to his partner, "Put her hard down! snatch her! snatch her!" The boat rasped and ground her way through the sand, hung upon the apex of disaster a single tremendous instant, and then over she went! And such a shout as went up at Mr. Bixby's back never loosened the roof of a pilot-house before!

There was no more trouble after that. Mr. Bixby was a hero that night; and it was some little time, too, before his exploit ceased to be talked about by river-men.

Fully to realize the marvelous precision required in laying the great steamer in her marks in that murky waste of water, one should know that not only must she pick her intricate way through snags and blind reefs, and then shave the head of the island so closely as to brush the overhanging foliage with her stern, but at one place she must pass almost within arm's reach of a sunken and invisible wreck that would snatch the hull timbers from under her if she should strike it, and destroy a quarter of a million dollars' worth of steamboat and cargo in five minutes, and maybe a hundred and fifty human lives into the bargain.

The last remark I heard that night was a compliment to Mr. Bixby, uttered in soliloquy and with unction by one of our guests. He said:

"By the Shadow of Death, but he's a lightning pilot!" » » »

When Sam Clemens the cub pilot was finishing his apprenticeship, he believed that without further ado he was ready to enter the fraternity of licensed river pilots and become one of the gods. Perhaps he was entitled to be a bit cocky, for months of careful study of every detail of the river throughout a thousand miles of its course lay behind him. He had at last mastered all of the channels by night and by day, going both upstream and down—so he thought. But Mr. Bixby, his master, thought otherwise. The result was a loss of face and a fallen pride which all overly eager young men suffer in all generations. The lesson that Bixby taught his apprentice was given in true Missouri style. Mark Twain tells the story of what happened with a mixture of amusement and chagrin that recurred whenever he recalled his young piloting experiences:

THE LESSON (from *Life on the Mississippi*)

« « « A pilot must have a memory; but there are two higher qualities which he must also have. He must have good and quick judgment and decision, and a cool, calm courage that no peril can shake. Give a man the merest trifle of pluck to start with, and by the time he has become a pilot he cannot be unmanned by any danger a steamboat can get into; but one cannot quite say the same for judgment. Judgment is a matter of brains, and a man must *start* with a good stock of that article or he will never succeed as a pilot.

The growth of courage in the pilot-house is steady all the time, but it does not reach a high and satisfactory condition until some time after the young pilot has been "standing his own watch" alone and under the staggering weight of all the responsibilities connected with the position. When the apprentice has become pretty thoroughly acquainted with the river, he goes clattering along so fearlessly with his steamboat, night or day, that he presently begins to imagine that it is *his* courage that animates him; but the first time the pilot steps out and leaves him to his own devices he finds out it was the other man's. He discovers that the article has been left out of his own cargo altogether. The whole river is bristling with exigencies in a moment; he is not prepared for them; he does not know how to meet them; all his knowledge forsakes him; and within fifteen minutes he is as white as a sheet and scared almost to death. Therefore pilots wisely train these cubs by various strategic tricks to look danger in the face a little more calmly. A favorite way of theirs is to play a friendly swindle upon the candidate.

Mr. Bixby served me in this fashion once, and for years afterward I used to blush, even in my sleep, when I thought of it. I had become a good steersman; so good, indeed, that I had all the work to do on our watch, night and day. Mr. Bixby seldom made a suggestion to me; all he ever did was to take the wheel on particularly bad nights or in particularly bad crossings, land the boat when she needed to be landed, play gentleman of leisure nine-tenths of the watch, and collect the wages. The lower river was about bankfull, and if anybody had questioned my ability to run any crossing between Cairo and New Orleans without help or instruction, I should have felt irreparably hurt. The idea of being afraid of any crossing in the lot, in the *daytime*, was a thing too preposterous for contemplation. Well, one matchless summer's day I was bowling down the bend above Island 66, brimful of self-conceit and carrying my nose as high as a giraffe's, when Mr. Bixby said:

"I am going below awhile. I suppose you know the next crossing?"

This was almost an affront. It was about the plainest and simplest crossing in the whole river. One couldn't come to any harm, whether he ran it right or not; and as for depth, there never had been any bottom there. I knew all this, perfectly well.

"Know how to *run* it? Why, I can run it with my eyes shut."

"How much water is there in it?"

"Well, that is an odd question. I couldn't get bottom there with a church steeple."

"You think so, do you?"

The very tone of the question shook my confidence. That was what Mr. Bixby was expecting. He left, without saying anything more. I began to imagine all sorts of things. Mr. Bixby, unknown to me, of course, sent somebody down to the forecastle with some mysterious instructions to the leadsmen, another messenger was sent to whisper among the officers, and then Mr. Bixby went into hiding behind a smoke-stack where he could observe results. Presently the captain stepped out on the hurricane-deck; next the chief mate appeared; then a clerk. Every moment or two a straggler was added to my audience; and before I got to the head of the island I had fifteen or twenty people assembled down there under my nose. I began to wonder what the trouble was. As I started across, the captain glanced aloft at me and said, with a sham uneasiness in his voice:

"Where is Mr. Bixby?"

"Gone below, sir."

But that did the business for me. My imagination began to construct dangers out of nothing, and they multiplied faster than I could keep the run of them. All at once I imagined that I saw shoal water ahead! The wave of coward agony that surged through me then came near dislocating every joint in me. All my confidence in that crossing vanished. I seized the bell-rope; dropped it, ashamed; seized it again; dropped it once more; clutched it tremblingly once again, and pulled it so feebly that I could hardly hear the stroke myself. Captain and mate sang out instantly, and both together:

"Starboard lead there! and quick about it!"

This was another shock. I began to climb the wheel like a squirrel; but I would hardly get the boat started to port before I would see new dangers on that side, and away I would spin to the other; only to find perils accumulating to starboard, and be crazy to get to port again. Then came the leadsman's sepulchral cry:

"D-e-e-p four!"

Deep four in a bottomless crossing! The terror of it took my breath away.

"M-a-r-k three! M-a-r-k three! Quarter-less-three! Half twain!"

This was frightful! I seized the bell-ropes and stopped the engines.

"Quarter twain! Quarter twain! *Mark* twain!"

I was helpless. I did not know what in the world to do. I was quaking from head to foot, and I could have hung my hat on my eyes, they stuck out so far.

"Quarter-*less*-twain! Nine-and-a-*half!*"

We were *drawing* nine! My hands were in a nerveless flutter. I could not ring a bell intelligibly with them. I flew to the speaking-tube and shouted to the engineer:

"Oh, Ben, if you love me, *back* her! Quick, Ben! Oh, back the immortal *soul* out of her!"

I heard the door close gently. I looked around, and there stood Mr. Bixby, smiling a bland, sweet smile. Then the audience on the hurricane-deck sent up a thundergust of humiliating laughter. I saw it all, now, and I felt meaner than the meanest man in human history. I laid in the lead, set the boat in her marks, came ahead on the engines, and said:

"It was a fine trick to play on an orphan, *wasn't* it? I suppose I'll never hear the last of how I was ass enough to heave the lead at the head of 66."

"Well, no, you won't, maybe. In fact I hope you won't; for I want you to learn something by that experience. Didn't you *know* there was no bottom in that crossing?"

"Yes, sir, I did."

"Very well, then. You shouldn't have allowed me or anybody else to shake your confidence in that knowledge. Try to remember that. And another thing: when you get into a dangerous place, don't turn coward. That isn't going to help matters any."

It was a good enough lesson, but pretty hardly learned. Yet about the hardest part of it was that for months I so often had to hear a phrase which I had conceived a particular distaste for. It was, "Oh, Ben, if you love me, back her!" » » »

Most of the glamour and high adventure of the Mississippi Valley in Sam Clemens's day were to be found afloat. When the cub pilot went ashore to visit the plantations and the small towns along the river, he stepped into quite a different world. A few small cities like St. Louis, Memphis, and New Orleans offered glimpses of culture and a taste of luxury. But the smaller settlements and isolated farms and plantations of the lower river still carried the primitive stamp of a semifrontier region. Mark Twain, through the eyes of the young Huck Finn, has left us a very real picture of that river-front world.

AN ARKANSAS PLANTATION (from *The Adventures of Huckleberry Finn*)

« « « Phelps's was one of these little one-horse cotton plantations, and they all look alike. A rail fence round a two-acre yard; a stile made out of logs sawed off and up-ended in steps, like barrels of a different length, to climb over the fence with, and for the women to stand on when they are going to jump onto a horse; some sickly grass-patches in the big yard, but mostly it was bare and smooth, like an old hat with the nap rubbed off; big double log house for the white folks—hewed logs, with the chinks stopped up with mud or mortar, and these mud-stripes been whitewashed some time or another; round-log kitchen, with a big broad, open but roofed passage joining it to the house; log smokehouse back of the kitchen; three little log nigger cabins in a row t'other side of the smokehouse; one little hut all by itself away down against the back fence, and some outbuildings down a piece the other side; ash-hopper and big kettle to bile soap in by the little hut; bench by the kitchen door, with bucket of water and a gourd; hound asleep there in the sun; more hounds asleep round about; about three shade trees away off in a corner; some currant bushes and gooseberry bushes in one place by the fence; outside of the fence a garden and a watermelon patch; then the cotton-fields begins, and after the fields the woods.

I went around and clumb over the back stile by the ash-hopper, and started for the kitchen. When I got a little ways I heard the dim hum of a spinning-wheel wailing along up and sinking along down again; and then I knowed for certain I wished I was dead— for that *is* the lonesomest sound in the whole world....

When I got half-way, first one hound and then another got up and went for me, and of course I stopped and faced them, and kept still. And such another powwow as they made! In a quarter of a minute I was a kind of a hub of a wheel, as you may say—

spokes made out of dogs—circle of fifteen of them packed together around me, with their necks and noses stretched up towards me, a-barking and howling; and more a-coming; you could see them sailing over fences and around corners from everywheres.

A nigger woman come tearing out of the kitchen with a rolling-pin in her hand, singing out, "Begone! *you* Tige! you Spot! begone sah!" and she fetched first one and then another of them a clip and sent them howling, and then the rest followed; and the next second half of them come back, wagging their tails around me, and making friends with me. There ain't no harm in a hound, nohow.

And behind the woman comes a little nigger girl and two little nigger boys without anything on but tow-linen shirts, and they hung on to their mother's gown, and peeped out from behind her at me, bashful, the way they always do. And here comes the white woman running from the house, about forty-five or fifty year old, bareheaded, and her spinning-stick in her hand; and behind her comes her little white children, acting the same way the little niggers was going. » » »

The typical small plantation of the Mississippi Valley in pre–Civil War days was still in the "backwoods" stage, but the typical river town was, if anything, more primitive. Even from the retrospect of forty years the author of *Huckleberry Finn* could not soften the harshest details of the village scenes. As he moved on down the river, in the person of Huck Finn, Sam Clemens lost the mellow atmosphere of his home town of Hannibal and saw only the ugly, the drab, and the sordid. The Arkansas river town that he describes through the eyes of Huck not only gives us a cross-section of the lower valley culture, but provides a fit setting for a not uncommon incident of that time and place, an attempted lynching.

RIVER TOWN (from *The Adventures of Huckleberry Finn*)

« « « Then we went loafing around town. The stores and houses was most all old, shackly, dried-up frame concerns that hadn't ever been painted; they was set up three or four foot above ground on stilts, so as to be out of reach of the water when the river was overflowed. The houses had little gardens around them, but they didn't seem to raise hardly anything in them but jimpson-weeds, and sunflowers, and ash-piles, and old curled-up boots and shoes, and pieces of bottles, and rags, and played-out tinware. The fences was made of different kinds of boards, nailed on at different times; and they leaned every which way, and had gates that didn't generly have but one hinge—a leather one. Some of the fences had been whitewashed some time or another, but the duke said it was in Columbus's time, like enough. There was generly hogs in the garden, and people driving them out.

All the stores was along one street. They had white domestic awnings in front, and the country-people hitched their horses to the awning-posts. There was empty dry-goods boxes under the awnings, and loafers roosting on them all day long, whittling them with their Barlow knives; and chawing tobacco, and gaping and yawning and stretching—a mighty ornery lot. They generly had on yellow straw hats most as wide as an umbrella, but didn't wear no coats nor waistcoats; they called one another Bill, and Buck, and Hank, and Joe, and Andy, and talked lazy and drawly, and used considerable many cuss-words. There was as many as one loafer leaning up against every awning-post; and he most always had his hands in his britches pockets, except when he fetched them out to lend a chaw of tobacco or scratch. . . .

All the streets and lanes was just mud; they warn't nothing else *but* mud—mud as black as tar and nigh about a foot deep in some places, and two or three inches deep in *all* the places. The hogs loafed and grunted around everywheres. You'd see a muddy sow and a litter of pigs come lazying along the street and whollop herself right down in the way, where folks had to walk around her, and she'd stretch out and shut her eyes and wave her ears whilst the pigs was milking her, and look as happy as if she was on salary. And pretty soon you'd hear a loafer sing out, "Hi! *so* boy, sick him, Tige!" and away the sow would go, squealing most horrible, with a dog or two swinging to each ear, and three or four dozen more a-coming; and then you would see all the loafers get up and watch the thing out of sight, and laugh at the fun and look grateful for the noise. Then they'd settle back again till there was a dog-fight....

On the river-front some of the houses was sticking out over the bank, and they was bowed and bent, and about ready to tumble in. The people had moved out of them. The bank was caved away under one corner of some others, and that corner was hanging over. People lived in them yet, but it was dangersome, because sometimes a strip of land as wide as a house caves in at a time. Sometimes a belt of land a quarter of a mile deep will start in and cave along and cave along till it all caves into the river in one summer. Such a town as that has to be always moving back, and back, and back, because the river's always gnawing at it. » » »

One could easily be deceived by the outward drabness and torpor of those little river towns. As Sam Clemens often idled away a day at a local hotel or roamed the streets of these settlements during brief boat landings, he looked shrewdly beneath the surface of things and found the lives of these villagers and country people charged with strong emotion. And occasionally their feelings would explode into violence as dramatic as anything one could experience on the river itself. Mark Twain recounts, with wry humor but with all the impact of present-day realism, one such episode in the lives of these people. At the beginning of this episode we find ourselves again in an Arkansas town of the 1840's, somewhere near noon of a marketing day:

COLONEL SHERBURN AND THE MOB[6] (from *The Adventures of Huckleberry Finn*)

« « « The nearer it got to noon that day the thicker and thicker was the wagons and horses in the streets, and more coming all the time. Families fetched their dinners with them from the country, and eat them in the wagons. There was considerable whiskey-drinking going on, and I seen three fights. By and by somebody sings out:

"Here comes old Boggs!—in from the country for his little old monthly drunk; here he comes, boys!"

All the loafers looked glad; I reckoned they was used to having fun out of Boggs. One of them says:

[6] Other expressions of Mark Twain's contempt for mobs and the craven submission of individuals to mass opinion may be found in *The Mysterious Stranger* and in "A Scrap of Curious History" (see Part II of this book).

"Wonder who he's a-gwyne to chaw up this time. If he'd a-chawed up all the men he's ben a-gwyne to chaw up in the last twenty year he'd have considerable reputation now."

Another one says, "I wisht old Boggs'd threaten me, 'cuz then I'd know I warn't gwyne to die for a thousan' year."

Boggs comes a-tearing along on his horse, whooping and yelling like an Injun, and singing out:

"Cler the track, thar. I'm on the waw-path, and the price uv coffins is a-gwyne to raise."

He was drunk, and weaving about in his saddle; he was over fifty year old, and had a very red face. Everybody yelled at him and laughed at him and sassed him, and he sassed back, and said he'd attend to them and lay them out in their regular turns, but he couldn't wait now because he'd come to town to kill old Colonel Sherburn, and his motto was, "Meat first, and spoon vittles to top off on."

He see me, and rode up and says:

"Whar'd you come f'm, boy? You prepared to die?"

Then he rode on. I was scared, but a man says:

"He don't mean nothing; he's always a-carryin' on like that when he's drunk. He's the best-naturedest old fool in Arkansaw—never hurt nobody, drunk nor sober."

Boggs rode up before the biggest store in town, and bent his head down so he could see under the curtain of the awning and yells:

"Come out here, Sherburn! Come out and meet the man you've swindled. You're the houn I'm after, and I'm a-gwyne to have you, too!"

And so he went on, calling Sherburn everything he could lay his tongue to, and the whole street packed with people listening and laughing and going on. By and by a proud-looking man about fifty-five—and he was a heap the best-dressed man in that town, too—steps out of the store, and the crowd drops back on each side to let him come. He says to Boggs, mighty ca'm and slow—he says:

"I'm tired of this, but I'll endure it till one o'clock. Till one o'clock, mind—no longer. If you open your mouth against me only once after that time you can't travel so far but I will find you."

Then he turns and goes in. The crowd looked mighty sober; no-

"Wooding up" on the Mississippi, from a lithograph by Currier and Ives.

Original pilot's license of Samuel Clemens.

body stirred, and there warn't no more laughing. Boggs rode off blackguarding Sherburn as loud as he could yell, all down the street; and pretty soon back he comes and stops before the store, still keeping it up. Some men crowded around him and tried to get him to shut up, but he wouldn't; they told him it would be one o'clock in about fifteen minutes, and so he *must* go home—he must go right away. But it didn't do no good. He cussed away with all his might, and threw his hat down in the mud and rode over it, and pretty soon away he went a-raging down the street again, with his gray hair a-flying. Everybody that could get a chance at him tried their best to coax him off his horse so they could lock him up and get him sober; but it warn't no use—up the street he would tear again, and give Sherburn another cussing. By and by somebody says:

"Go for his daughter!—quick, go for his daughter; sometimes he'll listen to her. If anybody can persuade him, she can."

So somebody started on a run. I walked down street a ways and stopped. In about five or ten minutes here comes Boggs again, but not on his horse. He was a-reeling across the street towards me, bareheaded, with a friend on both sides of him a-holt of his arms and hurrying him along. He was quiet, and looked uneasy; and he warn't hanging back any, but was doing some of the hurrying himself. Somebody sings out:

"Boggs!"

I looked over there to see who said it, and it was that Colonel Sherburn. He was standing perfectly still in the street, and had a pistol raised in his right hand—not aiming it, but holding it out with a barrel tilted up towards the sky. The same second I see a young girl coming on the run, and two men with her. Boggs and the men turned round to see who called him, and when they see the pistol the men jumped to one side, and the pistol-barrel come down slow and steady to a level—both barrels cocked. Boggs throws up both of his hands and says, "O Lord, don't shoot!" Bang! goes the first shot, and he staggers back, clawing at the air—bang! goes the second one, and he tumbles backwards onto the ground, heavy and solid, with his arms spread out. That young girl screamed out and comes rushing, and down she throws herself on her father, crying, and saying, "Oh, he's killed him, he's killed him!" The crowd closed up around them, and shouldered and jammed one another, with their necks stretched, trying to see, and people on the inside trying to shove them back and shouting, "Back, back! give him air! give him air!"

Colonel Sherburn he tossed his pistol onto the ground, and turned around on his heels and walked off.

They took Boggs to a little drug store, the crowd pressing around just the same, and the whole town following, and I rushed and got a good place at the window, where I was close to him and could see in. They laid him on the floor and put one large Bible under his head, and opened another one and spread it on his breast; but they tore open his shirt first, and I seen where one of the bullets went in. He made about a dozen long gasps, his breast lifting the Bible up when he drawed in his breath, and letting it down again when he breathed it out—and after that he laid still; he was dead. Then they pulled his daughter away from him, screaming and crying, and took her off. She was about sixteen, and very sweet and gentle looking, but awful pale and scared.

Well, pretty soon the whole town was there, squirming and scrouging and pushing and shoving to get at the window and have a look, but people that had the places wouldn't give them up, and folks behind them was saying all the time, "Say, now, you've looked enough, you fellows; 'tain't right and 'tain't fair for you to stay thar all the time, and never give nobody a chance; other folks has their rights as well as you."

There was considerable jawing back, so I slid out, thinking maybe there was going to be trouble. The streets was full, and everybody was excited. Everybody that seen the shooting was telling how it happened, and there was a big crowd packed around each one of these fellows, stretching their necks and listening. One long, lanky man, with long hair and a big white fur stovepipe hat on the back of his head, and a crooked-handled cane, marked out the places on the ground where Boggs stood and where Sherburn stood, and the people following him around from one place to t'other and watching everything he done, and bobbing their heads to show they understood, and stooping a little and resting their hands on their thighs to watch him mark the places on the ground with his cane; and then he stood up straight and stiff where Sherburn had stood, frowning and having his hat-brim down over his eyes, and sung out, "Boggs!" and then fetched his cane down slow to a level, and says "Bang!" staggered backwards, says "Bang!" again, and fell down flat on his back. The people that had seen the thing said he done it perfect; said it was just exactly the way it all happened. Then as much as a dozen people got out their bottles and treated him. » » »

Now, if this were pure fiction, Mark Twain might have ended the episode there; but this river-town tragedy was a part of real life, and just as the great river pursues its way relentlessly down its channel, Mark Twain follows this human action to its inevitable aftermath. The unexpected conclusion of the episode, however, provides a sardonic comment on human nature:

« « « Well, by and by somebody said Sherburn ought to be lynched. In about a minute everybody was saying it; so away they went, mad and yelling, and snatching down every clothes-line they come to to do the hanging with.

They swarmed up towards Sherburn's house, a-whooping and raging like Injuns, and everything had to clear the way or get run over and tromped to mush, and it was awful to see. Children was heeling it ahead of the mob, screaming and trying to get out of the way; and every window along the road was full of women's heads, and there was nigger boys in every tree, and bucks and wenches looking over every fence; and as soon as the mob would get nearly to them they would break and skaddle back out of reach. Lots of the women and girls was crying and taking on, scared most to death.

They swarmed up in front of Sherburn's palings as thick as they could jam together, and you couldn't hear yourself think for the noise. It was a little twenty-foot yard. Some sung out "Tear down the fence! tear down the fence!" Then there was a racket of ripping and tearing and smashing, and down she goes, and the front wall of the crowd begins to roll in like a wave.

Just then Sherburn steps out onto the roof of his little front porch, with a double-barreled gun in his hand, and takes his stand, perfectly ca'm and deliberate, not saying a word. The racket stopped, and the wave sucked back.

Sherburn never said a word—just stood there, looking down. The stillness was awful creepy and uncomfortable. Sherburn run his eye slow along the crowd; and wherever it struck the people tried a little to outgaze him, but they couldn't; they dropped their eyes and looked sneaky. Then pretty soon Sherburn sort of laughed; not the pleasant kind, but the kind that makes you feel like when you are eating bread that's got sand in it.

Then he says, slow and scornful:

"The idea of *you* lynching anybody! It's amusing. The idea of you thinking you had pluck enough to lynch a *man!* Because you're brave enough to tar and feather poor friendless cast-out women that come along here, did that make you think you had grit enough to lay your hands on a *man?* Why, a *man's* safe in the hands of ten thousand of your kind—as long as it's daytime and you're not behind him.

"Do I know you? I know you clear through. I was born and raised in the South, and I've lived in the North; so I know the average all around. The average man's a coward. In the North he lets anybody walk over him that wants to, and goes home and prays for a humble spirit to bear it. In the South one man, all by himself, has stopped a stage full of men in the daytime, and robbed the lot. Your newspapers call you a brave people so much that you think you *are* braver than any other people—whereas you're just *as* brave, and no braver. Why don't your juries hang murderers? Because they're afraid the man's friends will shoot them in the back, in the dark—and it's just what they *would* do.

"So they always acquit; and then a *man* goes in the night, with a hundred masked cowards at his back, and lynches the rascal. Your mistake is, that you didn't bring a man with you; that's one mistake, and the other is that you didn't come in the dark and fetch your masks. You brought *part* of a man—Buck Harkness, there—and if you hadn't had him to start you, you'd 'a' taken it out in blowing.

"You didn't want to come. The average man don't like trouble and danger. *You* don't like trouble and danger. But if only *half* a man—like Buck Harkness, there—shouts 'Lynch him! lynch him!'

you're afraid to back down—afraid you'll be found out to be what you are—*cowards*—and so you raise a yell, and hang yourselves onto that half-a-man's coat-tail, and come raging up here, swearing what big things you're going to do. The pitifulest thing out is a mob; that's what an army is—a mob; they don't fight with courage that's born in them, but with courage that's borrowed from their mass, and from their officers. But a mob without any *man* at the head of it is *beneath* pitifulness. Now the thing for *you* to do is to droop your tails and go home and crawl in a hole. If any real lynching's going to be done it will be done in the dark, Southern fashion; and when they come they'll bring their masks, and fetch a *man* along. Now *leave*—and take your half-a-man with you"— tossing his gun up across his left arm and cocking it when he says this.

The crowd washed back sudden, and then broke all apart, and went tearing off every which way, and Buck Harkness he heeled it after them, looking tolerable cheap. I could 'a' stayed if I wanted to, but I didn't want to. » » »

Colonel Sherburn faced down the mob and averted at least one lynching; and the rafts continued to float down the Mississippi, bearing Huckleberry Finns and other less vocal Missourians into other adventures of the River World; and the great floating palaces churned on their way under the pilotage of young Samuel Clemenses in a realm of plantations, bayous, and villages, where time seemed suspended and incidents like those related above were mere eddies from some vague world that always receded around the next bend of the river. But this halcyon life came to an end. The sudden outbreak of the Civil War blocked the river traffic, tied up the boats at the St. Louis and New Orleans wharves, and commandeered them for military operations. Armies soon moved up and down the valley and occupied the larger towns, and guerrilla warfare swept through the border states with slaughter and pillage. The spell was broken. The old life on the Mississippi was so disrupted by the war and later by the coming of the railroads that it never revived. In the meantime Samuel Clemens, son of Missouri and child of the river, left the valley to seek a new career.

Twenty-two years later, as Mark Twain, American writer, he revisited his river and recaptured something of the mood and exhilaration of his earlier days. But the old life was gone by the time he returned; he could not re-create it; he could only record it, but as one of the most colorful chapters in American history.

3. The West

IN THE SUMMER OF 1861, Sam Clemens set out across the Great Plains for the Far West. A short and inglorious service with Missouri Confederate irregulars had convinced him that he had no talent for soldiering. So when Orion Clemens, the new secretary of Nevada Territory, offered him a place as secretary to the Secretary, Sam seized the opportunity—an opportunity not so much to serve his brother as to see and explore the vast new mining frontier of the Pacific Coast. The resulting impressions and experiences of that western sojourn enriched Sam Clemens' stock of materials for future writing, sharpened his literary skills, leavened his native Missouri humor, broadened his horizons, and decided him on a literary career.[1] His original intention was to see the West for three months and then return to the river, but he remained in the West for over five years—years crowded with prospecting, silver mining, newspaper reporting, writing humorous sketches, lecturing, and travel into the faraway Pacific. Perhaps the most important result of these experiences was that, through the medium of Mark Twain's journalistic writing, these western years contributed to our heritage an authentic record of one of the great eras in American history—the migration into the Far West. For "Mark Twain" (as he began to sign himself shortly after his arrival in Nevada) wrote about everything he saw and heard, and he wrote realistically.[2] The present-day reader does not have to discount even the

[1] See Ivan Benson, *Mark Twain's Western Years* for an authoritative source of materials concerning this episode in Mark Twain's career.

exaggeration and burlesque that are woven into these western writings, for exaggeration and burlesque were just as much a part of western life as the boots and saddles and the tall tales that have always been identified with that region. Nor did Mark Twain try to romanticize or sentimentalize over the West as did such contemporaries as Bret Harte and Joaquin Miller. What he sought was the essential spirit of the people, the time, and the place. Whatever else Mark Twain's western writings caught, they caught the buoyancy, the optimism, the vigor and dynamic drive of the last American frontier, in a set of kaleidoscopic impressions, part narrative and part descriptive, that have not been equaled by any other writer of that period.

The most natural way to see Mark Twain's West is to join him as he sets out on the overland stagecoach from St. Joseph, Missouri, on his nineteen-day trip to Carson City:

OVERLAND STAGE[3] (from *Roughing It*[4])

« « « The first thing we did on that glad evening that landed us at St. Joseph was to hunt up the stage-office, and pay a hundred

---

[2] "He lived the Western experience to the full, and his response to it in his writings was personal and emotional," says Benson (*Mark Twain's Western Years, vii*). Convincing evidence of both the formative influence of the West on Mark Twain's literary development and his response to the West is contained in the selected "Mark Twain Western Items" included in Benson's study and in *Mark Twain's Letters from the Sandwich Islands Written for the "Sacramento Union"* (ed. by G. Ezra Dane). (San Francisco, The Grabhorn Press, 1937).

[3] The first stage line to the Far West was established in 1849, operating from Independence, Missouri, to Santa Fé, New Mexico. In 1857 a faster overland mail service was begun between Memphis and St. Louis as the eastern terminus and Sacramento, California, as the western terminus, over a southerly route through western Arkansas, El Paso, Texas, and Yuma, Arizona. However, the shortest and fastest overland service for mail and passengers was established in 1858 over the "central" route, via St. Joseph, the Platte River trail to Julesburg, Colorado, thence to Denver, the South Pass, Salt Lake City, Carson City, Nevada, and Sacramento, California. It was this latter stage route that Samuel and Orion Clemens took in the summer of 1861. See Frederic L. Paxson, *The Last American Frontier* (New York, The Macmillan Company, 1910).

[4] *Roughing It*, Mark Twain's second full-length book, was published in 1872. Although some of the material in this book was taken from his original journalistic accounts of the Hawaiian Island trip, most of the material lay fallow until after he wrote and published his *Innocents Abroad* in 1868–69. Consequently, the accounts of Mark Twain's trip to the West and of his early experiences in that region, reproduced in this book, were written from the retrospect of almost ten years, a remarkable testimony to the vividness of their author's memory.

and fifty dollars apiece for tickets per overland coach to Carson City, Nevada.

The next morning, bright and early, we took a hasty breakfast, and hurried to the starting-place. Then an inconvenience presented itself which we had not properly appreciated before, namely, that one cannot make a heavy traveling trunk stand for twenty-five pounds of baggage—because it weighs a good deal more. But that was all that we could take—twenty-five pounds each. So we had to snatch our trunks open, and make a selection in a good deal of a hurry. We put our lawful twenty-five pounds apiece all in one valise, and shipped the trunks back to St. Louis again. It was a sad parting, for now we had no swallow-tail coats and white kid gloves to wear at Pawnee receptions in the Rocky Mountains, and no stove-pipe hats nor patent-leather boots, nor anything else necessary to make life calm and peaceful. We were reduced to a war-footing. Each of us put on a rough, heavy suit of clothing, woolen army shirt and "stogy" boots included; and into the valise we crowded a few white shirts, some under-clothing and such things. My brother, the Secretary, took along about four pounds of United States statutes and six pounds of Unabridged Dictionary; for we did not know—poor innocents—that such things could be bought in San Francisco on one day and received in Carson City the next. I was armed to the teeth with a pitiful little Smith and Wesson's seven-shooter, which carried a ball like a homeopathic pill, and it took the whole seven to make a dose for an adult. But I thought it was grand. It appeared to me to be a dangerous weapon. It only had one fault—you could not hit anything with it. . . .

We took two or three blankets for protection against frosty weather in the mountains. In the matter of luxuries we were modest —we took none along but some pipes and five pounds of smoking-tobacco. We had two large canteens to carry water in, between stations on the Plains, and we also took with us a little shot-bag of silver coin for daily expenses in the way of breakfasts and dinners.

By eight o'clock everything was ready, and we were on the other side of the river. We jumped into the stage, the driver cracked his whip, and we bowled away and left "the States" behind us. It was a superb summer morning, and all the landscape was brilliant with sunshine. There was a freshness and breeziness, too, and an exhilarating sense of emancipation from all sorts of cares and responsibilities, that almost made us feel that the years that we had spent in the close, hot city, toiling and slaving, had been wasted and thrown away. We were spinning along through Kansas, and in the course of an hour and a half we were fairly abroad on the great Plains. Just here the land was rolling—a grand sweep of regular elevations and depressions as far as the eye could reach— like the stately heave and swell of the ocean's bosom after a storm. And everywhere were corn-fields, accenting with squares of deeper green this limitless expanse of grassy land. But presently this sea upon dry ground was to lose its "rolling" character and stretch away for seven hundred miles as level as a floor!

Our coach was a great swinging and swaying stage, of the most sumptuous description—an imposing cradle on wheels. It was drawn by six handsome horses, and by the side of the driver sat the "conductor," the legitimate captain of the craft; for it was his business to take charge and care of the mails, baggage, express matter, and passengers. We three were the only passengers, this trip. We sat on the back seat, inside. About all the rest of the coach was full of mail-bags—for we had three days' delayed mails with us. Almost touching our knees, a perpendicular wall of mail matter rose up to the roof. There was a great pile of it strapped on top of the stage, and both the fore and hind boots were full. . . .

We changed horses every ten miles, all day long, and fairly flew over the hard, level road. We jumped out and stretched our legs every time the coach stopped, and so the night found us still vivacious and unfatigued. . . .

It was now just dawn; and as we stretched our cramped legs full length on the mail-sacks, and gazed out through the windows across the wide wastes of greensward clad in cool, powdery mist, to where there was an expectant look in the eastern horizon, our perfect enjoyment took the form of a tranquil and contented ecstasy. The stage whirled along at a spanking gait, the breeze flapping the curtains and suspended coats in a most exhilarating way; the cradle swayed and swung luxuriously, the pattering of the horses' hoofs, the cracking of the driver's whip, and his "Hi-yi! g'lang!" were music; the spinning ground and the waltzing trees appeared to give us a mute hurrah as we went by, and then slack up and look after us with interest, or envy, or something; and as we lay and smoked the pipe of peace and compared all this luxury with the years of tiresome city life that had gone before it, we felt that there was only one complete and satisfying happiness in the world, and we had found it. . . .

By and by we passed through Marysville, and over the Big Blue and Little Sandy; thence about a mile, and entered Nebraska. About a mile further on, we came to the Big Sandy—one hundred and eighty miles from St. Joseph. » » »

One sight that never failed to astonish and amuse the greenhorn traveler from Missouri was the ubiquitous jack rabbit. Mark Twain's quick eye and his strong sense of form and motion have left us an indelible and vivid picture of this little animal:

THE JACK RABBIT (from *Roughing It*)

« « « As the sun was going down, we saw the first specimen of an animal known familiarly over two thousand miles of mountain and desert—from Kansas clear to the Pacific Ocean—as the "jackass rabbit." He is well named. He is just like any other rabbit, except that he is from one-third to twice as large, has longer legs in proportion to his size, and has the most preposterous ears that ever were mounted on any creature *but* a jackass. When he is sitting quiet, thinking about his sins, or is absent-minded or unapprehensive of danger, his majestic ears project above him conspicuously; but the breaking of a twig will scare him nearly to death, and then he tilts his ears back gently and starts for home. All you can see, then, for the next minute, is his long gray form stretched out straight and "streaking it" through the low sage-brush, head erect, eyes right, and ears just canted a little to the rear, but showing you where the animal is, all the time, the same as if he carried a jib. Now and then he makes a marvelous spring with his long legs, high over the stunted sagebrush, and scores a leap that would make a horse envious. Presently, he comes down to a long, graceful "lope," and shortly he mysteriously disappears. He has crouched behind a sage-bush, and will sit there and listen and tremble until you get within six feet of him, when he will get under way again. But one must shoot at this creature once, if he wishes to see him throw his heart into his heels, and do the best he knows how. He is frightened clear through, now, and he lays his long ears down on his back, straightens himself out like a yardstick every spring he makes, and scatters miles behind him with an easy indifference that is enchanting. » » »

Farther westward along the trail Mark Twain discovered a new marvel—the coyote.[5] His description of this animal is a remarkable foretaste of the animated cartoon of the modern movies almost fifty years before another Missourian, Walt Disney, brought this art to the moving picture screen:

THE COYOTE (from *Roughing It*)

« « « Along about an hour after breakfast we saw the first prairie-dog villages, the first antelope, and the first wolf. If I remember rightly, this latter was the regular *coyote* (pronounced ky-*o*-te) of the farthest deserts. And if it *was*, he was not a pretty creature, or respectable either, for I got well acquainted with his race afterward, and can speak with confidence. The coyote is a long, slim, sick and sorry-looking skeleton, with a gray wolf-skin stretched over it, a tolerably bushy tail that forever sags down with a despairing expression of forsakenness and misery, a furtive and evil eye, and a long, sharp face, with slightly lifted lip and exposed teeth. He has a general slinking expression all over. The coyote is a living, breathing allegory of Want. He is *always* hungry. He is always poor, out of luck and friendless. The meanest creatures despise him, and even the fleas would desert him for a velocipede. He is so spiritless and cowardly that even while his exposed teeth are pretending a threat, the rest of his face is apologizing for it.

[5] For other specimens of Mark Twain's flair for animal description, see accounts of the cat and the pain-killer and the poodle dog and the pinch bug in *Tom Sawyer*, the Genuine Mexican Plug and the Syrian camel's appetite in *Roughing It*, the raven and Jim Baker's crow, Jim Baker's blue-jay yarn, and the stupidity of ants in *A Tramp Abroad*, sows in an Arkansas River town and hounds on an Arkansas plantation in *Huckleberry Finn*, the "Celebrated Jumping Frog" in *Sketches New and Old*, and the chameleon in *Following the Equator*. Most of these animal portraits are reprinted in this book.

And he is *so* homely!—so scrawny, and ribby, and coarse-haired, and pitiful. When he sees you he lifts his lip and lets a flash of his teeth out, and then turns a little out of the course he was pursuing, depresses his head a bit, and strikes a long, soft-footed trot through the sagebrush, glancing over his shoulder at you, from time to time, till he is about out of easy pistol range, and then he stops and takes a deliberate survey of you; he will trot fifty yards and stop again—another fifty and stop again; and finally the gray of his gliding body blends with the gray of the sage-brush, and he disappears. All this is when you make no demonstration against him; but if you do, he develops a livelier interest in his journey,

and instantly electrifies his heels and puts such a deal of real estate between himself and your weapon, that by the time you have raised the hammer you see that you need a minie rifle, and by the time you have got him in line you need a rifled cannon, and by the time you have "drawn a bead" on him you see well enough that nothing but an unusually long-winded streak of lightning could reach him where he is now. But if you start a swift-footed dog after him, you will enjoy it ever so much—especially if it is a dog that has a good opinion of himself, and has been brought up to think he knows something about speed. The coyote will go swinging gently off on that deceitful trot of his, and every little while he will smile a fraudful smile over his shoulder that will fill that dog entirely full of encouragement and worldly ambition, and make him lay his head still lower to the ground, and stretch his neck further to the front, and pant more fiercely, and stick his tail out straighter behind, and move his furious legs with a yet wilder frenzy, and leave a broader and broader, and higher and denser cloud of desert sand smoking behind, and marking his long wake across the level plain! And all this time the dog is only a short twenty feet behind the coyote, and to save the soul of him he cannot understand why it is that he cannot get perceptibly closer; and he begins to get aggravated, and it makes him madder and madder to see how gently the coyote glides along and never pants or sweats or ceases to smile; and he grows still more and more incensed to see how shamefully he has been taken in by an entire stranger, and what an ignoble swindle that long, calm, soft-footed trot is; and next he notices that he is getting fagged, and that the coyote actually has to slacken speed a little to keep from running away from him—and *then* that town-dog is mad in earnest, and he begins to strain and weep and swear, and paw the sand higher than ever, and reach for the coyote with concentrated and desperate energy. This "spurt" finds him six feet behind the gliding enemy, and two miles from his friends. And then, in the instant that a wild new hope is lighting up his face, the coyote turns and smiles blandly upon him once more, and with a something about it which seems to say: "Well, I shall have to tear myself away from you, bub—business is business, and it will not do for me to be fooling along this way all day"—and forthwith there is a rushing sound, and the sudden splitting of a long crack through the atmosphere, and behold that dog is solitary and alone in the midst of a vast solitude.

It makes his head swim. He stops, and looks all around; climbs the nearest sand-mound, and gazes into the distance; shakes his head reflectively, and then, without a word, he turns and jogs along back to his train, and takes up a humble position under the hindmost wagon, and feels unspeakably mean, and looks ashamed, and hangs his tail at half-mast for a week. And for as much as a year after that whenever there is a great hue and cry after a coyote, that dog will merely glance in that direction without emotion, and apparently observe to himself, "I believe I do not wish any of the pie." » » »

One of the most colorful but fleeting images that Mark Twain caught from the westward movement was the Pony Express rider.

The Missouri traveler had the good fortune to make his stagecoach journey over the route followed by the Pony Express (St. Joseph, Missouri, to Sacramento, California) and during just that brief interval in American history (1860–61), before the completion of the telegraph line and the coming of the transcontinental railroad, when those swift horsemen were the only means of communication between the East and the Far West.[6] The sight of one of those riders was one of the highlights of his trip west:

PONY EXPRESS (from *Roughing It*)

« « « In a little while all interest was taken up in stretching our necks and watching for the "pony-rider"—the fleet messenger who sped across the continent from St. Jo to Sacramento, carrying letters nineteen hundred miles in eight days! Think of that for perishable horse and human flesh and blood to do! The pony-rider was usually a little bit of a man, brimful of spirit and endurance. No matter what time of the day or night his watch came on, and no matter whether it was winter or summer, raining, snowing, hailing, or sleeting, or whether his "beat" was a level straight road or a crazy trail over mountain crags and precipices, or whether it led through peaceful regions or regions that swarmed with hostile Indians, he must be always ready to leap into the saddle, and be off like the wind! There was no idling-time for a pony-rider on duty. He rode fifty miles without stopping, by daylight, moonlight, starlight, or through the blackness of darkness—just as it happened. He rode a splendid horse that was born for a racer and fed and lodged like a gentleman; kept him at his utmost speed for ten miles, and then, as he came crashing up to the station where stood two men holding fast a fresh, impatient steed, the transfer of

---

[6] Pony Express mail service was started between Placerville, California, and St. Joseph, Missouri, on April 3, 1860, with a schedule of ten days between the two termini. The riders followed a well-established trail through Forts Kearny, Laramie, and Bridger to Salt Lake City, and thence to Carson City, Placerville, and Sacramento, in the summer of 1861 at the time of Mark Twain's overland stage trip, after being transferred from a southern route made hazardous by the outbreak of the Civil War. In October of 1861 the Pony Express service was discontinued when the completion of the transcontinental telegraph line assured communication between the East and the Far West. See Frederic L. Paxson, *The Last American Frontier*.

rider and mail-bag was made in the twinkling of an eye, and away flew the eager pair and were out of sight before the spectator could get hardly the ghost of a look. Both rider and horse went "flying light." The rider's dress was thin, and fitted close; he wore a "roundabout," and a skull-cap, and tucked his pantaloons into his boot-tops like a race-rider. He carried no arms—he carried nothing that was not absolutely necessary, for even the postage on his literary freight was worth *five dollars a letter*. He got but little frivolous correspondence to carry—his bag had business letters in it, mostly. His horse was stripped of all unnecessary weight, too. He wore a little wafer of a racing-saddle, and no visible blanket. He wore light shoes, or none at all. The little flat mail-pockets strapped under the rider's thighs would each hold about the bulk of a child's primer. They held many and many an important busines chapter and newspaper letter, but these were written on paper as airy and thin as gold-leaf, nearly, and thus bulk and weight were economized. The stage-coach traveled about a hundred to a hundred and twenty-five miles a day (twenty-four hours), the pony-rider about two hundred and fifty. There were about eighty pony-riders in the saddle all the time, night and day, stretching in a long, scattering procession from Missouri to California, forty flying eastward, and forty toward the west, and among them making four hundred gallant horses earn a stirring livelihood and see a deal of scenery every single day in the year.

We had had a consuming desire, from the beginning, to see a pony-rider, but somehow or other all that passed us and all that met us managed to streak by in the night, and so we heard only a whiz and a hail, and the swift phantom of the desert was gone before we could get our heads out of the windows. But now we were expecting one along every moment, and would see him in broad daylight. Presently the driver exclaims:

"HERE HE COMES!"

Every neck is stretched further, and every eye strained wider. Away across the endless dead level of the prairie a black speck appears against the sky, and it is plain that it moves. Well, I should think so! In a second or two it becomes a horse and rider, rising and falling, rising and falling—sweeping toward us nearer and nearer—growing more and more distinct, more and more sharply defined—nearer and still nearer, and the flutter of the hoofs comes faintly to the ear—another instant a whoop and a hurrah from our upper deck, a wave of the rider's hand, but no reply, and man and horse burst past our excited faces, and go swinging away like a belated fragment of a storm!

So sudden is it all, and so like a flash of unreal fancy, that but for the flake of white foam left quivering and perishing on a mailsack after the vision had flashed by and disappeared, we might have doubted whether we had seen any actual horse and man at all, maybe. » » »

Mile after mile, as the stagecoach spun across the plains and threaded its way through the mountains, Sam Clemens gathered new and marvelous impressions. His spirits rose with each exciting experience, and each day seemed to add a more exhilarating scene to the unfolding panorama of the West—until he came to the great deserts beyond Salt Lake City. It was here that the West took on a grimmer aspect that threatened to dispel the romance of the whole adventure for the Missourian and his companions. He describes the desert with honesty and unmitigated realism:

THE DESERT—A HARSH REALITY (from *Roughing It*)

« « « Now we were to cross a desert in *daylight*. This was fine—novel — romantic — dramatically adventurous — *this,* indeed, was worth living for, worth traveling for! We would write home all about it.

This enthusiasm, this stern thirst for adventure, wilted under the sultry August sun and did not last above one hour. One poor little hour—and then we were ashamed that we had "gushed" so. The poetry was all in the anticipation—there is none in the reality. Imagine a vast, waveless ocean stricken dead and turned to ashes; imagine this solemn waste tufted with ashdusted sage-bushes; imagine the lifeless silence and solitude that belong to such a place; imagine a coach, creeping like a bug through the midst of this shoreless level, and sending up tumbled volumes of dust as if it were a bug that went by steam; imagine this aching monotony of toiling and plowing kept up hour after hour, and the shore still as far away as ever, apparently; imagine team, driver, coach, and passengers so deeply coated with ashes that they are all one colorless color; imagine ash-drifts roosting above mustaches and eyebrows like snow accumulations on boughs and bushes. This is the reality of it.

The sun beats down with dead, blistering, relentless malignity; the perspiration is welling from every pore in man and beast, but scarcely a sign of it finds its way to the surface—it is absorbed before it gets there; there is not the faintest breath of air stirring; there is not a merciful shred of cloud in all the brilliant firmament; there is not a living creature visible in any direction whither one searches the blank level that stretches its monotonous miles on every hand; there is not a sound—not a sigh—not a whisper—not a buzz, or a whir of wings, or distant pipe of bird—not even a sob from the lost souls that doubtless people that dead air. And so the occasional sneezing of the resting mules and the champing of the bits, grate harshly on the grim stillness, not dissipating the spell, but accenting it and making one feel more lonesome and forsaken than before.

The mules, under violent swearing, coaxing, and whip-cracking, would make at stated intervals a "spurt," and drag the coach a hundred or maybe two hundred yards, stirring up a billowy cloud of dust that rolled back, enveloping the vehicle to the wheel-tops or higher, and making it seem afloat in a fog. Then a rest followed, with the usual sneezing and bit-champing. Then another "spurt" of a hundred yards and another rest at the end of it. All day long we kept this up, without water for the mules and without ever changing the team. At least we kept it up ten hours, which, I take it, is a day, and a pretty honest one, in an alkali desert. It was from four in the morning till two in the afternoon. And it was so hot! and so close! and our water canteens went dry in the middle of the day and we got so thirsty! It was so stupid and tiresome and dull! and the tedious hours did lag and drag and limp along with such a cruel deliberation! It was so trying to give one's watch a good long undisturbed spell and then take it out and find that it had been fooling away the time and not trying to get ahead any! The alkali dust cut through our lips, it persecuted our eyes, it ate through the delicate membranes and made our noses bleed and *kept* them bleeding—and truly and seriously the romance all faded far away and disappeared, and left the desert trip nothing but a harsh reality—a thirsty, sweltering, longing, hateful reality! » » »

Not all of Mark Twain's journey into the West was as bleak as the episode described above. In contrast to the grim stretches of desert, much of his ride was across the mountain tops and through the passes, where the grandeur of the peaks and the far-flung valleys made the ordeal of the desert lands worth suffering. The young Missourian, brought up in the flatlands of the Mississippi Valley, was enchanted by the Rocky Mountains:

SOUTH PASS (from *Roughing It*)

« « « Two miles beyond South Pass City we saw for the first time that mysterious marvel which all Western untraveled boys have heard of and fully believe in, but are sure to be astounded at when they see it with their own eyes, nevertheless—banks of snow in dead summer-time. We were now far up toward the sky, and knew all the time that we must presently encounter lofty summits clad in the "eternal snow" which was so commonplace a matter of mention in books, and yet when I did see it glittering in the sun on stately domes in the distance and knew the month was August and that my coat was hanging up because it was too warm to wear it, I was full as much amazed as if I had never heard of snow in August before....

In a little while quite a number of peaks swung into view with long claws of glittering snow clasping them; and with here and there, in the shade, down the mountainside, a little solitary patch of snow looking no larger than a lady's pocket-handkerchief but being in reality as large as a "public square."

And now, at last, we were fairly in the renowned SOUTH PASS, and whirling gaily along high above the common world. We were perched upon the extreme summit of the great range of the Rocky Mountains, toward which we had been climbing, patiently climbing, ceaselessly climbing, for days and nights together —and about us was gathered a convention of Nature's kings that stood ten, twelve, and even thirteen thousand feet high—grand old fellows who would have to stoop to see Mount Washington, in the twilight. We were in such an airy elevation above the creeping populations of the earth, that now and then when the obstructing crags stood out of the way it seemed that we could look around and abroad and contemplate the whole great globe, with its dissolving views of mountains, seas, and continents stretching away through the mystery of the summer haze.

As a general thing the Pass was more suggestive of a valley than a suspension-bridge in the clouds—but it strongly suggested the latter at one spot. At that place the upper third of one or two majestic purple domes projected above our level on either hand and gave us a sense of a hidden great deep of mountains and plains and valleys down about their bases which we fancied we might see if we could step to the edge and look over. These Sultans of the fastnesses were turbaned with tumbled volumes of cloud, which shredded away from time to time and drifted off fringed and torn, trailing their continents of shadow after them; and catching presently on an intercepting peak, wrapped it about and brooded there —then shredded away again and left the purple peak, as they had left the purple domes, downy and white with new-laid snow. In passing, these monstrous rags of cloud hung low and swept along right over the spectator's head, swinging their tatters so nearly in his face that his impulse was to shrink when they came closest. In the one place I speak of, one could look below him upon a world of diminishing crags and canyons leading down, down, and away to a vague plain with a thread in it which was a road, and bunches of feathers in it which were trees—a pretty picture sleeping in the sunlight—but with a darkness stealing over it and glooming its features deeper and deeper under the frown of a coming storm; and then, while no film or shadow marred the noon brightness of his high perch, he could watch the tempest break forth down there and see the lightnings leap from crag to crag and the sheeted rain drive along the canyon-sides, and hear the thunders peal and crash and roar. » » »

Mark Twain's admiration for the mountain storms was equaled by his love of the beauty and solitude of the mountain lakes. Nowhere in his later travels around the world did he find any scenery that could inspire him as much as the pristine valleys and lakes of these western mountains. One of his most picturesque descriptions is of the gem of the Sierras, Lake Tahoe:[7]

LAKE TAHOE (from *The Innocents Abroad*)

« « « In the early morning one watches the silent battle of dawn and darkness upon the waters of Tahoe with a placid interest; but when the shadows sulk away and one by one the hidden beauties of the shore unfold themselves in the full splendor of noon; when the still surface is belted like a rainbow with broad bars of blue and green and white, half the distance from the circumference to the center; when, in the lazy summer afternoon, he lies in a boat, far out to where the dead blue of the deep water begins, and smokes the pipe of peace and idly winks at the distant crags and patches of snow from under his cap-brim; when the boat drifts shoreward to the white water, and he lolls over the gunwale and gazes by the hour down through the crystal depths and notes the colors of the pebbles and reviews the finny armies gliding in procession a hundred feet below; when at night he sees moon and stars, mountain ridges feathered with pines, jutting white capes, bold promontories, grand sweeps of rugged scenery topped with bald, glimmering peaks, all magnificently pictured in the polished mirror of the lake, in richest, softest detail, the tranquil interest that was born with the morning deepens and deepens, by sure degrees, till it culminates at last in resistless fascination. » » »

---

[7] Mark Twain's visit to Lake Tahoe, with a young friend from Cincinnati, John D. Kinney, lasted for only a few days in August of 1861, but it brought him into the real western wilderness for the first time. This interlude between his long, hard ride over the plains and deserts and his feverish life as a silver prospector came into his life as a refreshing and totally new experience. The sublimity and solitude of the mountain lake so appealed to his love of natural beauty that in later life he recalled the scene more often than any of his other western impressions. See Ivan Benson's *Mark Twain's Western Years* for a full account of the Lake Tahoe episode. Benson points out: "Previous to this trip he had not been particularly impressed with the desirability of staying in the West . . . . Then Clemens came to Lake Tahoe! The glory of the lake and the mountain fastness was overpowering" (Benson, *Mark Twain's Western Years*, 29). Mark Twain makes an interesting comparison between Tahoe and Alpine lakes in his later travel accounts in *The Innocents Abroad*.

As Mark Twain explored the western frontier of the 1860's, he found much more than deserts, snow-capped peaks, and solitary mountain lakes. The people and the animals of the region—miners, gamblers, desperadoes, politicians, pioneers, jack rabbits, coyotes, blue jays, horses—everything, in fact, that gave life to the West— continually caught his eye and absorbed his interest. And as anyone brought up on the western "tradition" of the modern movies and pulp fiction might expect, the horseman became Mark Twain's first and most vivid symbol of the West. The Missouri traveler's first glimpse of western glamour had been the Pony Express rider, whose skill and hardiness outmatched those of even the stagecoach drivers. When he reached Carson City, Nevada, Mark Twain determined to westernize himself in one bold step. As with many a tenderfoot, his ambition was deflated because of two things he was unacquainted with: the shrewdness of horse traders and the dynamics of horseflesh. If the following account of his first experience with a western horse is not absolutely true, at least it *might* have happened to him and it certainly *could* have happened to many a greenhorn; and even if it never actually *did* happen, at least it expresses the real spirit of Mark Twain's West!

THE GENUINE MEXICAN PLUG (from *Roughing It*)

« « « I resolved to have a horse to ride. I had never seen such wild, free, magnificent horsemanship outside of a circus as these picturesquely clad Mexicans, Californians, and Mexicanized Americans displayed in Carson streets every day. How they rode! Leaning just gently forward out of the perpendicular, easy and nonchalant, with broad slouch-hat brim blown square up in front, and long *riata* swinging above the head, they swept through the town like the wind! The next minute they were only a sailing puff of dust on the far desert. If they trotted, they sat up gallantly and gracefully, and seemed part of the horse; did not go jiggering up and down after the silly Miss-Nancy fashion of the riding-schools. I had quickly learned to tell a horse from a cow, and was full of anxiety to learn more. I was resolved to buy a horse.

While the thought was rankling in my mind, the auctioneer came scurrying through the plaza on a black beast that had as many humps and corners on him as a dromedary, and was necessarily uncomely; but he was "going, going, at twenty-two!—horse, saddle and bridle at twenty-two dollars, gentlemen!" and I could hardly resist.

A man whom I did not know (he turned out to be the auc-

tioneer's brother) noticed the wistful look in my eye, and observed that that was a very remarkable horse to be going at such a price; and added that the saddle alone was worth the money. It was a Spanish saddle, with ponderous *tapidaros*, and furnished with the ungainly sole-leather covering with the unspellable name. I said I had half a notion to bid. Then this keen-eyed person appeared to me to be "taking my measure"; but I dismissed the suspicion when he spoke, for his manner was full of guileless candor and truthfulness. Said he:

"I know that horse—know him well. You are a stranger, I take it, and so you might think he was an American horse, maybe, but I assure you he is not. He is nothing of the kind; but—excuse my speaking in a low voice, other people being near—he is, without the shadow of a doubt, a Genuine Mexican Plug!"

I did not know what a Genuine Mexican Plug was, but there was something about this man's way of saying it, that made me swear inwardly that I would own a Genuine Mexican Plug, or die.

"Has he any other—er—advantages?" I inquired, suppressing what eagerness I could.

He hooked his forefinger in the pocket of my army shirt, led me to one side, and breathed in my ear impressively these words:

"He can out-buck anything in America!"

"Going, going, going—at *twent-ty*-four dollars and a half, gen-"

"Twenty-seven!" I shouted, in a frenzy.

"And sold!" said the auctioneer, and passed over the Genuine Mexican Plug to me.

I could scarcely contain my exultation. I paid the money, and put the animal in a neighboring livery stable to dine and rest himself.

In the afternoon I brought the creature into the plaza, and certain citizens held him by the head, and others by the tail, while I mounted him. As soon as they let go, he placed all his feet in a bunch together, lowered his back, and then suddenly arched it upward, and shot me straight into the air a matter of three or four feet! I came as straight down again, lit in the saddle, went instantly up again, came down almost in the high pommel, shot up again, and came down on the horse's neck—all in the space of three or four seconds. Then he rose and stood almost straight up on his hind feet, and I, clasping his lean neck desperately, slid back into the saddle, and held on.
He came down, and immediately hoisted his heels into the air, delivering a vicious kick at the sky, and stood on his fore feet. And then down he came once more, and began the original exercise of shooting me straight up again.

The third time I went up I heard a stranger say: "Oh, *don't* he buck, though!"

While I was up, somebody struck the horse a sounding thwack with a leathern strap, and when I arrived again the Genuine Mexican Plug was not there. A Californian youth chased him up and caught him, and asked if he might have a ride. I granted him that luxury. He mounted the Genuine, got lifted into the air once, but sent his spurs home as he descended, and the horse darted away like a telegram. He soared over three fences like a bird, and disappeared down the road toward the Washoe Valley.

I sat down on a stone with a sigh, and by a natural impulse one of my hands sought my forehead, and the other the base of my stomach. I believe I never appreciated, till then, the poverty of the human machinery—for I still needed a hand or two to place elsewhere. Pen cannot describe how I was jolted up. Imagination cannot conceive how disjointed I was—how internally, externally, and universally I was unsettled, mixed up, and ruptured. . . .

After a gallop of sixteen miles the Californian youth and the Genuine Mexican Plug came tearing into town again, shedding foam-flakes like the spume-spray that drives before a typhoon, and, with one final skip over a wheel-barrow and a Chinaman, cast anchor in front of the "ranch."

Such panting and blowing! Such spreading and contracting of the red equine nostrils, and glaring of the wild equine eye! But was the imperial beast subjugated? Indeed, he was not. His lordship the Speaker of the House thought he was, and mounted him to go down to the Capitol; but the first dash the creature made was over a pile of telegraph-poles half as high as a church; and his time to the Capitol —one mile and three-quarters—remains unbeaten to this day. But

then he took an advantage—he left out the mile, and only did the three-quarters. That is to say, he made a straight cut across lots, preferring fences and ditches to a crooked road; and when the Speaker got to the Capitol he said he had been in the air so much he felt as if he had made the trip on a comet. . . .

Of course, I . . . tried to sell him; but that was a stretch of simplicity which met with little sympathy. The auctioneer stormed up and down the streets on him for four days, dispersing the populace, interrupting business, and destroying children, and never got a bid—at least never any but the eighteen-dollar one he hired a notoriously substanceless bummer to make. The people only smiled pleasantly, and restrained their desire to buy, if they had any. Then the auctioneer brought in his bill, and I withdrew the horse from the market. We tried to trade him off at private vendue next, offering him at a sacrifice for second-hand tombstones, old iron, temperance tracts—any kind of property. But holders were stiff, and we retired from the market again. I never tried to ride the horse any more. Walking was good enough exercise for a man like me, that had nothing the matter with him except ruptures, internal injuries, and such things. Finally I tried to *give* him away. But it was a failure. Parties said earthquakes were handy enough on the Pacific coast—they did not wish to own one. . . . » » »

Along with the bucking horse, the Old West introduced Mark Twain to the inevitable bad man, or "desperado," as he was then called. As any teen-ager of today, the young journalist from Missouri devoured all the newspaper accounts of these villains, legendary or otherwise, and listened with fascination to the local tales of their deadly deeds and desperate deaths. When he saw them in the flesh during some of their leisure moments in Virginia City, their flashy dress, "flush" manners, and poise earned the following admiring portrayal from Mark Twain:

PORTRAIT OF A DESPERADO (from *Roughing It*)

« « « The desperado stalked the streets with a swagger graded according to the number of his homicides, and a nod of recognition from him was sufficient to make a humble admirer happy for the rest of the day. The deference that was paid to a desperado of wide reputation, and who "kept his private graveyard," as the phrase went, was marked, and cheerfully accorded. When he moved along the sidewalk in his excessively long-tailed frock-coat, shiny stump-toed boots, and with dainty little slouch hat tipped over left eye, the small-fry roughs made room for his majesty; when he entered the restaurant, the waiters deserted bankers and merchants to overwhelm him with obsequious service; when he shouldered his way to a bar, the shouldered parties wheeled indignantly, recognized him, and—apologized. They got a look in return that froze their marrow, and by that time a curled and breast-pinned barkeeper was beaming over the counter, proud of the established acquaintanceship that permitted such a familiar form of speech as:

"How're ye, Billy, old fel? Glad to see you. What'll you take—the old thing? » » »

Mark Twain recounts the exploits and the violent endings of many of these western desperadoes. Like most red-blooded Americans, he felt in awe of such characters, but he did not try to improve upon them in his writing—they were already only too real for that time.[8] The westerner for whom Mark Twain had both a genuine admiration and a warm feeling was the strong man with the rough exterior and the noble heart. This character, who was a product of the same environment as the desperado and shared his love of adventure and rough-and-tumble tactics, was an entirely different species: a "type" popularized by Bret Harte and Owen Wister and later glamorized by Hollywood and writers of "westerns" in order to provide proper heroes for the frontier setting.[9]

[8] Mark Twain gives a full account of J. A. Slade, the most notorious desperado of those days, in Chaps. IX–X of *Roughing It*. The two men met briefly at Julesburg, Colorado, where Slade was working at the time for the Overland Stagecoach line.

[9] Mark Twain's portraits of western types make an interesting comparison with Bret Harte's characterizations of these same people of the mining frontier. In contrast to Bret Harte's sentimentalized treatment, Mark Twain humanizes his "characters" but permits them to remain true to life and true to their real social context. Kentuck of Harte's "The Luck of Roaring Camp" and Oakhurst of his "Outcasts of Poker Flat" would hardly have felt at home with Mark Twain's Scotty Briggs in Virginia City.

Mark Twain saw in this westerner's virility and high spirits a significant kind of local color. Unlike the dandified gamblers and the coolheaded highwaymen, this native son of the western mining towns was slow to move, but impassioned when aroused. He was usually humble in dress, backward in manner, and especially reticent among his betters. His greatest social handicap, but his most colorful trait, was his language, a language highly colored by inept grammar, plentiful slang, and rough-and-ready imagery, interlaced with mild and well-meant profanity. Distorted grammar and slang had already come to stereotype the Georgia "cracker" and the Pike County men of the Old Southwest and the backwoodsmen of the early frontier. The colorful speech of these goodhearted "roughs" of the mining towns became the hallmark of the westerner. It so captivated Mark Twain's interest that his portrayals of this type of character subordinate everything else to his peculiarities of speech:

BUCK FANSHAW'S FUNERAL (from *Roughing It*)

« « « Somebody has said that in order to know a community, one must observe the style of its funerals and know what manner of men they bury with most ceremony. I cannot say which class we buried with most eclat in our "flush times," the distinguished public benefactor or the distinguished rough—possibly the two chief grades or grand divisions of society honored their illustrious dead about equally. . . .

There was a grand time over Buck Fanshaw when he died. He was a representative citizen. He had "killed his man"—not in his own quarrel, it is true, but in defense of a stranger unfairly beset by numbers. He had kept a sumptuous saloon. He had been the proprietor of a dashing helpmeet whom he could have discarded without the formality of a divorce. He had held a high position in the fire department and been a very Warwick in politics. When he died there was great lamentation throughout the town, but especially in the vast bottom-stratum of society. . . .

After Buck Fanshaw's inquest, a meeting of the shorthaired brotherhood was held, for nothing can be done on the Pacific coast without a public meeting and an expression of sentiment. Regretful resolutions were passed and various committees appointed; among others, a committee of one was deputed to call on the minister, a fragile, gentle, spiritual new fledgling from an Eastern theological seminary, and as yet unacquainted with the ways of the mines. The committeeman, "Scotty" Briggs, made his visit; and in after days it was worth something to hear the minister tell about it. Scotty was a stalwart rough, whose customary suit, when on weighty official business, like committee work, was a fire-helmet, flaming red flannel shirt, patent-leather belt with spanner and revolver attached, coat hung over arm, and pants stuffed into boot-tops.... He was on a sorrowful mission, now, and his face was the picture of woe. Being admitted to the presence he sat down before the clergyman, placed his fire-hat on an unfinished manuscript sermon under the minister's nose, took from it a red silk handkerchief, wiped his brow and heaved a sigh of dismal impressiveness, explanatory of his business. He choked, and even shed tears; but with an effort he mastered his voice and said in lugubrious tones:

"Are you the duck that runs the gospel-mill next door?"

"Am I the—pardon me, I believe I do not understand?"

With another sigh and a half-sob, Scotty rejoined:

"Why you see we are in a bit of trouble, and the boys thought maybe you would give us a lift, if we'd tackle you—that is, if I've got the rights of it and you are the head clerk of the doxology-works next door."

"I am the shepherd in charge of the flock whose fold is next door."

"The which?"

"The spiritual adviser of the little company of believers whose sanctuary adjoins these premises."

Scotty scratched his head, reflected a moment, and then said:

"You ruther hold over me, pard. I reckon I can't call that hand. Ante and pass the buck."

"How? I beg pardon. What did I understand you to say?"

"Well, you've ruther got the bulge on me. Or maybe we've both got the bulge, somehow. You don't smoke me and I don't smoke you. You see, one of the boys has passed in his checks, and we want to give him a good send-off, and so the thing I'm on now is to roust out somebody to jerk a little chin-music for us and waltz him through handsome."

"My friend, I seem to grow more and more bewildered. Your observations are wholly incomprehensible to me. Cannot you simplify them in some way? At first I thought perhaps I understood you, but I grope now. Would it not expedite matters if you restricted yourself to categorical statements of fact unencumbered with obstructing accumulations of metaphor and allegory?"

Another pause, and more reflection. Then, said Scotty:

"I'll have to pass, I judge."

"How?"

"You've raised me out, pard."

"I still fail to catch your meaning."

"Why, that last lead of yourn is too many for me—that's the idea. I can't neither trump nor follow suit."

The clergyman sank back in his chair perplexed. Scotty leaned his head on his hand and gave himself up to thought. Presently his face came up, sorrowful but confident.

"I've got it now, so's you can savvy," he said. "What we want is a gospel-sharp. See?"

"A what?"

"Gospel-sharp. Parson."

"Oh! Why did you not say so before? I am a clergyman—a parson."

"Now you talk! You see my blind and straddle it like a man. Put it there!"—extending a brawny paw, which closed over the minister's small hand and gave it a shake indicative of fraternal sympathy and fervent gratification.

"Now we're all right, pard. Let's start fresh. Don't you mind my snuffling a little—becuz we're in a power of trouble. You see, one of the boys has gone up the flume—"

"Gone where?"

"Up the flume—throwed up the sponge, you understand."

"Thrown up the sponge?"

"Yes—kicked the bucket—"

"Ah—has departed to that mysterious country from whose bourne no traveler returns."

"Return! I reckon not. Why, pard, he's *dead!*"

"Yes, I understand."

"Oh, you do? Well I thought you might be getting tangled some more. Yes, you see he's dead again—"

"*Again!* Why, has he ever been dead before?"

"Dead before? No! Do you reckon a man has got as many lives as a cat? But you bet you he's awful dead now, poor old boy, and I wish I'd never seen this day. I don't want no better friend than Buck Fanshaw. I knowed him by the back; and when I know a man and like him, I freeze to him—you hear *me*. Take him all round, pard, there never was a bullier man in the mines. No man ever knowed Buck Fanshaw to go back on a friend. But it's all up, you know, it's all up. It ain't no use. They've scooped him."

"Scooped him?"

"Yes—death has. Well, well, well, we've got to give him up. Yes, indeed. It's a kind of a hard world, after all, *ain't* it? But pard, he was a rustler! You ought to seen him get started once. He was a bully boy with a glass eye! Just spit in his face and give him room according to his strength, and it was just beautiful to see him peel and go in. He was the worst son of a thief that ever drawed breath. Pard, he was *on* it! He was on it bigger than an Injun!"

"On it? On what?"

"On the shoot. On the shoulder. On the fight, you understand. *He* didn't give a continental for *any*body. *Beg* your pardon, friend, for coming so near saying a cussword—but you see I'm on an awful strain, in this palaver, on account of having to cramp down and draw everything so mild. But we've got to give him up. There ain't any getting around that, I don't reckon. Now if we can get you to help plant him—"

"Preach the funeral discourse? Assist at the obsequies?"

"Obs'quies is good. Yes. That's it—that's our little game. We are going to get the thing up regardless, you know. He was always nifty himself, and so you bet you his funeral ain't going to be no slouch—solid-silver door-plate on his coffin, six plumes on the hearse, and a nigger on the box in a biled shirt and a plug hat—how's that for high? And we'll take care of *you*, pard. We'll fix you, all right. There'll be a kerridge for you; and whatever you want, you just 'scape out and we'll tend to it. We've got a shebang fixed up for you to stand behind, in No. I's house, and don't you be afraid.

Just go in and toot your horn, if you don't sell a clam. Put Buck through as bully as you can, pard, for anybody that knowed him will tell you that he was one of the whitest men that was ever in the mines. You can't draw it too strong. He never could stand it to see things going wrong. He's done more to make this town quiet and peaceable than any man in it. I've seen him lick four Greasers in eleven minutes, myself. If a thing wanted regulating, *he* warn't a man to go browsing around after somebody to do it, but he would prance in and regulate it himself. He warn't a Catholic. Scasely. He was down on 'em. His word was, 'No Irish need apply!' But it didn't make no difference about that when it came down to what a man's rights was—and so, when some roughs jumped the Catholic boneyard and started in to stake out town lots in it he *went* for 'em! And he *cleaned* 'em, too! I was there, pard, and I seen it myself."

"That was very well indeed—at least the impulse was—whether the act was strictly defensible or not. Had deceased any religious convictions? That is to say, did he feel a dependence upon, or acknowledge allegiance to a higher power?"

More reflection.

"I reckon you've stumped me again, pard. Could you say it over once more, and say it slow?"

"Well, to simplify it somewhat, was he, or rather had he ever been connected with any organization sequestered from secular concerns and devoted to self-sacrifice in the interests of morality?"

"All down but nine—set 'em up on the other alley, pard."

"What did I understand you to say?"

"Why, you're most too many for me, you know. When you get in with your left I hunt grass every time. Every time you draw, you fill; but I don't seem to have any luck. Let's have a new deal."

"How? Begin again?"

"That's it."

"Very well. Was he a good man, and—"

"There—I see that; don't put up another chip till I look at my hand. A good man, says you? Pard, it ain't no name for it. He was the best man that ever—pard, you would have doted on that man. He could lam any galoot of his inches in America. It was him that put down the riot last election before it got a start; and everybody said he was the only man that could have done it. He waltzed in with a spanner in one hand and a trumpet in the other, and sent fourteen men home on a shutter in less than three minutes. He had that riot all broke up and prevented nice before anybody ever got a chance to strike a blow. He was always for peace, and he would *have* peace—he could not stand disturbances. Pard, he was a great loss to this town. It would please the boys if you could chip in something like that and do him justice. Here once when the Micks got to throwing stones through the Methodis' Sunday-school windows, Buck Fanshaw, all of his own notion, shut up his saloon and took a couple of six-shooters and mounted guard over the Sunday-school. Says he, 'No Irish need apply!' And they didn't. He was the bulliest man in the mountains, pard! He could run faster, jump higher, hit harder, and hold more tanglefoot whiskey without spilling it than any man in seventeen counties. Put that in, pard—it'll please the boys more than anything you could say. And you can say, pard, that he never shook his mother."

"Never shook his mother?"

"That's it—any of the boys will tell you so."

"Well, but why *should* he shake her?"

"That's what *I* say—but some people does."

"Not people of any repute?"

"Well, some that averages pretty so-so."

"In my opinion the man that would offer personal violence to his own mother, ought to—"

"Cheese it, pard; you've banked your ball clean outside the string. What I was drivin' at, was, that he never *throwed off* on his mother—don't you see? No indeedy. He give her a house to live in, and town lots, and plenty of money; and he looked after her and took care of her all the time; and when she was down with the smallpox I'm d—d if he didn't set up nights and nuss her himself! *Beg* your pardon for saying it, but it hopped out too quick for yours truly. You've treated me like a gentleman, pard, and I ain't the man to hurt your feelings intentional. I think you're white. I think you're a square man, pard. I like you, and I'll lick any man that don't. I'll lick him till he can't tell himself from a last year's corpse! Put it *there!* [Another fraternal hand-shake—and exit.]

The obsequies were all that "the boys" could desire. Such a

marvel of funeral pomp had never been seen in Virginia [City]. The plumed hearse, the dirge-breathing brass-bands, the closed marts of business, the flags drooping at half-mast, the long, plodding procession of uniformed secret societies, military battalions and fire companies, draped engines, carriages of officials, and citizens in vehicles and on foot, attracted multitudes of spectators to the sidewalks, roofs, and windows; and for years afterward, the degree of grandeur attained by any civic display in Virginia was determined by comparison with Buck Fanshaw's funeral. » » »

In his particular mediums of the anecdote, the yarn, or the tall tale, Mark Twain was unexcelled. His masterful craftsmanship shaped the raw materials of his experience and his observation into narratives which, viewed objectively, can be fully enjoyed simply as "story." But the careful reader often discovers that the story itself also serves as a framework within which the writer evolves an intriguing character. Usually this character is the storyteller himself. By means of his novel point of view, or his observations, or his digressions, and especially by means of his dialect, the teller of the story can even absorb almost all of the reader's interest. The foregoing account of Buck Fanshaw's funeral illustrates the type in a rather obvious way. Simon Wheeler's *Jumping Frog* story, presented elsewhere in this volume,[10] is the classic example of this art. Mark Twain exhibits this same skill of blending character and plot against a California background in another literary nugget of his western years:

JIM BAKER'S BLUEJAY YARN[11] (from *A Tramp Abroad*)

« « « When I first begun to understand jay language correctly, there was a little incident happened here. Seven years ago, the

[10] See Part II, Mark Twain, Missouri Humorist.

[11] Although the "Bluejay Yarn" appeared in 1880 embedded in his European travel accounts in *A Tramp Abroad,* this anecdote was born of Mark Twain's western years. He first picked up the story, which he attributes to Jim Baker, from a literary prospector friend, Jim Gillis, while he was hibernating in Gillis' cabin on Jackass Hill near San Francisco in the winter of 1864-65. Together with the "Jumping Frog Yarn," this story is typical of the fine art with which Mark Twain wrought so many little masterpieces out of the raw materials of his frontier experience. The reader

last man in this region but me moved away. There stands his house —been empty ever since; a log house, with a plank roof—just one big room, and no more; no ceiling—nothing between the rafters and the floor. Well, one Sunday morning I was sitting out here in front of my cabin, with my cat, taking the sun, and looking at the blue hills, and listening to the leaves rustling so lonely in the trees, and  thinking of the home away yonder in the states, that I hadn't heard from in thirteen years, when a bluejay lit on that house, with an acorn in his mouth, and says, "Hello, I reckon I've struck something." When he spoke, the acorn dropped out of his mouth and rolled down the roof, of course, but he didn't care; his mind was all on the thing he had struck. It was a knot-hole in the roof. He cocked his head to one side, shut one eye and put the other one to the hole, like a possum looking down a jug; then he glanced up with his bright eyes, gave a wink or two with his wings—which signifies gratification, you understand—and says, "It looks like a hole, it's located like a hole—blamed if I don't believe it *is* a hole!"

Then he cocked his head down and took another look; he glances up perfectly joyful, this time; winks his wings and his tail both, and says, "Oh, no, this ain't no fat thing, I reckon! If I ain't in luck!—why it's a perfectly elegant hole!" So he flew down and got that acorn, and fetched it up and dropped it in, and was just tilting his head back, with the heavenliest smile on his face, when all of a sudden he was paralyzed into a listening attitude and that smile faded gradually out of his countenance like breath off'n a razor, and the queerest look of surprise took its place. Then he says, "Why, I didn't hear it fall!" He cocked his eye at the hole again, and took a long look; raised up and shook his head; stepped around to the other side of the hole and took another look from

will find these highly descriptive anecdotes scattered throughout most of Mark Twain's later books, especially the travel books, and often with little relevance to the subject at hand.

that side; shook his head again. He studied a while, then he just went into the *de*tails—walked round and round the hole and spied into it from every point of the compass. No use. Now he took a thinking attitude on the comb of the roof and scratched the back of his head with his right foot a minute, and finally says, "Well, it's too many for *me*, that's certain; must be a mighty long hole; however, I ain't got no time to fool around here, I got to tend to business; I reckon it's all right—chance it, anyway."

So he flew off and fetched another acorn and dropped it in, and tried to flirt his eye to the hole quick enough to see what become of it, but he was too late. He held his eye there as much as a minute; then he raised up and sighed, and says, "Confound it, I don't seem to understand this thing, no way; however, I'll tackle her again." He fetched another acorn, and done his level best to see what become of it, but he couldn't. He says, "Well *I* never struck no such a hole as this before; I'm of the opinion it's a totally new kind of a hole." Then he begun to get mad. He held in for a spell, walking up and down the comb of the roof and shaking his head and muttering to himself; but his feelings got the upper hand of him, presently, and he broke loose and cussed himself black in the face. I never see a bird take on so about a little thing. When he got through he walks to the hole and looks in again for half a minute; then he says, "Well, you're a long hole, and a deep hole, and a mighty singular hole altogether—but I've started in to fill you, and I'm d——d if I *don't* fill you, if it takes a hundred years!"

And with that, away he went. You never see a bird work so since you was born. He laid into his work like a nigger, and the way he hove acorns into that hole for about two hours and a half was one of the most exciting and astonishing spectacles I ever struck. He never stopped to take a look anymore—he just hove 'em in and went for more. Well, at last he could hardly flop his wings, he was so tuckered out. He comes a-drooping down, once more, sweating like an ice-pitcher, drops his acorn in and says, "*Now* I guess I've got the bulge on you by this time!" So he bent down for a look. If you'll believe me, when his head come up again he was just pale with rage. He says, "I've shoveled acorns enough in there to keep the family thirty years, and if I can see a sign of one of 'em I wish I may land in a museum with a belly full of sawdust in two minutes!"

He just had strength enough to crawl up on to the comb and lean his back agin the chimbly, and then he collected his impressions and begun to free his mind. I see in a second that what I had mistook for profanity in the mines was only just the rudiments, as you may say.

Another jay was going by, and heard him doing his devotions, and stops to inquire what was up. The sufferer told him the whole circumstance, and says, "Now yonder's the hole, and if you don't believe me, go and look for yourself." So this fellow went and looked, and comes back and says, "How many did you say you put in there?" "Not any less than two tons," says the sufferer. The other jay went and looked again. He couldn't seem to make it out, so he raised a yell, and three more jays come. They all examined the hole, they all made the sufferer tell it over again, then they all discussed it, and got off as many leather-headed opinions about it as an average crowd of humans could have done.

They called in more jays; then more and more, till pretty soon this whole region 'peared to have a blue flush about it. There must have been five thousand of them; and such another jawing and disputing and ripping and cussing, you never heard. Every jay in the whole lot put his eye to the hole and delivered a more chuckle-headed opinion about the mystery than the jay that went there before him. They examined the house all over, too. The door was standing half open, and at last one old jay happened to go and light on it and look in. Of course, that knocked the mystery galley-west in a second. There lay the acorns, scattered all over the floor. He flopped his wings and raised a whoop. "Come here!" he says. "Come here, everybody; hang'd if this fool hasn't been trying to fill up a house with acorns!" They all came a-swooping down like a blue cloud, and as each fellow lit on the door and took a glance, the whole absurdity of the contract that that first jay had tackled hit him home and he fell over backward suffocating with laughter, and the next jay took his place and done the same.

Well, sir, they roosted around here on the housetop and the trees for an hour, and guffawed over that thing like human beings. It ain't any use to tell me a bluejay hasn't got a sense of humor, because I know better. And memory, too. They brought jays here from all over the United States to look down that hole, every summer for three years. Other birds, too. And they could all see the point, except an owl that come from Nova Scotia to visit the Yo Semite, and he took this thing in on his way back. He said he couldn't see anything funny in it. But then he was a good deal disappointed about Yo Semite, too. » » »

Fables of the Jim Baker type are scattered all through Mark Twain's work: stories and sketches of frogs, rabbits, coyotes, horses, dogs, birds, camels, even chameleons and ants. The best of these fables, however, came out of their writer's earlier experiences in western America—those years when life was vibrant and when every event, however incidental, seemed full of meaning. Unlike his owl from Nova Scotia, Mark Twain was everywhere "impressed" by, and frequently amused by, western life and western scenes during the whole of this American odyssey across the plains, through the mountains and deserts, into the wonderland of California, and across the sea to the exotic islands of the mid-Pacific.

The time inevitably came when the fledgling writer of stories and sketches, loaded with his western impressions, should return to the East. In spite of his attempts at prospecting and mining and in spite of his territorial newspaper reporting, Mark Twain never became a naturalized Westerner. It was not any homing instinct that drew him away. It was simply a kind of temperamental virus that infects many Americans in their youth: restlessness of spirit, an unsatisfied craving for ever new experiences. By 1867, Mark Twain was headed back east with literary ambitions. New sights, new friendships, new encounters lured him on, as always, into an ever expanding world. Before he was to finish exploring that world, many misfortunes would dampen his optimism and even his enthusiasm for life. Perhaps that is why, in later years, he looked back upon his western days with almost as much nostalgia as he suffered when he recalled his Missouri boyhood. The West had given the young man from Missouri a tremendous "lift"—almost a second youth—and he had seen that region when it was still young and still the great American promise.[12]

4. The Magic Land

IN HIS FIRST TRIP to England in 1872,[1] Mark Twain wrote back to his sister-in-law, Mrs. Crane, in America: "If you and Theodore will come over in the spring with Livy and me, and spend the summer, you will see a country that *is* so beautiful that you will be obliged to believe in fairyland. There is nothing like it elsewhere on the globe. . . . I would a good deal rather live here if I could get the rest of you over." A quarter of a century later, that first impression of England was as strong as ever in Mark Twain's mind. In his account of "Queen Victoria's Jubilee" in 1897,

---

[12] At the time he left California to begin his career in the East as a truly freelance writer, Mark Twain could have had little doubt about his prospects of a national reputation if he read the *Alta California* of December 15, 1866: "That his [travel] letters will be read with interest needs no assurance from us—his reputation has been made here in California, and his great ability is well known; but he has been known principally as a humorist, while he really has no superior as a descriptive writer—a keen observer of men and their surroundings—and we feel confident his letters to the *Alta*, from his new field of observation, will give him a world-wide reputation." Quoted in Benson, *Mark Twain's Western Years*, 213.

[1] Mark Twain's immediate purpose in going to England the first time was to secure English copyright for his previous writings in order to prevent future piracies of his works by British publishers. Another object of this visit was to gather material at first hand for a book he had been planning on "The Oddities and Eccentricities of the English." This literary project never materialized, probably because the American was so well received from the very beginning in all British circles that he lost all desire to satirize or burlesque contemporary England. For a full treatment of this matter, see R. M. Rodney, "Mark Twain in England."

he spoke of "that unapproachable beauty which has been the monopoly of sylvan England since the creation." In spite of the enchantment of such faraway places as India, Australia, and South Africa, Mark Twain was compelled to write in his *Following the Equator*:

"INCOMPARABLE" ENGLAND

« « « There is only one England. Now that I have sampled the globe, I am not in doubt. There is a beauty of Switzerland, and it is repeated in the glaciers and snowy ranges of many parts of the earth; there is a beauty of the fiord, and it is repeated in New Zealand and Alaska; there is a beauty of Hawaii, and it is repeated in ten thousand islands of the Southern Seas; there is a beauty of the prairie and the plain, and it is repeated here and there in the earth; each of these is worshipful, each is perfect in its way, yet holds no monopoly of its beauty; but that beauty which is England is alone—it has no duplicate. It is made up of very simple details—just grass, and trees, and shrubs, and roads, and hedges, and gardens, and houses, and vines, and churches, and castles, and here and there a ruin—and over it all a mellow dream-haze of history. But its beauty is incomparable, and all its own. » » »

A year after his first arrival in England, Mark Twain was so struck by the beauty and picturesqueness of the countryside and the ruins of southern England as he traveled from London to Dover, that he recorded the following impression in an article that was intended to satirize English customs and manners:

AN ENGLISH JOURNEY (from *Europe and Elsewhere*)

« « « We took the Dover train and went whistling along over the housetops at the rate of fifty miles an hour, and just as smoothly and pleasantly, too, as if we were in a sleigh. One can never have anything but a very vague idea of what speed is until he travels over an English railway. Our "lightning" expresses are sleepy and indolent by comparison. We looked into the back windows of the endless ranks of houses abreast and below us, and saw many a homelike little family of early birds sitting at their breakfasts. New views and new aspects of London were about me; the mighty city seemed to spread farther and wider in the clear morning air than it had ever done before. There is something awe-inspiring about the mere look of the figures that express the population of London when one comes to set them down in a good large hand—4,000,000! It takes a body's breath away, almost.

We presently left the city behind. We had started drowsy, but we did not stay so. How could we, with the brilliant sunshine pouring down, the balmy wind blowing through the open windows, and the Garden of Eden spread all abroad? We swept along through rolling expanses of growing grain—not a stone or a stump to mar their comeliness, not an unsightly fence or an ill-kept hedge; through broad meadows covered with fresh green grass as clean swept as if a broom had been at work there—little brooks wandering up and down them, noble trees here and there, cows in the shade, groves in the distance and church spires projecting out of them; and there were the quaintest old-fashioned houses set in the midst of smooth lawns or partly hiding themselves among fine old forest trees; and there was one steep-roofed ancient cottage whose walls all around, and whose roof, and whose chimneys, were clothed in a shining mail of ivy leaves!—so thoroughly, indeed, that only one little patch of roof was visible to prove that the house was not a mere house of leaves, with glass windows in it. Imagine those dainty little homes surrounded by flowering shrubs and bright green grass and all sorts of old trees—and then go on and try to imagine something more bewitching.

By and by we passed Rochester, and, sure enough, right there, on the highest ground in the town and rising imposingly up from among clustering roofs, was the gray old castle—roofless, ruined, ragged, the sky beyond showing clear and blue through the glassless windows, the walls partly clad with ivy—a time-scarred, weather-beaten old pile, but ever so picturesque and ever so majestic, too. There it was, a whole book of English history. I had read of Rochester Castle a thousand times, but I had never really believed there was any such building before.

Presently we reached the sea and came to a stand far out on a pier; and here was Dover and more history. The chalk cliffs of England towered up from the shore and the French coast was visible. On the tallest hill sat Dover Castle, stately and spacious and superb, looking just as it has always looked any time these ten or fifteen thousand years—I do not know its exact age, and it does not matter, anyway.

We stepped aboard the little packet and steamed away. The sea was perfectly smooth, and painfully brilliant in the sunshine. » » »

On his return from the Continent, Mark Twain accompanied a group of correspondents covering the arrival of the Persian Shah on a state visit to England. For the first time, the American witnessed an awesome spectacle that many Englishmen themselves never had seen—a naval review and escort by the very heads of Britain's sea power. At the time of this experience England was still "mistress of the seas" and had converted most of her men-of-war into iron-clad vessels. This tremendous display of naval power symbolized and dramatized English tradition so forcefully to the young American traveler that he was already becoming an ardent convert to what he later lauded as "English history, English growth, English achievement, the accumulated power and renown and dignity of twenty centuries of strenuous effort."

A NAVAL SALUTE (from *Europe and Elsewhere*)

« « « When we were a mile or so out from Ostend conversation ceased, an expectant look came into all faces, and opera glasses began to stand out from above all noses. This impressive hush lasted a few minutes, and then some one said:

"There they are!"

"Where?"

"Away yonder ahead—straight ahead."

Which was true. Three huge shapes smothered in the haze—the *Vanguard*, the *Audacious*, and the *Devastation*—all great ironclads. They were to do escort duty. The officers and correspondents gathered on the forecastle and waited for the next act. A red spout of fire issued from the *Vanguard*'s side, another flashed from the *Au-*

dacious. Beautiful these red tongues were against the dark haze. Then there was a long pause—ever so long a pause and not a sound, not the suspicion of a sound; and now, out of the stillness, came a deep, solemn "boom! boom!" It had not occurred to me that at so great a distance I would not hear the report as soon as I saw the flash. The two crimson jets were very beautiful, but not more so than the rolling volumes of white smoke that plunged after them, rested a moment over the water, and then went wreathing and curling up among the webbed rigging and the tall masts, and left only glimpses of these things visible, high up in the air, projecting as if from a fog.

Now the flashes came thick and fast from the black sides of both vessels. The muffled thunders of the guns mingled together in one continued roll, the two ships were lost to sight, and in their places two mountains of tumbled smoke rested upon the motionless water, their bases in the hazy twilight and their summits shining in the sun. It was good to be there and to see so fine a spectacle as that.

We closed up fast upon the ironclads. They fell apart to let our flotilla come between, and as the *Vigilant* ranged up the rigging of the ironclads was manned to salute the Shah. And, indeed, that was something to see. The shrouds, from the decks clear to the trucks, away up toward the sky, were black with men. On the lower rounds of these rope ladders they stood five abreast, holding each other's hands, and so the tapering shrouds formed attenuated pyramids of humanity, six pyramids of them towering into the upper air, and clear up on the top of each dizzy mast stood a little creature like a clothes pin—a mere black peg against the sky—and that mite was a sailor waving a flag like a postage stamp. All at once the pyramids of men burst into a cheer, and followed it with two more, given with a will. . . . » » »

The naval salute and escort across the English channel was climaxed by a colorful and dynamic scene that would have delighted the heart of Tom Sawyer himself:

A DOVER SPECTACLE (from *Europe and Elsewhere*)

« « « The sea scene grew little by little, until presently it was very imposing. We drew up into the midst of a waiting host of vessels. Enormous five-masted men-of-war, great turret ships, steam packets, pleasure yachts—every sort of craft, indeed—the sea was thick with them; the yards and rigging of the warships loaded with men, the packets crowded with people, the pleasure ships rainbowed with brilliant flags all over and over—some with flags strung thick on lines stretching from bowsprit to foremast, thence to mainmast, thence to mizzenmast, and thence to stern. All the ships were in motion—gliding hither and thither, in and out, mingling and parting—a bewildering whirl of flash and color. Our leader, the vast, black, ugly, but very formidable *Devastation*, plowed straight through the gay throng, our Shah-ships following, the lines of big men-of-war saluting, the booming of the guns drowning the cheering, stately islands of smoke towering everywhere. And so, in this condition of unspeakable grandeur, we swept into the harbor of Dover, and saw the English princes and the long ranks of red-coated soldiers waiting on the pier, civilian multitudes behind them, the lofty hill front by the castle swarming with spectators, and there was the crash of cannon and a general hurrah all through the air. » » »

From his earliest boyhood Mark Twain had loved pageantry and spectacle of any kind almost to the point of obsession. The annual circus and minstrel show had been the most delectable experiences of his childhood. His pride in his own showmanship is evident in incident after incident in his autobiographical novels *Tom Sawyer* and *Huckleberry Finn*. The legends of King Arthur and the triumphs of Joan of Arc not only released the boy's imagination for all kinds of escapades with his playmates but also provided the materials for some of his later novels. As a young man, he read Cervantes' *Don Quixote* and Lecky's *History of European Morals* and had so steeped himself in medieval European history that he gradually merged the present with the past until he came to identify modern England with ancient and medieval Britain.

This foreshortened view of history is the only way to explain his treatment of monarchy and the church in such books as *The Prince and the Pauper, Joan of Arc,* and *A Connecticut Yankee.* But the rough edges of English history were softened for Mark Twain by the continuous pomp and pageantry that cloaked all of English life down through the centuries. To the end of his life, Mark Twain, with his poetic hypersensitivity to color and form and movement, saw all of England through his "mellow dream-haze of history."

His romantic image of England was strengthened by his first experience in that fabled land. In his letters home during his first visit to England the Yankee visitor overflowed with all the enthusiasm of a young boy seeing his first three-ring circus:

> I have been received in a sort of tremendous way, tonight, by all the brains of London, assembled at the annual dinner of the sheriffs of London—mine being (between you and me) a name which was received with a flattering outburst of spontaneous applause when the long list of guests was called.[2]

And later in the season he wrote:

> I came here to take notes for a book, but I haven't done much but attend dinners and make speeches. But have had a jolly good time and I do hate to go away from these English folks; they make a stranger feel entirely at home—and they laugh so easily that it is a comfort to make after-dinner speeches here. I have made hundreds of friends; and last night in the crush of the opening of the new Guild-hall Library and Museum, I was surprised to meet a familiar face every few steps.
> ... I would sail on Saturday, but this is the day of the Lord Mayor's annual grand state dinner, when they say 900 of the great men of the city sit down to table, a great many of them in their fine official and court paraphernalia, so I must not miss it.[3]

His enthusiasm for England and all things English increased as he met and hobnobbed with the most celebrated writers and artists of England, was applauded by the lecture crowds, was hailed and toasted at banquets, and was accepted by the English people more

---
[2] *Mark Twain's Letters* (ed. by Albert Bigelow Paine), I, 199–200 (September 28, 1872).
[3] *Ibid.*, I, 201 (November 6, 1872).

heartily than he was by Americans. The exhilaration of his first reception in England lasted him all of his life and possibly explains those passages in his books in which he glamorizes the foreground of English political life.

In the person of Tom Canty of Offal Court in *The Prince and the Pauper*,[4] we can discover some of the long-suppressed desires of Samuel Clemens of Missouri:

DREAMS OF SPLENDOR (from *The Prince and the Pauper*)

« « « By and by Tom's reading and dreaming about princely life wrought such a strong effect upon him that he began to *act* the prince, unconsciously. His speech and manners became curiously ceremonious and courtly, to the vast admiration and amusement of his intimates. But Tom's influence among these young people began to grow now, day by day; and in time he came to be looked up to by them with a sort of wondering awe, as a superior being. He seemed to know so much! and he could do and say such marvelous things! and withal, he was so deep and wise! Tom's remarks and Tom's performances were reported by the boys to their elders; and these, also, presently began to discuss Tom Canty, and to regard him as a most gifted and extraordinary creature. Full-grown people brought their perplexities to Tom for solution, and were often astonished at the wit and wisdom of his decisions. In fact, he was become a hero to all who knew him except his own family—these only saw nothing in him.

Privately, after a while, Tom organized a royal court! He was

[4] *The Prince and the Pauper* was published in 1881, after Mark Twain had made three prolonged visits to England. Charlotte Yonge's *The Prince and the Page* (1865) first suggested the idea of the story to him. He evolved much of the plot through after-dinner storytelling sessions with his wife and children in 1877, but did not write the story in its final form until 1880. In the interval, Mark Twain's literary purpose changed, from the intention, avowed in the title, to offer simple amusement for "young people of all ages," to a much more serious purpose: "My idea is to afford a realizing sense of the exceeding severity of the laws of that day by inflicting some of their penalties upon the king himself and allowing him a chance to see the rest of them applied to others—all of which is to account for certain mildnesses which distinguished Edward VI's reign from those that preceded it and followed it" (*Letters*, I, 377, March 11, 1880). By the time he finished the novel, it had become a mixture of romance, pseudo-history, and social protest. See Rodney, "Mark Twain in England," for the genesis of the novel and its reception by English readers.

the prince; his special comrades were guards, chamberlains, equerries, lords and ladies in waiting, and the royal family. Daily the mock prince was received with elaborate ceremonials borrowed by Tom from his romantic readings; daily the great affairs of the mimic kingdom were discussed in the royal council, and daily his mimic highness issued decrees to his imaginary armies, navies, and viceroyalties.

After which he would go forth in his rags and beg a few farthings, eat his poor crust, take his customary cuffs and abuse, and then stretch himself upon his handful of foul straw, and resume his empty grandeurs in his dreams.

And still his desire to look just once upon a real prince, in the flesh, grew upon him, day by day, and week by week, until at last it absorbed all other desires, and became the one passion of his life.

One January day, on his usual begging tour, he tramped despondently up and down the region round about Mincing Lane and Little East Cheap, hour after hour, barefooted and cold, looking in at cook-shop windows and longing for the dreadful pork-pies and other deadly inventions displayed there—for to him these were dainties fit for the angels; that is, judging by the smell, they were—for it had never been his good luck to own and eat one. There was a cold drizzle of rain; the atmosphere was murky; it was a melancholy day. At night Tom reached home so wet and tired and hungry that it was not possible for his father and grandmother to observe his forlorn condition and not be moved—after their fashion; wherefore they gave him a brisk cuffing at once and sent him to bed. For a long time his pain and hunger, and the swearing and fighting going on in the building, kept him awake; but at last his thoughts drifted away to far, romantic lands, and he fell asleep in the company of jeweled and gilded princelings who lived in vast palaces, and had servants salaaming before them or flying to execute their orders. And then, as usual, he dreamed that *he* was a princeling himself.

All night long the glories of his royal estate shone upon him; he moved among great lords and ladies, in a blaze of light, breathing perfumes, drinking in delicious music, and answering the reverent obeisances of the glittering throng as it parted to make way for him, with here a smile, and there a nod of his princely head.

And when he awoke in the morning and looked upon the wretchedness about him, his dream had had its usual effect—it had intensified the sordidness of his surroundings a thousandfold. Then came bitterness, and heartbreak, and tears. » » »

Just as Mark Twain had set out for the enchanted land of nineteenth-century England, Tom Canty wanders far from home, drawn by his desire for a glimpse of the never-never land of palaces and nobility and pageantry:

A PRINCE IN A PALACE (from *The Prince and the Pauper*)

« « « He wandered here and there in the city, hardly noticing where he was going, or what was happening around him. People jostled him and some gave him rough speech; but it was all lost on the musing boy. By and by he found himself at Temple Bar, the farthest from home he had ever traveled in that direction. He stopped and considered a moment, then fell into his imaginings again, and passed on outside the walls of London. . . .

Tom discovered Charing Village presently, and rested himself at the beautiful cross built there by a bereaved king of earlier days; then idled down a quiet, lovely road, past the great cardinal's stately palace, toward a far more mighty and majestic palace beyond—Westminster. Tom stared in glad wonder at the vast pile of masonry, the wide-spreading wings, the frowning bastions and turrets, the huge stone gateway, with its gilded bars and its magnificent array of colossal granite lions, and the other signs and symbols of English royalty. Was the desire of his soul to be satisfied at last? Here, indeed, was a king's palace. Might he not hope to see a prince now—a prince of flesh and blood, if Heaven were willing?

At each side of the gilded gate stood a living statue, that is to say, an erect and stately and motionless man-at-arms, clad from head to heel in shining steel armor. At a respectful distance were many countryfolk, and people from the city, waiting for any chance glimpse of royalty that might offer. Splendid carriages, with splendid people in them and splendid servants outside, were arriving and departing by several other noble gateways that pierced the royal inclosure.

Poor little Tom, in his rags, approached, and was moving slowly and timidly past the sentinels, with a beating heart and a rising hope, when all at once he caught sight through the golden bars of a spectacle that almost made him shout for joy. Within was a comely boy, tanned and brown with sturdy outdoor sports and exercises, whose clothing was all of lovely silks and satins, shining with jewels; at his hip a little jeweled sword and dagger; dainty buskins on his feet, with red heels; and on his head a jaunty crimson cap, with drooping plumes fastened with a great sparkling gem. Several gorgeous gentlemen stood near—his servants, without a doubt. Oh! he was a prince—a prince, a living prince, a real prince—without the shadow of a question; and the prayer of the pauper boy's heart was answered at last. » » »

The dream comes true, of course. Befriended by young Edward VI, the pauper exchanges places with the prince and admires himself in his new-found splendor:

« « « Tom Canty, left alone in the prince's cabinet, made good use of his opportunity. He turned himself this way and that before the great mirror, admiring his finery; then walked away, imitating the prince's high-bred carriage, and still observing results in the glass. Next he drew the beautiful sword, and bowed, kissing the blade, and laying it across his breast, as he had seen a noble knight do, by way of salute to the lieutenant of the Tower, five or six weeks before, when delivering the great lords of Norfolk and Surrey into his hands for captivity. Tom played with the jeweled dagger that hung upon his thigh; he examined the costly and exquisite ornaments of the room; he tried each of the sumptuous chairs, and thought how proud he would be if the Offal Court herd could only peep in and see him in his grandeur. » » »

In this enchanted land of pauper-turned-prince, Mark Twain *alias* Tom Canty indulged himself in years of accumulated fancy and historical romance. In his novel, Mark Twain takes his readers on a royal progress down the Thames River by night to the Old City of London. The elaborate stage-setting for the entrance of the young prince sets the lavish tone and creates the resplendent atmosphere for all that follows:

THE RIVER PAGEANT (from *The Prince and the Pauper*)

« « « At nine in the evening the whole vast river-front of the palace was blazing with light. The river itself, as far as the eye could reach cityward, was so thickly covered with watermen's boats and with pleasure barges, all fringed with colored lanterns, and gently agitated by the waves, that it resembled a glowing and limitless garden of flowers stirred to soft motion by summer winds. The grand terrace of stone steps leading down to the water, spacious enough to mass the army of a German principality upon, was a picture to see, with its ranks of royal halberdiers in polished armor, and its troops of brilliantly costumed servitors flitting up and down, and to and fro, in the hurry of preparation.

Presently a command was given, and immediately all living creatures vanished from the steps. Now the air was heavy with the hush of suspense and expectancy. As far as one's vision could carry, he might see the myriads of people in the boats rise up, and shade their eyes from the glare of lanterns and torches, and gaze toward the palace.

A file of forty or fifty state barges drew up to the steps. They were richly gilt, and their lofty prows and sterns were elaborately carved. Some of them were decorated with banners and streamers; some with cloth-of-gold and arras embroidered with coats of arms; others with silken flags that had numberless little silver bells fastened to them, which shook out tiny showers of joyous music whenever the breezes fluttered them; others of yet higher pretensions, since they belonged to nobles in the prince's immediate service, had their sides picturesquely fenced with shields gorgeously emblazoned with armorial bearings. Each state barge was towed by a tender. Besides the rowers, these tenders carried each a number of men-at-arms in glossy helmet and breastplate, and a company of musicians. . . .

There was a flourish of trumpets within; and the prince's uncle, the future great Duke of Somerset, emerged from the gateway, arrayed in a "doublet of black cloth-of-gold, and a cloak of crimson satin flowered with gold, and ribanded with nets of silver." He turned, doffed his plumed cap, bent his body in a low reverence, and began to step backward, bowing at each step. A prolonged trumpet-blast followed, and a proclamation, "Way for the high and mighty, the Lord Edward, Prince of Wales!" High aloft on the palace walls a long line of red tongues of flame leaped forth with a thunder-crash; the massed world on the river burst into a mighty roar of welcome; and Tom Canty, the cause and hero of it all, stepped into view, and slightly bowed his princely head.

He was "magnificently habited in a doublet of white satin, with a front-piece of purple cloth-of-tissue, powdered with diamonds, and edged with ermine. Over this he wore a mantle of white cloth-of-gold, pounced with the triple-feather crest, lined with blue satin, set with pearls and precious stones, and fastened with a clasp of brilliants. About his neck hung the order of the Garter, and several princely foreign orders"; and wherever light fell upon him jewels responded with a blinding flash. » » »

All of this was just a prelude to the scenes that followed: the progress down the river to the London Guildhall, where Tom Canty, playing young Prince Edward, is to preside over a banquet, a night of revelry like something out of the *Arabian Nights,* and a dramatic climax suggestive of Shakespearean comedy or an Elizabethan masque:

AT GUILDHALL[5] (from *The Prince and the Pauper*)

« « « The royal barge, attended by its gorgeous fleet, took its stately way down the Thames through the wilderness of illuminated boats. The air was laden with music; the river-banks were beruffled with joy-flames; the distant city lay in a soft luminous glow from its countless invisible bonfires; above it rose many a slender spire into the sky, incrusted with sparkling lights, wherefore in

[5] Mark Twain himself banqueted and spoke at the Guildhall in November of 1872 with nine hundred other guests at the Lord Mayor's annual grand state dinner. He attended dinners and gave after-dinner speeches during his many London residences at other such famous places as the Mansion House, the Whitefriars Club, the Savage Club, the Scottish Corporation, the Garrick Club, the Bath Club, and the inner sanctum of *Punch.*

AT GUILDHALL

their remoteness they seemed like jeweled lances thrust aloft; as the fleet swept along, it was greeted from the banks with a continuous hoarse roar of cheers and the ceaseless flash and boom of artillery.

Arrived at the Dowgate, the fleet was towed up the limpid Walbrook (whose channel has now been for two centuries buried out of sight under acres of buildings) to Bucklersbury, past houses and under bridges populous with merry-makers and brilliantly lighted, and at last came to a halt in a basin where now is Barge Yard, in the center of the ancient city of London. Tom disembarked, and he and his gallant procession crossed Cheapside and made a short march through the Old Jewry and Basinghall Street to the Guildhall.

Tom and his little ladies [the princesses] were received with due ceremony by the Lord Mayor and the Fathers of the City, in their gold chains and scarlet robes of state, and conducted to a rich canopy of state at the head of the great hall, preceded by heralds making proclamation, and by the Mace and the City Sword. The lords and ladies who were to attend upon Tom and his two small friends took their places behind their chairs.

At a lower table the court grandees and other guests of noble degree were seated, with the magnates of the city; the commoners took places at a multitude of tables on the main floor of the hall. From their lofty vantage ground, the giants Gog and Magog, the ancient guardians of the city, contemplated the spectacle below them with eyes grown familiar to it in forgotten generations. There was a bugle-blast and a proclamation, and a fat butler appeared in a high perch in the leftward wall, followed by his servitors bearing with impressive solemnity a royal Baron of Beef, smoking hot and ready for the knife.

After grace, Tom (being instructed) rose—and the whole house with him—and drank from a portly golden loving-cup with the Princess Elizabeth; from her it passed to the Lady Jane, and then traversed the general assemblage. So the banquet began.

By midnight the revelry was at its height. Now came one of those picturesque spectacles so admired in that old day. A description of it is still extant in the quaint wording of a chronicler who witnessed it:

"Space being made, presently entered a baron and an earl appareled after the Turkish fashion in long robes of bawdkin powdered with gold; hats on their heads of crimson velvet, with great rolls of gold, girded with two swords called simitars, hanging by great bawdricks of gold. Next came another baron and another earl, in two long gowns of yellow satin, traversed with white satin, and in every bend of white was a bend of crimson satin, after the fashion of Russia, with furred hats of gray on their heads; either of them having an hatchet in their hands, and boots with *pykes*" (points a foot long), "turned up. And after them came a knight, then the Lord High Admiral, and with him five nobles, in doublets of crimson velvet, voyded low on the back and before to the cannel-bone, laced on the breasts with chains of silver; and, over that, short cloaks of crimson satin, and on their heads hats after the dancers' fashion, with pheasants' feather in them. These were appareled after the fashion of Prussia. The torch-bearers, which were about an hundred, were appareled in crimson satin and green, like Moors, their faces black. Next came in a *mommarye*. Then the minstrels, which were disguised, danced; and the lords and ladies did wildly dance also, that it was a pleasure to behold." . . .

Suddenly, high above the jubilant roar and thunder of the revel, broke the clear peal of a bugle-note. There was instant silence—a deep hush; then a single voice rose—that of the messenger from the palace—and began to pipe forth a proclamation, the whole multitude standing, listening. The closing words, solemnly pronounced, were:

"The king is dead!"

The great assemblage bent their heads upon their breasts with one accord; remained so, in profound silence, a few moments; then all sunk upon their knees in a body, stretched out their hands toward Tom, and a mighty shout burst forth that seemed to shake the building:

"Long live the king!"

Poor Tom's dazed eyes wandered abroad over this stupefying spectacle, and finally rested dreamily upon the kneeling princesses beside him a moment, then upon the Earl of Hertford. A sudden purpose dawned in his face. He said, in a low tone, at Lord Hertford's ear:

"Answer me truly, on thy faith and honor! Uttered I here a command, the which none but a king might hold privilege and prerogative to utter, would such commandment be obeyed, and none rise up to say me nay?"

"None, my liege, in all these realms. In thy person bides the majesty of England. Thou art the king—thy word is law."

Tom responded, in a strong, earnest voice, and with great animation:

"Then shall the king's law be law of mercy, from this day, and never more be law of blood! Up from thy knees and away! To the Tower and say the king decrees the Duke of Norfolk shall not die!"

The words were caught up and carried eagerly from lip to lip far and wide over the hall, and as Hertford hurried from the presence, another prodigious shout burst forth:

"The reign of blood is ended! Long live Edward, king of England!" » » »

As imaginary king of England, Mark Twain indulged his boyhood fancies almost to the point of fantasy—assisted by historian Hume and various early English chroniclers. The pomp and ceremony of court life hedged in the young King Tom Canty–Clemens at every turn, from his moment of rising to the end of his royal day. Mark Twain, the Missouri humorist, cannot resist the temptation to do a bit of spoofing, even at the expense of the royal household, but behind his humor lies the ever enchanted spirit of Samuel Clemens:

THE ROYAL BEDCHAMBER (from *The Prince and the Pauper*)

« « « He opened his eyes—the richly clad First Lord of the Bedchamber was kneeling by his couch. The gladness of the lying dream faded away—the poor boy recognized that he was still a captive and a king. The room was filled with courtiers clothed in purple mantles—the mourning color—and with the noble servants of the monarch. Tom sat up in bed and gazed out from the heavy silken curtains upon this fine company.

The weighty business of dressing began, and one courtier after another knelt and paid his court and offered to the little king his condolences upon his heavy loss, while the dressing proceeded. In the beginning, a shirt was taken up by the Chief Equerry in Waiting, who passed it to the First Lord of the Buckhounds, who passed it to the Second Gentleman of the Bedchamber, who passed it to the Head Ranger of Windsor Forest, who passed it to the Third Groom of the Stole, who passed it to the Chancellor Royal of the Duchy of Lancaster, who passed it to the Master of the Wardrobe, who passed it to Norroy King-at-Arms, who passed it to the Constable of the Tower, who passed it to the Chief Steward of the Household, who passed it to the Hereditary Grand Diaperer, who passed it to the Lord High Admiral of England, who passed it to the Archbishop of Canterbury, who passed it to the First Lord of the Bedchamber, who took what was left of it and put it on Tom. Poor little wondering chap, it reminded him of passing buckets at a fire.

Each garment in its turn had to go through this slow and solemn process; consequently Tom grew very weary of the ceremony; so weary that he felt an almost gushing gratefulness when he at last saw his long silken hose begin the journey down the line and knew that the end of the matter was drawing near. But he exulted too soon. The First Lord of the Bedchamber received the hose and was about to incase Tom's legs in them, when a sudden flush invaded his face and he hurriedly hustled the things back into the hands of the Archbishop of Canterbury with an astonished look and a whispered, "See, my lord!"—pointing to a something connected with the hose. The Archbishop paled, then flushed, and passed the hose to the Lord High Admiral, whispering, "See, my lord!" The Admiral passed the hose to the Hereditary Grand Diaperer, and had hardly breath enough in his body to ejaculate, "See, my lord!" The hose drifted backward along the line, to the Chief Steward of the Household, the Constable of the Tower, Norroy King-at-Arms, the Master of the Wardrobe, the Chancellor Royal of the Duchy of Lancaster, the Third Groom of the Stole, the Head Ranger of Windsor Forest, the Second Gentleman of the Bedchamber, the First Lord of the Buckhounds—accompanied always with that amazed and frightened "See! see!"—till they finally reached the hands of the Chief Equerry in Waiting, who gazed a moment, with a pallid face, upon what had caused all this dismay, then hoarsely whispered, "Body of my life, a tag gone from a truss point!—to the Tower with the Head Keeper of the King's Hose!"—after which he leaned upon the shoulder of the First Lord of the Buckhounds to regather his vanished strength while fresh hose, without any damaged strings to them, were brought.

But all things must have an end, and so in time Tom Canty was in a condition to get out of bed. The proper official poured water, the proper official engineered the washing, the proper official stood by with a towel, and by and by Tom got safely through the purifying stage and was ready for the services of the Hairdresser-royal. When he at length emerged from his master's hands, he was a gracious figure and as pretty as a girl, in his mantle and trunks of purple satin, and purple-plumed cap. He now moved in state toward his breakfast-room, through the midst of the courtly assemblage; and as he passed, these fell back, leaving his way free, and dropped upon their knees. » » »

In Mark Twain's fantasy we next see Prince Tom at dinner—another strictly "private" affair of the royal household:

A STATE DINNER[6] (from *The Prince and the Pauper*)

« « « Let us privileged ones hurry to the great banqueting-room and have a glance at matters there while Tom is being made ready for the imposing occasion. It is a spacious apartment, with gilded pillars and pilasters, and pictured walls and ceilings. At the door stand tall guards, as rigid as statues, dressed in rich and picturesque costumes, and bearing halberds. In a high gallery which runs all around the place is a band of musicians and a packed company of citizens of both sexes, in brilliant attire. In the center of the room, upon a raised platform, is Tom's table. Now let the ancient chronicler speak:

[6] Mark Twain's principal source of information about the life and customs of fifteenth-century England was Hume's *History of England*.

"A gentleman enters the room bearing a rod, and along with him another bearing a table-cloth, which, after they have both kneeled three times with the utmost veneration, he spreads upon the table, and after kneeling again they both retire; then come two others, one with the rod again, the other with a salt-cellar, a plate, and bread; when they have kneeled as the others had done, and placed what was brought upon the table, they too retire with the same ceremonies performed by the first; at last come two nobles, richly clothed, one bearing a tasting-knife, who, after prostrating themselves in the most graceful manner, approach and rub the table with bread and salt, with as much awe as if the king had been present."

So end the solemn preliminaries. Now, far down the echoing corridors we hear a bugle-blast, and the indistinct cry, "Place for the king! way for the king's most excellent majesty!" These sounds are momently repeated—they grow nearer and nearer—and presently, almost in our faces, the martial note peals and the cry rings out, "Way for the king!" At this instant the shining pageant appears, and files in at the door, with a measured march. Let the chronicler speak again:

"First come Gentlemen, Barons, Earls, Knights of the Garter, all richly dressed and bareheaded; next comes the Chancellor, between two, one of which carries the royal scepter, the other the Sword of State in a red scabbard, studded with golden fleurs-de-lis, the point upwards; next comes the King himself—whom, upon his appearing, twelve trumpets and many drums salute with a great burst of welcome, whilst all in the galleries rise in their places, crying 'God save the King!' After him come nobles attached to his person, and on his right and left march his guard of honor, his fifty Gentlemen Pensioners, with gilt battle-axes."

This was all fine and pleasant. Tom's pulse beat high and a glad light was in his eye. He bore himself right gracefully, and all the more so because he was not thinking of how he was doing it, his mind being charmed and occupied with the blithe sights and sounds about him—and besides, nobody can be very ungraceful in nicely fitting beautiful clothes after he has grown a little used to them—especially if he is for the moment unconscious of them. Tom remembered his instructions, and acknowledged his greeting with a slight inclination of his plumed head, and a courteous "I thank ye, my good people."

He seated himself at table without removing his cap; and did it without the least embarrassment: for to eat with one's cap on was the one solitary royal custom upon which the kings and the Cantys met upon common ground, neither party having any advantage over the other in the matter of old familiarity with it. The pageant broke up and grouped itself picturesquely, and remained bareheaded.

Now, to the sound of gay music, the Yeomen of the Guard entered—"the tallest and mightiest men in England, they being selected in this regard"—but we will let the chronicler tell about it:

"The Yeomen of the Guard entered bareheaded, clothed in scarlet, with golden roses upon their backs; and these went and came, bringing in each turn a course of dishes, served in plate. These dishes were received by a gentleman in the same order they were brought, and placed upon the table, while the taster gave to each guard a mouthful to eat of the particular dish he had brought, for fear of any poison."

Tom made a good dinner, notwithstanding he was conscious that hundreds of eyes followed each morsel to his mouth and watched him eat it with an interest which could not have been more intense if it had been a deadly explosive and was expected to blow him up and scatter him all over the place. He was careful not to hurry, and equally careful not to do anything whatever for himself, but wait till the proper official knelt down and did it for him. He got through without a mistake—flawless and precious triumph.

When the meal was over at last and he marched away in the midst of his bright pageant, with the happy noises in his ears of blaring bugles, rolling drums, and thundering acclamations, he felt that if he had seen the worst of dining in public, it was an ordeal which he would be glad to endure several times a day if by that means he could but buy himself free from some of the more formidable requirements of his royal office. » » »

Mark Twain himself, during his many stays in England, dined often at Lord Mayors' banquets and enjoyed the hospitality and entertainment of aristocracy and even royalty on several occasions.[7] His many trips about London made him familiar with the Tower, London Bridge, the Parliament buildings, the Guildhall, Westminster Abbey, and all the other great landmarks of English history. He steeped himself in guidebooks and old chronicles until he knew every corner of the Old City, and he watched the royal processions and official ceremonies that embodied English tradition until English history became, in his mind, a kind of continuous pageant marching out of the past into the present. It made little difference to him whether he was witnessing an actual pageant or reading about and fabricating one several centuries old—his imagination was captivated by either. When, in the latter part of *The Prince and the Pauper*, Mark Twain describes a royal procession of the time of Edward VI, it is all a part of his Magic Land:

THE RECOGNITION PROCESSION (from *The Prince and the Pauper*)

« « « When Tom Canty awoke the next morning, the air was heavy with a thunderous murmur; all the distances were charged with it. It was music to him; for it meant that the English world was out in its strength to give loyal welcome to the great day.

Presently Tom found himself once more the chief figure in a wonderful floating pageant on the Thames; for by ancient custom the "recognition procession" through London must start from the Tower, and he was bound thither.

When he arrived there, the sides of the venerable fortress seemed suddenly rent in a thousand places, and from every rent leaped a red tongue of flame and a white gush of smoke; a deafening explosion followed, which drowned the shoutings of the multitude, and made the ground tremble; the flame-jets, the smoke, and the explosions were repeated over and over again with marvelous celerity, so that in a few moments the old Tower disappeared in the vast fog of its own smoke, all but the very top of the tall pile called the White Tower; this, with its banners, stood out above

---

[7] Mark Twain met and dined with Emperor Wilhelm II of Germany and the Prince of Wales in Homburg in 1891. He encountered the English prince again in 1907, when, as Edward VII, he and the Queen cordially greeted the American during a garden party at Windsor Castle.

the dense bank of vapor as a mountain peak projects above a cloud-rack.

Tom Canty, splendidly arrayed, mounted a prancing war-steed, whose rich trappings almost reached to the ground; his "uncle," the Lord Protector Somerset, similarly mounted, took place in his rear; the King's Guard formed in single ranks on either side, clad in burnished armor; after the Protector followed a seemingly interminable procession of resplendent nobles attended by their vassals; after these came the lord mayor and the aldermanic body, in crimson velvet robes, and with their gold chains across their breasts; and after these the officers and members of all the guilds of London, in rich raiment, and bearing the showy banners of the several corporations. Also in the procession, as a special guard of honor through the city, was the Ancient and Honorable Artillery Company—an organization already three hundred years old at that time, and the only military body in England possessing the privilege (which it still possesses in our day) of holding itself independent of the commands of Parliament. It was a brilliant spectacle, and was hailed with acclamations all along the line, as it took its stately way through the packed multitudes of citizens. 》 》 》

The royal procession winds its way to its climax at Westminster Abbey for the king's coronation.[8] Here, in the inner sanctum of six centuries of English royalty, Mark Twain lifts his "dream-haze of history" to re-create the climactic scenes of his historical romance:

CORONATION DAY (from *The Prince and the Pauper*)

《 《 《 Let us go backward a few hours, and place ourselves in Westminster Abbey, at four o'clock in the morning of this memorable Coronation Day. We are not without company; for although it is still night, we find the torch-lighted galleries already filling up

[8] The Recognition Procession and the Coronation ceremony are still essentially the same today as they were when the first Edward was crowned in 1272. Mark Twain's description may not catch all of the detail of the ritual as television audiences may now see it, but his absorption of the symbolism and tradition provide the modern reader more of the spirit of the ceremony than the camera-eye can possibly record.

with people who are well content to sit still and wait seven or eight hours till the time shall come for them to see what they may not hope to see twice in their lives—the coronation of a king. Yes, London and Westminster have been astir ever since the warning guns boomed at three o'clock, and already crowds of untitled rich folk who have bought the privilege of trying to find sittingroom in the galleries are flocking in at the entrances reserved for their sort.

The hours drag along, tediously enough. All stir has ceased for some time, for every gallery has long ago been packed. We may sit now, and look and think at our leisure. We have glimpses, here and there and yonder, through the dim cathedral twilight, of portions of many galleries and balconies, wedged full with people, the other portions of these galleries and balconies being cut off from sight by intervening pillars and architectural projections. We have in view the whole of the great north transept—empty, and waiting for England's privileged ones. We see also the ample area or platform, carpeted with rich stuffs, whereon the throne stands. The throne occupies the center of the platform, and is raised above it upon an elevation of four steps. Within the seat of the throne is enclosed a rough flat rock—the stone of Scone—which many generations of Scottish kings sat on to be crowned, and so it in time became holy enough to answer a like purpose for English monarchs. Both the throne and its footstool are covered with cloth-of-gold.

Stillness reigns, the torches blink dully, the time drags heavily. But at last the lagging daylight asserts itself, the torches are extinguished, and a mellow radiance suffuses the great spaces. All features of the noble building are distinct now, but soft and dreamy, for the sun is lightly veiled with clouds.

At seven o'clock the first break in the drowsy monotony occurs; for on the stroke of this hour the first peeress enters the transept, clothed like Solomon for splendor, and is conducted to her appointed place by an official clad in satins and velvets, whilst a duplicate of him gathers up the lady's long train, follows after, and, when the lady is seated, arranges the train across her lap for her. He then places her footstool according to her desire, after which he puts her coronet where it will be convenient to her hand when the time for the simultaneous coroneting of the nobles shall arrive.

By this time the peeresses are flowing in in a glittering stream, and satin-clad officials are flitting and glinting everywhere, seating them and making them comfortable. The scene is animated enough now. There is stir and life, and shifting color everywhere. After a time, quiet reigns again; for the peeresses are all come, and are all in their places—a solid acre, or such a matter, of human flowers, resplendent in variegated colors, and frosted like a Milky Way with diamonds. There are all ages here: brown, wrinkled, white-haired dowagers who are able to go back, and still back, down the stream of time, and recall the crowning of Richard III and the troublous days of that old forgotten age; and there are handsome middle-aged dames; and lovely and gracious young matrons; and gentle and beautiful young girls, with beaming eyes and fresh complexions, who may possibly put on their jeweled coronets awkwardly when the great time comes; for the matter will be new to them, and their excitement will be a sore hindrance. Still, this may not happen, for the hair of all these ladies has been arranged with a special view to the swift and successful lodging of the crown in its place when the signal comes.

We have seen that this massed array of peeresses is sown thick with diamonds, and we also see that it is a marvelous spectacle—but now we are about to be astonished in earnest. About nine, the clouds suddenly break away and a shaft of sunshine cleaves the mellow atmosphere and drifts slowly along the ranks of ladies; and every rank it touches flames into a dazzling splendor of many-colored fires, and we tingle to our finger-tips with the electric thrill that is shot through us by the surprise and the beauty of the spectacle! Presently a special envoy from some distant corner of the Orient, marching with the general body of foreign ambassadors, crosses this bar of sunshine, and we catch our breath, the glory that streams and flashes and palpitates about him is so overpowering; for he is crusted from head to heels with gems, and his slightest movement showers a dancing radiance all around him.

Let us change the tense for convenience. The time drifted along —one hour—two hours—two hours and a half; then the deep booming of artillery told that the king and his grand procession had arrived at last; so the waiting multitude rejoiced. All knew that a further delay must follow, for the king must be prepared and robed for the solemn ceremony; but this delay would be pleasantly occupied by the assembling of the peers of the realm in their stately robes. These were conducted ceremoniously to their seats, and their coronets placed conveniently at hand; and meanwhile the multitude in the galleries were alive with interest, for most of them were beholding for the first time, dukes, earls, and barons, whose names had been historical for five hundred years. When all were finally seated, the spectacle from the galleries and all coigns of vantage was complete; a gorgeous one to look upon and to remember.

Now the robed and mitered great heads of the church, and their attendants, filed in upon the platform and took their appointed places; these were followed by the Lord Protector and other great officials, and these again by a steel-clad detachment of the Guard.

There was a waiting pause; then, at a signal, a triumphant peal of music burst forth, and Tom Canty, clothed in a long robe of cloth-of-gold, appeared at a door, and stepped upon the platform. The entire multitude rose, and the ceremony of the Recognition ensued.

Then a noble anthem swept the Abbey with its rich waves of sound; and thus heralded and welcomed, Tom Canty was conducted to the throne. The ancient ceremonies went on with impressive solemnity, whilst the audience gazed; and as they drew nearer and nearer to completion, Tom Canty grew pale, and still paler, and a deep and steadily deepening woe and despondency settled down upon his spirits and upon his remorseful heart.

At last the final act was at hand. The Archbishop of Canterbury lifted up the crown of England from its cushion and held it out over the trembling mock king's head. In the same instant a rainbow radiance flashed along the spacious transept; for with one impulse every individual in the great concourse of nobles lifted a coronet and poised it over his or her head—and paused in that attitude. 》 》 》

Within the framework of the story, the coronation ceremony is intended to be simply another backdrop for the dramatic action, which now reaches its climax with the reappearance of the true prince and the release of the pauper Tom Canty from a distressing situation. In another sense, though, the coronation and all the ceremony and pageantry that precede it provide the truer climax because it is an emotional climax. For Mark Twain, at least, fancy and history finally merge into intense and immediate reality in these descriptive passages.

England was ever the Magic Land for Mark Twain, whether he saw it through the eyes of Tom Canty of Offal Court or through the eyes of Samuel Clemens, American traveler. Even though he made frontal attacks on what he considered to be the evils of monarchy and institutionalized religion in *A Connecticut Yankee* and in parts of *The Prince and the Pauper,* nevertheless, he loved the legendary lore and the historical glamour of Britain. Six times Mark Twain visited and revisited England during the thirty-five years between his first and his last trips. He often stayed for a year or more, in residence in London or its suburbs, to revive his spirit and to gather fresh materials for his books. His last trip to England, at the invitation of Oxford University to receive an honorary degree, was a four-week celebration unequaled by any reception ever given by the English to an American up to that time. All of Tom Sawyer's dreams of colorful pomp and ceremony, of recognition and honors, finally came true when the elderly Mark Twain stood in the Sheldonian Theater at Oxford and was acclaimed as the peer of England's most famous nineteenth-century writers. Only an American who saw England with romantic vision could write about England as Mark Twain did, and only an American who had so absorbed the English tradition and had responded so imaginatively and sympathetically to the beauty of old England could be accepted so entirely by the English people.

5. The World Outside

IN THE PUBLIC MIND, Mark Twain is so closely identified with things American, that it often surprises his reader to learn that this "son of Missouri" spent twelve years abroad. Over three of these years he spent in England, and about six months of his wandering was on excursions to such places as the Hawaiian Islands and Bermuda. But he traveled and lived for eight years altogether in Europe, principally in Germany and Italy, with side trips to Paris, Belgium, Switzerland, Austria, Sweden, Greece, Palestine, Egypt, and North Africa. In later life he gave more than a year to his lecture tour around the world, with visits to the South Pacific, Australia, New Zealand, Tasmania, Ceylon, India, Madagascar, and South Africa. These various foreign travels and residences kept him away from America on five occasions for more than a year at a time, once for as long as two and one-half years. Yet he never lost the American touch and the American point of view.[1] His ties with his homeland remained so strong that a compelling nostalgia always drew him back to America in spite of his tremendous popularity and unstinted welcome everywhere abroad. Most Americans who left their country as frequently and

---

[1] Nineteenth-century America produced a succession of "literary ambassadors" who served her cause well, not only in England, but also in many European countries. Actual diplomatic posts were given to James Fenimore Cooper, who spent seven years in France as U. S. consul at Lyons; Washington Irving, who served for four years as U. S. minister to Spain; Nathaniel Hawthorne, for four years the American consul at Liverpool; William Dean Howells, Mark Twain's closest literary friend, who served as Venetian consul during the Civil War years; and most notable of all, James Russell Lowell, who was the American minister to Spain for three years and the American minister to Great Britain for five years. All of these writers spent many more years abroad than the terms of their diplomatic posts. Other noted American writers went to Europe without diplomatic commissions, but with such strong literary reputations that they became some of our most effective good-will ambassadors: William Cullen Bryant, Ralph Waldo Emerson, Henry Wadsworth Longfellow, and Henry James. With the exception of Irving and James, none of these American writers went abroad more often or spent more time in European residence than Mark Twain; yet that essential Americanism within him, the very quality that endeared him to British and European audiences, made him always feel alien when he was abroad.

for as long as Mark Twain did eventually became expatriates. They usually sought something abroad that they felt America lacked, something so essential to their lives that it made foreign residence and citizenship a spiritual necessity. But in the world outside of America and England, Mark Twain never found anything sufficiently "soul-satisfying," as he would put it. His travels in the world outside his native environment and his enchanted land of England were only an experience of progressive disillusionment.

However, during his travels in that outside world Mark Twain saw much that fired his imagination, much that at least partially appeased his hunger for new experience, and much that appealed to his sensitive love of color, form, and movement. Wherever he saw a picturesque scene or found some relic of a great historical event, whether it was in Italy or India, Austria or Tasmania, his feelings rose, often to the point of fervor, and poured themselves into pages of intense description. With his ear for good narrative he re-created in his travel books many tales and local legends, gathered from both Europe and the East, that are highly entertaining because of the way he retold them. And whenever Mark Twain found evidence of sham or injustice or cruelty, his indignation worked itself out in smoldering sarcasm or biting satire, and sometimes in pure burlesque. Whatever his shortcomings as a journalist, his travel accounts constantly seethe and frequently erupt with a great variety of phenomena in a most unpredictable way. And throughout the accounts runs that essential strain of his humor, with which he can be counted on to enliven the flatter, more pedestrian stretches of his travels. The high lights of these reports from the outside world are usually his descriptions, written with an objective eye and a perfectly serious intention, but often with a strong emotional undertone.

In order to glimpse the world outside, as Mark Twain saw it, the reader should start with his first trip to Europe. In the summer of 1867 we find him in northern Italy, on his "Quaker City" excursion to the Holy Land, viewing the sub-Alpine lakes and mountains of Lombardy. Although he at first instinctively compares the scene with his familiar American rivers and mountains, his Yankee skepticism is quickly overcome by the beauty of the region and he comes totally under its spell.

LAKE COMO (from *The Innocents Abroad*)

« « « ...I always had an idea that Como was a vast basin of water, like Tahoe, shut in by great mountains. Well, the border of huge mountains is here, but the lake itself is not a basin. It is as crooked as any brook, and only from one-quarter to two-thirds as wide as the Mississippi. There is not a yard of low ground on either side of it—nothing but endless chains of mountains that spring abruptly from the water's edge, and tower to altitudes varying from a thousand to two thousand feet. Their craggy sides are clothed with vegetation, and white specks of houses peep out from the luxuriant foliage everywhere; they are even perched upon jutting and picturesque pinnacles a thousand feet above your head.

Again, for miles along the shores, handsome country-seats surrounded by gardens and groves, sit fairly in the water, sometimes in nooks carved by Nature out of the vine-hung precipices, and with no ingress or egress save by boats. Some have great broad stone staircases leading down to the water, with heavy stone balustrades ornamented with statuary and fancifully adorned with creeping vines and bright-colored flowers—for all the world like a drop-curtain in a theater, and lacking nothing but long-waisted, high-heeled women and plumed gallants in silken tights coming down to go serenading in the splendid gondola in waiting.

A great feature of Como's attractiveness is the multitude of pretty houses and gardens that cluster upon its shores and on its mountainsides. They look so snug and so homelike, and at eventide when everything seems to slumber, and the music of the vesper-bells comes stealing over the water, one almost believes that nowhere else than on the Lake of Como can there be found such a paradise of tranquil repose.

From my window here in Ballagio, I have a view of the other side of the lake now, which is as beautiful as a picture. A scarred and wrinkled precipice rises to a height of eighteen hundred feet; on a tiny bench half-way up its vast wall, sits a little snowflake of a church, no bigger than a martin-box, apparently; skirting the base of the cliff are a hundred orange groves and gardens, flecked with glimpses of the white dwellings that are buried in them; in front, three or four gondolas lie idle upon the water—and in the burnished mirror of the lake, mountain, chapel, houses, groves, and boats are counterfeited so brightly and so clearly that one scarce knows where the reality leaves off and the reflection begins!

The surroundings of this picture are fine. A mile away, a grove-plumed promontory juts far into the lake and glasses its palace in the blue depths; in midstream a boat is cutting the shining surface and leaving a long track behind, like a ray of light; the mountains beyond are veiled in a dreamy purple haze; far in the opposite direction a tumbled mass of domes and verdant slopes and valleys bars the lake, and here, indeed, does distance lend enchantment to the view—for on this broad canvas, sun and clouds and the richest of atmospheres have blended a thousand tints together, and over its surface the filmy lights and shadows drift, hour after hour, and glorify it with a beauty that seems reflected out of Heaven itself. Beyond all question, this is the most voluptuous scene we have yet looked upon. » » »

This same first visit to Europe took Mark Twain in rapid progression through all the renowned cities of Italy: Genoa, Milan, Venice, Bologna, Florence, Pisa, Leghorn, Rome, and Naples. With his fellow American travelers he had to admire ancient ruins, palaces, churches by the dozen, and—as he expressed it—"acres of historical paintings." He saw much to astound him and much to appall him in this "wretchedest, princeliest land on earth," but very little that he could genuinely admire. He frankly admitted that he was glad to get away from such centers of art and power as Florence and Rome. The mixture of splendor and squalor that met him at every turn in these cities, in addition to the Colosseum and other reminders of cruelty and injustice, offended his progressive and democratic spirit.[2] One monument to wealth and religious as-

[2] *The Innocents Abroad,* published in 1869, almost two years after the Holy Land trip, was Mark Twain's first full-fledged book. The influence of the writer's earlier journalistic experience on the book is obvious: it is primarily the observations of a roving reporter, partly serious and objective, partly flippant and humorous. The essential element of *Innocents Abroad*—an element most unusual in travel books of the time—is Mark Twain's skepticism. At times, this skepticism breaks out into a rash of sarcasms, caustic remarks, and indignations that forecast his bitter protests against social injustice in *The Prince and the Pauper, A Connecticut Yankee,* and other later works. This spirit of skepticism and protest became more and more

piration, however, made him catch his breath—the great cathedral at Milan. For fervency of feeling and rhapsodic description, the following passage from his impressions of Milan surpasses anything he wrote about the other cultural antiquities of Europe:

MILAN—A POEM IN MARBLE (from *The Innocents Abroad*)

« « « Toward dusk we drew near Milan, and caught glimpses of the city and the blue mountain-peaks beyond. But we were not caring for these things—they did not interest us in the least. We were in a fever of impatience; we were dying to see the renowned cathedral! We watched—in this direction and that—all around—everywhere. We needed no one to point it out—we did not wish any one to point it out—we would recognize it, even in the desert of the great Sahara.

At last, a forest of graceful needles, shimmering in the amber sunlight, rose slowly above the pygmy housetops, as one sometimes sees, in the far horizon, a gilded and pinnacled mass of cloud lift itself above the waste of waves, at sea,—the cathedral! We knew it in a moment.

Half of that night, and all of the next day, this architectural autocrat was our sole object of interest.

What a wonder it is! So grand, so solemn, so vast! And yet so delicate, so airy, so graceful! A very world of solid weight, and yet it seems in the soft moonlight only a fairy delusion of frostwork that might vanish with a breath! How sharply its pinnacled angles and its wilderness of spires were cut against the sky, and how richly their shadows fell upon its snowy roof! It was a vision!—a miracle!—an anthem sung in stone, a poem wrought in marble!

Howsoever you look at the great cathedral, it is noble, it is beautiful! Wherever you stand in Milan, or within seven miles of Milan, it is visible—and when it is visible, no other obejct can chain your whole attention. Leave your eyes unfettered by your will but a single instant and they will surely turn to seek it. It is

---

volatile in Mark Twain until it culminated in the pessimism and futilitarianism of his old age. See Part II of this book for a fuller treatment of this evolution in Mark Twain.

the first thing you look for when you rise in the morning, and the last your lingering gaze rests upon at night. Surely, it must be the princeliest creation that ever brain of man conceived.

At nine o'clock in the morning we went and stood before this marble colossus. The central one of its five great doors is bordered with a bas-relief of birds and fruits and beasts and insects, which have been so ingeniously carved out of the marble that they seem like living creatures—and the figures are so numerous and the design so complex, that one might study it a week without exhausting its interest. On the great steeple—surmounting the myriad of spires—inside of the spires—over the doors, the windows—in nooks and corners—everywhere that a niche or a perch can be found about the enormous building, from summit to base, there is a marble statue, and every statue is a study in itself! Raphael, Angelo, Canova—giants like these gave birth to the designs, and their own pupils carved them. Every face is eloquent with expression, and every attitude is full of grace. Away above, on the lofty roof, rank on rank of carved and fretted spires spring high in the air, and through their rich tracery one sees the sky beyond. In their midst the central steeple towers proudly up like the mainmast of some great Indiaman among a fleet of coasters.

We wished to go aloft. The sacristan showed us a marble stairway (of course it was marble, and of the purest and whitest—there is no other stone, no brick, no wood, among its building-materials), and told us to go up one hundred and eighty-two steps and stop till he came. It was not necessary to say stop—we should have done that anyhow. We were tired by the time we got there. This was the roof. Here, springing from its broad marble flagstones, were the long files of spires, looking very tall close at hand, but diminishing in the distance like the pipes of an organ. We could see, now, that the statue on the top of each was the size of a large man, though they all looked like dolls from the street. We could see, also, that from the inside of each and every one of these hollow spires, from sixteen to thirty-one beautiful marble statues looked out upon the world below.

From the eaves to the comb of the roof stretched in endless succession great curved marble beams, like the fore-and-aft braces of a steamboat, and along each beam from end to end stood up a row of richly carved flowers and fruits—each separate and distinct in kind, and over 15,000 species represented. At a little distance these rows seem to close together like the ties of a railroad track, and then the mingling together of the buds and blossoms of this marble garden forms a picture that is very charming to the eye.

We descended and entered. Within the church, long rows of fluted columns, like huge monuments, divided the building into broad aisles, and on the figured pavement fell many a soft blush from the painted windows above. I knew the church was very large, but I could not fully appreciate its great size until I noticed that the men standing far down by the altar looked like boys, and seemed to glide, rather than walk. We loitered about gazing aloft at the monster windows all aglow with brilliantly colored scenes in the lives of the Saviour and His followers. Some of these pictures are mosaics, and so artistically are their thousand particles of tinted glass or stone put together that the work has all the smoothness and finish of a painting. We counted sixty panes of glass in one window, and each pane was adorned with one of these master achievements of genius and patience. . . .

I like to revel in the dryest details of the great cathedral. The building is five hundred feet long by one hundred and eighty wide, and the principal steeple is in the neighborhood of four hundred feet high. It has 7,148 marble statues, and will have upward of three thousand more when it is finished. In addition, it has one thousand five hundred bas-reliefs. It has one hundred and thirty-six spires—twenty-one more are to be added. Each spire is surmounted by a statue six and a half feet high. Everything about the church is marble, and all from the same quarry; it was bequeathed to the Archbishopric for this purpose centuries ago. So nothing but the mere workmanship costs; still that is expensive—the bill foots up six hundred and eighty-four millions of francs, thus far (considerably over a hundred millions of dollars), and it is estimated that it will take a hundred and twenty years yet to finish the cathedral. It looks complete, but is far from being so. We saw a new statue put in its niche yesterday, alongside of one which had been standing these four hundred years, they said. There are four staircases leading up to the main steeple, each of which cost a hundred thousand dollars, with the four hundred and eight statues which adorn them. Marcoda Campione was the architect who designed the wonderful structure more than five hundred years ago, and it took him forty-six years to work out the plan and get it ready to hand over to the builders. He is dead now. The building was begun a little less than five hundred years ago, and the third generation hence will not see it completed.

The building looks best by moonlight, because the older portions of it being stained with age, contrast unpleasantly with the newer and whiter portions. It seems somewhat too broad for its height, but maybe familiarity with it might dissipate this impression.

They say that the Cathedral of Milan is second only to St. Peter's at Rome. I cannot understand how it can be second to anything made by human hands. » » »

Picturesque landscape and an occasional piece of soaring architecture furnished Mark Twain much material for the enthusiastic descriptions of his travel books. But the subject that most often excited his pen was the crowd of a great city, the color and dynamics of humanity in the mass. Although his study of history and his survey of the Old World civilization only convinced him of man's inhumanity to man, the great procession of mankind always fascinated him, wherever he found it. In Italy he found it most strikingly in Naples.

NAPLES (from *The Innocents Abroad*)

« « « "See Naples and die." Well, I do not know that one would necessarily die after merely seeing it, but to attempt to live there might turn out a little differently. To see Naples as we saw it in the early dawn from far up on the side of Vesuvius, is to see a picture of wonderful beauty. At that distance its dingy buildings looked white—and so, rank on rank of balconies, windows, and roofs, they piled themselves up from the blue ocean till the colossal castle of St. Elmo topped the grand white pyramid and gave the picture symmetry, emphasis, and completeness. And when its lilies turned to roses—when it blushed under the sun's first kiss—it was beautiful beyond all description. One might well say, then, "See Naples and die." The frame of the picture was charming, itself. In front, the smooth sea—a vast mosaic of many colors; the lofty island swimming in a dreamy haze in the distance; at our end of the city the stately double peak of Vesuvius, and its strong black ribs and seams of lava stretching down to the limitless level campagna—a green carpet that enchants the eye and leads it on and on, past clusters of trees, and isolated houses, and snowy villages, until it shreds out in a fringe of mist and general vagueness far away. It is from the Hermitage, there on the side of Vesuvius, that one should "see Naples and die."

But do not go within the walls and look at it in detail. That takes away some of the romance of the thing. The people are filthy in their habits, and this makes filthy streets and breeds disagreeable sights and smells. There never was a community so prejudiced against the cholera as these Neapolitans are. But they have good reason to be. The cholera generally vanquishes a Neapolitan when it seizes him, because, you understand, before the doctor can dig through the dirt and get at the disease the man dies. The upper classes take a sea-bath every day, and are pretty decent.

The streets are generally about wide enough for one wagon, and how they do swarm with people! It is Broadway repeated in every street, in every court, in every alley! Such masses, such throngs, such multitudes of hurrying, bustling, struggling humanity! We never saw the like of it, hardly even in New York, I think. There are seldom any sidewalks, and when there are, they are not often wide enough to pass a man on without caroming on him. So everybody walks in the street—and where the street is wide enough, carriages are forever dashing along. Why a thousand people are not run over and crippled every day is a mystery that no man can solve.

But if there is an eighth wonder in the world, it must be the dwelling-houses of Naples. I honestly believe a good majority of them are a hundred feet high! And the solid brick walls are seven feet through. You go up nine flights of stairs before you get to the "first" floor. No, not nine, but there or thereabouts. There is a little bird-cage of an iron railing in front of every window clear away up, up, up, among the eternal clouds, where the roof is, and there is always somebody looking out of every window—people of ordinary size looking out from the first floor, people a shade smaller from the second, people that look a little smaller yet from the third—and from thence upward they grow smaller and smaller by a regularly graduated diminution, till the folks in the topmost windows seem more like birds in an uncommonly tall martin-box than anything else. The perspective of one of these narrow cracks of streets, with its rows of tall houses stretching away till they come together in the distance like railway-tracks; its clothes-lines crossing over at all altitudes and waving their bannered raggedness over the swarms of people below; and the white-dressed women perched in balcony railings all the way from the pavement up to the heavens—a perspective like that is really worth going into Neapolitan details to see.

Naples, with its immediate suburbs, contains six hundred and twenty-five thousand inhabitants, but I am satisfied it covers no more ground than an American city of one hundred and fifty thousand. It reaches up into the air infinitely higher than three American cities, though, and there is where the secret of it lies. I will observe here, in passing, that the contrasts between opulence and poverty, and magnificence and misery, are more frequent and more striking in Naples than in Paris even. One must go to the Bois de Boulogne to see fashionable dressings, splendid equipages, and stunning liveries, and to the Faubourg St. Antoine to see vice, misery, hunger, rags, dirt—but in the thoroughfares of Naples these things are all mixed together. Naked boys of nine years and the fancy-dressed children of luxury; shreds and tatters, and brilliant uniforms; jackass carts and state carriages; beggars, princes, and bishops, jostle each other in every street. At six o'clock every evening, all Naples turns out to drive on the Riviera di Chiaja (whatever that may mean); and for two hours one may stand there and see the motliest and the worst-mixed procession go by that ever eyes beheld. Princes (there are more princes than policemen in Naples—the city is infested with them)—princes who live up seven flights of stairs and don't own any principalities, will keep a carriage and go hungry; and clerks, mechanics, milliners, and strumpets will go without their dinners and squander the money on a hack-ride in the Chiaja; the ragtag and rubbish of the city stack themselves up, to the number of twenty or thirty, on a rickety little go-cart hauled by a donkey not much bigger than a cat, and *they* drive in the Chiaja; dukes and bankers in sumptuous carriages and with gorgeous drivers and footmen, turn out, also, and so the furious procession goes. For two hours rank and wealth, and obscurity and poverty, clatter along side by side in the wild procession, and then go home serene, happy, covered with glory! » » »

Mark Twain was like any other American tourist in Italy: he must see all the sights. And one of the indispensable sights of any Italian tour at that time was Mount Vesuvius. The excursion up the famous volcano was begun as a lark, and it is obvious that this particular American tourist was not going to let himself be "taken in" by Vesuvius any more than he had been by religious relics or the great masters of painting or any other Italian marvels so highly touted for the tourist trade. But once he had left the dingy streets of Naples behind, and the world of sky and sea and plains and mountains had begun to unfold before him, Mark Twain quickly lost his skepticism, and his ascent of the mountain led him into an enchantment that never failed to cast itself about him whenever he left the cities of men and sordid realities. What he saw on Vesuvius gave his descriptive talents full scope.[3]

MOUNT VESUVIUS (from *The Innocents Abroad*)

« « « We got our mules and horses, after an hour and a half of bargaining with the population of Annunciation, and started sleepily up the mountain, with a vagrant at each mule's tail who pretended to be driving the brute along, but was really holding on and getting himself dragged up instead. I made slow headway at first, but I began to get dissatisfied at the idea of paying my minion five francs to hold my mule back by the tail and keep him from going up the hill, and so I discharged him.

[3] An interesting companion piece to this description of Vesuvius is Mark Twain's account of his visit to Kilauea in the Hawaiian Islands (*Roughing It*, II, Chaps. XXXIII–XXXIV). Just as Lake Como in Italy must take second place to the spectacular Lake Tahoe in California, so Vesuvius suffers by comparison to Kilauea: "I have seen Vesuvius since, but it was a mere toy, a child's volcano, a soup-kettle, compared to this."

We had one magnificent picture of Naples from a high point on the mountainside. We saw nothing but the gas-lamps, of course—two-thirds of a circle, skirting the great Bay—a necklace of diamonds glinting up through the darkness from the remote distance—less brilliant than the stars overhead, but more softly, richly beautiful—and over all the great city the lights crossed and recrossed each other in many and many a sparkling line and curve. And back of the town, far around and abroad over the miles of level campagna, were scattered rows, and circles, and clusters of lights, all glowing like so many gems, and marking where a score of villages were sleeping. About this time, the fellow who was hanging on to the tail of the horse in front of me and practising all sorts of unnecessary cruelty upon the animal, got kicked some fourteen rods, and this incident, together with the fairy spectacle of the lights far in the distance, made me serenely happy, and I was glad I started to Vesuvius. . . .

At the Hermitage we were about fifteen or eighteen hundred feet above the sea, and thus far a portion of the ascent had been pretty abrupt. For the next two miles the road was a mixture—sometimes the ascent was abrupt and sometimes it was not; but one characteristic it possessed all the time, without failure—without modification—it was all uncompromisingly and unspeakably infamous. It was a rough, narrow trail, and led over an old lava-flow—a black ocean which was tumbled into a thousand fantastic shapes—a wild chaos of ruin, desolation, and barrenness—a wilderness of billowy upheavals, of furious whirlpools, of miniature mountains rent asunder—of knarled and knotted, wrinkled and twisted masses of blackness that mimicked branching roots, great vines, trunks of trees, all interlaced and mingled together; and all these weird shapes, all this turbulent panorama, all this stormy, far-stretching waste of blackness, with its thrilling suggestiveness of life, of action, of boiling, surging, furious motion, was petrified!—all stricken dead and cold in the instant of its maddest rioting!—fettered, paralyzed, and left to glower at heaven in impotent rage forevermore!

Finally we stood in a level, narrow valley (a valley that had been created by the terrific march of some old-time eruption) and on either hand towered the two steep peaks of Vesuvius. The one we had to climb—the one that contains the active volcano—seemed about eight hundred or one thousand feet high, and looked almost too straight-up-and-down for any man to climb, and certainly no mule could climb it with a man on his back. Four of these native pirates will carry you up to the top in a sedan-chair, if you wish it, but suppose they were to slip and let you fall,—is it likely that you would ever stop rolling? Not this side of eternity, perhaps. We left the mules, sharpened our fingernails, and began the ascent I have been writing about so long, at twenty minutes to six in the morning. The path led straight up a rugged sweep of loose chunks of pumice-stone, and for about every two steps forward we took, we slid back one. It was so excessively steep that we had to stop, every fifty or sixty steps, and rest a moment. To see our comrades, we had to look very nearly straight up at those above us, and very nearly straight down at those below. We stood on the summit at last—it had taken an hour and fifteen minutes to make the trip.

What we saw there was simply a circular crater—a circular ditch, if you please—about two hundred feet deep, and four or five hundred feet wide, whose inner wall was about half a mile in circumference. In the center of the great circus-ring thus formed was a torn and ragged upheaval a hundred feet high, all snowed over with a sulphur crust of many and many a brilliant and beautiful color, and the ditch enclosed this like the moat of a castle, or surrounded it as a little river does a little island, if the simile is gaudy in the extreme—all mingled together in the richest confusion were red, blue, brown, black, yellow, white—I do not know that there was a color, or shade of a color, or combination of colors, unrepresented—and when the sun burst through the morning mists and fired this tinted magnificence, it topped imperial Vesuvius like a jeweled crown! » » »

Mark Twain stopped at Greece on his way to the Holy Land in the hope that Greece, unlike Italy, would still reflect some of that glory of the Ancient World which American tourists of the mid nineteenth century fondly expected to find somewhere in the Near East. But his expectations were more quickly dashed here than in Italy. Greece he found to be "a bleak, unsmiling desert," without any suggestion of its former glory—at least in the harsh light of day. Only a night trip to the Parthenon provided a momentary illusion of the beauty he sought in this fabled land.

ATHENS BY MOONLIGHT (from *The Innocents Abroad*)

« « « The full moon was riding high in the cloudless heavens now. We sauntered carelessly and unthinkingly to the edge of the lofty battlements of the citadel, and looked down—a vision! And such a vision! Athens by moonlight! The prophet that thought the splendors of the New Jerusalem were revealed to him, surely saw this instead! It lay in the level plain right under our feet—all spread abroad like a picture—and we looked down upon it as we might have looked from a balloon. We saw no semblance of a street, but every house, every window, every clinging vine, every projection, was as distinct and sharply marked as if the time were noonday; and yet there was no glare, no glitter, nothing harsh or repulsive—the noiseless city was flooded with the mellowest light that ever streamed from the moon, and seemed like some living creature wrapped in peaceful slumber. On its further side was a little temple, whose delicate pillars and ornate front glowed with a rich luster that chained the eye like a spell; and nearer by, the palace of the king reared its creamy walls out of the midst of a great garden of shrubbery that was flecked all over with a random shower of amber lights—a spray of golden sparks that lost their brightness in the glory of the moon, and glinted softly upon the sea of dark foliage like the pallid stars of the milky way. Overhead the stately columns, majestic still in their ruin—underfoot the dreaming city—in the distance the silver sea—not on the broad earth is there another picture half so beautiful! » » »

Twenty-nine chapters later in this same account of *The Innocents Abroad* we find Mark Twain again enraptured by the beauty of the natural scene. As a traveling correspondent, he has given most of his space to quips and satire and burlesque and scornful, even bitter, commentary on European culture and traditions. But occasionally, in the very midst of his mock-reporting, a glimpse of beauty catches him up short, and under its spell he indulges in a descriptive passage that is surpassing in its sense of color and form, and movement. These descriptions often seem to belie the realism and skepticism that dominate the rest of the travel accounts. A strong, underlying sentiment emerges at such moments and carries away both Mark Twain and his most hardened readers with its refreshing spontaneity. The following is his brief impression of a picturesque landfall after days of monotonous sea voyage:

FUNCHAL (from *The Innocents Abroad*)

« « « At last we anchored in the open roadstead of Funchal, in the beautiful islands we call the Madeiras.

The mountains looked surpassingly lovely, clad as they were in living green; ribbed with lava ridges; flecked with white cottages; riven by deep chasms purple with shade; the great slopes dashed with sunshine and mottled with shadows flung from the drifting squadrons of the sky, and the superb picture fitly crowned by towering peaks whose fronts were swept by the trailing fringes of the clouds. » » »

Seventeen years later, while on his famous world tour, Mark Twain could write even more buoyantly and with greater flair about the splendors of India:[4]

---

[4] Mark Twain's lecture tour around the world in 1895–96 took him to Hawaii, the Fiji Islands, Australia, Tasmania, New Zealand, Ceylon, India, Mauritius, and South Africa. Although he was received with enthusiasm everywhere he visited and lectured, he had little zest for these Far Eastern travels. He was depressed by the failure of his business ventures and was suffering from poor health. "He was himself in such wretched physical health that a large proportion of his lectures had to be canceled [in South Africa]," says a contemporary journalist, "and the audiences whom he did meet little realized at what cost their amusement was provided" (Poultney Bigelow, "God Speed Mark Twain!," *The Independent*, October 25, 1900). Much of his account of this trip in *Following the Equator* is the most pedestrian kind of journalism, highlighted only occasionally by flashes of his humor and even less frequently by the emotional response that kindled so many of the fine descriptive passages in his earlier travel books. The warmth, the color, and the humanity of India were one of the few experiences of the trip that liberated the American traveler from his preoccupation with the history and statistics of imperialism. It is also interesting to note that his description of an icestorm, recalled from his childhood days by his view of the Taj Mahal, is a much more moving and spontaneous description than his description of the Taj Mahal itself.

JEYPORE (from *Following the Equator*)

« « « We drove often to the city [Jeypore] from the hotel Kaiser-i-Hand, a journey which was always full of interest, both night and day, for that country road was never quiet, never empty, but was always India in motion, always a streaming flood of brown people clothed in smouchings from the rainbow, a tossing and moiling flood, happy, noisy, a charming and satisfying confusion of strange human and strange animal life and equally strange and outlandish vehicles.

And the city itself is a curiosity. Any Indian city is that, but this one is not like any other that we saw. It is shut up in a lofty turreted wall; the main body of it is divided into six parts by perfectly straight streets that are more than a hundred feet wide; the blocks of houses exhibit a long frontage of the most taking architectural quaintnesses, the straight lines being broken everywhere by pretty little balconies, pillared and highly ornamented, and other cunning and cozy and inviting perches and projections, and many of the fronts are curiously pictured by the brush, and the whole of them have the soft rich tint of strawberry ice-cream. One cannot look down the far stretch of the chief street and persuade himself that these are real houses, and that it is all out-of-doors—the impression that it is an unreality, a picture, a scene in a theater, is the only one that will take hold.

Then there came a great day when this illusion was more pronounced than ever. A rich Hindu had been spending a fortune upon the manufacture of a crowd of idols and accompanying paraphernalia whose purpose was to illustrate scenes in the life of his especial god or saint, and this fine show was to be brought through the town in processional state at ten in the morning. As we passed through the great public pleasure garden on our way to the city we found it crowded with natives. That was one sight. Then there was another. In the midst of the spacious lawns stands the palace which contains the museum—a beautiful construction of stone which shows arched colonnades, one above another, and receding, terrace-fashion, toward the sky. Every one of these terraces, all the way to the top one, was packed and jammed with natives. One must try to imagine those solid masses of splendid color, one above another, up and up, against the blue sky, and the Indian sun turning them all to beds of fire and flame.

Later, when we reached the city, and glanced down the chief avenue, smoldering in its crushed-strawberry tint, those splendid effects were repeated; for every balcony, and every fanciful birdcage of a snuggery countersunk in the housefronts, and all the long lines of roofs, were crowded with people, and each crowd was an explosion of brilliant color.

Then the wide street itself, away down and down and down into the distance, was alive with gorgeously clothed people—not still, but moving, swaying, drifting, eddying, a delirious display of all colors and all shades of color, delicate, lovely, pale, soft, strong, stunning, vivid, brilliant, a sort of storm of sweet-pea blossoms passing on the wings of a hurricane; and presently, through this storm of color, came swaying and swinging the majestic elephants, clothed in their Sunday best of gaudinesses, and the long procession of fanciful trucks freighted with their groups of curious and costly images, and then the long rear-guard of stately camels, with their picturesque riders.

For color, and picturesqueness, and novelty, and outlandishness, and sustained interest and fascination, it was the most satisfying show I had ever seen, and I suppose I shall not have the privilege of looking upon its like again. » » »

In the midst of his travels, Mark Twain often took time out from his admiration of scenery and his indulgence in romantic legends and historical ruins to comment on things of more immediate and pressing interest, such as the sanitation of European cities, the working conditions of women abroad, the decrepitude of German coffee, and hundreds of other miscellaneous problems that were always diverting his attention from the world as he would have it to the world as he found it. Whatever his subject, if his sensibilities were sufficiently offended, his descriptive comment, reinforced by his humor, could be as graphic as any of his descriptions of Alpine mountains or moonlit Acropolis. In a fit of gastronomic depression over hotel cooking while he was "tramping" through Germany,

Mark Twain tried to raise his spirits by recalling the horrors of "New England Pie," which in turn suggested his own "Recipe for German Coffee":

RECIPES (from A *Tramp Abroad*)

« « « *Recipe for New England Pie*: To make this excellent breakfast dish, proceed as follows: Take a sufficiency of water and a sufficiency of flour, and construct a bullet-proof dough. Work this into the form of a disk, with the edges turned up some three-fourths of an inch. Toughen and kiln-dry it a couple of days in a mild but unvarying temperature. Construct a cover for this redoubt in the same way and of the same material. Fill with stewed dried apples; aggravate with cloves, lemon-peel, and slabs of citron; add two portions of New Orleans sugar, then solder on the lid and set in a safe place till it petrifies. Serve cold at breakfast and invite your enemy.

Recipe for German Coffee: Take a barrel of water and bring it to a boil; rub a chickory berry against a coffee berry, then convey the former into the water. Continue the boiling and evaporation until the intensity of the flavor and aroma of the coffee and chickory has been diminished to a proper degree; then set aside to cool. Now unharness the remains of a once cow from the plow, insert them in a hydraulic press, and when you shall have acquired a teaspoonful of that pale-blue juice which a German superstition regards as milk, modify the malignity of its strength in a bucket of tepid water and ring up the breakfast. Mix the beverage in a cold cup, partake with moderation, and keep a wet rag around your head to guard against over-excitement. » » »

On a trip down the Neckar River during this same tour of Germany, Mark Twain was astounded by the amount of physical labor performed by European women on the farms and in menial tasks in town:

WOMAN'S WORK ON THE CONTINENT (from *A Tramp Abroad*)

« « « The women do all kinds of work on the continent. They dig, they hoe, they reap, they sow, they bear monstrous burdens on their backs, they shove similar ones long distances on wheelbarrows, they drag the cart when there is no dog or lean cow to drag it—and when there is, they assist the dog or cow. Age is no matter—the older the woman the stronger she is, apparently. On the farm a woman's duties are not defined—she does a little of everything; but in the towns it is different, there she only does certain things, the men do the rest. For instance, a hotel chambermaid has nothing to do but make beds and fires in fifty or sixty rooms, bring towels and candles, and fetch several tons of water up several flights of stairs, a hundred pounds at a time, in prodigious metal pitchers. She does not have to work more than eighteen or twenty hours a day, and she can always get down on her knees and scrub the floors of halls and closets when she is tired and needs a rest. » » »

During his "Quaker City" tour of Italy, the landscape and a few monuments of that country appealed to Mark Twain, but on the whole Italy impressed him as "one vast museum of magnificence and misery." The squalor of certain towns aroused his indignation to the point of revulsion in his description of what he saw:

CIVITA VECCHIA (from *The Innocents Abroad*)

« « « This Civita Vecchia is the finest nest of dirt, vermin, and ignorance we have found yet, except that African perdition they call Tangier, which is just like it. The people here live in alleys two yards wide, which have a smell about them which is peculiar but not entertaining. It is well the alleys are not wider, because they hold as much smell now as a person can stand, and, of course, if they were wider they would hold more, and then the people would die. These alleys are paved with stone, and carpeted with deceased cats, and decayed rags, and decomposed vegetable tops, and remnants of old boots, all soaked with dish-water, and the people sit around on stools and enjoy it. They are indolent, as a general thing, and yet have few pastimes. They work two or three hours at a time, but not hard, and then they knock off and catch flies. This does not require any talent, because they only have to grab—if they do not get the one they are after, they get another. It is all the same to them. They have no partialities. Whichever one they get is the one they want. » » »

Mark Twain was always ready to confess that he knew next to nothing about good music and painting. He would pass no serious judgment on the arts of Europe.[5] But he often resented the European's pride in his rivers, particularly little rivers, for with his background of Mississippi piloting the American could justifiably lay claim to an expert knowledge of rivers.

THE ARNO (from *The Innocents Abroad*)

« « « Between times we used to go and stand on the bridges and admire the Arno. It is popular to admire the Arno. It is a great historical creek with four feet in the channel and some scows floating around. It would be a very plausible river if they would pump some water into it. They all call it a river, and they honestly think it *is* a river, do these dark and bloody Florentines. They even help out the delusion by building bridges over it. I do not see why they are too good to wade. » » »

The farther Mark Twain explored among the modern peoples, cities, and cultures of Europe and the Near East, the more disillusioned he became with the world outside of America and England. He entered Palestine with the hope that there at least, in a Moslem and Arab world uncontaminated by the lower-class wretchedness

---

[5] Two possible exceptions are his little excursus on Joseph Turner's painting of "The Slave Ship" (*A Tramp Abroad*, I, Chap. XXIV) and his mock diatribe against opera (see p. 157 of this book).

of European civilization, the reality of things would measure up to their reputation. His progress through the Holy Land, however, was a succession of disenchantments.

THE ARABS OF JEZREEL[6] (from *The Innocents Abroad*)

« « « Picturesque Arabs sat upon the ground, in groups, and solemnly smoked their long-stemmed chibouks. Other Arabs were filling black hogskins with water—skins which, well filled, and distended with water till the short legs projected painfully out of the proper line, looked like the corpses of hogs bloated by drowning. Here was a grand Oriental picture which I had worshiped a thousand times in soft, rich steel engravings! But in the engraving there was no desolation; no dirt; no rags; no fleas; no ugly features; no sore eyes; no feasting flies; no besotted ignorance in the countenances; no raw places on the donkeys' backs; no disagreeable jabbering in unknown tongues; no stench of camels; no suggestion that a couple of tons of powder placed under the party and touched off would heighten the effect and give to the scene a genuine interest and a charm which it would always be pleasant to recall, even though a man lived a thousand years. . . .

As we trotted across the Plain of Jezreel, we met half a dozen Digger Indians (Bedouins) with very long spears in their hands, cavorting around on old crow-bait horses, and spearing imaginary enemies, whooping, and fluttering their rags in the wind, and carrying on in every respect like a pack of hopeless lunatics. At last, here were the "wild, free sons of the desert, speeding over the plain like the wind, on their beautiful Arabian mares" we had read so much about and longed so much to see! Here were the "picturesque costumes"! This was the "gallant spectacle"! Tatterdemalion vagrants—cheap braggadocio—"Arabian mares" spined and necked like the ichthyosaurus in the museum, and humped and cornered like a dromedary! To glance at the genuine son of the desert is to take the romance out of him forever—to behold his steed

[6] This description of the Arabs suggests Mark Twain's earlier description of the Goshute Indians (*Roughing It*, I, Chap. XIX). The depravity of savage peoples and the insensitivity of certain ignorant and backward elements in civilized countries always disgusted Mark Twain as much as the pomposity and arrogance of noblemen and aristocrats.

is to long in charity to strip his harness off and let him fall to pieces. » » »

One of the pastimes of Europeans—and Americans traveling in Europe—that always remained incomprehensible to Mark Twain was the opera. He left no evidence of how many operatic performances he sat through during his years on the Continent, but few or many, it is evident that he suffered from each such experience. Mark Twain's description of a German opera in the 1870's may not do justice to its art, but it vividly describes his state of mind during the ordeal:

MARK TWAIN AT THE OPERA (from *A Tramp Abroad*)

« « « One day we took the train and went down to Mannheim to see "King Lear" played in German. It was a mistake. We sat in our seats three whole hours and never understood anything but the thunder and lightning; and even that was reversed to suit German ideas, for the thunder came first and the lightning followed after. . . .

Another time, we went to Mannheim and attended a shivaree—otherwise an opera—the one called "Lohengrin." The banging and slamming and booming and crashing were something beyond belief. The racking and pitiless pain of it remains stored up in my memory alongside the memory of the time that I had my teeth fixed. There were circumstances which made it necessary for me to stay through the four hours to the end, and I stayed; but the recollection of that long, dragging, relentless season of suffering is indestructible. To have to endure it in silence, and sitting still, made it all the harder. I was in a railed compartment with eight or ten strangers, of the two sexes, and this compelled repression; yet at times the pain was so exquisite that I could hardly keep the tears back. At those times, as the howlings and wailings and shriekings of the singers, and the ragings and roarings and explosions of the vast orchestra rose higher and higher, and wilder and wilder, and fiercer and fiercer, I could have cried if I had been alone. Those strangers would not have been surprised to see a man do such a thing who was being gradually skinned, but they would have marveled at it here, and made remarks about it no doubt, whereas there was nothing in the present case which was an advantage over being skinned. There was a wait of half an hour at the end of the first act, and I could have gone out and rested during that time, but I could not trust myself to do it, for I felt that I should desert and stay out. There was another wait of half an hour toward nine o'clock, but I had gone through so much by that time that I had no spirit left, and so had no desire but to be let alone. . . .

It was a curious sort of a play. In the matter of costumes and scenery it was fine and showy enough; but there was not much action. That is to say, there was not much really done, it was only talked about; and always violently. It was what one might call a narrative play. Everybody had a narrative and a grievance, and none were reasonable about it, but all in an offensive and ungovernable state. There was little of that sort of customary thing where the tenor and the soprano stand down by the footlights, warbling, with blended voices, and keep holding out their arms toward each other and drawing them back and spreading both hands over first one breast and then the other with a shake and a pressure—no, it was every rioter for himself and no blending. Each sang his indictive narrative in turn, accompanied by the whole orchestra of sixty instruments, and when this had continued for some time, and one was hoping they might come to an understanding and modify the noise, a great chorus composed entirely of maniacs would suddenly break forth, and then during two minutes, and sometimes three, I lived over again all that I had suffered the time the orphan asylum burned down. » » »

A European custom that struck Mark Twain as even more ridiculous and irrational than opera-going was dueling.[7] The old code

[7] Mark Twain gives an account of his own "duel" on the mining frontier during his western days, in his *Autobiography*, I, 350–61. Although the affair was abortive and its "principal" gives it a burlesque treatment, his challenge to a rival newspaper editor of Virginia City violated a new territorial law against dueling, brought on himself the threat of arrest and imprisonment, and hastened his departure from Nevada. The full story of the affair is given, more reliably, by Ivan Benson in *Mark Twain's Western Years*. For Mark Twain's observations on student dueling in Germany, see *A Tramp Abroad*, I, Chaps. V–VII.

of honor that required two intelligent human beings to face each other with swords or pistols and draw each other's blood and frequently take each other's life, for any insult or offense however trivial, appalled his nineteenth-century reason and sense of justice. He could understand vigorous young students of the German universities dueling for sport and heroic scars, but he could not seriously accept the artificialities into which French dueling had degenerated. Fortunately for his readers, Mark Twain did not resort to sarcasm or invective when he decided to expose the imposture of French dueling. He chose instead the weapon of narrative burlesque and wrote one of the most entertaining episodes in all of his travel accounts.

THE GREAT FRENCH DUEL (from *A Tramp Abroad*)

« « « Much as the modern French duel is ridiculed by certain smart people, it is in reality one of the most dangerous institutions of our day. Since it is always fought in the open air, the combatants are nearly sure to catch cold. M. Paul de Cassagnac, the most inveterate of the French duelists, had suffered so often in this way that he is at last a confirmed invalid; and the best physician in Paris has expressed the opinion that if he goes on dueling for fifteen or twenty years more—unless he forms the habit of fighting in a comfortable room where damps and draughts cannot intrude—he will eventually endanger his life. This ought to moderate the talk of those people who are so stubborn in maintaining that the French duel is the most health-giving of recreations because of the open-air exercise it affords. And it ought also to moderate that foolish talk about French duelists and socialist-hated monarchs being the only people who are immortal.

But it is time to get at my subject. As soon as I heard of the late fiery outbreak between M. Gambetta and M. Fourtou in the French Assembly, I knew that trouble must follow. I knew it because a long personal friendship with M. Gambetta had revealed to me the desperate and implacable nature of the man. Vast as are his physical proportions, I knew that the thirst for revenge would penetrate to the remotest frontiers of his person.

I did not wait for him to call on me, but went at once to him.

As I had expected, I found the brave fellow steeped in a profound French calm. I say French calm, because French calmness and English calmness have points of difference. He was moving swiftly back and forth among the debris of his furniture, now and then staving chance fragments of it across the room with his foot; grinding a constant grist of curses through his set teeth; and halting every little while to deposit another handful of his hair on the pile which he had been building of it on the table.

He threw his arms around my neck, bent me over his stomach to his breast, kissed me on both cheeks, hugged me four or five times, and then placed me in his own arm-chair. As soon as I had got well again, we began business at once.

I said I supposed he would wish me to act as his second, and he said, "Of course." I said I must be allowed to act under a French name, so that I might be shielded from obloquy in my country, in case of fatal results. He winced here, probably at the suggestion that dueling was not regarded with respect in America. However, he agreed to my requirement. This accounts for the fact that in all the newspaper reports M. Gambetta's second was apparently a Frenchman.

First, we drew up my principal's will. I insisted upon this, and stuck to my point. I said I had never heard of a man in his right mind going out to fight a duel without first making his will. He said he had never heard of a man in his right mind doing anything of the kind. When he had finished the will, he wished to proceed to a choice of his "last words." He wanted to know how the following words, as a dying exclamation, struck me:

"I die for my God, for my country, for freedom of speech, for progress, and the universal brotherhood of man!"

I objected that this would require too lingering a death; it was a good speech for a consumptive, but not suited to the exigencies of the field of honor. We wrangled over a good many ante-mortem outbursts, but I finally got him to cut his obituary down to this, which he copied into his memorandum-book, purposing to get it by heart:

"I DIE THAT FRANCE MAY LIVE."

I said that this remark seemed to lack relevancy; but he said relevancy was a matter of no consequence in last words, what you wanted was thrill.

The next thing in order was the choice of weapons. My principal said he was not feeling well, and would leave that and the other details of the proposed meeting to me. Therefore I wrote the following note and carried it to M. Fourtou's friend:

> Sir: M. Gambetta accepts M. Fourtou's challenge, and authorizes me to propose Plessis-Piquet as the place of meeting; tomorrow morning at daybreak as the time; and axes as the weapons.
> I am, sir, with great respect,
>
> MARK TWAIN

M. Fourtou's friend read this note, and shuddered. Then he turned to me, and said, with a suggestion of severity in his tone:

"Have you considered, sir, what would be the inevitable result of such a meeting as this?"

"Well, for instance, what *would* it be?"

"Bloodshed!"

"That's about the size of it," I said. "Now, if it is a fair question, what was your side proposing to shed?"

I had him there. He saw he had made a blunder, so he hastened to explain it away. He said he had spoken jestingly. Then he added that he and his principal would enjoy axes, and indeed prefer them, but such weapons were barred by the French code, and so I must change my proposal.

I walked the floor, turning the thing over in my mind, and finally it occurred to me that Gatling-guns at fifteen paces would be a likely way to get a verdict on the field of honor. So I framed this idea into a proposition.

But it was not accepted. The code was in the way again. I proposed rifles; then double-barreled shotguns; then Colt's navy revolvers. These being all rejected, I reflected awhile, and sarcastically suggested brickbats at three-quarters of a mile. I always hate to fool away a humorous thing on a person who has no perception of humor; and it filled me with bitterness when this man went soberly away to submit the last proposition to his principal.

He came back presently and said his principal was charmed

with the idea of brickbats at three-quarters of a mile, but must decline on account of the danger to disinterested parties passing between. Then I said:

"Well, I am at the end of my string, now. Perhaps *you* would be good enough to suggest a weapon? Perhaps you have even had one in your mind all the time?"

His countenance brightened, and he said with alacrity:

"Oh, without doubt, monsieur!"

So he fell to hunting in his pockets—pocket after pocket, and he had plenty of them—muttering all the while, "Now, what could I have done with them?"

At last he was successful. He fished out of his vest pocket a couple of little things which I carried to the light and ascertained to be pistols. They were single-barreled and silver-mounted, and very dainty and pretty. I was not able to speak for emotion. I silently hung one of them on my watch-chain, and returned the other. My companion in crime now unrolled a postage-stamp containing several cartridges, and gave me one of them. I asked if he meant to signify by this that our men were to be allowed but one shot apiece. He replied that the French code permitted no more. I then begged him to go on and suggest a distance, for my mind was growing weak and confused under the strain which had been put upon it. He named sixty-five yards. I nearly lost my patience. I said:

"Sixty-five yards, with these instruments? Squirt-guns would be deadlier at fifty. Consider, my friend, you and I are banded together to destroy life, not make it eternal."

But with all my persuasions, all my arguments, I was only able to get him to reduce the distance to thirty-five yards; and even this concession he made with reluctance, and said with a sigh, "I wash my hands of this slaughter; on your head be it."

There was nothing for me but to go home to my old lion-heart and tell my humiliating story. When I entered, M. Gambetta was laying his last lock of hair upon the altar. He sprang toward me, exclaiming:

"You have made the fatal arrangements—I see it in your eye!"

"I have."

His face paled a trifle, and he leaned upon the table for support.

He breathed thick and heavily for a moment or two, so tumultuous were his feelings; then he hoarsely whispered:

"The weapon, the weapon! Quick! what is the weapon!"

"This!" and I displayed that silver-mounted thing. He cast but one glance at it, then swooned ponderously to the floor.

When he came to, he said mournfully:

"The unnatural calm to which I have subjected myself has told upon my nerves. But away with weakness! I will confront my fate like a man and a Frenchman."

He rose to his feet, and assumed an attitude which for sublimity has never been approached by man, and has seldom been surpassed by statues. Then he said, in his deep bass tones:

"Behold, I am calm, I am ready; reveal to me the distance."

"Thirty-five yards." . . .

I could not lift him up, of course; but I rolled him over, and poured water down his back. He presently came to, and said:

"Thirty-five yards—without a rest? But why ask? Since murder was that man's intention, why should he palter with small details? But mark you one thing: in my fall the world shall see how the chivalry of France meets death."

After a long silence he asked:

"Was nothing said about that man's family standing up with him, as an offset to my bulk? But no matter; I would not stoop to make such a suggestion; if he is not noble enough to suggest it himself, he is welcome to this advantage, which no honorable man would take."

He now sank into a sort of stupor of reflection, which lasted some minutes; after which he broke silence with:

"The hour—what is the hour fixed for the collision?"

"Dawn, to-morrow."

He seemed greatly surprised, and immediately said:

"Insanity! I never heard of such a thing. Nobody is abroad at such an hour."

"That is the reason I named it. Do you mean to say you want an audience?"

"It is no time to bandy words. I am astonished that M. Fourtou should ever have agreed to so strange an innovation. Go at once and require a later hour."

I ran down-stairs, threw open the front door, and almost plunged into the arms of M. Fourtou's second. He said:

"I have the honor to say that my principal strenuously objects to the hour chosen, and begs you will consent to change it to half past nine."

"Any courtesy, sir, which it is in our power to extend is at the service of your excellent principal. We agree to the proposed change of time."

"I beg you to accept the thanks of my client." Then he turned to a person behind him, and said, "You hear, M. Noir, the hour is altered to half past nine." Whereupon M. Noir bowed, expressed his thanks, and went away. My accomplice continued:

"If agreeable to you, your chief surgeons and ours shall proceed to the field in the same carriage, as is customary."

"It is entirely agreeable to me, and I am obliged to you for mentioning the surgeons, for I am afraid I should not have thought of them. How many shall I want? I suppose two or three will be enough?"

"Two is the customary number for each party. I refer to 'chief' surgeons; but considering the exalted positions occupied by our clients, it will be well and decorous that each of us appoint several consulting surgeons, from among the highest in the profession. These will come in their own private carriages. Have you engaged a hearse?"

"Bless my stupidity, I never thought of it! I will attend to it right away. I must seem very ignorant to you; but you must try to overlook that, because I have never had any experience of such a swell duel as this before. I have had a good deal to do with duels on the Pacific coast, but I see now that they were crude affairs. A hearse—sho! we used to leave the elected lying around loose, and let anybody cord them up and cart them off that wanted to. Have you anything further to suggest?"

"Nothing, except that the head undertakers shall ride together, as is usual. The subordinates and mutes will go on foot, as is also usual. I will see you at eight o'clock in the morning, and we will then arrange the order of the procession. I have the honor to bid you a good day."

I returned to my client, who said, "Very well; at what hour is the engagement to begin?"

"Half past nine."

"Very good indeed. Have you sent the fact to the newspapers?"

"*Sir!* If after our long and intimate friendship you can for a moment deem me capable of so base a treachery—"

"Tut, tut! What words are these, my dear friend? Have I wounded you? Ah, forgive me; I am overloading you with labor. Therefore go on with the other details, and drop this one from your list. The bloody-minded Fourtou will be sure to attend to it. Or I myself—yes, to make certain, I will drop a note to my journalistic friend, M. Noir—"

"Oh, come to think of it, you may save yourself the trouble; that other second has informed M. Noir."

"H'm! I might have known it. It is just like that Fourtou, who always wants to make a display."

At half past nine in the morning, the procession approached the field of Plessis-Piquet in the following order: first came our carriage—nobody in it but M. Gambetta and myself; then a carriage containing M. Fourtou and his second; then a carriage containing two poet-orators who did not believe in God, and these had MS funeral orations projecting from their breast pockets; then a carriage containing the head surgeons and their cases of instruments; then eight private carriages containing consulting surgeons; then a hack containing a coroner; then the two hearses; then a carriage containing the head undertakers; then a train of assistants and mutes on foot; and after these came plodding through the fog a long procession of camp followers, police, and citizens generally. It was a noble turnout, and would have made a fine display if we had had thinner weather.

There was no conversation. I spoke several times to my principal, but I judge he was not aware of it, for he always referred to his note-book and muttered absently, "I die that France may live."

Arrived on the field, my fellow-second and I paced off the thirty-five yards, and then drew lots for choice of position. This latter was but an ornamental ceremony, for all the choices were alike in such weather. These preliminaries being ended, I went to my principal and asked him if he was ready. He spread himself out to his full width, and said in a stern voice, "Ready! Let the batteries be charged."

The loading was done in the presence of duly constituted witnesses. We considered it best to perform this delicate service with the assistance of a lantern, on account of the state of the weather. We now placed our men.

At this point the police noticed that the public had massed themselves together on the right and left of the field; they therefore begged a delay, while they should put these poor people in a place of safety.

The request was granted.

The police having ordered the two multitudes to take positions behind the duelists, we were once more ready. The weather growing still more opaque, it was agreed between myself and the other second that before giving the fatal signal we should each deliver a loud whoop to enable the combatants to ascertain each other's whereabouts.

I now returned to my principal, and was distressed to observe that he had lost a good deal of his spirit. I tried my best to hearten him. I said, "Indeed, sir, things are not as bad as they seem. Considering the character of the weapons, the limited number of shots allowed, the generous distance, the impenetrable solidity of the fog, and the added fact that one of the combatants is one-eyed and the other cross-eyed and near-sighted, it seems to me that this conflict need not necessarily be fatal. There are chances that both of you may survive. Therefore, cheer up; do not be downhearted."

This speech had so good an effect that my principal immediately stretched forth his hand and said, "I am myself again; give me the weapon."

I laid it, all lonely and forlorn, in the center of the vast solitude of his palm. He gazed at it and shuddered. And still mournfully contemplating it, he murmured in a broken voice:

"Alas, it is not death I dread, but mutilation."

I heartened him once more, and with such success that he presently said, "Let the tragedy begin. Stand at my back; do not desert me in this solemn hour, my friend."

I gave him my promise. I now assisted him to point his pistol toward the spot where I judged his adversary to be standing, and cautioned him to listen well and further guide himself by my fellow-second's whoop. Then I propped myself against M. Gambetta's back, and raised a rousing "Whoop-ee!" This was answered from out the far distances of the fog, and I immediately shouted:

"One—two—three—*fire!*"

Two little sounds like *spit! spit!* broke upon my ear, and in the same instant I was crushed to the earth under a mountain of flesh. Bruised as I was, I was still able to catch a faint accent from above, to this effect:

"I die for . . . for . . . perdition take it, what *is* it I die for? . . . oh, yes—FRANCE! I die that France may live!"

The surgeons swarmed around with their probes in their hands, and applied their microscopes to the whole area of M. Gambetta's person, with the happy result of finding nothing in the nature of a wound. Then a scene ensued which was in every way gratifying and inspiriting.

The two gladiators fell upon each other's neck, with floods of proud and happy tears; that other second embraced me; the surgeons, the orators, the undertakers, the police, everybody embraced, everybody congratulated, everybody cried, and the whole atmosphere was filled with praise and with joy unspeakable.

It seemed to me then that I would rather be a hero of a French duel than a crowned and sceptered monarch.

When the commotion had somewhat subsided, the body of surgeons held a consultation, and after a good deal of debate decided that with proper care and nursing there was reason to believe that I would survive my injuries. My internal hurts were deemed the most serious, since it was apparent that a broken rib had penetrated my left lung, and that many of my organs had been pressed out so far to one side or the other of where they belonged, that it was doubtful if they would ever learn to perform their functions in such remote and unaccustomed localities. They then set my left arm in two places, pulled my right hip into its socket again, and re-elevated my nose. I was an object of great interest, and even admiration; and many sincere and warm-hearted persons had themselves introduced to me, and said they were proud to know the only man who had been hurt in a French duel in forty years.

I was placed in an ambulance at the very head of the procession; and thus with gratifying *eclat* I was marched into Paris, the most conspicuous figure in that great spectacle, and deposited at the hospital.

The cross of the Legion of Honor has been conferred upon me. However, few escape that distinction.

Such is the true version of the most memorable private conflict of the age.

I have no complaints to make against anyone. I acted for myself, and I can stand the consequences.

Without boasting, I think I may say I am not afraid to stand before a modern French duelist, but as long as I keep in my right mind I will never consent to stand behind one again. » » »

During his many tours of western and central Europe, Mark Twain enjoyed brief interludes of spiritual satisfaction despite his continuing disillusionment about civilization and humanity. Much of what he wrote about Europe and Europeans was from the point of view of the jaded and skeptical American correspondent who finds even more foibles and stupidities abroad than at home. His early good-natured humor and spirit of burlesque changed gradually into a strong strain of satire, irony, and scorn that culminated in his pseudo-Germanic legend, *The Mysterious Stranger.* During the thirty years between the appearance of *The Innocents Abroad* and his composition of *What Is Man?* and *The Mysterious Stranger,* Mark Twain met many hundreds of celebrated Europeans; he observed and lived among thousands of common, everyday Europeans; and he closely appraised the whole pattern of European living—its traditions, customs, manners, morals, aesthetics, and social, economic, and political life. As he traveled about the Continent and recorded his impressions, he found little to commend in European civilization. Mark Twain's disapproval of things European had been veiled by his farcical humor in *The Innocents Abroad,* but the disapproval is not so well masked in *A Tramp Abroad* twelve years later in 1880, and the *Connecticut Yankee* of

1889 is sheer invective against European institutions.[8] His *Following the Equator* of 1897 is mainly an indictment of European imperialism, and his posthumous *Europe and Elsewhere* is an undisguised rejection of European society. But even in the midst of this corrupt society, Mark Twain could always discover a glimpse of beauty, a momentary charm. Almost invariably he found them in the lowly life of peasants, the evidences of historical antiquity, and the picturesque background. To these facets of Europe Mark Twain responded with the imaginative appreciation and enthusiasm of a confirmed romantic right up until his last years. When he began an article on the watering place of Aix-les-Bains in 1891, he remarked with his usual king phobia: "Aix-les-Bains. Certainly this is an enchanting place. It is a strong word, but I think the facts justify it. True, there is a rabble of nobilities, big and little, here all the time, and often a king or two; but as these behave quite nicely and also keep mainly to themselves, they are little or no annoyance." After many caustic remarks about the gambling and commercialism of the place and the lack of etiquette of the natives and the hypochondria of the visitors, he suddenly breaks out into an ecstatic description of the countryside, which apparently was a much greater tonic to him than the baths:

AIX-LES-BAINS (from *Europe and Elsewhere*[9])

« « « There are many beautiful drives about Aix, many interesting places to visit, and much pleasure to be found in paddling around the little Lake Bourget on the small steamers, but the excursion which satisfied me best was a trip to Annecy and its neighborhood. You go to Annecy in an hour by rail, through a garden land that has not had its equal for beauty perhaps since Eden; and certainly not Eden was cultivated as this garden is. The charm and loveliness of the whole region are bewildering. Picturesque rocks, forest-clothed hills, slopes richly bright in the cleanest and greenest grass, fields of grain without fleck or flaw, dainty of color and as shiny and shimmery as silk, old gray mansions and towers, half buried

[8] Mark Twain's opinion of European civilization was strongly colored by his reading of W. E. H. Lecky's *History of European Morals.*
[9] These observations of modern Europe, under the title of *Europe and Elsewhere*, did not appear until 1923, thirteen years after Mark Twain's death.

in foliage and sunny eminences, deep chasms with precipitous walls, and a swift stream of pale-blue water between, with now and then a tumbling cascade, and always noble mountains in view, with vagrant white clouds curling about their summits.

Then at the end of an hour you come to Annecy and rattle through its old crooked lanes, built solidly up with curious old houses that are a dream of the Middle Ages, and presently you come to the main object of your trip—Lake Annecy. It is a revelation; it is a miracle. It brings the tears to a body's eyes, it affects you just as all things that you instantly recognize as perfect affect you—perfect music, perfect eloquence, perfect art, perfect joy, perfect grief. It stretches itself out there in a caressing sunlight, and away toward its border of majestic mountains, a crisped and radiant plain of water of the divinest blue that can be imagined. All the blues are there, from the faintest shoalwater suggestion of the color, detectable only in the shadow of some overhanging object, all the way through, a little blue and a little bluer still, and again a shade bluer, till you strike the deep, rich Mediterranean splendor which breaks the heart in your bosom, it is so beautiful.

And the mountains, as you skim along on the steamboat, how stately their forms, how noble their proportions, how green their velvet slopes, how soft the mottlings of the sun and shadow that play about the rocky ramparts that crown them, how opaline the vast upheavals of snow banked against the sky in the remotenesses beyond—Mont Blanc and the others—how shall anybody describe? Why, not even the painter can quite do it, and the most the pen can do is to suggest. » » »

Some of the most delightful passages in Mark Twain have already been found in his animal stories drawn from recollections of western days—anecdotes about rabbits, coyotes, horses, and bluejays. This penchant for animal life runs all through his later writings and asserts itself, in fable-like anecdotes, at the most unexpected places. The result is usually not a true narrative, or "story," like "The Celebrated Jumping Frog" or "The Genuine Mexican Plug," but simply an account of some incident in which the interest centers on the animal as a "character." Two such characters emerge from his early travels in Europe and the Middle East. When added to the collection of his animal portraits, they demonstrate Mark Twain's peculiar ability to remove himself and his reader from the immediate context of time and place and momentarily to enter a realm as old as Aesop and as perennial as youth itself. Mark Twain's humor, of course, strongly colors the anecdote in each case and often provides, through the medium of the story, some of his pithiest observations on life and human nature.

THE SYRIAN CAMEL'S APPETITE (from *Roughing It*)

« « « In Syria, once, at the headwaters of the Jordan, a camel took charge of my overcoat while the tents were being pitched, and examined it with a critical eye, all over, with as much interest as if he had an idea of getting one made like it; and then, after he was done figuring on it as an article of apparel, he began to

A tough statement.

contemplate it as an article of diet. He put his foot on it, and lifted one of the sleeves out with his teeth, and chewed and chewed at it, gradually taking it in, and all the while opening and closing his eyes in a kind of religious ecstasy, as if he had never tasted anything as good as an overcoat before in his life. Then he smacked his lips once or twice, and reached after the other sleeve. Next he tried the velvet collar, and smiled a smile of such contentment that it was plain to see that he regarded that as the daintiest thing about an overcoat. The tails went next, along with some percussion-caps and cough-candy, and some fig-paste from Constantinople. And then my newspaper correspondence dropped out, and he took a chance in that—manuscript letters written for the home papers. But he was treading on dangerous ground, now. He began to come across solid wisdom in those documents that was rather weighty on his stomach; and occasionally he would take a joke that would shake him up till it loosened his teeth; it was getting to be perilous times with him, but he held his grip with good courage and hopefully, till at last he began to stumble on statements that not even a camel could swallow with impunity. He began to gag and gasp, and his eyes to stand out, and his forelegs to spread, and in about a quarter of a minute he fell over as stiff as a carpenter's workbench, and died a death of indescribable agony. I went and pulled the manuscript out of his mouth, and found that the sensitive creature had choked to death on one of the mildest and gentlest statements of fact that I ever laid before a trusting public. » » »

The next piece of animal-lore interrupts Mark Twain's account of his travels through the Black Forest of Germany, for no apparent reason other than that he happened to be intensely interested in ants and the implications of their strange behavior.

ANTS' ANTICS[10] (from *A Tramp Abroad*)

« « « Now and then, while we rested, we watched the laborious ant at his work. I found nothing new in him—certainly nothing to

[10] For accuracy of observation and for the writer's deductions concerning the nature of ants, Mark Twain's description bears comparison with Henry Thoreau's description of a battle of the ants in *Walden*, Chap. XII.

change my opinion of him. It seems to me that in the matter of intellect the ant must be a strangely overrated bird. During many summers, now, I have watched him, when I ought to have been in better business, and I have not yet come across a living ant that seemed to have any more sense than a dead one. I refer to the ordinary ant, of course; I have had no experience of those wonderful Swiss and African ones which vote, keep drilled armies, hold slaves, and dispute about religion. Those particular ants may be all that the naturalist paints them, but I am persuaded that the average ant is a sham. I admit his industry, of course; he is the hardest-working creature in the world—when anybody is looking—but his leather-headedness is the point I make against him. He goes out foraging, he makes a capture, and then what does he do? Go home? No—he goes anywhere but home. He doesn't know where home is. His home may be only three feet away—no matter, he can't find it. He makes his capture, as I have said; it is generally something which can be of no sort of use to himself or anybody else; it is usually

seven times bigger than it ought to be; he hunts out the awkwardest place to take hold of it; he lifts it bodily up in the air by main force, and starts; not toward home, but in the opposite direction; not calmly and wisely, but with a frantic haste which is wasteful of his strength; and he fetches up against a pebble, and instead of going around it, he climbs over it backward dragging his booty after him, tumbles down on the other side, jumps up in a passion, kicks the dust off his clothes, moistens his hands, grabs his property viciously, yanks it this way, then that, shoves it ahead of him a moment, turns tail and lugs it after him another moment, gets madder and madder, then presently hoists it into the air and goes tearing away in an entirely new direction; comes to a weed; it never occurs to him to go around it; no, he must climb it; and he does climb it, dragging his worthless property to the top—which is as bright a thing to do as it would be for me to carry a sack of flour from Heidelberg to Paris by way of Strasburg steeple; when he gets up there he finds that is not the place; takes a cursory glance at the scenery and either climbs down again or tumbles down, and starts off once more—as usual, in a new direction. At the end of half an hour, he fetches up within six inches of the place he started from and lays his burden down; meantime he has been over all the ground for two yards around, and climbed all the weeds and pebbles he came across. Now he wipes the sweat from his brow, strokes his limbs, and marches aimlessly off, in as violent a hurry as ever. He traverses a good deal of zigzag country, and by and by stumbles

on his same booty again. He does not remember to have ever seen it before; he looks around to see which is not the way home, grabs his bundle and starts; he goes through the same adventures he had before; finally stops to rest, and a friend comes along. Evidently the friend remarks that a last year's grasshopper leg is a very noble acquisition, and inquires where he got it. Evidently the proprietor does not remember exactly where he did get it, but thinks he got it "around here somewhere." Evidently the friend contracts to help him freight it home. Then, with a judgment peculiarly antic (pun not intentional), they take hold of opposite ends of that grasshopper leg and begin to tug with all their might in opposite directions. Presently they take a rest and confer together. They decide that something is wrong, they can't make out what. Then they go at it again, just as before. Same result. Mutual recriminations follow. Evidently each accuses the other of being an obstructionist. They warm up, and the dispute ends in a fight. They lock themselves together and chew each other's jaws for awhile; then they roll and tumble on the ground till one loses a horn or a leg and has to haul off for repairs. They make up and go to work again in the same old insane way, but the crippled ant is at a disadvantage; tug as he may, the other one drags off the booty and him at the end of it. Instead of giving up, he hangs on, and gets his shins bruised against every obstruction that comes in the way. By and by, when that grasshopper leg has been dragged all over the same old ground once more, it is finally dumped at about the spot where it originally lay, the two perspiring ants inspect it thoughtfully and decide that dried grasshopper legs are a poor sort of property

after all, and then each starts off in a different direction to see if he can't find an old nail or something else that is heavy enough to afford entertainment and at the same time valueless enough to make an ant want to own it.

There in the Black Forest, on the mountainside, I saw an ant go through with such a performance as this with a dead spider of fully ten times his own weight. The spider was not quite dead, but too far gone to resist. He had a round body the size of a pea. The little ant—observing that I was noticing—turned him on his back, sunk his fangs into his throat, lifted him into the air and started vigorously off with him, stumbling over little pebbles, stepping on the spider's legs and tripping himself up, dragging him backward, shoving him bodily ahead, dragging him up stones six inches high instead of going around them, climbing weeds twenty times his own height and jumping from their summits—and finally leaving him in the middle of the road to be confiscated by any other fool of an ant that wanted him. I measured the ground which this ass traversed, and arrived at the conclusion that what he had accomplished inside of twenty minutes would constitute some such job as this—relatively speaking—for a man; to wit: to strap two eight-hundred-pound horses together, carry them eighteen hundred feet, mainly over (not around) boulders averaging six feet high, and in the course of the journey climb up and jump from the top of one precipice like Niagara, and three steeples, each a hundred and twenty feet high; and then put the horses down, in an exposed place, without anybody to watch them, and go off to indulge in some other idiotic miracle for vanity's sake.

Science has recently discovered that the ant does not lay up anything for winter use. This will knock him out of literature, to some extent. He does not work, except when people are looking, and only then when the observer has a green, naturalistic look, and seems to be taking notes. This amounts to deception, and will injure him for the Sunday-schools. He has not judgment enough to know what is good to eat from what isn't. This amounts to ignorance, and will impair the world's respect for him. He cannot stroll around a stump and find his way home again. This amounts to idiocy, and once the damaging fact is established, thoughtful people will cease to look up to him, the sentimental will cease to fondle him. His vaunted industry is but a vanity and of no effect, since he never gets home with anything he starts with. This disposes of the last remnant of his reputation and wholly destroys his main usefulness as a moral agent, since it will make the sluggard hesitate to go to him any more. It is strange, beyond comprehension, that so manifest a humbug as the ant has been able to fool so many nations and keep it up so many ages without being found out. 》 》 》

As late as 1896, while he was on his lecture tour around the world, Mark Twain could still find time to pause in the midst of a hurried tour of South Africa to study the most commonplace species of insects and animals. No account of his literary collection from the animal kingdom would be complete without his portrait of the chameleon he saw at a Durban hotel. Just as in his early western sketches of the jack rabbit, the coyote, and the Mexican plug,[11]

[11] See pages 82–85 and 93–97 of this book.

Mark Twain preserves a delicate balance between objective description and caricature that gives his animal character plausibility without the pathetic fallacy that vitiates so much modern animated cartooning.

THE CHAMELEON (from *Following the Equator*)

« « « *The chameleon in the hotel court.* He is fat and indolent and contemplative; but is businesslike and capable when a fly comes about—reaches out a tongue like a teaspoon and takes him in. He gums his tongue first. He is always pious, in his looks. And pious and thankful both, when Providence or one of us sends him a fly. He has a froggy head, and a back like a new grave—for shape; and hands like a bird's toes that have been frost-bitten. But his eyes are his exhibition feature. A couple of skinny cones project from the sides of his head, with a wee shiny bead of an eye set in the apex of each; and these cones turn bodily like pivot-guns and point every which way, and they are independent of each other; each has its own exclusive machinery. When I am behind him and C. in front of him, he whirls one eye rearward and the other forward—which gives him a most Congressional expression (one eye on the constituency and one on the swag); and then if something happens above and below him he shoots out one eye upward like a telescope and the other downward—and this changes his expression, but does not improve it. » » »

Mark Twain's round-the-world lecture tour at the close of the nineteenth century brought him full circle both literally and figuratively. He returned to Europe and finally America a disenchanted man, for whatever "ultimate" he sought in his many years abroad, he never found it. A restlessness and hunger for experience as driving as his would never have permitted him to follow Voltaire's advice to stay at home and cultivate his own garden. He was fated to be a wanderer. But since he never found the climactic and soul-satisfying experience, it is perhaps just as appropriate to leave him observing a chameleon in a South African courtyard as it would be to leave him contemplating the world from the top of Mount Vesuvius. These various glimpses of Mark Twain's world reveal that at least through long wanderings, keen observation, and faithful recording of experiences his creative urge was fulfilled. His hypersensitivity, his sense of beauty, and his highly developed imagination enriched his writings with much fine narrative and description. For a better appreciation of the contributing force of that most essential element in Mark Twain—his native humor—the reader is invited into the second part of this book.

PART II

Mark Twain, Missouri Humorist

MARK TWAIN, MISSOURI HUMORIST

1. Early Humor in Missouri

It was to be expected that Missouri, at the crossroads of the nation and at the confluence of its two greatest rivers, would catch the rollicking spirit of adventurers into the West after the Revolutionary War—of boatmen who drew up at her wharves; of the government army men who came to put down Indian uprisings; of trappers who were to make St. Louis the leading fur market of the world; of itinerant people, actors, peddlers, roustabouts, and a little later, lawyers, judges, and preachers on the circuit. All of these on "lagging, dragging journeys" amused each other and made themselves welcome to men marooned on the outposts of civilization with stories, often connected with their occupation—a boat race, a "varmint theatre" (forerunner of Barnum and Bailey), practical jokes on the backwoodsman or the dapper city man; and the antics of strange and outlandish characters on the border, where fugitives from justice and all sorts of down-and-outers mingled with more reputable wanderers and officials.

In general, these tales were not pretty stories. Told by men for men, they had to do with boasting bouts, with fights of men "liquored up," with escapes from the terrifying John Murrell, with Mike Fink's shot that killed his friend. In all, whatever could get a laugh from the travel-weary was valued most. It might be the story of the pioneer woman in central Missouri who was called the Great Interrogator because of her habit of hailing every passer-by. "What's the news of the Indians?" she called to an army officer. "Very, very bad, Madam," he replied. "Tecumseh and his band have put handspikes under Lake Michigan and are going to upset it and drown us all." When living conditions on the border were difficult, often desperate, there was all the more reason for people to brace themselves with a laugh.

By 1800 newspapers in Cincinnati, the earliest publishing center west of the Alleghenies, were beginning to fill out an occasional column with one of these anecdotes, but always with the editor's apology for giving recognition to material of such poor literary quality.

If we accept Hobbes's definition of humor that its source is in a feeling of superiority arising from the perception of an incongruity or ineptitude (the "sudden glory" theory), it accounts for much of the humor on the Missouri border. Here the more sophisticated man is depicted telling a tale about an ignoramus. This story-within-a-story pattern, of course, is not new. Addison's Mr. Spectator introduces Will Wimble in much the same spirit. "Odd and uncommon characters are the game I look for and most delight in," he says, "for which reason I was much pleased with the novelty of the person that talked with me." Many of the narrative devices in frontier humorous stories were those used by good storytellers the world over.

But in such a democratic atmosphere as that on the Missouri frontier, where the dregs of civilization could thrive as parasites on adventurers and where a "squatter" could clear a few acres of forest land, grow a patch of corn for hominy and liquor, and raise a few pigs to support his family, the only recourse of the superior man, when irritated at having to rub shoulders with inferiors, was in a laugh. Many of these wrote down stories of their encounters to send to friends back home.

These were the men through whom tales of Missouri backwoods characters first got into print. Usually they were young professional men who had come west to find a stake, journalists hoping to start newspapers, lawyers and doctors to hang out their shingles. In many cases it was an interest in stories of the folk that caused them to take up writing as an avocation. These found themselves in a rough border society where every man was an individualist, quick to take offense when his rights were threatened. He was capable of taking the law into his own hands to assert his freedom. In such society men dared to express themselves more profanely and picturesquely than in an older, more conventional society. A young army paymaster stationed at Old Franklin reports a settler saying: "There's a right smart sprinkle of snakes in these parts. I and my brother-in-law went out snakin' a few days ago, and we killed three hundred and fifty rattlesnakes, and two yearlin' copperheads, and it warn't a very good morning for snakin', neither." They were given to boasting and tall talk.

The hero-boaster was Mike Fink, king of the keelboatmen: "I'm a snapping-turtle—I can lick five times my own weight in wildcats ... I can swallow niggers whole, raw and cooked. I can out-run, out-dance, out-jump, out-drink, out-holler, and out-lick any white thing in the shape o' human that's ever put foot within two thousand miles o' the big Massasip. Whoop! Holler, you varmints! ... I'm in fur a fight!"

By the time Missouri became a state, her papers were beginning to give space to western stories and anecdotes, sometimes with apologies from the editor. In Old Franklin, where he lived for fourteen years, Alphonso Wetmore, in 1820, contributed to the *Missouri Intelligencer* a sketch of Mike Shuckwell and his pet bear. In the early 1830's stories of this colorful society began to appear in New York in William T. Porter's *Spirit of the Times* (1831–56), a weekly *Chronicle of the Turf, Agriculture, Field Sports, Literature, and the Stage*.

Such early tales were not peculiar to Missouri. Whatever can be said about a heterogeneous new society's finding expression here could probably be duplicated in the literary beginnings of almost any state of what has come to be known as the Old Southwest (capital: Memphis, Tennessee). Most of the others, in fact, produced humorists who attained greater local contemporary fame.

In the 1840's a brilliant group of young men became associated in St. Louis who found in the folk tales related there a wealth of material awaiting a recorder: Alphonso Wetmore, Charles Keemle, a newspaperman, Joseph M. Field, Matthew C. Field, Noah M. Ludlow, "pioneers of the drama in the West," according to Franklin J. Meine, author of *Tall Tales of the Southwest*, and John S. Robb. The stories they wrote down were a sort of natural expression of the frontier.

Charles Keemle (1800–65) published Alphonso Wetmore's *Gazetteer of the State of Missouri* (1837), and to it they appended tales of bear hunts, Indian attacks, and other "true stories." In their "Sketch of Mountain Life," a beaver trapper, Gall Buster, and his companion, Joseph Cutting, a singing Yankee who carries a cookbook and a peddler's pack, tell of their adventures in the vernacular. While these cannot be classed as humorous tales, they are forerunners of the tall tales or "whopper stories" in several respects: (1) they are told in a light, easy tone different from that of conventional Missouri writings of the period; (2) such characters as Joseph Cutting and Gall Buster anticipate the "characters" so popular in tall tales; and (3) some of their heroes are represented as narrators of the stories in language peculiar to the frontier.

Joseph M. Field (1810–56), actor-manager, playwright, and editor, was associated with Matthew C. Field and Charles Keemle in founding the St. Louis *Reveille*, in which tales and sketches of western life were to be found. He became known outside the borders of Missouri for his stories of Mike Fink and in 1847 published *The Drama in Pokerville; The Bench and Bar of Jurytown and Other Stories*, a collection of frontier tales.

Noah M. Ludlow (1795–1886), who, with the actor Sol Smith, built the first theatre in St. Louis, in *Dramatic Life as I Found It* (1880) contributed to our knowledge of early humor in the state. But it was Solomon Franklin Smith (1801–65), actor-manager, lawyer, and preacher, who most nearly embodied the spirit of this early humor. Matt Field wrote of him, "Orally Old Sol tells the story with droll and irresistible effect, much of which may be lost in attempts to record his stories." He was "a born wag." "We verily believe that when he is going to his grave he will play some droll trick upon the pall-bearers," Field says, after a tale about how the actor had betrayed an irascible patron into taking the checks at the door of his theatre. When Smith himself wrote about people who had amused him, it was one eccentric writing of another. In "A Bully Boat and a Brag Captain," he tells of the captain of the "Caravan" absorbed in a game of brag, though he remonstrated at every woodyard all night with yellow-faced wood merchants because of their repeated overcharge, only to discover, when the morning sun dispelled the fog, that he had been "wooding all night at the same wood-yard."

The one of these early St. Louisans who most nearly belonged to the class of professional writers was John S. Robb, a St. Louis lawyer, afterwards Judge Robb of California. He wondered why the "incident and humor" in which the West abounded was so seldom sought by "the finished and graphic writers of our country." He published tall tales that he had originally contributed to the New York *Spirit of the Times*, the New Orleans *Picayune*, and the St. Louis *Reveille* in a volume entitled *Streaks of Squatter Life and Far Western Scenes*. One of his best-known stories was "The Standing Candidate." Old Sugar, "an odd-looking old man" who appeared at a political barbecue, declared that when he saw "Jake Simons settin' close bang-up agin Sofy," whom he was courtin', "I war so enormous mad that the new silk handkercher round my neck lost its color."

But his "Swallowing an Oyster Alive" was the most popular of these tales. A "hero from the Sucker State" who has never seen an "ister" before "stalks" into a St. Louis oyster house and, after managing to swallow a "bivalve" alive, is warned by a wag looking on that it will eat out his "innards." Terrified, he gets the better of it with a bottle of pepper sauce. "He fairly squealed from its effects . . . and pitched and twisted. . . . 'If that ister critter's dyin' agonies didn't stir a 'ruption in me equal to a small earthquake!' he recounted. 'It squirmed like a sarpent when that killin' stuff touched it.'"

It was a western man who finally proved to America and the rest of the world that the original vein which literary prospectors had been seeking in the new country lay in this very ore which had been ignored by critics as journalistic and subliterary. Rufus W. Griswold in 1845 had suggested that the productions of the South and West gave "abundant promise for the future," but many of those who enjoyed the frontier tales were as apologetic for their taste as Sir Philip Sidney in Shakespeare's England was for enjoying the old ballads.

When "The Jumping Frog of Calaveras County" appeared in the New York *Saturday Press* the year the Civil War came to an end and was copied extensively not only in American but also in European papers, the vein that Mark Twain was supposed to have unearthed in California was revealed. But it was in his brother's printing office in Hannibal, Missouri, that young Sam Clemens, through exchanges and books lying about, had become acquainted with the tricks and the manners of western humor. In the Jumping Frog story one odd character yarns it off in western dialect about how another odd character lost in a frog race. Mark Twain had grown up where frontier wit and buffoonery were depended upon to win social recognition. When he was seventeen years old, he had experimented with an anecdote about how a countryman got the best of a sophisticate, ironically entitled "The Dandy Frightening a Squatter," which he had published in the Boston *Carpet Bag*, May 1, 1852.

The influence of the tall tales is noticeable in most of Mark Twain's shorter and longer fiction. His autobiographical narratives as well as his more nearly conventional stories partake of the manner and matter of these tales. The story of Tom Blankenship's discomfiture at falling into the pans of taffy which Pamela Clemens's girl friends had put out to cool has something of the boisterous quality of John S. Robb's "Nettle Bottom Ball," or Betsy Jones's "Tumble in the Mush Pan." In "The Private History of a Campaign that Failed," Mark Twain, an odd character, tells of Sam Clemens's brief Civil War experience as if unaware that his "slacker" confession redounds to his discredit. "The Man That Corrupted Hadleyburg" is the story of a tremendous practical joke played by the Devil upon a whole village. In *Huckleberry Finn*—a collection of short stories, really—are constant reminders of the method and subject matter of early Missouri tales. In fact, it was the irreverence and crude buffoonery of these tales holding over in the style and tone of most of his early writing that delayed the recognition of Mark Twain as a major American writer.

2. Mark Twain's Development as a Humorist

MARK TWAIN STARTED his writing career as a professional funmaker, and Bernard De Voto insisted that to the end of his life his leading motive was to make people laugh. But, as has often been pointed out, not one of his books, with the possible exception of the earliest sketches, is primarily a humorous book. The steps by which he progressed from the boisterous extravaganzas of the 1860's to the bitter satire and the more delicate irony of the early 1900's cannot be clearly marked, for he was likely to drop into frontier spoofing almost to the end of his fifty years of writing and entertaining. The term "fun-maker" does not apply to him, however, after he has suffered through business failure and family tragedy. There is a vast difference between the kind of laugh called forth by "The Dutch Nick Massacre" (1863) or "To Raise Poultry" (1870) and that aroused by "Eve's Diary" (1905) or "The Last Lotos Club Speech" (1908). If one allows for much overlapping, five, or possibly six, stages can be discovered in Mark Twain's development as a humorist.

The first might be called the stage of exaggeration, burlesque, and understatement (a kind of inverse exaggeration) caught from the frontier tellers of tall tales—uppermost in his writing through *Roughing It* (1870): "I went away from there," he writes in *Innocents Abroad* (1869), recalling in Milan his boyhood experience of discovering a corpse in his father's office, where he had taken refuge for the night. "I do not say that I went in any kind of hurry, but I simply went. That is sufficient. I went out of the window. I carried the sash along with me. I did not want the sash, but it was handier to take it than to leave it. I was not scared, but I was considerably agitated." This is a higher type of humor than the cacography (distorted spelling, pronunciation, and grammar) which was the chief stock in trade of such contemporaries of Mark Twain's as Artemus Ward. The Missourian depends upon their favorite tricks in such dialect pieces as "The Jumping Frog"—though with a difference. They are seen in "Dan Murphy," one of the *Galaxy* sketches. Dan's inconsolable widow has consented to his being embalmed, but when, at the wake, the bill comes, she exclaims, "Sivinty-five dollars for stuffin' Dan, blister their souls! Did them divils suppose I was goin' to stairt a musaim that I'd be dalin' in such expinsive curiassities?"

While the broad extravaganza of "Journalism in Tennessee" (1869), characteristic of his early humor, is the kind of fun-making that delighted his early audiences, mere verbal witticisms such as he fell back on in "To Raise Poultry" (1870) are comparatively rare in the writings of Mark Twain. "The last and saddest evidence of intellectual poverty is the pun," he once said, but he was always likely to fall from grace, as in the implied pun in the speech on "The Babies" (1880); "In another [cradle] the future renowned astronomer is blinking at the shining milky way with but languid interest—poor little chap!—and wondering what has become of that other one they call the wet-nurse."

A new development of his humor with a more serious purpose became apparent with his publication, with Charles Dudley Warner, of *The Gilded Age* in 1871. It is the gayer, blither satirical vein of a young man, but its barbs at business chicanery and Congressional obliquity were so timely that even critics who find the book amateurish as a novel testify to its historical value. It was so effective, in fact, that its title has become the name of the period of inflated business ambitions following the Civil War. The half-whimsical satire at the expense of Colonel Sellers' promotion of a visionary scheme with the assurance "There's millions in it!" doesn't appeal to our deepest disapproval. Colonel Sellers is the greatest achievement of Mark Twain's creative genius before Tom Sawyer.

Because he was dissatisfied with the reception of *The Gilded Age,* Mark Twain turned to a different humorous device in *Tom Sawyer* (1876) and *Huckleberry Finn* (1884). Nowhere is to be found more effective dramatic irony than that at the expense of Tom and Huck. The author puts the reader in the way of having a point of view on the two boys which they are blissfully unaware of. Sometimes Aunt Polly also comes in for a satirical implication. When Huck tells her about a steamboat accident,

"Good gracious!" she exclaims, "anybody hurt?"

"No'm," he answers. "Killed a nigger."

"Well, it's lucky," she replies, "because people sometimes do get hurt."

In "The Facts Concerning the Recent Carnival of Crime in Connecticut" (1876) of this third stage, the irony is directed at himself. In this allegory he gets even with his conscience, the imp that has nagged at him relentlessly all his life, by killing it off.

The fourth step in Mark Twain's development as a humorist (his second period of purposeful satire) may be said to have begun with the publication of "The Campaign that Failed" (1885), whose purpose is to hold up to ridicule his own brief Civil War experience; but in that autobiographical sketch in his earlier satirical vein is to be found his first thrust at the irrational business of war (to culminate later in the scathing irony of the War Prayer). It is *A Connecticut Yankee* (1889), however, that marks this as the really transitional stage of the humorist's career. In *The Prince and the Pauper* (1881) he had shown his tendency to take a shot at tyrannical institutions in England and, by implication, in America. But in *A Connecticut Yankee* he set out to use all the resources of his humor to vent his indignation at the cruelty and injustice of those who sit in the seats of the mighty, in the England of King Arthur, ostensibly; but one feels that he is leveling his shafts at tyranny and injustice wherever they are found.

Here the comedy and serious purpose are fairly well balanced. There is much irreverence and coarse burlesque. The Yankee found his coat of mail galling, especially on horseback. "When I trotted I rattled like a crate of dishes. . . . I dropped into a walk . . . and as we didn't create any breeze . . . I was like to get fried in that stove. . . . When you itch, you are inside and your hands are outside." Fantastic figures of speech are frequent: people gave vent to their gratitude in "typhoons and cyclones of frantic joy and whole Niagaras of happy tears." The King, dressed in peasant disguise, looked as "humble as the Leaning Tower of Pisa." "The grandstand was clothed in flags, streamers and rich tapestry. . . . British Aristocracy . . . every individual a flashing prism of gaudy silks and velvets—well I never saw anything to begin with it but a fight between an upper Mississippi sunset and the Aurora Borealis." Of Sandy's talkativeness, a machinist, The Boss, complained: "She could grind, and pump, and churn, and buzz by the week, and never stop to oil or blow out."

Along with these are some of the author's most characteristic serious passages. He accounts for the injustice of Arthurians, whom he admires in a digression on heredity and training: "Training—training is everything; training is all there is *to* a person. We speak of nature; it is folly; . . . What we call by that misleading name is merely heredity and training. We have no thoughts of our own, no opinions of our own.... All that is original in us, and therefore fairly creditable or discreditable to us, can be covered up and hidden by the point of a cambric needle, all the rest being atoms contributed by, and inherited from, a procession of ancestors that stretches back a billion years to the Adam-clan or grass-hopper or monkey from whom our race has been so tediously and ostentatiously and unprofitably developed. And as for me, all that I think about this plodding sad pilgrimage, this frantic drift between the eternities, is to look out and humbly live a pure and high and blameless life, and save that one microscopic atom in me that is truly me: the rest may land in Sheol and welcome, for all I care."

This more serious purpose served by his humor in *A Connecticut Yankee* is seen in *Pudd'nhead Wilson* (1892) in one of the most successful portrayals of his creative imagination. None of the characters in his former fiction is a more convincing individual than the Negro woman, Roxana, struggling with her derelict son, who would "sell her down the river." And nothing from Mark Twain's pen has been more often quoted than the aphorisms of the Pudd'nhead Wilson calendar, with their satirical anticlimax and comic figures of speech:

"Cauliflower is cabbage with a college education."

"If you pick up a starving dog and make him prosperous, he will not bite you. This is the principal difference between a dog and a man."

"April 1 This is the day on which we are reminded of what we are on the other three hundred and sixty-four."

"It is better to be a young June Bug than an old bird of paradise."

From the time of his writing *Joan of Arc* (1895), in what may be called the fifth step in his development as a humorist, although he could not wholly give up the old drolling, Mark Twain shows finer feeling. However sharp his invective against the treatment of Joan becomes, there is less buffoonery. The tender feeling of the first chapter of the book, in the description of the maid's childhood joys around the Fairy Tree, is like that which he had bestowed upon his own small daughters: "There was a very small squirrel on her shoulder, sitting up as those creatures do and turning a rocky fragment of prehistoric chestnut-cake over and over in its knotty hands ... and giving its elevated bushy tail a flirt and its painted ears a toss." The nearest approach in the novel to his old fun-making is in the story of Uncle Laxart's riding a bull to a funeral and the bull's knocking over a beehive and bringing down upon himself and the rider the vengeance of the bees.

While "The Man That Corrupted Hadleyburg" (1899) is the story of a practical joke practiced by the Devil, Prince of Spoofers, upon a whole village, the tone of this allegorical legend, written in the author's sixties, shows growth in human sympathy and in literary feeling.

His growth in taste can be noted by comparing such a hoax as that in "The Petrified Man" (1862) with that embedded in "The Double-Barrelled Detective Story" (1902).

"It was a crisp and spicy morning in early October. The lilacs and laburnams, lit with the glory-fires of autumn, hung burning and flashing in the upper air, a fairy bridge provided by kind nature for the wingless wild things that have their homes in the tree-tops and would visit together; the larch and the pomegranate flung their purple and yellow flames in brilliant broad splashes along the slanting sweep of the woodland; the sensuous fragrance of innumerable deciduous flowers rose upon the swooning atmosphere; far in the empty sky a solitary esophagus slept upon motionles wing; everywhere brooded stillness, serenity, and the peace of God." It is not until the reader is jerked out of his more or less passive acceptance of the words by the resounding word "esophagus" that he discovers what a trick the author has been playing upon him with this trumped-up description. Even the much sobered Mark Twain could not resist the temptation to betray his too trustful reader shamefully.

To account for the last writings of the humorist is not easy. All that was paradoxical in his mind and character came full circle in his last years. The beautiful old man sitting on the verandah of his summer retreat in New Hampshire is a puzzling figure. There was the same alertness and impulse to amuse when he was surrounded by people, but it became easier day by day for him to lapse into bitterness at the thought of all that was wrong with the world. Prophetically he was a mid-twentieth-century American puzzling over how this sorry scheme of things has come about. The humor most characteristic of this period is of two kinds, representing two facets of his nature: the mordant satire of the essay "What is Man?" and *The Mysterious Stranger*, both written in 1898, and the gracious irony of "The Last Lotus Club Speech" (1908).

However despairing his conclusion was for himself and for the race, he defended to the last the medium which his endowment had led him to choose for striking at evil. Satire was the great purifying weapon. "For your race in its poverty," Satan says in *The Mysterious Stranger*, "has one really effective weapon—laughter. Power, money, persuasion, supplication, persecution—these can lift a colossal humbug—push it a little—weaken it a little century by century; but only laughter can blow it to atoms at a blast."

The implied definition of humor in his essay on William Dean Howells (*Harper's Magazine*, July, 1908) shows how his feeling about what its quality should be had changed in the course of his fifty-year experiment: "I do not think that anyone else can play with humorous fancies so gracefully and delicately and deliciously as he does.... His is a humor that flows round about and over and through the mesh of the page, pervading, refreshing, health-giving, and makes no more show and no more noise than does the circulation of the blood."

An incident which he read in Dana's *Two Years Before the Mast* suggested to him the farewell words of his "Last Lotos Club Speech," more heartening to his admirers than his recommendation of his dream philosophy at the end of *The Mysterious Stranger*. The irony at his own expense is an example of his finest humor:

« « « There was a presumptuous little self-important skipper in a coasting sloop, engaged in the dryed-apple and kitchen-furniture trade, and he was always hailing every ship that came in sight. He did it just to hear himself talk and to air his own grandeur.

One day a majestic Indiaman came ploughing by with course on course of canvas towering into the sky, her decks and yards swarming with sailors, her hull burdened to the Plimeal line with a rich freightage of precious spices, lading the breezes with gracious and mysterious odors of the Orient. It was a noble spectacle, a sublime spectacle! Of course the little skipper popped into the shrouds and squeaked out a hail, "Ship Ahoy! What ship is that? And whence and whither?" In a deep and thunderous bass the voice came back through the speaking trumpet, "The *Begum*, of Bengal, one hundred and forty-two days out of Canton, homeward bound! What ship is that?" Well, it just crushed the poor little creature's vanity flat, and he squeaked back most humbly, "Only the *Mary Ann* fourteen hours out from Boston, bound for Kittery Point—with nothing to speak of!" Oh, what an eloquent word that word "only," to express the depth of his humbleness! That is just my case. During just one hour in the twenty-four—not more—I pause and reflect in the stillness of the night with echoes of your English welcome still lingering in my ears, and then I am humble. Then I am properly meek, and for that little while I am only the *Mary Ann*, fourteen hours out, cargoed with vegetables and tinware; but during all the twenty-three hours my vain self-complacency rides high on the white crest of your approval, and then I am a stately Indiaman, ploughing the great seas under a cloud of canvas and laden with the kindest words that have ever been vouchsafed to any wondering alien in this world, I think; then my twenty-six fortunate days on this old Mother Soil seem to be multiplied by six, and *I* am the *Begum* of Bengal, one hundred forty-six days out of Canton, homeward bound! » » »

"The Dandy Frightening the Squatter," submitted by Sam Clemens to an eastern comic weekly when he was sixteen years old, is evidence that even then he had had contact with the broader American tradition in humor. The idea of an unsophisticated person getting the better of a sophisticated one had delighted the folk from the 1700's. It had been depended upon by the early American theatre for the comic relief element. In Royall Tyler's *The Contrast* (1787), the first American comedy, the most important character is the Yankee, Jonathan, who makes the simple native dignity of his master, Colonel Manly, apparent when he is contrasted with pretentious foreigners. Whereas Tyler's contrast amused a more sophisticated eastern audience, Sam Clemens's "Dandy" is typical of the newspaper humor of the Old Southwest, and his "Squatter" was calculated to delight the folk of that backwoods region.

THE DANDY FRIGHTENING THE SQUATTER[1]

« « « About thirteen years ago, when the now flourishing young city of Hannibal, on the Mississippi River, was but a "woodyard,"

[1] "The Dandy Frightening the Squatter" was published by the Boston *Carpet Bag*, May 1, 1852, when Sam Clemens was sixteen years old (his seventeenth birthday was November 30 [see Bernard De Voto's *Mark Twain's America*, 78–91]), four months before his writings for the *Hannibal Journal*. It was discovered by Franklin J. Meine and reprinted in his *Tall Tales of the Southwest: An Anthology of Western and Southwestern Humor 1830–1860*. Mr. Meine found also that Charles Farrar Browne, whom Mark Twain was to know in California as Artemus Ward and who was the first to encourage him to submit jokes to an eastern paper, was a compositor on the *Carpet Bag*, and might have set the type for Sam Clemens's first writing experiment. Young Browne also contributed sketches to the *Carpet Bag* under the pseudonym "Lieut Chub" (see Edgar M. Branch, *The Literary Apprenticeship of Mark Twain*, 4–7; also Fred W. Lorch, "A Source for Mark Twain's 'The Dandy Frightening the Squatter,'" *American Literature*, Vol. III (1931), 309-13). Sam was fast learning the ways of the world. His first full-time job, as printer and self-appointed columnist on the family newspaper in Hannibal, gave him his first real taste of journalism and his start toward a literary career—but at an age of indiscretion, as the mature Mark Twain later confesses:

MY FIRST LITERARY VENTURE
(from *Sketches New and Old*)

I was a very smart child at the age of thirteen—an unusually smart child, I thought at the time. It was then that I did my first newspaper scribbling, and most unexpectedly to me it stirred up a fine sensation in the community. It did, indeed, and I was very proud of it, too. I was a printer's "devil," and a progressive and aspiring one. My uncle had me on his paper (the *Weekly Hannibal Journal*, two dollars a year in advance—five hundred subscribers, and they paid in cordwood, cabbages, and unmarketable turnips), and on a lucky summer's day he left town to be gone a week, and asked me if I thought I could edit one issue of the paper judiciously. Ah! didn't I want to try! Higgins was the editor on the rival paper. He had lately been jilted, and one night a friend found an open note on the poor fellow's bed, in which he stated that he could not longer endure life and had drowned himself in Bear Creek. The friend ran down there and discovered Higgins wading back to shore. He had concluded he wouldn't. The village was full of it for several days, but Higgins did not suspect it. I thought this was a fine opportunity. I wrote an elaborately wretched account of the whole matter, and then illustrated it with villainous cuts engraved on the bottoms of wooden type with a jackknife—one of them a picture of Higgins wading out into the Creek in his shirt, with a lantern, sounding the depth of the water with a walking-stick. I thought it was desperately funny, and was densely unconscious that there was any moral obliquity about such a publication. Being satisfied with this effort, I looked around for other worlds to conquer, and it struck me that it would make good, interesting matter to charge the editor of a neighboring country paper with a piece of gratuitous rascality and "see him squirm."

I did it, putting the article into the form of a parody on the "Burial of Sir John Moore"—and a pretty crude parody it was, too.

Then I lampooned two prominent citizens outrageously—not because they had done anything to deserve but merely because I thought it was my duty to make the paper lively.

Next I gently touched up the newest stranger—the lion of the day, the gorgeous surrounded by a few huts, belonging to some hardy "*squatters*," and such a thing as a steamboat was considered quite a sight, the following incident occurred:

A tall, brawny woodsman stood leaning against a tree which stood upon the bank of the river, gazing at some approaching object, which our readers would easily have discovered to be a steamboat.

About half an hour elapsed, and the boat was moored, and the hands busily engaged in taking on wood.

Now among the many passengers on this boat, both male and female, was a spruce young dandy, with a killing moustache, &c., who seemed bent on making an impression upon the hearts of the young ladies on board, and to do this, he thought he must perform some heroic deed. Observing our squatter friend, he imagined this to be a fine opportunity to bring himself into notice; so, stepping into the cabin, he said:

journeyman tailor from Quincy. He was a simpering coxcomb of the first water, and the "loudest" dressed man in the state. He was an inveterate woman-killer. Every week he wrote lushy "poetry" for the *Journal*, about his newest conquest. His rhymes for my week were headed, "TO MARY IN H——L," meaning to Mary in Hannibal, of course. But while setting up the piece I was suddenly riven from head to heel by what I regarded as a perfect thunderbolt of humor, and I compressed it into a snappy footnote at the bottom—thus: "We will let this thing pass, just this once; but we wish Mr. J. Gordon Runnels to understand distinctly that we have a character to sustain, and from this time forth when he wants to commune with his friends in h——l, he must select some other medium than the columns of this journal!"

The paper came out, and I never knew any little thing attract so much attention as those playful trifles of mine.

For once the *Hannibal Journal* was in demand—a novelty it had not experienced before. The whole town was stirred. Higgins dropped in with a double-barreled shotgun early in the forenoon. When he found that it was an infant (as he called me) that had done him the damage, he simply pulled my ears and went away; but he threw up his situation that night and left town for good. The tailor came with his goose and a pair of shears; but he despised me, too, and departed for the South that night. The two lampooned citizens came with threats of libel, and went away incensed at my insignificance. The country editor pranced in with a war-whoop next day, suffering for blood to drink; but he ended by forgiving me cordially and inviting me down to the drug store to wash away all animosity in a friendly bumper of "Fahnestock's Vermifuge." It was his little joke. My uncle was very angry when he got back—unreasonably so, I thought, considering what an impetus I had given the paper, and considering also that gratitude for his preservation ought to have been uppermost in his mind, inasmuch as by his delay he had so wonderfully escaped dissection, tomahawking, libel, and getting his head shot off. But he softened when he looked at the accounts and saw that I had actually booked the unparalleled number of thirty-three new subscribers, and had the vegetables to show for it, cordwood, cabbages, beans, and unsalable turnips enough to run the family for two years!

"Ladies, if you wish to enjoy a good laugh, step out on the guards. I intend to frighten that gentleman into fits, who stands on the bank."

The ladies complied with the request, and our dandy drew from his bosom a formidable looking bowie-knife, and thrust it into his belt; then, taking a large horse-pistol in each hand, he seemed satisfied that all was right. Thus equipped, he strode on shore, with an air which seemed to say—"The hopes of a nation depend on me." Marching up to the woodsman he exclaimed:

"Found you at last, have I? You are the very man I've been looking for these three weeks! Say your prayers!" he continued, presenting his pistols, "you'll make a capital barn door, and I shall drill the key-hole myself!"

The squatter calmly surveyed him a moment, and then, drawing back a step, he planted his huge fist directly between the eyes of his astonished antagonist, who, in a moment, was floundering in the turbid waters of the Mississippi.

Every passenger on the boat had by this time collected on the guards, and the shout that now went up from the crowd speedily restored the crest-fallen hero to his senses, and, as he was sneaking off towards the boat, was thus accosted by his conqueror:

"I say, yeou, next time yeou come around drillin' key-holes, don't forget your old acquaintances!"

The ladies unanimously voted the knife and pistols to the victor. » » »

"The Jumping Frog," the second of young Samuel Clemens' writings to appear in an eastern paper, is considered to be his masterpiece in the field of folk humor.[2] Edward Wagenknecht, in his chapter entitled "The Divine Amateur" (*Mark Twain: The Man and His Work*), makes it clear how important folklore and folk speech were in forming Mark Twain's genius. These folk elements

[2] As Charles Neider points out (*The Complete Short Stories of Mark Twain*, xvi), Mark Twain's short stories "are part of our folklore. Twain is our writer closest to folklore.... "The Jumping Frog" is a living American fairy tale, acted out annually in Calaveras County. Whatever may be its dim origins (it has been claimed to be close kin to an old Greek tale; but the latter probably descended from a Hindu one, and so on), it is now *our* story, mirroring something in us." Mark Twain later in life said he had found it was 2,000 years old.

were acquired unconsciously in Hannibal, Missouri, as a printer's devil, at his Uncle John Quarles' farm near Florida, Missouri, at wharves along the Mississippi River, and on river boats. Wagenknecht quotes Gamaliel Bradford, who says that Mark Twain resembles "the bard . . . the old epic popular singer, who gathered up in himself, almost unconsciously, the life and spirit of a whole nation and poured it forth more as a voice, an instrument, than as a deliberate artist." "The Jumping Frog" might be called the culmination of its author's experiments with early American folk humor, though the folk element gave character to his writing almost to the end.[3] Though regarded subliterary when it was published, as discerning a critic as James Russell Lowell said of it, "It is the finest piece of humorous writing yet produced in America."

THE CELEBRATED JUMPING FROG OF CALAVERAS COUNTY[4]

« « « In compliance with the request of a friend of mine, who wrote me from the East, I called on good-natured, garrulous old Simon Wheeler, and inquired after my friend's friend, *Leonidas W. Smiley*, as requested to do, and I hereunto append the result. I have a lurking suspicion that *Leonidas W. Smiley* is a myth; that my friend never knew such a personage; and that he only

[3] The importance of this tale in the development of Mark Twain as a humorist is stressed by two leading Mark Twain students: "At Angel's Camp [in 1865] he made what was for him probably the greatest scoop of his career. For he heard Ben Coon tell about the jumping frog, and he sensed that it would make a good story. . . . it became the foundation of his literary fame" (Ivan Benson, *Mark Twain's Western Years*, 126). " 'The Jumping Frog' was the turning point in [Mark Twain's] literary career. He had told plenty of funny stories before, but he had created no characters. . . . For the first time Mark Twain had projected vividly recognized characters upon paper; a commonplace folktale had become literature because it was restated in terms of recognizable human personalities. He had found the first half of his art: the ability so to transfer speech to paper that the speaker came alive for the reader" (DeLancey Ferguson, *Mark Twain: Man and Legend*, 104).

[4] "The Celebrated Jumping Frog of Calaveras County" was first published in the New York *Saturday Press*, November 18, 1865, under the title "Jim Smiley and His Jumping Frog." It was almost immediately reprinted in European papers. At thirty, almost to the day, Mark Twain became known to the world. But, as in his attitude twenty years later toward *Huckleberry Finn*, he did not realize what he had done. He wrote to his mother: "To think that after writing many an article a man might be excused for thinking tolerably good, those New York people should single out a villainous backwoods sketch to compliment me on!" (*Letters*, I, 101, January 20, 1866).

conjectured that, if I asked old Wheeler about him, that it would remind him of his infamous *Jim Smiley*, and he would go to work and bore me nearly to death with some infernal reminiscence of him as long and tedious as it would be useless to me. If that was the design, it certainly succeeded.

I found Simon Wheeler dozing comfortably by the bar-room stove of the old dilapidated tavern in the ancient mining camp of Angel's, and I noted that he was fat and bald-headed, and had an expression of winning gentleness and simplicity upon his tranquil countenance. He roused up and gave me good-day. I told him a friend of mine had commissioned me to make some inquiries about a cherished companion of his boyhood named *Leonidas W. Smiley—Rev. Leonidas W.* Smiley—a young minister of the Gospel, who he had heard was at one time a resident of Angel's Camp. I added that, if Mr. Wheeler could tell me anything about this Rev. Leonidas W. Smiley, I would feel under many obligations to him.

Simon Wheeler backed me into a corner and blockaded me there with his chair, and then sat me down and reeled off the monotonous narrative which follows this paragraph. He never smiled, he never frowned, he never changed his voice from the gentle-flowing key to which he tuned the initial sentence, he never betrayed the slightest suspicion of enthusiasm; but all through the interminable narrative there ran a vein of impressive earnestness and sincerity, which showed me plainly that, so far from his imagining that there was anything ridiculous or funny about his story, he regarded it as a really important matter, and admitted its two heroes as men of transcendent genius in *finesse*. To me, the spectacle of a man drifting serenely along through such a queer yarn without ever smiling, was exquisitely absurd. As I said before, I asked him to tell me what he knew of Rev. Leonidas W. Smiley, and he replied as follows. I let him go on in his own way, and never interrupted him once:

There was a feller here once by the name of *Jim* Smiley, in the winter of '49—or maybe it was the spring of '50—I don't recollect exactly, somehow, though what makes me think it was one or the other is because I remember the big flume wasn't finished when he first came to the camp; but anyway, he was the curiousest man about always betting on anything that turned up you ever see, if he could get anybody to bet on the other side; and if he couldn't, he'd change sides. Any way that suited the other man would suit him—any way just so's he got a bet, *he* was satisfied. But still he was lucky, uncommon lucky—he most always come out winner. He was always ready and laying for a chance; there couldn't be no solit'ry thing mentioned but that feller'd offer to bet on it, and take any side you please, as I was just telling you. If there was a horse-race, you'd find him flush, or you'd find him busted at the end of it; if there was a dog-fight, he'd bet on it; if there was a cat-fight, he'd bet on it; if there was a chicken-fight, he'd bet on it; why, if there was two birds sitting on a fence, he would bet you which one would fly first; or if there was a camp-meeting, he would be there reg'lar, to bet on Parson Walker, which he judged to be the best exhorter about here, and so he was, too, and a good man. If he even seen a straddle-bug start to go anywheres, he would bet you how long it would take him to get wherever he was going to, and if you took him up, he would foller that straddle-bug to Mexico but what he would find out where he was bound for and how long he was on the road. Lots of the boys here has seen that Smiley, and can tell you about him. Why, it never made no difference to *him*—he would bet on *any*thing—the dangdest feller. Parson Walker's wife laid very sick once, for a good while, and it seemed as if they warn't going to save her; but one morning he came in, and Smiley asked how she was, and he said she was considerable better—thank the Lord for his inf'nit mercy—and coming on so smart that, with the blessing of Prov'dence, she'd get well yet; and Smiley, before he thought, says, "Well, I'll risk two-and-a-half that she don't anyway."

Thish-yer Smiley had a mare—the boys called her the fifteen-minute nag, but that was only in fun, you know, because, of course, she was faster than that—and he used to win money on that horse, for all she was so slow and always had the asthma, or the distemper, or the consumption, or something of that kind. They used to give her two or three hundred yards start, and then pass her under way; but always at the fag-end of the race she'd get excited and desperate-like, and come cavorting and straddling up, and scattering her legs around limber, sometimes in the air, and sometimes out to one side amongst the fences, and kicking up m-o-r-e dust, and raising m-o-r-e racket with her coughing and sneezing and blowing her nose—and always fetch up at the stand just about a neck ahead, as near as you could cipher it down.

And he had a little bull pup, that to look at him you'd think he wan't worth a cent but to set around and look ornery and lay for a chance to steal something. But as soon as money was up on him, he was a different dog; his under-jaw'd begin to stick out like the fo-castle of a steamboat, and his teeth would uncover, and shine savage like the furnaces. And a dog might tackle him, and bully-rag him, and bite him, and throw him over his shoulder two or three times, and Andrew Jackson—which was the name of the pup—Andrew Jackson would never let on but what *he* was satisfied, and hadn't expected nothing else—and the bets being doubled and doubled on the other side all the time, till the money was all up; and then all of a sudden he would grab that other dog jest by the j'int of his hind leg and freeze to it—not claw, you understand, but only jest grip and hang on till they throwed up the sponge, if it was a year. Smiley always come out winner on that pup, till he harnessed a dog once that didn't have no hind legs, because they'd been sawed off by a circular saw, and when the thing had gone along far enough, and the money was all up, and he come to make a snatch for his pet holt, he saw in a minute how he'd been imposed on, and how the other dog had him in the door, so to speak, and he 'peared surprised, and then he looked sorter discouraged-like, and didn't try no more to win the fight, and so he got shucked out bad. He gave Smiley a look, as much as to say his heart was broke and it was *his* fault for putting up a dog that hadn't no hind legs for him to take holt of, which was his main dependence in a fight, and then he limped off a piece and laid down and died. It was a good pup, was that Andrew Jackson, and would have made a name for hisself if he'd lived, for the stuff was in him, and he had genius—I know it, because he hadn't no opportunities to speak of, and it don't stand to reason that a dog could make such a fight as he could under them circumstances, if he hadn't no talent. It always makes me feel sorry when I think of that last fight of his'n, and the way it turned out.

Well, thish-yer Smiley had rat-tarriers and chicken-cocks, and tom-cats, and all them kind of things, till you couldn't rest, and you couldn't fetch nothing for him to bet on but he'd match you. He ketched a frog one day, and took him home, and said he cal'klated to edercate him; and so he never done nothing for these three months but set in his back yard and learn that frog to jump. And you bet you he *did* learn him, too. He'd give him a little punch behind, and the next minute you'd see that frog whirling in the air like a doughnut—see him turn one summerset, or maybe a couple, if he got a good start, and come down flat-footed and all right, like a cat. He got him up so in the matter of catching flies, and kept him in practice so constant, that he'd nail a fly every time as far as he could see him. Smiley said all a frog wanted was education, and he could do most anything—and I believe him. Why, I've seen him set Dan'l Webster down here on this floor—Dan'l Webster was the name of the frog—and sing out, "Flies, Dan'l, flies!" and quicker'n you could wink, he'd spring straight up, and snake a fly off'n the counter there, and flop down on the floor again as solid as a gob of mud, and fall to scratching the side of his head with his hind foot as indifferent as if he hadn't no idea he's been doin' any more'n any frog might do. You never see a frog so modest and straightfor'ard as he was, for all he was so gifted. And when it come to fair and square jumping on the dead level, he could get over more ground at one straddle than any animal of his breed you ever see. Jumping on a dead level was his strong suit, you understand; and when it come to that, Smiley would ante up money on him as long as he had a red. Smiley was monstrous proud of his frog, and well he might be, for fellers that had traveled and been everywhere all said he laid over any frog that ever *they* see.

Well, Smiley kept the beast in a little lattice box, and he used to fetch him downtown sometimes and lay for a bet. One day a feller —a stranger in the camp, he was—come across him with his box, and says:

"What might it be that you've got in the box?"

And Smiley says, sorter indifferent like, "It might be a parrot, or it might be a canary, maybe, but it ain't—it's only just a frog."

An' the feller took it, and looked at it careful, and turned it round this way and that, and says, "H'm—so 'tis. Well, what's *he* good for?"

"Well," Smiley says, easy and careless, "he's good enough for *one* thing, I should judge—he can outjump any frog in Calaveras county."

The feller took the box again, and took another long, particular look, and give it back to Smiley, and says, very deliberate, "Well, I don't see no p'ints about that frog that's any better'n any other frog."

"Maybe you don't," Smiley says. "Maybe you understand frogs, and maybe you don't understand 'em; maybe you've had experience, and maybe you ain't only a amature, as it were. Anyways, I've got *my* opinion, and I'll risk forty dollars that he can outjump any frog in Calaveras county."

And the feller studied a minute, and then says, kinder sad like, "Well, I'm only a stranger here, and I ain't got no frog; but if I had a frog, I'd bet you."

And then Smiley says, "That's all right—that's all right—if you'll hold my box a minute, I'll go and get you a frog." And so the feller took the box, and put up his forty dollars along with Smiley's, and set down to wait.

So he set there a good while thinking and thinking to hisself, and then he got the frog out and prized his mouth open and took a teaspoon and filled him full of quail shot—filled him pretty near up to his chin—and set him on the floor. Smiley he went to the swamp and slopped around in the mud for a long time, and finally he ketched a frog, and fetched him in, and give him to this feller, and says:

"Now, if you're ready, set him alongside of Dan'l, with his forepaws just even with Dan'l, and I'll give the word." Then he says, "One—two—three—jump!" and him and the feller touched up the frogs from behind, and the new frog hopped off, but Dan'l gave a heave, and hysted up his shoulders—so—like a Frenchman, but it wasn't no use—he couldn't budge; he was planted as solid as an anvil, and he couldn't no more stir than if he was anchored out. Smiley was a good deal surprised, and he was disgusted, too, but he didn't have no idea what the matter was, of course.

The feller took the money and started away; and when he was going out at the door, he sorter jerked his thumb over his shoulder—this way—at Dan'l, and says again, very deliberate, "Well, *I* don't see no p'ints about that frog that's any better'n any other frog."

Smiley he stood scratching his head and looking down at Dan'l a long time, and at last he says, "I do wonder what in the nation that frog throw'd off for—I wonder if there ain't something the matter with him—he 'pears to look mighty baggy, somehow." And he ketched Dan'l by the nap of the neck, and lifted him up and says, "Why, blame my cats, if he don't weigh five pounds!" and turned him upside down, and he belched out a double handful of shot. And then he see how it was, and he was the maddest man—he set the frog down and took out after that feller, but he never ketched him. And—

(Here Simon Wheeler heard his name called from the front yard, and got up to see what was wanted.) And turning to me as he moved away, he said: "Just set where you are, stranger, and rest easy—I ain't going to be gone a second."

But, by your leave, I did not think that a continuation of the history of the enterprising vagabond *Jim* Smiley would be likely to afford me much information concerning the Rev. *Leonidas W. Smiley*, and so I started away.

At the door I met the sociable Wheeler returning, and he buttonholed me and recommenced:

"Well, thish-yer Smiley had a yeller one-eyed cow that didn't have no tail, only jest a short stump like a bannanner, and—"

"Oh, hang Smiley and his afflicted cow!" I muttered goodnaturedly, and bidding the old gentleman good-day, I departed.[5] » » »

"To Raise Poultry" is an example of the early, pot-boiler type of humor which, even at the time of its writing, Mark Twain was hoping to abandon. He preferred not to be known as a punster and seldom indulged in this form of cleverness, but when an

---

[5] Fifteen years after the appearance of Mark Twain's celebrated frog story, H. R. Haweis, a British critic, wrote, "What, I should like to know, is the fun of saying that a frog who has been caused to swallow a quantity of shot cannot jump so high as he could before" (*American Humorist*, 50). In spite of Haweis' reaction, the "jumping frog" story quickly spread throughout the British Empire and established Mark Twain's literary fame in all parts of the English-speaking world (see R. M. Rodney, "Mark Twain in England"). The story was eventually translated into many languages. For the absurdities that resulted from its translation into French and Mark Twain's reaction, see "The Jumping Frog in English, Then in French, Then Clawed Back into A Civilized Language Once More by Patient, Unremunerated Toil" in *Sketches New and Old*.

honorary membership was conferred upon him by a poultry society, he enlivened the pages of the *Buffalo Express* with this letter.

TO RAISE POULTRY[6] (from *Sketches New and Old*)

« « « Seriously, from early youth I have taken an especial interest in the subject of poultry-raising, and so this membership touches a ready sympathy in my breast. Even as a school-boy, poultry-raising was a study with me, and I may say without egotism that as early as the age of seventeen I was acquainted with all the best and speediest methods of raising chickens, from raising them off a roost by burning lucifer matches under their noses, down to lifting them off a fence on a frosty night by insinuating the end of a warm board under their heels. By the time I was twenty years old, I really suppose I had raised more poultry than any one individual in all the section round about there. The very chickens came to know my talent by and by. The youth of both sexes ceased to paw the earth for worms, and old roosters that came to crow, "remained to pray," when I passed by.

I have had so much experience in the raising of fowls that I cannot but think that a few hints from me might be useful to the society. The two methods I have already touched upon are very simple, and are only used in the raising of the commonest class of fowls; one is for summer, the other for winter. In the one case you start out with a friend along about eleven o'clock on a summer's night (not later, because in some states—especially in California and Oregon—chickens always rouse up just at midnight and crow from ten to thirty minutes, according to the ease or difficulty they experience in getting the public waked up), and your friend carries with him a sack. Arrived at the henroost (your neighbor's, not your own), you light a match and hold it under first one and then another pullet's nose until they are willing to go into that bag without making any trouble about it. You then return home, either taking the bag with you or leaving it behind, according as circum-

---

[6] "To Raise Poultry" was first published in the *Buffalo Express*, June 4, 1870, under the title "More Distinction." It was later included in the miscellaneous collection of Mark Twain's writings entitled *Sketches New and Old* (1875).

stances dictate. N.B.—I *have* seen the time when it was eligible and appropriate to leave the sack behind and walk off with considerable velocity, without ever leaving any word where to send it.

In the case of the other method mentioned for raising poultry, your friend takes along a covered vessel with a charcoal fire in it, and you carry a long slender plank. This is a frosty night, understand. Arrived at the tree, or fence, or other hen-roost (your own if you are an idiot), you warm the end of your plank in your friend's fire vessel, and then raise it aloft and ease it up gently against a slumbering chicken's foot. If the subject of your attentions is a true bird, he will infallibly return thanks with a sleepy cluck or two, and step out and take up quarters on the plank, thus becoming so conspicuously accessory before the fact to his own murder as to make it a grave question in our minds, as it once was in the mind of Blackstone, whether he is not really and deliberately committing suicide in the second degree. But you enter into a contemplation of these legal refinements subsequently—not then.

When you wish to raise a fine, large, donkey-voiced Shanghai rooster, you do it with a lasso, just as you would a bull. It is because he must be choked, and choked effectually, too. It is the only good, certain way, for whenever he mentions a matter which he is cordially interested in, the chances are ninety-nine in a hundred that he secures somebody else's immediate attention to it too, whether it be day or night.

The Black Spanish is an exceedingly fine bird and a costly one. Thirty-five dollars is the usual figure, and fifty a not uncommon price for a specimen. Even its eggs are worth from a dollar to a dollar and a half apiece, and yet are so unwholesome that the city physician seldom or never orders them for the workhouse. Still I have once or twice procured as high as a dozen at a time for nothing, in the dark of the moon. The best way to raise the Black Spanish fowl is to go late in the evening and raise coop and all. The reason I recommend this method is that, the birds being so valuable, the owners do not permit them to roost around promiscuously, but put them in a coop as strong as a fireproof safe, and keep it in the kitchen at night. The method I speak of is not always a bright and satisfying success, and yet there are so many little articles of *vertu* about a kitchen, that if you fail on the coop you can generally bring away something else. I brought away a nice steel trap one night, worth ninety cents.

But what is the use in my pouring out my whole intellect on this subject? I have shown the Western New York Poultry Society that they have taken to their bosom a party who is not a spring chicken by any means, but a man who knows all about poultry, and is just as high up in the most efficient methods of raising it as the president of the institution himself. I thank these gentlemen for the honorary membership that they have conferred upon me, and shall stand at all times ready and willing to testify my good feeling and my official zeal by deeds as well as by this hastily penned advice and information. Whenever they are ready to go to raising poultry, let them call for me any evening after eleven o'clock, and I shall be on hand promptly. » » »

It is doubtful whether any other American writer creates in his reader, as a sort of by-product, such a sense of personal attachment as Mark Twain does. Perhaps because of the autobiographical element in so much that he has written, his readers carry away a sense not only of the joy of his humor, but also of the charm and gaiety of his personality. A sense of proprietorship also may contribute to our attachment. As Archibald Henderson wrote at the time of Mark Twain's death, he "realized his own country and his own age as no other American has so completely done." Even the student members of the Hawaiian University Quill Club felt this proprietorship when, in 1931, they dedicated their yearbook "To the memory of Mark Twain, most beloved of our American humorists, for his tireless crusade against the forces of gloom and melancholy, that dispersed the darkness as dawn dispatches night . . . for the immortal sunshine of his words, cheering the jaded soul to-day as it did half a century ago . . . for the music of laughter that was his gift to posterity."

It is a commonplace of Mark Twain criticism to say that the force of his prose style had its origin in his experiences as a public speaker. Mr. Lionel Trilling, in his introduction to *Huckleberry Finn*, says that Mark Twain "established for written prose the virtues of Americal colloquial speech. . . . Out of his knowledge of the actual speech of America he forged a classic prose. . . . He is the master of the style that escapes the fixity of the printed page, that sounds in our ears with the immediacy of the heard voice."

SPEECH ON THE BABIES[7] (At the banquet, in Chicago, given by The Army of the Tennessee to their first commander, General U. S. Grant, November, 1879.)

The fifteenth regular toast was "The Babies—as they comfort us in our sorrows, let us not forget them in our festivities."

« « « I like that. We have not all had the good fortune to be ladies. We have not all been generals, or poets, or statesmen; but when the toast works down to the babies, we stand on common ground. It is a shame that for a thousand years the world's banquets have utterly ignored the baby, as if he didn't amount to

[7] The scene was a Chicago banquet hall, November 13, 1879. General Grant, on returning from his trip around the world, after a journey from San Francisco which had been like a royal progress, was guest of honor at a banquet given by the Army of the Tennessee to honor their first commander. When Mark Twain had met General Grant the day before, both men remembered a trying moment some years before in Washington when Mark Twain had first met Grant. Mark Twain had broken down the formality of the occasion by saying, "General, I seem to be a little embarrassed. Are you?" Now when Carter Harrison, master of ceremonies, said, "General, let me present Mr. Clemens, a man almost as great as yourself," Grant said very gravely, "Mr. Clemens, I am not embarrassed, are you?"
   Although there were fourteen toasts before Mark Twain's and it was two o'clock in the morning and the seven hundred guests were sleepy (Mark Twain had been scheduled to speak last in order to hold the crowd), there was continual applause throughout the speech. But as he progressed with the last sentence, his audience showed itself to be uncertain about the outcome. When, however, after a dramatic pause, he pronounced the last clause, "the house came down with a crash," his biographer writes. "The linking of their hero's great military triumph with that earliest of all conquests was so moving that even Grant's iron serenity broke; he rocked and laughed while the tears streamed down his cheeks" (Albert Bigelow Paine's chapter on the occasion, *Mark Twain: A Biography*, II, 652-55.)
   Writing to William Dean Howells about having been asked to speak about the reception for General Grant, Mark Twain recalled: "I choke up with the memory of it—to talk of it would simply be impossible. Imagine what it would be like to see a bullet-shredded old battle flag reverently unfolded to the gaze of a thousand middle-aged soldiers most of whom hadn't seen it since they saw it advancing over victorious fields when they were in their prime. And imagine what it was like when Grant, their first commander, stepped into view while they were still going mad over the flag—and then, right in the midst of it all, somebody struck up 'When we were marching through Georgia'" (*Letters*, I, 370, November 12, 1879).

anything. If you will stop and think a minute—if you will go back fifty or a hundred years to your early married life and recontemplate your first baby—you will remember that he amounted to a good deal, and even something over. You soldiers all know that when that little fellow arrived at family headquarters you had to hand in your resignation. He took entire command. You became his lackey, his mere body-servant, and you had to stand around, too. He was not a commander who made allowances for time, distance, weather, or anything else. You had to execute his order whether it was possible or not. And there was only one form of marching in his manual of tactics, and that was the double-quick. He treated you with every sort of insolence and disrespect, and the bravest of you didn't dare say a word. You could face the death-storm at Donelson and Vicksburg, and give back blow for blow; but when he clawed your whiskers, and pulled your hair, and twisted your nose, you had to take it. When the thunders of war were sounding in your ears you set your faces toward the batteries, and advanced with steady tread; but when he turned on the terrors of his war-whoop you advanced in the other direction, and mighty glad of the chance, too. When he called for soothing-syrup, did you venture to throw out any side remarks about certain services being unbecoming an officer and a gentleman? No. You got up and *got* it. When he ordered his pap-bottle and it was not warm, did you talk back? Not you. You went to work and *warmed* it. You even descended so far in your menial office as to take a suck at that warm, insipid stuff yourself, to see if it was right—three parts water to one of milk, a touch of sugar to modify the colic, and a drop of peppermint to kill those hiccoughs. I can taste that stuff yet. And how many things you learned as you went along! Sentimental young folks still take stock in that beautiful old saying that when the baby smiles in his sleep, it is because the angels are whispering to him. Very pretty, but too thin—simply wind on the stomach, my friends. If the baby proposed to take a walk at his usual hour, two o'clock in the morning, didn't you rise up promptly and remark, with a mental addition which would not improve a Sunday-school book *much*, that that was the very thing you were about to propose yourself? Oh! you were under good discipline, and as you went fluttering up and down the room in your undress uniform, you not only prattled undignified baby-talk, but even tuned up your martial voices and tried to *sing!*—"Rock-a-by baby in the tree-top," for instance. What a spectacle for an Army of the Tennessee! And what an affliction for the neighbors, too; for it is not everybody within a mile around that likes military music at three in the morning. And when you had been keeping this sort of thing up two or three hours, and your little velvet-head intimated that nothing suited him like exercise and noise, what did you do? ["*Go on!*"] You simply *went* on until you dropped in the last ditch. The idea that a *baby* doesn't *amount* to anything! Why, *one* baby is just a house and a front yard full by itself. *One* baby can furnish more business than you and your whole Interior Department can attend to. He is enterprising, irrepressible, brimful of lawless activities. Do what you please, you can't make him stay on the reservation. Sufficient unto the day is one baby. As long as you are in your right mind don't you ever pray for twins. Twins amount to a permanent riot. And there ain't any real difference between triplets and an insurrection.

Yes, it was high time for a toastmaster to recognize the importance of the babies. Think what is in store for the present crop! Fifty years from now we shall all be dead, I trust, and then this flag, if it still survive (and let us hope it may), will be floating over a Republic numbering 200,000,000 souls, according to the settled laws of our increase. Our present schooner of State will have grown into a political leviathan—a *Great Eastern*. The cradled babies of to-day will be on deck. Let them be well trained, for we are going to leave a big contract on their hands. Among the three or four million cradles now rocking in the land are some which this nation would preserve for ages as sacred things, if we could know which ones they are. In one of these cradles the unconscious Farragut of the future is at this moment teething—think of it!—and putting in a world of dead earnest, unarticulated, but perfectly justifiable profanity over it, too. In another the future renowned astronomer is blinking at the shining Milky Way with but a languid interest—poor little chap!—and wondering what has become of that other one they call the wet-nurse. In another the future great historian is lying—and doubtless will continue to lie until his earthly mission is ended. In another the future President is busying himself with no profounder problem of state than what the mischief has become of his hair so early; and in a mighty array of other cradles there are now some 60,000 future office-seekers, getting ready to furnish him occasion to grapple with that same old problem a second time. And in still one more cradle, somewhere under the flag, the future illustrious commander-in-chief of the American armies is so little burdened with his approaching grandeurs and responsibilities as to be giving his whole strategic mind at this moment to trying to find out some way to get his big toe into his mouth—an achievement which, meaning no disrespect, the illustrious guest of this evening turned *his* entire attention to some fifty-six years ago; and if the child is but a prophecy of the man, there are mighty few who will doubt that he *succeeded.* » » »

In "The Campaign That Failed,"[8] Mark Twain describes the twenty-six-year-old Sam Clemens drifting into and out of a second lieutenancy in a band of Confederate volunteers. The humor of it is much the same kind of dramatic irony that he had been experimenting with in *Tom Sawyer* and *Huckleberry Finn*. A successful author with convictions about the evils of war writes something of an apologia[9] for his brief Civil War experience, and shows what

[8] Published first in *Century Magazine*, December 1885, "A Campaign That Failed" was written in the author's best creative period. His nephew Samuel Moffett, in "Mark Twain: A Biographical Sketch" (*The Writings of Mark Twain*, Author's National Edition, XXII, 395), writes: "Brought up in a slaveholding atmosphere, Mark Twain naturally sympathized at first with the South. In June [1861] he joined the Confederates in Ralls County, Missouri, under General Tom Harris. His military career lasted two weeks. Narrowly missing the distinction of being captured by Colonel Ulysses S. Grant, he resigned, explaining that he had become 'incapacitated by fatigue' through persistent retreating. . . . The official reports and correspondence of the Confederate commanders speak very respectfully of the work of the raw countrymen of the Harris Brigade" (see also Jerry Allen's *The Adventures of Mark Twain*, 95–100). That Mark Twain's brief Civil War experience was not such an irresponsible escapade as "A Campaign That Failed" might lead the reader to infer is indicated in a letter of 1891 (*Letters*, II, 541): "I was a *soldier* two weeks once in the beginning of the war, and I was hunted like a rat the whole time. Familiar? My splendid Kipling himself hasn't a more burnt-in, hard-baked, and unforgettable unfamiliarity with that death-on-the-pale-horse-with-hell-following-after, which is a raw soldier's first fortnight in the field—and which, without any doubt, is the most tremendous fortnight and the vividest he is ever going to see."

[9] At the time the Mark Twain memorial stamp was issued (1935), the question arose in Congress whether Hartford, Connecticut, or Hannibal, Missouri, should

the pride, pomp, and circumstance of war amounted to in the case of the "Marion Rangers."[10]

THE PRIVATE HISTORY OF A CAMPAIGN THAT FAILED

« « « You have heard from a great many people who did something in the war; is it not fair and right that you listen a little moment to one who started out to do something in it, but didn't? Thousands entered the war, got just a taste of it, and then stepped out again permanently. These, by their very numbers, are respectable, and are therefore entitled to a sort of voice—not a loud one, but a modest one; not a boastful one, but an apologetic one. They ought not to be allowed much space among better people—people who did something. I grant that; but they ought at least to be allowed to state why they didn't do anything, and also to explain the process by which they didn't do anything. Surely this kind of light must have a sort of value.

Out West there was a good deal of confusion in men's minds during the first months of the great trouble—a good deal of unsettledness, of leaning first this way, then that, then the other way. It was hard for us to get our bearings. I call to mind an instance of this. I was piloting on the Mississippi when the news came that South Carolina had gone out of the Union on the 20th of December, 1860. My pilot mate was a New-Yorker. He was strong for the Union; so was I. But he would not listen to me with any patience; my loyalty was smirched, to his eye, because my father had owned slaves. I said, in palliation of this dark fact, that I had heard my father say, some years before he died, that slavery was a great wrong, and that he would free the solitary negro he then owned if he could think it right to give away the property of the

---

sell the first covers. Representative Shannon of Kansas City, in a speech which he circulated over the state, asserted heatedly that Missouri wanted none of the honor; that if Sam Clemens had not been a "slecker," he would have stayed in Missouri to fight for the Confederacy instead of running away to California.

[10] The band of "Marion Rangers" may have felt themselves to be following in the footsteps of a band of Marion County men who, in the 1840's, went forth to the Mexican War, calling themselves the "Marion Rangers." For the reader today, the real irony lies in the smiling author's regarding the inglorious episode as an amusing youthful adventure.

family when he was so straitened in means. My mate retorted that a mere impulse was nothing—anybody could pretend to a good impulse; and went on decrying my Unionism and libeling my ancestry. A month later the secession atmosphere had considerably thickened on the Lower Mississippi, and I became a rebel; so did he. We were together in New Orleans the 26th of January, when Louisiana went out of the Union. He did his full share of the rebel shouting, but was bitterly opposed to letting me do mine. He said that I came of bad stock—of a father who had been willing to set slaves free. In the following summer he was piloting a Federal gunboat and shouting for the Union again, and I was in the Confederate army. I held his note for some borrowed money. He was one of the most upright men I ever knew, but he repudiated that note without hesitation because I was a rebel and the son of a man who owned slaves.

In that summer—of 1861—the first wash of the wave of war broke upon the shores of Missouri. Our state was invaded by the Union forces. They took possession of St. Louis, Jefferson Barracks, and some other points. The Governor, Claib Jackson, issued his proclamation calling out fifty thousand militia to repel the invader.

I was visiting in the small town where my boyhood had been spent—Hannibal, Marion County. Several of us got together in a secret place by night and formed ourselves into a military company. One Tom Lyman, a young fellow of a good deal of spirit but of no military experience, was made captain; I was made second lieutenant. We had no first lieutenant; I do not know why; it was long ago. There were fifteen of us. By the advice of an innocent connected with the organization we called ourselves the Marion Rangers. I do not remember that any one found fault with the name. I did not; I thought it sounded quite well. The young fellow who proposed this title was perhaps a fair sample of the kind of stuff we were made of. He was young, ignorant, goodnatured, well-meaning, trivial, full of romance, and given to reading chivalric novels and singing forlorn love-ditties. He had some pathetic little nickel-plated aristocratic instincts, and detested his name, which was Dunlap; detested it, partly because it was nearly as common in that region as Smith, but mainly because it had a plebeian sound to his ear. So he tried to ennoble it by writing it in this way:

d'Unlap. That contented his eye, but left his ear unsatisfied, for people gave the new name the same old pronunciation—emphasis on the front end of it. He then did the bravest thing that can be imagined—a thing to make one shiver when one remembers how the world is given to resenting shams and affectations; he began to write his name so: *d'Un Lap*. And he waited patiently through the long storm of mud that was flung at this work of art, and he had his reward at last; for he lived to see that name accepted, and the emphasis put where he wanted it by the people who had known him all his life, and to whom the tribe of Dunlaps had been as familiar as the rain and the sunshine for forty years. So sure of victory at last is the courage that can wait. He said he had found, by consulting some ancient French chronicles, that the name was rightly and originally written d'Un Lap; and said that if it were translated into English it would mean Peterson: Lap, Latin or Greek, he said, for stone or rock, same as the French *pierre*, that is to say, Peter: *d'* of or from; *un*, a or one; hence d'Un Lap, of or from a stone or a Peter; that is to say, one who is the son of a stone, the son of a Peter—Peterson. Our militia company were not learned, and the explanation confused them; so they called him Peterson Dunlap. He proved useful to us in his way; he named our camps for us, and he generally struck a name that was "no slouch," as the boys said.

That is one sample of us. Another was Ed Stevens, son of the town jeweler—trim-built, handsome, graceful, neat as a cat; bright, educated, but given over entirely to fun. There was nothing serious in life to him. As far as he was concerned, this military expedition of ours was simply a holiday. I should say that about half of us looked upon it in the same way; not consciously, perhaps, but unconsciously. We did not think; we were not capable of it. As for myself, I was full of unreasoning joy to be done with turning out of bed at midnight and four in the morning for a while; grateful to have a change, new scenes, new occupations, a new interest. In my thoughts that was as far as I went; I did not go into the details; as a rule, one doesn't at twenty-four.

Another sample was Smith, the blacksmith's apprentice. This vast donkey had some pluck, of a slow and sluggish nature, but a soft heart; at one time he would knock a horse down for some impropriety, and at another he would get homesick and cry. However, he had one ultimate credit to his account which some of us hadn't; he stuck to the war, and was killed in battle at last.

Jo Bowers, another sample, was a huge, good-natured, flax-headed lubber; lazy, sentimental, full of harmless brag, a grumbler by nature; an experienced, industrious, ambitious, and often quite picturesque liar, and yet not a successful one, for he had had no intelligent training, but was allowed to come up just any way. This life was serious enough to him, and seldom satisfactory. But he was a good fellow, anyway, and the boys all liked him. He was made orderly sergeant; Stevens was made corporal.

These samples will answer—and they are quite fair ones. Well, this herd of cattle started for the war. What could you expect of them? They did as well as they knew how; but, really, what was justly to be expected of them? Nothing, I should say. That is what they did.

We waited for a dark night, for caution and secrecy were necessary; then, toward midnight, we stole in couples and from various directions to the Griffith place, beyond the town; from that point we set out together on foot. Hannibal lies at the extreme southeastern corner of Marion County, on the Mississippi River; our objective point was the hamlet of New London, ten miles away, in Ralls County.

The first hour was all fun, all idle nonsense and laughter. But that could not be kept up. The steady trudging came to be like work; the play had somehow oozed out of it; the stillness of the woods and the somberness of the night began to throw a depressing influence over the spirits of the boys, and presently the talking died out and each person shut himself up in his own thoughts. During the last half of the second hour nobody said a word.

Now we approached a log farm-house where, according to report, there was a guard of five Union soldiers. Lyman called a halt; and there, in the deep gloom of the overhanging branches, he began to whisper a plan of assault upon that house, which made the gloom more depressing than it was before. It was a crucial moment; we realized, with a cold suddenness, that here was no jest—we were standing face to face with actual war. We were equal to the occasion. In our response there was no hesitation, no indecision: we said that if Lyman wanted to meddle with those soldiers, he could go ahead and do it; but if he waited for us to follow him, he would wait a long time.

Lyman urged, pleaded, tried to shame us, but it had no effect. Our course was plain, our minds were made up: we would flank the farm-house—go out around. And that was what we did.

We struck into the woods and entered upon a rough time, stumbling over roots, getting tangled in vines, and torn by briers. At last we reached an open place in a safe region, and sat down, blown and hot, to cool off and nurse our scratches and bruises. Lyman was annoyed, but the rest of us were cheerful; we had flanked the farm-house, we had made our first military movement, and it was a success; we had nothing to fret about, we were feeling just the other way. Horse-play and laughing began again; the expedition was become a holiday frolic once more.

Then we had two more hours of dull trudging and ultimate silence and depression; then, about dawn, we straggled into New London, soiled, heel-blistered, fagged with our little march, and all of us except Stevens in a sour and raspy humor and privately down on the war. We stacked our shabby old shotguns in Colonel Ralls's barn, and then went in a body and breakfasted with that veteran of the Mexican War. Afterward he took us to a distant meadow, and there in the shade of a tree we listened to an old-fashioned speech from him, full of gunpowder and glory, full of that adjective-piling, mixed metaphor and windy declamation which were regarded as eloquence in that ancient time and that remote region; and then he swore us on the Bible to be faithful to the State of Missouri and drive all invaders from her soil, no matter whence they might come or under what flag they might march. This mixed us considerably, and we could not make out just what service we were embarked in; but Colonel Ralls, the practised politician and phrase-juggler, was not similarly in doubt; he knew quite clearly that he had invested us in the cause of the Southern Confederacy. He closed the solemnities by belting around me the sword which his neighbor, Colonel Brown, had worn at Buena Vista and Molino del Rey; and he accompanied this act with another impressive blast.

Then we formed in line of battle and marched four miles to a shady and pleasant piece of woods on the border of the far-reaching expanses of a flowery prairie. It was an enchanting region for war—our kind of war.

We pierced the forest about half a mile, and took up a strong position, with some low, rocky, and wooded hills behind us, and a purling, limpid creek in front. Straightway half the command were in swimming and the other half fishing. The ass with the French name gave this position a romantic title, but it was too long, so the boys shortened and simplified it to Camp Ralls.

We occupied an old maple-sugar camp, whose half-rotted troughs were still propped against the trees. A long corn-crib served for sleeping quarters for the battalion. On our left, half a mile away, were Mason's farm and house; and he was a friend to the cause. Shortly after noon the farmers began to arrive from several directions, with mules and horses for our use, and these they lent us for as long as the war might last, which they judged would be about three months. The animals were of all sizes, all colors, and all breeds. They were mainly young and frisky, and nobody in the command could stay on them long at a time; for we were town boys, and ignorant of horsemanship. The creature that fell to my share was a very small mule, and yet so quick and active that it could throw me without difficulty; and it did this whenever I got on it. Then it would bray—stretching its neck out, laying its ears back, and spreading its jaws till you could see down to its works. It was a disagreeable animal in every way. If I took it by the bridle and tried to lead it off the grounds, it would sit down and brace back, and no one could budge it. However, I was not entirely destitute of military resources, and I did presently manage to spoil this game; for I had seen many a steamboat aground in my time, and knew a trick or two which even a grounded mule would be obliged to respect. There was a well by the corn-crib; so I substituted thirty fathom of rope for the bridle, and fetched him home with the windlass.

I will anticipate here sufficiently to say that we did learn to ride, after some days' practice, but never well. We could not learn to like our animals; they were not choice ones, and most of them had annoying peculiarities of one kind or another. Stevens's horse would carry him, when he was not noticing, under the huge excrescences which form on the trunks of oak-trees, and wipe him out of the saddle; in this way Stevens got several bad hurts. Sergeant Bowers's horse was very large and tall, with slim, long legs, and looked like a railroad bridge. His size enabled him to reach all about, and as far as he wanted to, with his head; so he was always biting Bowers's legs. On the march, in the sun, Bowers slept a good deal; and as soon as the horse recognized that he was asleep he would reach around and bit him on the leg. His legs were black and blue with bites. This was the only thing that could ever make him swear, but this always did; whenever his horse bit him he always swore, and of course Stevens, who laughed at everything, laughed at this, and would even get into such convulsions over it as to lose his balance and fall off his horse; and then Bowers, already irritated by the pain of the horse-bite, would resent the laughter with hard language, and there would be a quarrel; so that horse made no end of trouble and bad blood in the command.

However, I will get back to where I was—our first afternoon in the sugarcamp. The sugar-troughs came very handy as horse-troughs, and we had plenty of corn to fill them with. I ordered Sergeant Bowers to feed my mule; but he said that if I reckoned he went to war to be a dry-nurse to a mule it wouldn't take me very long to find out my mistake. I believed that this was insubordination, but I was full of uncertainties about everything military, and so I let the thing pass, and went and ordered Smith, the blacksmith's apprentice, to feed the mule; but he merely gave me a large, cold, sarcastic grin, such as an ostensibly seven-year-old horse gives you when you lift his lip and find he is fourteen, and turned his back on me. I then went to the captain, and asked if it were not right and proper and military for me to have an orderly. He said it was, but as there was only one orderly in the corps, it was but right that he himself should have Bowers on his staff. Bowers said he wouldn't serve on anybody's staff; and if anybody thought he could make him, let him try it. So, of course, the thing had to be dropped; there was no other way.

Next, nobody would cook; it was considered a degradation; so we had no dinner. We lazied the rest of the pleasant afternoon away, some dozing under the trees, some smoking cob-pipes and talking sweethearts and war, some playing games. By late supper-time all hands were famished; and to meet the difficulty all hands turned to, on an equal footing, and gathered wood, built fires, and cooked the meal. Afterward everything was smooth for a while; then trouble broke out between the corporal and the sergeant, each claiming to rank the other. Nobody knew which was the higher office; so Lyman had to settle the matter by making the rank of both officers equal. The commander of an ignorant crew like that has many troubles and vexations which probably do not occur in the regular army at all. However, with the song-singing and yarn-spinning around the camp-fire, everything presently became serene again; and by and by we raked the corn down level in one end of the crib, and all went to bed on it, tying a horse to the door, so that he would neigh if any one tried to get in.*

We had some horsemanship drill every forenoon; then, afternoons, we rode off here and there in squads a few miles, and visited the farmers' girls, and had a youthful good time, and got an honest good dinner or supper, and then home again to camp, happy and content.

For a time life was idly delicious, it was perfect; there was nothing to mar it. Then came some farmers with an alarm one day. They said it was rumored that the enemy were advancing in our direction from over Hyde's prairie. The result was a sharp stir among us, and general consternation. It was a rude awakening from our pleasant trance. The rumor was but a rumor—nothing definite about it; so, in the confusion, we did not know which way to retreat. Lyman was for not retreating at all in these uncertain circumstances; but he found that if he tried to maintain that attitude he would fare badly, for the command were in no humor to put up with insubordination. So he yielded the point and called a council of war—to consist of himself and the three other officers; but the privates made such a fuss about being left out that we had to allow them to remain, for they were already present, and doing

---

* It was always my impression that that was what the horse was there for, and I know that it was also the impression of at least one other of the command, for we talked about it at the time, and admired the military ingenuity of the device; but when I was out West, three years ago, I was told by Mr. A. G. Fuqua, a member of our company, that the horse was his; that the leaving of him tied at the door was a matter of mere forgetfulness, and that to attribute it to intelligent invention was to give him quite too much credit. In support of his position he called my attention to the suggestive fact that the artifice was not employed again. I had not thought of that before.—Mark Twain's footnote.

the most of the talking too. The question was, which way to retreat; but all were so flurried that nobody seemed to have even a guess to offer. Except Lyman. He explained in a few calm words that, inasmuch as the enemy were approaching from over Hyde's prairie, our course was simple: all we had to do was not to retreat *toward* him; any other direction would answer our needs perfectly. Everybody saw in a moment how true this was, and how wise; so Lyman got a great many compliments. It was now decided that we should fall back on Mason's farm.

It was after dark by this time, and as we could not know how soon the enemy might arrive, it did not seem best to try to take the horses and things with us; so we only took the guns and ammunition, and started at once. The route was very rough and hilly and rocky, and presently the night grew very black and rain began to fall; so we had a troublesome time of it, struggling and stumbling along in the dark; and soon some person slipped and fell, and then the next person behind stumbled over him and fell, and so did the rest, one after the other; and then Bowers came, with the keg of powder in his arms, while the command were all mixed together, arms and legs, on the muddy slope; and so he fell, of course, with the keg, and this started the whole detachment down the hill in a body, and they landed in the brook at the bottom in a pile, and each that was undermost pulling the hair and scratching and biting those that were on top of him; and those that were being scratched and bitten scratching and biting the rest in their turn, and all saying they would die before they would ever go to war again if they ever got out of this brook this time, and the invader might rot for all they cared, and the country along with him—and all such talk as that, which was dismal to hear and take part in, in such smothered, low voices, and such a grisly dark place and so wet, and the enemy, maybe, coming any moment.

The keg of powder was lost, and the guns, too; so the growling and complaining continued straight along while the brigade pawed around the pasty hillside and slopped around in the brook hunting for these things; consequently we lost considerable time at this; and then we heard a sound, and held our breath and listened, and it seemed to be the enemy coming, though it could have been a cow, for it had a cough like a cow; but we did not wait, but left a couple of guns behind and struck out for Mason's again as briskly as we could scramble along in the dark. But we got lost presently among the rugged little ravines, and wasted a deal of time finding the way again, so it was after nine when we reached Mason's stile at last; and then before we could open our mouths to give the countersign several dogs came bounding over the fence, with great riot and noise, and each of them took a soldier by the slack of his trousers and began to back away with him. We could not shoot the dogs without endangering the persons they were attached to; so we had to look on helpless at what was perhaps the most mortifying spectacle of the Civil War. There was light enough, and to spare, for the Masons had now run out on the porch with candles in their hands. The old man and his son came and undid the dogs without difficulty, all but Bowers's; but they couldn't undo his dog, they didn't know his combination; he was of the bull kind, and seemed to be set with a Yale time-lock; but they got him loose at last with some scalding water, of which Bowers got his share and returned thanks. Peterson Dunlap afterward made up a fine name for this engagement, and also for the night march which preceded it, but both have long ago faded out of my memory.

We now went into the house, and they began to ask us a world of questions, whereby it presently came out that we did not know anything concerning who or what we were running from; so the old gentleman made himself very frank, and said we were a curious breed of soldiers, and guessed we could be depended on to end up the war in time, because no government could stand the expense of the shoe-leather we should cost it trying to follow us around. "Marion *Rangers!* good name, b'gosh!" said he. And he wanted to know why we hadn't had a picket-guard at the place where the road entered the prairie, and why we hadn't sent out a scouting party to spy out the enemy and bring us an account of his strength, and so on, before jumping up and stampeding out of a strong position upon a mere vague rumor—and so on, and so forth, till he made us all feel shabbier than the dogs had done, not half so enthusiastically welcome. So we went to bed shamed and low-spirited; except Stevens. Soon Stevens began to devise a garment for Bowers which could be made to automatically display his battle-scars to the grateful, or conceal them from the envious, according to his occasions; but Bowers was in no humor for this, so there was a fight, and when it was over Stevens had some battle-scars of his own to think about.

Then we got a little sleep. But after all we had gone through, our activities were not over for the night; for about two o'clock in the morning we heard a shout of warning from down the lane, accompanied by a chorus from all the dogs, and in a moment everybody was up and flying around to find out what the alarm was about. The alarmist was a horseman who gave notice that a detachment of Union soldiers was on its way from Hannibal with orders to capture and hang any bands like ours which it could find, and said we had no time to lose. Farmer Mason was in a flurry this time himself. He hurried us out of the house with all haste, and sent one of his negroes with us to show us where to hide ourselves and our telltale guns among the ravines half a mile away. It was raining heavily.

We struck down the lane, then across some rocky pasture-land which offered good advantages for stumbling; consequently we were down in the mud most of the time, and every time a man went down he blackguarded the war, and the people that started it, and everybody connected with it, and gave himself the master dose of all for being so foolish as to go into it. At last we reached the wooded mouth of a ravine, and there we huddled ourselves under the streaming trees, and sent the negro back home. It was a dismal and heart-breaking time. We were like to be drowned with the rain, deafened with the howling wind and the booming thunder, and blinded by the lightning. It was, indeed, a wild night. The drenching we were getting was misery enough, but a deeper misery still was the reflection that the halter might end us before we were a day older. A death of this shameful sort had not occurred to us as being among the possibilities of war. It took the romance all out of the campaign, and turned our dreams of glory into a repulsive nightmare. As for doubting that so barbarous an order had been given, not one of us did that.

The long night wore itself out at last, and then the negro came to us with the news that the alarm had manifestly been a false one, and that breakfast would soon be ready. Straightaway we were light-hearted again, and the world was bright, and life as full of hope and promise as ever—for we were young then. How long ago that was! Twenty-four years.

The mongrel child of philology named the night's refuge Camp Devastation, and no soul objected. The Masons gave us a Missouri country breakfast, in Missourian abundance, and we needed it: hot biscuits; hot "wheatbread," prettily criss-crossed in a lattice pattern on top; hot corn-pone; fried chicken; bacon, coffee, eggs, milk, buttermilk, etc.; and the world may be confidently challenged to furnish the equal of such a breakfast, as it is cooked in the South.

We stayed several days at Mason's; and after all these years the memory of the dullness, and stillness, and lifelessness of that slumberous farm-house still oppresses my spirit as with a sense of the presence of death and mourning. There was nothing to do, nothing to think about; there was no interest in life. The male part of the household were away in the fields all day, the women were busy and out of our sight; there was no sound but the plaintive wailing of a spinning-wheel, forever moaning out from some distant room— the most lonesome sound in nature, a sound steeped and sodden with homesickness and the emptiness of life. The family went to bed about dark every night, and as we were not invited to intrude any new customs we naturally followed theirs. Those nights were a hundred years long to youths accustomed to being up till twelve. We lay awake and miserable till that hour every time, and grew old and decrepit waiting through the still eternities for the clock-strikes. This was no place for town boys. So at last it was with something very like joy that we received news that the enemy were on our track again. With a new birth of the old warrior spirit we sprang to our places in line of battle and fell back on Camp Ralls.

Captain Lyman had taken a hint from Mason's talk, and he now gave orders that our camp should be guarded against surprise by the posting of pickets. I was ordered to place a picket at the forks of the road in Hyde's prairie. Night shut down black and threatening. I told Sergeant Bowers to go out to that place and stay till midnight; and, just as I was expecting, he said he wouldn't do it. I tried to get others to go, but all refused. Some excused themselves on account of the weather; but the rest were frank enough to say they wouldn't go in any kind of weather. This kind of thing sounds odd now, and impossible, but there was no surprise in it at the time.

On the contrary, it seemed a perfectly natural thing to do. There were scores of little camps scattered over Missouri where the same thing was happening. These camps were composed of young men who had been born and reared to a sturdy independence, and who did not know what it meant to be ordered about by Tom, Dick, and Harry, whom they had known familiarly all their lives, in the village or on the farm. It is quite within the probabilities that this same thing was happening all over the South. James Redpath recognized the justice of this assumption, and furnished the following instance in support of it. During a short stay in East Tennessee he was in a citizen colonel's tent one day talking, when a big private appeared at the door, and, without salute or other circumlocution, said to the colonel:

"Say, Jim, I'm a-goin' home for a few days."

"What for?"

"Well, I hain't b'en there for a right smart while, and I'd like to see how things is comin' on."

"How long are you going to be gone?"

" 'Bout two weeks."

"Well, don't be gone longer than that; and get back sooner if you can."

That was all, and the citizen officer resumed his conversation where the private had broken it off. This was in the first months of the war, of course. The camps in our part of Missouri were under Brigadier-General Thomas H. Harris. He was a townsman of ours, a first-rate fellow, and well liked; but we had all familiarly known him as the sole and modest-salaried operator in our telegraph-office, where he had to send about one despatch a week in ordinary times, and two when there was a rush of business; consequently, when he appeared in our midst one day, on the wing, and delivered a military command of some sort, in a large military fashion, nobody was surprised at the response which he got from the assembled soldiery:

"Oh, now, what'll you take to *don't*, Tom Harris?"

It was quite the natural thing. One might justly imagine that we were hopeless material for war. And so we seemed, in our ignorant state; but there were those among us who afterward learned the grim trade; learned to obey like machines; became valuable soldiers, fought all through the war, and came out at the end with excellent records. One of the very boys who refused to go out on picket duty that night, and called me an ass for thinking he would expose himself to danger in such a foolhardy way, had become distinguished for intrepidity before he was a year older.

I did secure my picket that night—not by authority, but by diplomacy. I got Bowers to go by agreeing to exchange ranks with him for the time being, and go along and stand the watch with him as his subordinate. We stayed out there a couple of dreary hours in the pitchy darkness and the rain, with nothing to modify the dreariness but Bowers's monotonous growlings at the war and the weather; then we began to nod, and presently found it next to impossible to stay in the saddle; so we gave up the tedious job, and went back to the camp without waiting for the relief guard. We rode into camp without interruption or objection from anybody, and the enemy could have done the same, for there were no sentries. Everybody was asleep; at midnight there was nobody to send out another picket, so none was sent. We never tried to establish a watch at night again, as far as I remember, but we generally kept a picket out in the daytime.

In that camp the whole command slept on the corn in the big corn-crib; and there was usually a general row before morning, for the place was full of rats, and they would scramble over the boys' bodies and faces, annoying and irritating everybody; and now and then they would bite some one's toe, and the person who owned the toe would start up and magnify his English and begin to throw corn in the dark. The ears were half as heavy as bricks, and when they struck they hurt. The persons struck would respond, and inside of five minutes every man would be locked in a death-grip with his neighbor. There was a grievous deal of blood shed in the corn-crib, but this was all that was spilt while I was in the war. No, that is not quite true. But for one circumstance it would have been all. I will come to that now.

Our scares were frequent. Every few days rumors would come that the enemy were approaching. In these cases we always fell back on some other camp of ours; we never stayed where we were. But the rumors always turned out to be false; so at last even we began to grow indifferent to them. One night a negro was sent to our corn-crib with the same old warning; the enemy was hovering in our neighborhood. We all said let him hover. We resolved to stay still and be comfortable. It was a fine war-like resolution, and no doubt we all felt the stir of it in our veins—for a moment. We had been having a very jolly time, that was full of horse-play and school-boy hilarity; but that cooled down now, and presently the fast-waning fire of forced jokes and forced laughs died out altogether, and the company became silent. Silent and nervous. And soon uneasy—worried—apprehensive. We had said we would stay, and we were committed. We could have been persuaded to go, but there was nobody brave enough to suggest it. An almost noiseless movement presently began in the dark by a general but unvoiced impulse. When the movement was completed each man knew that he was not the only person who had crept to the front wall and had his eye at a crack between the logs. No, we were all there; all there with our hearts in our throats, and staring out toward the sugar-troughs where the forest footpath came through. It was late, and there was a deep woodsy stillness everywhere. There was a veiled moonlight, which was only just strong enough to enable us to mark the general shape of objects. Presently a muffled sound caught our ears, and we recognized it as the hoofbeats of a horse or horses. And right away a figure appeared in the forest path; it could have been made of smoke, its mass had so little sharpness of outline. It was a man on horseback, and it seemed to me that there were others behind him. I got hold of a gun in the dark, and pushed it through a crack between the logs, hardly knowing what I was doing, I was so dazed with fright. Somebody said "Fire!" I pulled the trigger. I seemed to see a hundred flashes and hear a hundred reports; then I saw the man fall down out of the saddle. My first feeling was of surprised gratification; my first impulse was an apprentice-sportsman's impulse to run and pick up his game. Somebody said, hardly audible, "Good—we've got him!—wait for the rest." But the rest did not come. We waited—listened—still no more came. There was not a sound, not the whisper of a leaf; just perfect stillness; an uncanny kind of stillness, which was all the more uncanny on account of the damp, earthy, late-night smells now rising and pervading it. Then, wondering, we crept stealthily out, and approached the man. When we got to him the moon revealed him distinctly. He was lying on his back, with his arms abroad; his mouth was open and his chest heaving with long gasps, and his white shirtfront was all splashed with blood. The thought shot through me that I was a murderer; that I had killed a man—a man who had never done me any harm. That was the coldest sensation that ever went through my marrow. I was down by him in a moment, helplessly stroking his forehead; and I would have given anything then—my own life freely—to make him again what he had been five minutes before. And all the boys seemed to be feeling in the same way; they hung over him, full of pitying interest, and tried all they could to help him, and said all sorts of regretful things. They had forgotten all about the enemy; they thought only of this one forlorn unit of the foe. Once my imagination persuaded me that the dying man gave me a reproachful look out of his shadowy eyes, and it seemed to me that I could rather he had stabbed me than done that. He muttered and mumbled like a dreamer in his sleep about his wife and his child; and I thought with a new despair, "This thing that I have done does not end with him; it falls upon *them* too, and they never did me any harm, any more than he."

In a little while the man was dead. He was killed in war; killed in fair and legitimate war; killed in battle, as you may say; and yet he was as sincerely mourned by the opposing force as if he had been their brother. The boys stood there a half-hour sorrowing over him, and recalling the details of the tragedy, and wondering who he might be, and if he were a spy, and saying that if it were to do over again they would not hurt him unless he attacked them first. It soon came out that mine was not the only shot fired; there were five others—a division of the guilt which was a great relief to me, since it in some degree lightened and diminished the burden I was carrying. There were six shots fired at once; but I was not in my right mind at the time, and my heated imagination had magnified my one shot into a volley.

The man was not in uniform, and was not armed. He was a stranger in the country; that was all we over found out about him. The thought of him got to preying upon me every night; I could not get rid of it. I could not drive it away, the taking of that unoffending life seemed such a wanton thing. And it seemed an epitome of war; that all war must be just that—the killing of strangers against whom you feel no personal animosity; strangers whom, in other circumstances, you would help if you found them in trouble, and who would help you if you needed it. My campaign was spoiled. It seemed to me that I was not rightly equipped for this awful business; that war was intended for men, and I for a child's nurse. I resolved to retire from this avocation of sham soldiership while I could save some remnant of my self-respect. These morbid thoughts clung to me against reason; for at bottom I did not believe I had touched that man. The law of probabilities decreed me guiltless of his blood; for in all my small experience with guns I had never hit anything I had tried to hit, and I knew I had done my best to hit him. Yet there was no solace in the thought. Against a diseased imagination demonstration goes for nothing.

The rest of my war experience was of a piece with what I have already told of it. We kept monotonously falling back upon one camp or another, and eating up the farmers and their families. They ought to have shot us; on the contrary, they were as hospitably kind and courteous to us as if we had deserved it. In one of these camps we found Ab Grimes, an Upper Mississippi pilot, who afterward became famous as a dare-devil rebel spy, whose career bristled with desperate adventures. The look and style of his comrades suggested that they had not come into the war to play, and their deeds made good the conjecture later. They were fine horsemen and good revolver shots; but their favorite arm was the lasso. Each had one at his pommel, and could snatch a man out of the saddle with it every time, on a full gallop, at any reasonable distance.

In another camp the chief was a fierce and profane old blacksmith of sixty, and he had furnished his twenty recruits with gigantic home-made bowieknives, to be swung with two hands, like the *machetes* of the Isthmus. It was a grisly spectacle to see that earnest band practising their murderous cuts and slashes under the eye of that remorseless old fanatic.

The last camp which we fell back upon was in a hollow near the village of Florida, where I was born—in Monroe County. Here we were warned one day that a Union colonel was sweeping down on us with a whole regiment at his heel. This looked decidedly serious. Our boys went apart and consulted; then we went back and told the other companies present that the war was a disappointment to us, and we were going to disband. They were getting ready themselves to fall back on some place or other, and we were only waiting for General Tom Harris, who was expected to arrive at any moment; so they tried to persuade us to wait a little while, but the majority of us said no, we were accustomed to falling back, and didn't need any of Tom Harris's help; we could get along perfectly well without him—and save time, too. So about half of our fifteen, including myself, mounted and left on the instant; the others yielded to persuasion and stayed—stayed through the war.

An hour later we met General Harris on the road, with two or three people in his company—his staff, probably, but we could not tell; none of them were in uniform; uniforms had not come into vogue among us yet. Harris ordered us back; but we told him there was a Union colonel coming with a whole regiment in his wake, and it looked as if there was going to be a disturbance; so we had concluded to go home. He raged a little, but it was of no use; our minds were made up. We had done our share; had killed one man, exterminated one army, such as it was; let him go and kill the rest, and that would end the war. I did not see that brisk young general again until last year; then he was wearing white hair and whiskers.

In time I came to know that Union colonel whose coming frightened me out of the war and crippled the Southern cause to that extent—General Grant. I came within a few hours of seeing him when he was as unknown as I was myself; at a time when anybody could have said, "Grant—Ulysses S. Grant? I do not remember hearing the name before." It seems difficult to realize that there was once a time when such a remark could be rationally made; but there *was*, and I was within a few miles of the place and the occasion, too, though proceeding in the other direction.

The thoughtful will not throw this war paper of mine lightly aside as being valueless. It has this value: it is a not unfair picture of what went on in many and many a militia camp in the first months of the rebellion, when the green recruits were without discipline, without the steadying and heartening influence of trained leaders; when all their circumstances were new and strange, and charged with exaggerated terrors, and before the invaluable experience of actual collision in the field had turned them from rabbits into soldiers. If this side of the picture of that early day has not before been put into history, then history has been to that degree incomplete, for it had and has its rightful place there. There was more Bull Run material scattered through the early camps of this country than exhibited itself at Bull Run. And yet it learned its trade presently, and helped to fight the great battles later. I could have become a soldier myself if I had waited. I had got part of it learned; I knew more about retreating than the man that invented retreating. » » »

In "The Facts Concerning the Recent Carnival of Crime in Connecticut" Mark Twain indulges in drollery at the expense of his tormenting conscience, which he treats as his alter ego declaring its independence. Writing of the experiment twenty years later, however, and comparing it with *Dr. Jekyll and Mr. Hyde,* he says that conscience is "a mere machine; the creature of *training;* it is whatever one's mother, and Bible, and comrades, and laws, and system of government, and habitat and heredities have made it. It is not a separate person, it has no originality, no independence."[11] The allegory or apologue was a favorite literary form of the author's, employed here, he said, to set forth "an exasperating metaphysical question in the guise of a literary extravaganza."[12]

[11] See *Notebook,* 348–50. In his *Autobiography,* II, 8–9, Mark Twain says it is a lie "that conscience, man's moral medicine chest, is not only created by the Creator, but is put into man ready charged with the right and only true and authentic correctives of conduct—and the duplicate chest, with the self-same correctives, unchanged, unmodified, distributed to all nations and all epochs."

[12] "The Facts Concerning the Recent Carnival of Crime in Connecticut" was written to be read at the Monday Club in Hartford in January, 1876. In a letter to his friend Howells, dated January 11, 1876 (*Letters,* I, 271), Mark Twain says that he has been working on "an *Atlantic* article . . . less than two days' work [but] I have spent three more days trimming, altering and working at it. I shall put in one more day's work polishing on it, and then read it before our club. . . . I think it will bring out considerable discussion among the gentlemen of the club—though the title of the article will not give them much notion of what is to follow . . . 'The Facts Concerning the Recent Carnival of Crime in Connecticut.'" In a letter to Howells a week later he urges his friend to "hear the club toot their horns over the exasperating metaphysical question which I mean to lay before them in the disguise of a literary extravaganza; it would brace you up like a cordial."

THE FACTS CONCERNING THE RECENT CARNIVAL OF CRIME IN CONNECTICUT

« « « I was feeling blithe, almost jocund. I put a match to my cigar, and just then the morning's mail was handed in. The first superscription I glanced at was in a handwriting that sent a thrill of pleasure through and through me. It was Aunt Mary's; and she was the person I loved and honored most in all the world, outside of my own household. She had been my boyhood's idol; maturity, which is fatal to so many enchantments, had not been able to dislodge her from her pedestal; no, it had only justified her right to be there, and placed her dethronement permanently among the impossibilities. To show how strong her influence over me was, I will observe that long after everybody else's "*do*-stop-smoking" had ceased to affect me in the slightest degree, Aunt Mary could still stir my torpid conscience into faint signs of life when she touched upon the matter. But all things have their limit in this world. A happy day came at last, when even Aunt Mary's words could no longer move me. I was not merely glad to see that day arrive; I was more than glad—I was grateful; for when its sun had set, the one alloy that was able to mar my enjoyment of my aunt's society was gone. The remainder of her stay with us that winter was in every way a delight. Of course she pleaded with me just as earnestly as ever, after that blessed day, to quit my pernicious habit, but to no purpose whatever; the moment she opened the subject I at once became calmly, peacefully, contentedly indifferent—absolutely, adamantinely indifferent. Consequently the closing weeks of that memorable visit melted away as pleasantly as a dream, they were so freighted for me with tranquil satisfaction. I could not have enjoyed my pet vice more if my gentle tormentor had been a smoker herself, and an advocate of the practice. Well, the sight of her handwriting reminded me that I was getting very hungry to see her again. I easily guessed what I should find in her letter. I opened it. Good! just as I expected; she was coming! Coming this very day, too, and by the morning train; I might expect her any moment.

I said to myself, "I am thoroughly happy and content now. If my most pitiless enemy could appear before me at this moment, I would freely right any wrong I may have done him."

Straightway the door opened, and a shriveled, shabby dwarf entered. He was not more than two feet high. He seemed to be about forty years old. Every feature and every inch of him was a trifle out of shape; and so, while one could not put his finger upon any particular part and say, "This is a conspicuous deformity," the spectator perceived that this little person was a deformity as a whole—a vague, generally, evenly blended, nicely adjusted deformity. There was a fox-like cunning in the face and the sharp little eyes, and also alertness and malice. And yet, this vile bit of human rubbish seemed to bear a sort of remote and ill-defined resemblance to me! It was dully perceptible in the mean form, the countenance, and even the clothes, gestures, manner, and attitudes of the creature. He was a far-fetched, dim suggestion of a burlesque upon me, a caricature of me in little. One thing about him struck me forcibly and most unpleasantly: he was covered all over with a fuzzy, greenish mold, such as one sometimes sees upon mildewed bread. The sight of it was nauseating.

He stepped along with a chipper air, and flung himself into a doll's chair in a very free-and-easy way, without waiting to be asked. He tossed his hat into the waste-basket. He picked up my old chalk pipe from the floor, gave the stem a wipe or two on his knee, filled the bowl from the tobacco-box at his side, and said to me in a tone of pert command:

"Gimme a match!"

I blushed to the roots of my hair; partly with indignation, but mainly because it somehow seemed to me that this whole performance was very like an exaggeration of conduct which I myself had sometimes been guilty of in my intercourse with familiar friends—but never, never with strangers, I observed to myself. I wanted to kick the pygmy into the fire, but some incomprehensible sense of being legally and legitimately under his authority forced me to obey his order. He applied the match to the pipe, took a contemplative whiff or two, and remarked, in an irritatingly familiar way:

"Seems to me it's devilish odd weather for this time of year."

I flushed again, and in anger and humiliation as before; for the language was hardly an exaggeration of some that I have uttered in my day, and moreover was delivered in a tone of voice and with an exasperating drawl that had the seeming of a deliberate travesty of my style. Now there is nothing I am quite so sensitive about as a mocking imitation of my drawling infirmity of speech. I spoke up sharply and said:

"Look here, you miserable ash-cat! you will have to give a little more attention to your manners, or I will throw you out of the window!"

The manikin smiled a smile of malicious content and security, puffed a whiff of smoke contemptuously toward me, and said, with a still more elaborate drawl:

"Come—go gently now; don't put on *too* many airs with your betters."

This cool snub rasped me all over, but it seemed to subjugate me, too, for a moment. The pygmy contemplated me awhile with his weasel eyes, and then said, in a peculiarly sneering way: "You turned a tramp away from your door this morning."

I said crustily:

"Perhaps I did, perhaps I didn't. How do *you* know?"

"Well, I know. It isn't any matter *how* I know."

"Very well. Suppose I *did* turn a tramp away from the door—what of it?"

"Oh, nothing; nothing in particular. Only you lied to him."

"I *didn't!* That is, I——"

"Yes, but you did; you lied to him."

I felt a guilty pang—in truth, I had felt it forty times before that tramp had traveled a block from my door—but still I resolved to make a show of feeling slandered; so I said:

"This is a baseless impertinence. I said to the tramp—"

"There—wait. You were about to lie again. *I* know what you said to him. You said the cook was gone down-town and there was nothing left from breakfast. Two lies. You knew the cook was behind the door, and plenty of provisions behind *her*."

This astonishing accuracy silenced me; and it filled me with wondering speculations, too, as to how this cub could have got his information. Of course he could have culled the conversation from the tramp, but by what sort of magic had he contrived to find out about the concealed cook? Now the dwarf spoke again:

"It was rather pitiful, rather small, in you to refuse to read that poor young woman's manuscript the other day, and give her an opinion as to its literary value; and she had come so far, too, and *so* hopefully. Now *wasn't* it?"

I felt like a cur! And I had felt so every time the thing had recurred to my mind, I may as well confess. I flushed hotly and said:

"Look here, have you nothing better to do than prowl around prying into other people's business? Did that girl tell you that?"

"Never mind whether she did or not. The main thing is, you did that contemptible thing. And you felt ashamed of it afterward. Aha! you feel ashamed of it *now!*"

This was a sort of devilish glee. With fiery earnestness I responded:

"I told that girl, in the kindest, gentlest way, that I could not consent to deliver judgment upon *any* one's manuscript, because an individual's verdict was worthless. It might underrate a work of high merit and lose it to the world, or it might overrate a trashy production and so open the way for its infliction upon the world. I said that the great public was the only tribunal competent to sit in judgment upon a literary effort, and therefore it must be best to lay it before that tribunal in the outset, since in the end it must stand or fall by that mighty court's decision anyway."

"Yes, you said all that. So you did, you juggling, small-souled shuffler! And yet when the happy hopefulness faded out of that poor girl's face, when you saw her furtively slip beneath her shawl the scroll she had so patiently and honestly scribbled at—so ashamed of her darling now, so proud of it before—when you saw the gladness go out of her eyes and the tears come there, when she crept away so humbly who had come so——"

"Oh, peace! peace! peace! Blister your merciless tongue, haven't all these thoughts tortured me enough without *your* coming here to fetch them back again!"

Remorse! Remorse! It seemed to me that it would eat the very heart out of me! And yet that small fiend only sat there leering at me with joy and contempt, and placidly chuckling. Presently he began to speak again. Every sentence was an accusation, and every accusation a truth. Every clause was freighted with sarcasm and derision, every slow-dropping word burned like vitriol. The dwarf reminded me of times when I had flown at my children in anger and punished them for faults which a little inquiry would have taught me that others, and not they, had committed. He reminded me of how I had disloyally allowed old friends to be traduced in my hearing, and been too craven to utter a word in their defense. He reminded me of many dishonest things which I had done; of many which I had procured to be done by children and other irresponsible persons; of some which I had planned, thought upon, and longed to do, and been kept from the performance by fear of consequences only. With exquisite cruelty he recalled to my mind, item by item, wrongs and unkindnesses I had inflicted and humiliations I had put upon friends since dead, "who died thinking of those injuries, maybe, and grieving over them," he added, by way of poison to the stab.

"For instance," said he, "take the case of your younger brother, when you two were boys together, many a long year ago. He always lovingly trusted in you with a fidelity that your manifold treacheries were not able to shake. He followed you about like a dog, content to suffer wrong and abuse if he might only be with you; patient under these injuries so long as it was your hand that inflicted them. The latest picture you have of him in health and strength must be such a comfort to you! You pledged your honor that if he would let you blindfold him no harm should come to him; and then, giggling and choking over the rare fun of the joke, you led him to a brook thinly glazed with ice, and pushed him in; and how you did laugh! Man, you will never forget the gentle, reproachful look he gave you as he struggled shivering out, if you live a thousand years! Oho! you see it now, you see it *now!*"

"Beast, I have seen it a million times, and shall see it a million more! and may you rot away piecemeal, and suffer till doomsday what I suffer now, for bringing it back to me again!"

The dwarf chuckled contentedly, and went on with his accusing history of my career. I dropped into a moody, vengeful state, and suffered in silence under the merciless lash. At last this remark of his gave me a sudden rouse:

"Two months ago, on a Tuesday, you woke up, away in the night, and fell to thinking, with shame, about a peculiarly mean and pitiful act of yours toward a poor ignorant Indian in the wilds of the Rocky Mountains in the winter of eighteen hundred and—"

"Stop a moment, devil! Stop! Do you mean to tell me that even my very *thoughts* are not hidden from you?"

"It seems to look like that. Didn't you think the thoughts I have just mentioned?"

"If I didn't, I wish I may never breathe again! Look here, friend—look me in the eye. Who *are* you?"

"Well, who do you think?"

"I think you are Satan himself. I think you are the devil."

"No."

"No? Then who *can* you be?"

"Would you really like to know?"

"*Indeed* I would."

"Well, I am your *Conscience!*"

In an instant I was in a blaze of joy and exultation. I sprang at the creature, roaring:

"Curse you. I have wished a hundred million times that you were tangible, and that I could get my hands on your throat once! Oh, but I will wreak a deadly vengeance on——"

Folly! Lightning does not move more quickly than my Conscience did! He darted aloft so suddenly that in the moment my fingers clutched the empty air he was already perched on the top of the high bookcase, with his thumb at his nose in token of derision. I flung the poker at him, and missed. I fired the bootjack. In a blind rage I flew from place to place, and snatched and hurled any missile that came handy; the storm of books, inkstands, and chunks of coal gloomed the air and beat about the manikin's perch relentlessly, but all to no purpose; the nimble figure dodged every shot; and not only that, but burst into a cackle of sarcastic and triumphant laughter as I sat down exhausted. While I puffed and gasped with fatigue and excitement, my Conscience talked to this effect:

"My good slave, you are curiously witless—no, I mean characteristically so. In truth, you are always consistent, always yourself, always an ass. Otherwise it must have occurred to you that if you attempted this murder with a sad heart and a heavy conscience, I would droop under the burdening influence instantly. Fool, I should have weighed a ton, and could not have budged from the floor; but instead, you are so cheerfully anxious to kill me that your conscience is as light as a feather; hence I am away up here out of your reach. I can almost respect a mere ordinary sort of fool; but *you*—pah!"

I would have given anything, then, to be heavy-hearted, so that I could get this person down from there and take his life, but I could no more be heavy-hearted over such a desire than I could have sorrowed over its accomplishment. So I could only look longingly up at my master, and rave at the ill luck that denied me a heavy conscience the one only time that I had ever wanted such a thing in my life. By and by I got to musing over the hour's strange adventure, and of course my human curiosity began to work. I set myself to framing in my mind some questions for this fiend to answer. Just then one of my boys entered, leaving the door open behind him, and exclaimed:

"My! what *has* been going on here? The bookcase is all one riddle of——"

I sprang up in consternation, and shouted:

"Out of this! Hurry! Jump! Fly! Shut the door! Quick, or my Conscience will get away!"

The door slammed to, and I locked it. I glanced up and was grateful, to the bottom of my heart, to see that my owner was still my prisoner. I said:

"Hang you, I might have lost you! Children are the heedlessest creatures. But look here, friend, the boy did not seem to notice you at all; how is that?"

"For a very good reason. I am invisible to all but you."

I made a mental note of that piece of information with a good deal of satisfaction. I could kill this miscreant now, if I got a chance, and no one would know it. But this very reflection made me so light-hearted that my Conscience could hardly keep his seat, but was like to float aloft toward the ceiling like a toy balloon. I said, presently:

"Come, my Conscience, let us be friendly. Let us fly a flag of truce for a while. I am suffering to ask you some questions."

"Very well. Begin."

"Well, then, in the first place, why were you never visible to me before?"

"Because you never asked to see me before; that is, you never asked in the right spirit and the proper form before. You were just in the right spirit this time, and when you called for your most pitiless enemy I was that person by a very large majority, though you did not suspect it."

"Well, did that remark of mine turn you into flesh and blood?"

"No. It only made me visible to you. I am unsubstantial, just as other spirits are."

This remark prodded me with a sharp misgiving. If he was unsubstantial, how was I going to kill him? But I dissembled, and said persuasively:

"Conscience, it isn't sociable of you to keep at such a distance. Come down and take another smoke."

This was answered with a look that was full of derision, and with this observation added:

"Come where you can get at me and kill me? The invitation is declined with thanks."

"All right," said I to myself; "so it seems a spirit *can* be killed, after all; there will be one spirit lacking in this world, presently, or I lose my guess." Then I said aloud:

"Friend——"

"There; wait a bit. I am not your friend, I am your enemy; I am not your equal, I am your master. Call me 'my lord,' if you please. You are too familiar."

"I don't like such titles. I am willing to call you *sir*. That is as far as——"

"We will have no argument about this. Just obey, that is all. Go on with your chatter."

"Very well, my lord—since nothing but my lord will suit you—I was going to ask you how long you will be visible to me?"

"Always!"

I broke out with strong indignation: "This is simply an outrage. That is what I think of it. You have dogged, and dogged, and *dogged* me, all the days of my life, invisible. That was misery enough; now to have such a looking thing as you tagging after me like another shadow all the rest of my days is an intolerable prospect. You have my opinion, my lord; make the most of it."

"My lad, there was never so pleased a conscience in this world as I was when you made me visible. It gives me an inconceivable advantage. *Now* I can look you straight in the eye, and call you names, and leer at you, jeer at you, sneer at you; and *you* know what eloquence there is in visible gesture and expression, more especially when the effect is heightened by audible speech. I shall always address you henceforth in your o-w-n s-n-i-v-e-l-i-n-g d-r-a-w-l—baby!"

I let fly with the coal-hod. No result. My lord said:

"Come, come! Remember the flag of truce!"

"Ah, I forgot that. I will try to be civil; and *you* try it, too, for a novelty. The idea of a *civil* conscience! It is a good joke; an excellent joke. All the consciences *I* have ever heard of were nagging, badgering, fault-finding, execrable savages! Yes; and always in a sweat about some poor little insignificant trifle or other—destruction catch the lot of them, *I* say! I would trade mine for the smallpox and seven kinds of consumption, and be glad of the chance. Now tell me, why *is* it that a conscience can't haul a man over the coals once, for an offense, and then let him alone? Why is it that it wants to keep on pegging at him, day and night and night and day, week in and week out, forever and ever, about the same old thing? There is no sense in that, and no reason in it. I think a conscience that will act like that is meaner than the very dirt itself."[13]

"Well, *we* like it; that suffices."

"Do you do it with the honest intent to improve a man?"

That question produced a sarcastic smile, and this reply:

"No, sir. Excuse me. We do it simply because it is 'business.' It is our trade. The *purpose* of it is to improve the man, but *we* are merely disinterested agents. We are appointed by authority, and haven't anything to say in the matter. We obey orders and leave the consequences where they belong. But I am willing to admit this much: We *do* crowd the orders a trifle when we get a chance, which is most of the time. We enjoy it. We are instructed to remind a man a few times of an error; and I don't mind acknowledging that we try to give pretty good measure. And when

---

[13] See *Huckleberry Finn:* "But that's always the way, it don't make no difference whether you do right or wrong, a person's conscience ain't got no sense, and just goes for him *anyway.* If I had a yaller dog that didn't know no more than a person's conscience does I would pison him. It takes up more room than all the rest of a person's insides, and yet ain't no good, nohow."

we get hold of a man of a peculiarly sensitive nature, oh, but we do haze him! I have consciences to come all the way from China and Russia to see a person of that kind put through his paces, on a special occasion. Why, I knew a man of that sort who had accidentally crippled a mulatto baby; the news went abroad, and I wish you may never commit another sin if the consciences didn't flock from all over the earth to enjoy the fun and help his master exorcise him. That man walked the floor in torture for forty-eight hours, without eating or sleeping, and then blew his brains out. The child was perfectly well again in three weeks."

"Well, you are a precious crew, not to put it too strong. I think I begin to see now why you have always been a trifle inconsistent with me. In your anxiety to get all the juice you can out of a sin, you make a man repent of it in three or four different ways. For instance, you found fault with me for lying to that tramp, and I suffered over that. But it was only yesterday that I told a tramp the square truth, to wit, that, it being regarded as bad citizenship to encourage vagrancy, I would give him nothing. What did you do *then*? Why, you made me say to myself, 'Ah, it would have been so much kinder and more blameless to ease him off with a little white lie, and send him away feeling that if he could not have bread, the gentle treatment was at least something to be grateful for!' Well, I suffered all day about *that*. Three days before I had fed a tramp, and fed him freely, supposing it a virtuous act. Straight off you said, 'Oh, false citizen, to have fed a tramp!' and I suffered as usual. I gave a tramp work; you objected to it—*after* the contract was made, of course; you never speak up beforehand. Next, I *refused* a tramp work; you objected to *that*. Next, I proposed to kill a tramp; you kept me awake all night, oozing remorse at every pore. Sure I was going to be right *this* time, I sent the next tramp away with my benediction; and I wish you may live as long as I do, if you didn't make me smart all night again because I didn't kill him. Is there *any* way of satisfying that malignant invention which is called a conscience?"

"Ha, ha! this is luxury! Go on!"

"But come, now, answer me that question. *Is* there any way?"

"Well, none that I propose to tell *you*, my son. Ass! I don't care *what* act you may turn your hand to, I can straightway whisper a word in your ear and make you think you have committed a dreadful meanness. It is my *business*—and my joy—to make you repent of *every*thing you do. If I have fooled away any opportunities it was not intentional; I beg to assure you it was not intentional!"

"Don't worry; you haven't missed a trick that *I* know of. I never did a thing in all my life, virtuous or otherwise, that I didn't repent of in twenty-four hours. In church last Sunday I listened to a charity sermon. My first impulse was to give three hundred and fifty dollars; I repented of that and reduced it a hundred; repented of that and reduced it another hundred; repented of that and reduced it another hundred; repented of that and reduced the remaining fifty to twenty-five; repented of that and came down to fifteen; repented of that and dropped to two dollars and a half; when the plate came around at last, I repented once more and contributed ten cents. Well, when I got home, I did wish to goodness I had that ten cents back again! You never *did* let me get through a charity sermon without having something to sweat about."

"Oh, and I never shall, I never shall. You can always depend on me."

"I think so. Many and many's the restless night I've wanted to take you by the neck. If I could only get hold of you now!"

"Yes, no doubt. But I am not an ass; I am only the saddle of an ass. But go on, go on. You entertain me more than I like to confess."

"I am glad of that. (You will not mind my lying a little, to keep in practice.) Look here; not to be too personal, I think you are about the shabbiest and most contemptible little shriveled-up reptile that can be imagined. I am grateful enough that you are invisible to other people, for I should die with shame to be seen with such a mildewed monkey of a conscience as *you* are. Now if you were five or six feet high, and——"

"Oh, come! who is to blame?"

"*I* don't know."

"Why, you are; nobody else."

"Confound you, I wasn't consulted about your personal appearance."

"I don't care, you had a good deal to do with it, nevertheless. When you were eight or nine years old, I was seven feet high, and as pretty as a picture."

"I wish you had died young! So you have grown the wrong way, have you?"

"Some of us grow one way and some the other. You had a large conscience once; if you've a small conscience now I reckon there are reasons for it. However, both of us are to blame, you and I. You see, you used to be conscientious about a great many things; morbidly so, I may say. It was a great many years ago. You probably do not remember it now. Well, I took a great interest in my work, and I so enjoyed the anguish which certain pet sins of yours afflicted you with that I kept pelting at you until I rather overdid the matter. You began to rebel. Of course I began to lose ground, then, and shrivel a little—diminish in stature, get moldy, and grow deformed. The more I weakened, the more stubbornly you fastened on to those particular sins; till at last the places on my person that represent those vices became as callous as shark-skin. Take smoking, for instance. I played that card a little too long, and I lost. When people plead with you at this late day to quit that vice, that old callous place seems to enlarge and cover me all over like a shirt of mail. It exerts a mysterious, smothering effect; and presently I, your faithful hater, your devoted Conscience, go sound asleep! Sound? It is no name for it. I couldn't hear it thunder at such a time. You have some few other vices—perhaps eighty, or maybe ninety—that affect me in much the same way."

"This is flattering; you must be asleep a good part of your time."

"Yes, of late years. I should be asleep *all* the time but for the help I get."

"Who helps you?"

"Other consciences. Whenever a person whose conscience I am acquainted with tries to plead with you about the vices you are callous to, I get my friend to give his client a pang concerning some villainy of his own, and that shuts off his meddling and starts him off to hunt personal consolation. My field of usefulness is about trimmed down to tramps, budding authoresses, and that line of goods now; but don't you worry—I'll harry you on *them* while they last! Just you put your trust in me."

"I think I can. But if you had only been good enough to mention these facts some thirty years ago, I should have turned my particular attention to sin, and I think that by this time I should not only have had you pretty permanently asleep on the entire list of human vices, but reduced to the size of a homeopathic pill, at that. That is about the style of conscience *I* am pining for. If I only had you shrunk down to a homeopathic pill, and could get my hands on you, would I put you in a glass case for a keepsake? No, sir, I would give you to a yellow dog! That is where *you* ought to be—you and all your tribe. You are not fit to be in society, in my opinion. Now another question. Do you know a good many consciences in this section?"

"Plenty of them."

"I would give anything to see some of them! Could you bring them here? And would they be visible to me?"

"Certainly not."

"I suppose I ought to have known that without asking. But no matter, you can describe them. Tell me about my neighbor Thompson's conscience, please."

"Very well. I know him intimately; have known him many years. I knew him when he was eleven feet high and of a faultless figure. But he is very rusty and tough and misshapen now, and hardly ever interests himself about anything. As to his present size—well, he sleeps in a cigar-box."

"Likely enough. There are few smaller, meaner men in this region than Hugh Thompson. Do you know Robinson's conscience?"

"Yes. He is a shade under four and a half feet high; used to be a blond; is a brunette now, but still shapely and comely."

"Well, Robinson is a good fellow. Do you know Tom Smith's conscience?"

"I have known him from childhood. He was thirteen inches high, and rather sluggish, when he was two years old—as nearly all of us are at that age. He is thirty-seven feet high now, and the stateliest figure in America. His legs are still racked with growing-pains, but he has a good time, nevertheless. Never sleeps. He is the most active and energetic member of the New England Conscience Club; is president of it. Night and day you can find him pegging away at Smith, panting with his labor, sleeves rolled up, countenance all alive with enjoyment. He has got his victim splendidly dragooned now. He can make poor Smith imagine that the most innocent little thing he does is an odious sin; and then he sets to work and almost tortures the soul out of him about it."

"Smith is the noblest man in all this section, and the purest; and yet is always breaking his heart because he cannot be good! Only a conscience *could* find pleasure in heaping agony upon a spirit like that. Do you know my aunt Mary's conscience?"

"I have seen her at a distance, but am not acquainted with her. She lives in the open air altogether, because no door is large enough to admit her."

"I can believe that. Let me see. Do you know the conscience of that publisher who once stole some sketches of mine for a 'series' of his, and then left me to pay the law expenses I had to incur in order to choke him off?"

"Yes. He has a wide fame. He was exhibited, a month ago, with some other antiquities, for the benefit of a recent Member of the Cabinet's conscience that was starving in exile. Tickets and fares were high, but I traveled for nothing by pretending to be the conscience of an editor, and got in for half-price by representing myself to be the conscience of a clergyman. However, the publisher's conscience, which was to have been the main feature of the entertainment, was a failure—as an exhibition. He was there, but what of that? The management had provided a microscope with a magnifying power of only thirty thousand diameters, and so nobody got to see him, after all. There was great and general dissatisfaction, of course, but——"

Just here there was an eager footstep on the stair; I opened the door, and my aunt Mary burst into the room. It was a joyful meeting and a cheery bombardment of questions and answers concerning family matters ensued. By and by my aunt said:

"But I am going to abuse you a little now. You promised me, the day I saw you last, that you would look after the needs of the poor family around the corner as faithfully as I had done it myself. Well, I found out by accident that you failed of your promise. *Was* that right?"

In simple truth, I never had thought of that family a second time! And now such a splintering pang of guilt shot through me! I glanced up at my Conscience. Plainly, my heavy heart was affecting him.

His body was drooping forward; he seemed about to fall from the bookcase. My aunt continued:

"And think how you have neglected my poor *protégé* at the almshouse, you dear, hard-hearted promise-breaker!" I blushed scarlet, and my tongue was tied. As the sense of guilty negligence waxed sharper and stronger, my Conscience began to sway heavily back and forth; and when my aunt, after a little pause, said in a grieved tone, "Since you never once went to see her, maybe it will not distress you now to know that that poor child died, months ago, utterly friendless and forsaken!" my Conscience could no longer bear up under the weight of my sufferings, but tumbled headlong from his high perch and struck the floor with a dull, leaden thump. He lay there writhing with pain and quaking with apprehension, but straining every muscle in frantic efforts to get up. In a fever of expectancy I sprang to the door, locked it, placed my back against it, and bent a watchful gaze upon my struggling master. Already my fingers were itching to begin their murderous work.

"Oh, what *can* be the matter!" exclaimed my aunt, shrinking from me, and following with her frightened eyes the direction of mine. My breath was coming in short, quick gasps now, and my excitement was almost uncontrollable. My aunt cried out:

"Oh, do not look so! You appal me! Oh, what can the matter be? What is it you see? Why do you stare so? Why do you work your fingers like that?"

"Peace, woman!" I said, in a hoarse whisper. "Look elsewhere; pay no attention to me; it is nothing—nothing. I am often this way. It will pass in a moment. It comes from smoking too much."

My injured lord was up, wild-eyed with terror, and trying to hobble toward the door. I could hardly breathe, I was so wrought up. My aunt wrung her hands, and said:

"Oh, I knew how it would be; I knew it would come to this at last! Oh, I impore you to crush out that fatal habit while it may yet be time! You must not, you shall not be deaf to my supplications longer!" My struggling Conscience showed sudden signs of weariness! "Oh, promise me you will throw off this hateful slavery of tobacco!" My Conscience began to reel drowsily, and grope with his hands—enchanting spectacle! "I beg you, I beseech you, I implore you! Your reason is deserting you! There is madness in your eye! It flames with frenzy! Oh, hear me, hear me, and be saved! See, I plead with you on my very knees!" As she sank before me my Conscience reeled again, and then drooped languidly to the floor, blinking toward me a last supplication for mercy, with heavy eyes. "Oh, promise, or you are lost! Promise, and be redeemed! Promise! Promise and live!" With a long-drawn sigh my conquered Conscience closed his eyes and fell fast asleep!

With an exultant shout I sprang past my aunt, and in an instant I had my lifelong foe by the throat. After so many years of waiting and longing, he was mine at last. I tore him to shreds and fragments. I rent the fragments to bits. I cast the bleeding rubbish into the fire, and drew into my nostrils the grateful incense of my burnt-offering. At last, and forever, my Conscience was dead!

I was a free man! I turned upon my poor aunt, who was almost petrified with terror, and shouted:

"Out of this with your paupers, your charities, your reforms, your pestilent morals! You behold before you a man whose life-conflict is done, whose soul is at peace; a man whose heart is dead to sorrow, dead to suffering, dead to remorse; a man WITHOUT A CONSCIENCE! In my joy I spare you, though I could throttle you and never feel a pang! Fly!"

She fled. Since that day my life is all bliss. Bliss, unalloyed bliss. Nothing in all the world could persuade me to have a conscience again. I settled all my old outstanding scores, and began the world anew. I killed thirty-eight persons during the first two weeks—all of them on account of ancient grudges. I burned a dwelling that interrupted my view. I swindled a widow and some orphans out of their last cow, which is a very good one, though not thoroughbred, I believe. I have also committed scores of crimes, of various kinds, and have enjoyed my work exceedingly, whereas it would formerly have broken my heart and turned my hair gray, I have no doubt.

In conclusion, I wish to state, by way of advertisement, that medical colleges desiring assorted tramps for scientific purposes, either by the gross, by cord measurement, or per ton, will do well to examine the lot in my cellar before purchasing elsewhere, as these were all selected and prepared by myself, and can be had at a low rate, because I wish to clear out my stock and get ready for the spring trade. » » »

While most of Mark Twain's writings have historical significance in one way or another, "A Scrap of Curious History" is a definite experiment with the historical short-story, somewhat like Hawthorne's "The Gray Champion," with the scene laid in Marion City, Missouri, which had become a ghost town, north of Hannibal, on the Mississippi River.[14] In Marion City in the 1830's was staged a miniature Civil War between abolitionists and slaveholders, with the victory to the slaveholders.[15] The humor of the story lies in the town's struggle with abolitionism as seen in the perspective of sixty years later. The story's conventional literary style makes it clear how far its author had departed from the folk elements that gave flavor to his early tales.

A SCRAP OF CURIOUS HISTORY[16] (from *What Is Man? and Other Essays*)

« « « Marion City, on the Mississippi River, in the State of Missouri—a village; time, 1845. La Bourboule-les-Bains, France—a village; time, the end of June, 1894. I was in the one village in that early time; I am in the other now. These times and places are sufficiently wide apart, yet today I have the strange sense of being thrust back into that Missourian village and of reliving certain stirring days that I lived there so long ago.

Last Saturday night the life of the President of the French Republic was taken by an Italian assassin. Last night a mob sur-

---

[14] "A Scrap of Curious History" and "A Campaign That Failed" are Mark Twain's only experiments with Civil War material. Some account of the events described in "Scrap" can be found in *The Missouri Historical Review*, Vol. XXIII (April, 1929), 361–79, "Palmyra and Its Historical Environment" by F. H. Sosey. The same author published earlier a historical novel based on those events, *Robert DeVoy: A Tale of the Palmyra Massacre* (1903). The story of Marion City, the ghost town, is to be found in *Mark Twain: Son of Missouri*, 66–75, by M. M. Brashear.

[15] Two men representing the American Colonization Society came into Marion County (of which Palmyra was the county seat) in 1836 with tracts, to educate the district in abolitionist principles. Dr. Nelson, president of Marion College and a Presbyterian preacher, spoke from the Presbyterian pulpit in a neighboring town about the feasibility of buying up slaves to be sent to a colony in Liberia in Africa. Dr. John Boseley, a large slaveowner, attacked Dr. Nelson and was himself stabbed by an abolitionist, though not fatally.

[16] "A Scrap of Curious History" was published posthumously in *Harper's Magazine*, October, 1914, and included in the volume entitled *What Is Man?* (1917). It was published with the note: "Written at La Bourboule-les-Bains, France, June, 1894."

rounded our hotel, shouting, howling, singing the "Marseillaise," and pelting our windows with sticks and stones; for we have Italian waiters, and the mob demanded that they be turned out of the house instantly—to be drubbed, and then driven out of the village. Everybody in the hotel remained up until far into the night, and experienced the several kinds of terror which one reads about in books which tell of night attacks by Italians and by French mobs: the growing roar of the oncoming crowd; the arrival, with rain of stones and crash of glass; the withdrawal to rearrange plans—followed by a silence ominous, threatening, and harder to bear than even the active siege and the noise. The landlord and the two village policemen stood their ground, and at last the mob was persuaded to go away and leave our Italians in peace. To-day four of the ringleaders have been sentenced to heavy punishment of a public sort—and are become local heroes, by consequence.

That is the very mistake which was at first made in the Missourian village half a century ago. The mistake was repeated and repeated —just as France is doing in these latter months.

In our village we had our Ravochals, our Henrys, our Vaillants; and in a humble way our Cesario—I hope I have spelled this name wrong. Fifty years ago we passed through, in all essentials, what France has been passing through during the past two or three years, in the matter of periodical frights, horrors, and shudderings.

In several details the parallels are quaintly exact. In that day, for a man to speak out openly and proclaim himself an enemy of negro slavery was simply to proclaim himself a madman. For he was blaspheming against the holiest thing known to a Missourian, and he could *not* be in his right mind. For a man to proclaim himself an anarchist in France, three years ago, was to proclaim himself a madman—he could not be in his right mind.

Now the original old first blasphemer against any institution profoundly venerated by a community is quite sure to be in earnest; his followers and imitators may be humbugs and self-seekers, but he himself is sincere—his heart is in his protest.

Robert Hardy was our first *abolitionist*—awful name! He was a journeyman cooper, and worked in the big cooper-shop belonging to the great pork-packing establishment which was Marion City's chief pride and sole source of prosperity. He was a New-Englander, a stranger. And, being a stranger, he was of course regarded as an inferior person—for that has been human nature from Adam down—and of course, also, he was made to feel unwelcome, for this is the ancient law with man and the other animals. Hardy was thirty years old, and a bachelor; pale, given to reverie and reading. He was reserved, and seemed to prefer the isolation which had fallen to his lot. He was treated to many side remarks by his fellows, but as he did not resent them it was decided that he was a coward.

All of a sudden he proclaimed himself an abolitionist—straight out and publicly! He said that negro slavery was a crime, an infamy. For a moment the town was paralyzed with astonishment; then it broke into a fury of rage and swarmed toward the cooper-shop to lynch Hardy. But the Methodist minister made a powerful speech to them and stayed their hands. He proved to them that Hardy was insane and not responsible for his words; that no man *could* be sane and utter such words.

So Hardy was saved. Being insane, he was allowed to go on talking. He was found to be good entertainment. Several nights running he made abolition speeches in the open air, and all the town flocked to hear and laugh. He implored them to believe him sane and sincere, and have pity on the poor slaves, and take measures for the restoration of their stolen rights, or in no long time blood would flow—blood, blood, rivers of blood!

It was great fun. But all of a sudden the aspect of things changed. A slave came flying from Palmyra, the county-seat, a few miles back, and was about to escape in a canoe to Illinois and freedom in the dull twilight of the approaching dawn, when the town constable seized him. Hardy happened along and tried to rescue the negro; there was a struggle, and the constable did not come out of it alive. Hardy crossed the river with the negro, and then came back to give himself up. All this took time, for the Mississippi is not a French brook, like the Seine, the Loire, and those other rivulets, but is a real river nearly a mile wide. The town was on hand in force now, but the Methodist preacher and the sheriff had already made arrangements in the interest of order; so Hardy was surrounded by a strong guard and safely conveyed to the village calaboose in spite of all the effort of the mob to get hold of him. The reader will have begun to perceive that this Methodist minister was a prompt man; a prompt man, with active hands and a good head-piece. Williams was his name—Damon Williams; Damon Williams in public, Damnation Williams in private, because he was so powerful on that theme and so frequent.

The excitement was prodigious. The constable was the first man who had ever been killed in the town. The event was by long odds the most imposing in the town's history. It lifted the humble village into sudden importance; its name was in everybody's mouth for twenty miles around. And so was the name of Robert Hardy— Robert Hardy, the stranger, the despised. In a day he was become the person of most consequence in the region, the only person talked about. As to those other coopers, they found their position curiously changed—they were important people, or unimportant, now, in proportion as to how large or how small had been their intercourse with the new celebrity. The two or three who had really been on a sort of familiar footing with him found themselves objects of admiring interest with the public and of envy with their shopmates.

The village weekly journal had lately gone into new hands. The new man was an enterprising fellow, and he had made the most of the tragedy. He issued an extra. Then he put up posters promising to devote his whole paper to matters connected with the great event —there would be a full and intensely interesting biography of the murderer, and even a portrait of him. He was as good as his word. He carved the portrait himself, on the back of a wooden type—and a terror it was to look at. It made a great commotion, for this was the first time the village paper had ever contained a picture. The village was very proud. The output of the paper was ten times as great as it had ever been before, yet every copy was sold.

When the trial came on, people came from all over the farms around, and from Hannibal, and Quincy, and even from Keokuk; and the court-house could hold only a fraction of the crowd that applied for admission. The trial was published in the village paper, with fresh and still more trying pictures of the accused.

Hardy was convicted, and hanged—a mistake. People came from miles around to see the hanging; they brought cakes and cider, also the women and children, and made a picnic of the matter. It was the largest crowd the village had ever seen. The rope that hanged

Hardy was eagerly bought up, in inch samples, for everybody wanted a memento of the memorable event.

Martyrdom gilded with notoriety has its fascinations. Within one week afterward four young light-weights in the village proclaimed themselves abolitionists! In life Hardy had not been able to make a convert; everybody laughed at him; but nobody could laugh at his legacy. The four swaggered around with their slouch-hats pulled down over their faces, and hinted darkly at awful possibilities. The people were troubled and afraid, and showed it. And they were stunned, too; they could not understand it. "Abolitionist" had always been a term of shame and horror; yet here were four young men who were not only not ashamed to bear that name, but were grimly proud of it. Respectable young men they were, too—of good families, and brought up in the church. Ed Smith, the printer's apprentice, nineteen, had been the head Sunday-school boy, and had once recited three thousand Bible verses without making a break. Dick Savage, twenty, the baker's apprentice; Will Joyce, twenty-two, journeyman blacksmith; and Henry Taylor, twenty-four, tobacco-stemmer—were the other three. They were all of a sentimental cast; they were all romance-readers; they all wrote poetry, such as it was; they were all vain and foolish; but they had never before been suspected of having anything bad in them.

They withdrew from society, and grew more and more mysterious and dreadful. They presently achieved the distinction of being denounced by names from the pulpit—which made an immense stir! This was grandeur, this was fame. They were envied by all the other young fellows now. This was natural. Their company grew—grew alarmingly. They took a name. It was a secret name, and was divulged to no outsider; publicly they were simply the abolitionists. They had pass-words, grips, and signs; they had secret meetings; their initiations were conducted with gloomy pomps and ceremonies, at midnight.

They always spoke of Hardy as "the Martyr," and every little while they moved through the principal street in procession—at midnight, black-robed, masked, to the measured tap of the solemn drum — on pilgrimage to the Martyr's grave, where they went through with some majestic fooleries and swore vengeance upon his murderers. They gave previous notice of the pilgrimage by small posters, and warned everybody to keep indoors and darken all houses along the route, and leave the road empty. These warnings were obeyed, for there was a skull and crossbones at the top of the poster.

When this kind of thing had been going on about eight weeks, a quite natural thing happened. A few men of character and grit woke up out of the nightmare of fear which had been stupefying their faculties, and began to discharge scorn and scoffings at themselves and the community for enduring this child's-play; and at the same time they proposed to end it straightway. Everybody felt an uplift; life was breathed into their dead spirits; their courage rose and they began to feel like men again. This was on a Saturday. All day the new feeling grew and strengthened; it grew with a rush; it brought inspiration and cheer with it. Midnight saw a united community, full of zeal and pluck, and with a clearly defined and welcome piece of work in front of it. The best organizer and bitterest talker on that great Saturday was the Presbyterian clergyman who had denounced the original four from his pulpit—Rev. Hiram Fletcher—and he promised to use his pulpit in the public interest again now. On the morrow he had revelations to make, he said—secrets of the dreadful society.

But the revelations were never made. At half past two in the morning the dead silence of the village was broken by a crashing explosion, and the town patrol saw the preacher's house spring in a wreck of whirling fragments into the sky. The preacher was killed, together with a negro woman, his only slave and servant.

The town was paralyzed again, and with reason. To struggle against a visible enemy is a thing worth while, and there is a plenty of men who stand always ready to undertake it; but to struggle against an invisible one—an invisible one who sneaks in and does his awful work in the dark and leaves no trace—that is another matter. That is a thing to make the bravest tremble and hold back.

The cowed populace were afraid to go to the funeral. The man who was to have had a packed church to hear him expose and denounce the common enemy had but a handful to see him buried. The coroner's jury had brought in a verdict of "death by the visitation of God," for no witness came forward; if any existed they prudently kept out of the way. Nobody seemed sorry. Nobody wanted to see the terrible secret society provoked into the commission of further terrible outrages. Everybody wanted the tragedy hushed up, ignored, forgotten, if possible.

And so there was a bitter surprise and an unwelcome one when Will Joyce, the blacksmith's journeyman, came out and proclaimed himself the assassin! Plainly he was not minded to be robbed of his glory. He made his proclamation, and stuck to it. Stuck to it, and insisted upon a trial. Here was an ominous thing; here was a new and peculiarly formidable terror, for a motive was revealed here which society could not hope to deal with successfully—*vanity*, thirst for notoriety. If men were going to kill for notoriety's sake, and to win the glory of newspaper renown, a big trial, and a showy execution, what possible invention of man could discourage or deter them? The town was in a sort of panic; it did not know what to do.

However, the grand jury had to take hold of the matter—it had no choice. It brought in a true bill, and presently the case went to the county court. The trial was a fine sensation. The prisoner was the principal witness for the prosecution. He gave a full account of the assassination; he furnished even the minutest particulars: how he deposited his keg of powder and laid his train—from the house to such-and-such a spot; how George Ronalds and Henry Hart came along just then, smoking, and he borrowed Hart's cigar and fired the train with it, shouting, "Down with all slave-tyrants!" and how Hart and Ronalds made no effort to capture him, but ran away, and had never come forward to testify yet.

But they had to testify now, and they did—and pitiful it was to see how reluctant they were, and how scared. The crowded house listened to Joyce's fearful tale with a profound and breathless interest, and in a deep hush which was not broken till he broke it himself, in concluding, with a roaring repetition of his "Death to all slave-tyrants!"—which came so unexpectedly and so startlingly that it made every one present catch his breath and gasp.

The trial was put in the paper, with biography and large portrait, with other slanderous and insane pictures, and the edition sold beyond imagination.

The execution of Joyce was a fine and picturesque thing. It drew a vast crowd. Good places in trees and seats on rail fences sold for half a dollar apiece; lemonade and gingerbread-stands had great prosperity. Joyce recited a furious and fantastic and denunciatory speech on the scaffold which had imposing passages of school-boy eloquence in it, and gave him a reputation on the spot as an orator, and the name, later, in the society's records, of the "Martyr Orator." He went to his death breathing slaughter and charging his society to "avenge his murder." If he knew anything of human nature he knew that to plenty of young fellows present in that great crowd he was a grand hero—and enviably situated.

He was hanged. It was a mistake. Within a month from his death the society which he had honored had twenty new members, some of them earnest, determined men. They did not court distinction in the same way, but they celebrated his martyrdom. The crime which had been obscure and despised had become lofty and glorified.

Such things were happening all over the country. Wild-brained martyrdom was succeeded by uprising and organization. Then, in natural order, followed riot, insurrection, and the wrack and restitutions of war. It was bound to come, and it would naturally come in that way. It has been the manner of reform since the beginning of the world. » » »

The practical joke played by the mysterious stranger upon a village of pious, unsuspecting people, with the hilarious surprise at the end, is a document in evidence to demonstrate what Mark Twain meant when he asserted at the beginning of his career as a humorist that a writer "can deliver a satire with telling force through the insidious medium of travesty." Whether it is destined to take a place among such parables as Addison's "The Vision of Mirza," or prove itself to have belonged on the local, ephemeral plane, like Elbert Hubbard's "A Message to Garcia" and Edward Everett Hale's *The Man Without a Country*, the literary fate of Mark Twain's story of Hadleyburg lies in the lap of the gods. We can say of it, however, that nothing its author wrote exhibits better the fine directions and clarity of his sentences;[17] that nothing writ-

[17] Archibald Henderson, one of Mark Twain's earliest biographers, calls "The Man That Corrupted Hadleyburg" "a contribution to world literature, an ironic fable of such originality and dexterous creation that it has no satisfactory parallel in literature."

ten in the United States shows up more relentlessly the insidious way in which money undermines human character;[18] and that nothing he wrote illustrates better what his friend William Dean Howells meant when he said that this humorist "pierced to the heart of life."[19]

THE MAN THAT CORRUPTED HADLEYBURG[20]

I

« « « It was many years ago. Hadleyburg was the most honest and upright town in all the region around about. It had kept that reputation unsmirched during three generations, and was prouder of it

---

[18] T. S. Eliot, in his Introduction to *Huckleberry Finn*, explains the darker side of the humorist in the following terms: "The pessimism which Mark Twain discharged in 'The Man That Corrupted Hadleyburg' and 'What Is Man' springs less from his observation of society than from his hatred of himself for allowing society to tempt and corrupt him and give him what he wanted." On this same matter, Dixon Wecter, in his *Sam Clemens of Hannibal*, 222, remarks: "Certainly 'The Man That Corrupted Hadleyburg,' along with *Pudd'nhead Wilson* and its overtones of village stupidity and venality, and *The Mysterious Stranger* in its unpublished draft with a Hannibal locale, report something about the river town of Mark Twain's dreams that the earlier *Tom Sawyer* and *Huckleberry Finn* had omitted or glossed over.... For all his continued loyalty to the integrity of boyhood, they suggest that the old dream world—in so far as it involved adults, at any rate, with their greeds and passions—was revealed at last to be illusory and rotten at heart."

[19] Owen Wister, in *The Favorite Works of Mark Twain*, xxi, offers the following comparison: "Suppose Hawthorne had been born in Florida, Missouri, and Mark Twain in Salem, Massachusetts.... You will notice that the *problem of evil* preoccupied one of them all his life, the other in his later years, and that both wrote masterpieces on that dark theme. You will readily recall *Young Goodman Brown* and *The Man That Corrupted Hadleyburg*." DeLancey Ferguson, in *Mark Twain: Man and Legend*, writes of the story: "It is a tragedy-trap, and not merely for the Richardsons who suffer the penalty of their undetected lie. It traps the reader, too, and at the end leaves him, if he is honest with himself, saying, 'There, with or without the grace of God, go I.' " Charles Neider, in *The Complete Short Stories of Mark Twain*, xvi, says: " 'The Man That Corrupted Hadleyburg' is part of our world heritage. A rebel American of creative kind, Frank Lloyd Wright, has written me that it is his favorite of all short stories."

[20] "The Man That Corrupted Hadleyburg" was written in Vienna in 1898. It was first published in *Harper's* in December, 1899. Probably the first hint for this story is contained in an 1897 entry in the *Notebook*, 342: "Buried treasure in a Missouri village—supposed by worn figures to be $980. Corrupts village, causes quarrels and murder, and when found at last is $9.80." An 1891 entry is "Hell or Heidelberg, whichever you come to first" (*Notebook*, 216). In the first draft of the story, the scene was laid in Hannibal. Entry in Mark Twain's *Notebook* of January 3, 1903, reads: "The offspring of riches: pride, vanity, ostentation, arrogance, tyranny." Entry of January 4, 1903, reads: "The offspring of poverty: greed, sordidness, envy, hate, malice, cruelty, meanness, lying, shirking, cheating, stealing, murder."

than of any other of its possessions. It was proud of it, and so anxious to insure its perpetuation, that it began to teach the principles of honest dealing to its babies in the cradle, and made the like teachings the staple of their culture thenceforward through all the years devoted to their education. Also, throughout the formative years temptations were kept out of the way of the young people, so that their honesty could have every chance to harden and solidify, and become a part of their very bone. The neighboring towns were jealous of this honorable supremacy, and affected to sneer at Hadleyburg's pride in it and call it vanity; but all the same they were obliged to acknowledge that Hadleyburg was in reality an incorruptible town; and if pressed they would also acknowledge that the mere fact that a young man hailed from Hadleyburg was all the recommendation he needed when he went forth from his natal town to seek for responsible employment.

But at last, in the drift of time, Hadleyburg had the ill luck to offend a passing stranger—possibly without knowing it, certainly without caring, for Hadleyburg was sufficient unto itself, and cared not a rap for strangers or their opinions. Still, it would have been well to make an exception in this one's case, for he was a bitter man and revengeful. All through his wanderings during a whole year he kept his injury in mind, and gave all his leisure moments to trying to invent a compensating satisfaction for it. He contrived many plans, and all of them were good, but none of them was quite sweeping enough; the poorest of them would hurt a great many individuals, but what he wanted was a plan which would comprehend the entire town, and not let so much as one person escape unhurt. At last he had a fortunate idea, and when it fell into his brain it lit up his whole head with an evil joy. He began to form a plan at once, saying to himself, "That is the thing to do—I will corrupt the town."

Six months later he went to Hadleyburg, and arrived in a buggy at the house of the old cashier of the bank about ten at night. He got a sack out of the buggy, shouldered it, and staggered with it through the cottage yard, and knocked at the door. A woman's voice said "Come in," and he entered, and set his sack behind the stove in the parlor, saying politely to the old lady who sat reading the *Missionary Herald* by the lamp:

"Pray keep your seat, madam, I will not disturb you. There—now it is pretty well concealed; one would hardly know it was there. Can I see your husband a moment, madam?"

No, he was gone to Brixton, and might not return before morning.

"Very well, madam, it is no matter. I merely wanted to leave that sack in his care, to be delivered to the rightful owner when he shall be found. I am a stranger; he does not know me; I am merely passing through the town to-night to discharge a matter which has been long in my mind. My errand is now completed, and I go pleased and a little proud, and you will never see me again. There is a paper attached to the sack which will explain everything. Good night, madam."

The old lady was afraid of the mysterious big stranger, and was glad to see him go. But her curiosity was roused, and she went straight to the sack and brought away the paper. It began as follows:

TO BE PUBLISHED; or, the right man sought out by private inquiry—either will answer. This sack contains gold coin weighing a hundred and sixty pounds four ounces——

"Mercy on us, and the door not locked!"

Mrs. Richards flew to it all in a tremble and locked it, then pulled down the window-shades and stood frightened, worried, and wondering if there was anything else she could do toward making herself and the money more safe. She listened awhile for burglars, then surrendered to curiosity and went back to the lamp and finished reading the paper:

I am a foreigner, and am presently going back to my own country, to remain there permanently. I am grateful to America for what I have received at her hands during my long stay under her flag; and to one of her citizens—a citizen of Hadleyburg—I am especially grateful for a great kindness done me a year or two ago. Two great kindnesses, in fact. I will explain. I was a gambler. I say I WAS. *I was a ruined gambler. I arrived in this village at night, hungry and without a penny. I asked for help—in the dark; I was ashamed to beg in the light. I begged of the right man. He gave me twenty* dollars—that is to say, he gave me life, as I considered it. He also gave me fortune; for out of that money I have made myself rich at the gaming-table. And finally a remark which he made to me has remained with me to this day, and has at last conquered me; and in conquering has saved the remnant of my morals; I shall gamble no more. Now I have no idea who that man was, but I want him found, and I want him to have this money, to give away, throw away, or keep, as he pleases. It is merely my way of testifying my gratitude to him. If I could stay, I would find him myself; but no matter, he will be found. This is an honest town, an incorruptible town, and I know I can trust it without fear. This man can be identified by the remark which he made to me; I feel persuaded that he will remember it.

And now my plan is this: If you prefer to conduct the inquiry privately, do so. Tell the contents of this present writing to any one who is likely to be the right man. If he shall answer, 'I am the man; the remark I made was so-and-so,' apply the test—to wit: open the sack, and in it you will find a sealed envelope containing that remark. If the remark mentioned by the candidate tallies with it, give him the money, and ask no further questions, for he is certainly the right man.

But if you shall prefer a public inquiry, then publish this present writing in the local paper—with these instructions added, to wit: Thirty days from now, let the candidate appear at the town-hall at eight in the evening (Friday), and hand his remark, in a sealed envelope, to the Rev. Mr. Burgess (if he will be kind enough to act); and let Mr. Burgess there and then destroy the seals of the sack, open it, and see if the remark is correct; if correct, let the money be delivered, with my sincere gratitude, to my benefactor thus identified.

Mrs. Richards sat down, gently quivering with excitement, and was soon lost in thinkings—after this pattern: "What a strange thing it is! . . . And what a fortune for that kind man who set his bread afloat upon the waters! . . . If it had only been my husband that did it!—for we are so poor, so old and poor! . . ." Then, with a sigh—"But it was not my Edward; no, it was not he that gave a stranger twenty dollars. It is a pity, too; I see it now. . . ." Then, with a shudder—"But it is *gambler's* money! the wages of sin: we couldn't take it; we couldn't touch it. I don't like to be near it; it seems a defilement." She moved to a farther chair. . . . "I wish Edward would come and take it to the bank; a burglar might come at any moment; it is dreadful to be here all alone with it."

At eleven Mr. Richards arrived, and while his wife was saying, "I am *so* glad you've come!" he was saying, "I'm so tired—tired clear out; it is dreadful to be poor, and have to make these dismal journeys at my time of life. Always at the grind, grind, grind, on a salary —another man's slave, and he sitting at home in his slippers, rich and comfortable."

"I am so sorry for you, Edward, you know that; but be comforted: we have our livelihood; we have our good name——"

"Yes, Mary, and that is everything. Don't mind my talk—it's just a moment's irritation and doesn't mean anything. Kiss me—there, it's all gone now, and I am not complaining any more. What have you been getting? What's in the sack?"

Then his wife told him the great secret. It dazed him for a moment; then he said:

"It weighs a hundred and sixty pounds? Why, Mary, it's for-ty thou-sand dollars—think of it—a whole fortune! Not ten men in this village are worth that much. Give me the paper."

He skimmed through it and said:

"Isn't it an adventure! Why, it's a romance; it's like the impossible things one reads about in books, and never sees in life." He was well stirred up now; cheerful, even gleeful. He tapped his old wife on the cheek, and said, humorously, "Why, we're rich, Mary, rich; all we've got to do is to bury the money and burn the papers. If the gambler ever comes to inquire, we'll merely look cold upon him and say: 'What is this nonsense you are talking? We have never heard of you and your sack of gold before'; and then he would look foolish, and——"

"And in the mean time, while you are running on with your jokes, the money is still here, and it is fast getting along toward burglar-time."

"True. Very well, what shall we do—make the inquiry private? No, not that: it would spoil the romance. The public method is better. Think what a noise it will make! And it will make all the other towns jealous; for no stranger would trust such a thing to any town but Hadleyburg, and they know it. It's a great card for us. I must get to the printing-office now, or I shall be too late."

"But stop—stop—don't leave me here alone with it, Edward!"

But he was gone. For only a little while, however. Not far from his own house he met the editor-proprietor of the paper, and gave him the document, and said, "Here is a good thing for you, Cox—put it in."

"It may be too late, Mr. Richards, but I'll see."

At home again he and his wife sat down to talk the charming mystery over; they were in no condition for sleep. The first question was, Who could the citizen have been who gave the stranger the twenty dollars? It seemed a simple one; both answered it in the same breath:

"Barclay Goodson."

"Yes," said Richards, "he could have done it, and it would have been like him, but there's not another in the town."

"Everybody will grant that, Edward—grant it privately, anyway. For six months, now, the village has been its own proper self once more—honest, narrow, self-righteous, and stingy."

"It is what he always called it, to the day of his death—said it right out publicly, too."

"Yes, and he was hated for it."

"Oh, of course; but he didn't care. I reckon he was the best-hated man among us, except the Reverend Burgess."

"Well, Burgess deserves it—he will never get another congregation here. Mean as the town is, it knows how to estimate *him*. Edward, doesn't it seem odd that the stranger should appoint Burgess to deliver the money?"

"Well, yes—it does. That is——"

"Why so much that-*is*-ing? Would *you* select him?"

"Mary, maybe the stranger knows him better than this village does."

"Much *that* would help Burgess!"

The husband seemed perplexed for an answer; the wife kept a steady eye upon him, and waited. Finally Richards said, with the hesitancy of one who is making a statement which is likely to encounter doubt:

"Mary, Burgess is not a bad man."

His wife was certainly surprised.

"Nonsense!" she exclaimed.

"He is not a bad man. I know. The whole of his unpopularity had its foundation in that one thing—the thing that made so much noise."

"That 'one thing,' indeed! As if that 'one thing' wasn't enough, all by itself."

"Plenty. Plenty. Only he wasn't guilty of it."

"How you talk! Not guilty of it! Everybody knows he *was* guilty."

"Mary, I give you my word—he was innocent."

"I can't believe it, and I don't. How do you know?"

"It is a confession. I am ashamed, but I will make it. I was the only man who knew he was innocent. I could have saved him, and—and—well, you know how the town was wrought up—I hadn't the pluck to do it. It would have turned everybody against me. I felt mean, ever so mean; but I didn't dare; I hadn't the manliness to face that."

Mary looked troubled, and for a while was silent. Then she said, stammeringly:

"I—I don't think it would have done for you to—to—One mustn't—er—public opinion—one has to be so careful—so—" It was a difficult road, and she got mired; but after a little she got started again. "It was a great pity, but—Why, we couldn't afford it, Edward—we couldn't indeed. Oh, I wouldn't have had you do it for anything!"

"It would have lost us the good will of so many people, Mary; and then—and then——"

"What troubles me now is, what *he* thinks of us, Edward."

"He? *He* doesn't suspect that I could have saved him."

"Oh," exclaimed the wife, in a tone of relief, "I am glad of that! As long as he doesn't know that you could have saved him, he—he—well, that makes it a great deal better. Why, I might have known he didn't know, because he *is* always trying to be friendly with us, as little encouragement as we give him. More than once people have twitted me with it. There's the Wilsons, and the Wilcoxes, and the Harknesses, they take a mean pleasure in saying, '*Your friend* Burgess,' because they know it pesters me. I wish he wouldn't persist in liking us so; I can't think why he keeps it up."

"I can explain it. It's another confession. When the thing was new and hot, and the town made a plan to ride him on a rail, my conscience hurt me so that I couldn't stand it, and I went privately and gave him notice, and he got out of the town and staid out till it was safe to come back."

"Edward! If the town had found it out——"

"*Don't!* It scares me yet, to think of it. I repented of it the minute it was done; and I was even afraid to tell you, lest your face might betray it to somebody. I didn't sleep any that night, for worrying. But after a few days I saw that no one was going to suspect me, and after that I got to feeling glad I did it. And I feel glad yet, Mary—glad through and through."

"So do I, now, for it would have been a dreadful way to treat him. Yes, I'm glad; for really you did owe him that, you know. But, Edward, suppose it should come out yet, some day!"

"It won't."

"Why?"

"Because everybody thinks it was Goodson."

"Of course they would!"

"Certainly. And of course *he* didn't care. They persuaded poor old Sawlsberry to go and charge it on him, and he went blustering over there and did it. Goodson looked him over, like as if he was hunting for a place on him that he would despise the most, then he says, 'So you are the Committee of Inquiry, are you?' Sawlsberry said that was about what he was. 'Hm. Do they require particulars, or do you reckon a kind of a *general* answer will do?' 'If they require particulars, I will come back, Mr. Goodson; I will take the general answer first.' 'Very well, then, tell them to go to hell—I reckon that's general enough. And I'll give you some advice, Sawlsberry; when you come back for the particulars, fetch a basket to carry the relics of yourself home in.'"

"Just like Goodson; it's got all the marks. He had only one vanity: he thought he could give advice better than any other person."

"It settled the business, and saved us, Mary. The subject was dropped."

"Bless you, I'm not doubting *that*."

Then they took up the gold-sack mystery again, with strong interest. Soon the conversation began to suffer breaks—interruptions caused by absorbed thinkings. The breaks grew more and more frequent. At last Richards lost himself wholly in thought. He sat long, gazing vacantly at the floor, and by and by he began to punctuate his thoughts with little nervous movements of his hands that seemed to indicate vexation. Meantime his wife too had relapsed into a thoughtful silence, and her movements were beginning to show a troubled discomfort. Finally Richards got up and strode aimlessly about the room, plowing his hands through his hair, much as a somnambulist might do who was having a bad dream. Then he seemed to arrive at a definite purpose; and without a word he put on his hat and passed quickly out of the house. His wife sat brooding, with a drawn face, and did not seem to be aware that she was alone. Now and then she murmured, "Lead us not into t–... but–but–we are so poor, so poor!... Lead us not into... Ah, who would be hurt by it?–and no one would ever know.... Lead us..." The voice died out in mumblings. After a little she glanced up and muttered in a half-frightened, half-glad way:

"He is gone! But, oh dear, he may be too late–too late.... Maybe not–maybe there is still time." She rose and stood thinking, nervously clasping and unclasping her hands. A slight shudder shook her frame, and she said, out of a dry throat, "God forgive me–it's awful to think such things–but... Lord, how we are made –how strangely we are made!"

She turned the light low, and slipped stealthily over and knelt down by the sack and felt of its ridgy sides with her hands, and fondled them lovingly; and there was a gloating light in her poor old eyes. She fell into fits of absence; and came half out of them at times to mutter, "If we had only waited!–oh, if we had only waited a little, and not been in such a hurry!"

Meantime Cox had gone home from his office and told his wife all about the strange thing that had happened, and they had talked it over eagerly, and guessed that the late Goodson was the only man in the town who could have helped a suffering stranger with so noble a sum as twenty dollars. Then there was a pause, and the two became thoughtful and silent. And by and by nervous and fidgety. At last the wife said, as if to herself:

"Nobody knows this secret but the Richardses... and us... nobody."

The husband came out of his thinkings with a slight start, and gazed wistfully at his wife, whose face was become very pale; then he hesitatingly rose, and glanced furtively at his hat, then at his wife—a sort of mute inquiry. Mrs. Cox swallowed once or twice, with her hand at her throat, then in place of speech she nodded her head. In a moment she was alone, and mumbling to herself.

And now Richards and Cox were hurrying through the deserted streets, from opposite directions. They met, panting, at the foot of the printing-office stairs; by the night light there they read each other's face. Cox whispered:

"Nobody knows about this but us?"

The whispered answer was,

"Not a soul—on honor, not a soul!"

"If it isn't too late to——"

The men were starting up-stairs; at this moment they were overtaken by a boy, and Cox asked:

"Is that you, Johnny?"

"Yes, sir."

"You needn't ship the early mail—nor *any* mail; wait till I tell you."

"It's already gone, sir."

"*Gone?*" It had the sound of an unspeakable disappointment in it.

"Yes, sir. Time-table for Bixton and all the towns beyond changed to-day, sir—had to get the papers in twenty minutes earlier than common. I had to rush; if I had been two minutes later——"

The men turned and walked slowly away, not waiting to hear the rest. Neither of them spoke during ten minutes; then Cox said, in a vexed tone: "What possessed you to be in such a hurry, *I* can't make out."

The answer was humble enough:

"I see it now, but somehow I never thought, you know, until it was too late. But the next time——"

"Next time be hanged! It won't come in a thousand years."

Then the friends separated without a good night, and dragged themselves home with the gait of mortally stricken men. At their homes their wives sprang up with an eager "Well?"—then saw the answer with their eyes and sank down sorrowing, without waiting for it to come in words. In both houses a discussion followed of a heated sort—a new thing; there had been discussions before, but not heated ones, not ungentle ones. The discussions to-night were a sort of seeming plagiarisms of each other. Mrs. Richards said,

"If you had only waited, Edward—if you had only stopped to think; but no, you must run straight to the printing-office and spread it all over the world."

"It *said* publish it."

"That is nothing; it also said do it privately, if you liked. There, now—is that true, or not?"

"Why, yes—yes, it is true; but when I thought what a stir it would make, and what a compliment it was to Hadleyburg that a stranger should trust it so——"

"Oh, certainly, I know all that; but if you had only stopped to think, you would have seen that you *couldn't* find the right man, because he is in his grave, and hasn't left chick nor child nor relation behind him; and as long as the money went to somebody that awfully needed it, and nobody would be hurt by it, and—and——"

She broke down, crying. Her husband tried to think of some comforting thing to say, and presently came out with this:

"But after all, Mary, it must be for the best—it *must* be; we know that. And we must remember that it was so ordered——"

"Ordered! Oh, everything's *ordered*, when a person has to find some way out, when he has been stupid. Just the same, it was *ordered* that the money should come to us in this special way, and it was you that must take it on yourself to go meddling with the designs of Providence—and who gave you the right? It was wicked, that is what it was—just blasphemous presumption, and no more becoming to a meek and humble professor of——"

"But, Mary, you know how we have been trained all our lives long, like the whole village, till it is absolutely second nature to us to stop not a single moment to think when there's an honest thing to be done——"

"Oh, I know it, I know it—it's been one everlasting training and training and training in honesty—honesty shielded, from the very cradle, against every possible temptation, and so it's *artificial* honesty, and weak as water when temptation comes, as we have seen this night. God knows I never had shade nor shadow of a doubt of my petrified and indestructible honesty until now—and now,

The famous Jumping Frog poster announcing a Brooklyn lecture, February 7, 1869.

Underwood and Underwood

Mark Twain in front of his cottage at Tuxedo Park, New York, wearing the white suit he adopted in later years for both summer and winter wear.

under the very first big and real temptation, I—Edward, it is my belief that this town's honesty is as rotten as mine is; as rotten as yours is. It is a mean town, a hard, stingy town, and hasn't a virtue in the world but this honesty it is so celebrated for and so conceited about; and so help me, I do believe that if ever the day comes that its honesty falls under great temptation, its grand reputation will go to ruin like a house of cards. There, now I've made confession, and I feel better; I am a humbug, and I've been one all my life, without knowing it. Let no man call me honest again—I will not have it."

"I—well, Mary, I feel a good deal as you do; I certainly do. It seems strange, too, so strange. I never could have believed it—never."

A long silence followed; both were sunk in thought. At last the wife looked up and said:

"I know what you are thinking, Edward."

Richards had the embarrassed look of a person who is caught.

"I am ashamed to confess it, Mary, but——"

"It's no matter, Edward, I was thinking the same question myself."

"I hope so. State it."

"You were thinking, if a body could only guess out *what the remark was* that Goodson made to the stranger."

"It's perfectly true. I feel guilty and ashamed. And you?"

"I'm past it. Let us make a pallet here; we've got to stand watch till the bank vault opens in the morning and admits the sack. . . . Oh dear, oh dear—if we hadn't made the mistake!"

The pallet was made, and Mary said:

"The open sesame—what could it have been? I do wonder what that remark could have been? But come; we will get to bed now."

"And sleep?"

"No: think."

"Yes, think."

By this time the Coxes too had completed their spat and their reconciliation, and were turning in—to think, to think, and toss, and fret, and worry over what the remark could possibly have been which Goodson made to the stranded derelict; that golden remark; that remark worth forty thousand dollars, cash.

The reason that the village telegraph-office was open later than usual that night was this: The foreman of Cox's paper was the local representative of the Associated Press. One might say its honorary representative, for it wasn't four times a year that he could furnish thirty words that would be accepted. But this time it was different. His despatch stating what he had caught got an instant answer:

Send the whole thing—all the details—twelve hundred words.

A colossal order! The foreman filled the bill; and he was the proudest man in the State. By breakfast-time the next morning the name of Hadleyburg the Incorruptible was on every lip in America, from Montreal to the Gulf, from the glaciers of Alaska to the orange-groves of Florida; and millions and millions of people were discussing the stranger and his money-sack, and wondering if the right man would be found, and hoping some more news about the matter would come soon—right away.

II

Hadleyburg village woke up world-celebrated — astonished — happy—vain. Vain beyond imagination. Its nineteen principal citizens and their wives went about shaking hands with each other, and beaming, and smiling, and congratulating, and saying *this* thing adds a new word to the dictionary—*Hadleyburg*, synonym for *incorruptible*—destined to live in dictionaries forever! And the minor and unimportant citizens and their wives went around acting in much the same way. Everybody ran to the bank to see the gold-sack; and before noon grieved and envious crowds began to flock in from Brixton and all neighboring towns; and that afternoon and next day reporters began to arrive from everywhere to verify the sack and its history and write the whole thing up anew, and make dashing free-hand pictures of the sack, and of Richards's house, and the bank, and the Presbyterian church, and the Baptist church, and the public square, and the town-hall where the test would be applied and the money delivered; and damnable portraits of the Richardses, and Pinkerton the banker, and Cox, and the foreman, and Reverend Burgess, and the postmaster—and even of Jack Halliday, who was the loafing, good-natured, no-account, irreverent fisherman, hunter, boys' friend, stray-dogs' friend, typical "Sam Lawson" of the town. The little mean, smirking, oily Pinkerton showed the sack to all comers, and rubbed his sleek palms together pleasantly, and enlarged upon the town's fine old reputation for honesty and upon this wonderful indorsement of it, and hoped and believed that the example would now spread far and wide over the American world, and be epoch-making in the matter of moral regeneration. And so on, and so on.

By the end of a week things had quieted down again; the wild intoxication of pride and joy had sobered to a soft, sweet, silent delight—a sort of deep, nameless, unutterable content. All faces bore a look of peaceful, holy happiness.

Then a change came. It was a gradual change: so gradual that its beginnings were hardly noticed; maybe were not noticed at all, except by Jack Halliday, who always noticed everything; and always made fun of it, too, no matter what it was. He began to throw out chaffing remarks about people not looking quite so happy as they did a day or two ago; and next he claimed that the new aspect was deepening to positive sadness; next, that it was taking on a sick look; and finally he said that everybody was become so moody, thoughtful, and absent-minded that he could rob the meanest man in town of a cent out of the bottom of his breeches pocket and not disturb his revery.

At this stage—or at about this stage—a saying like this was dropped at bedtime—with a sigh, usually—by the head of each of the nineteen principal households: "Ah, what *could* have been the remark that Goodson made?"

And straightway—with a shudder—came this, from the man's wife:

"Oh, *don't!* What horrible thing are you mulling in your mind? Put it away from you, for God's sake!"

But that question was wrung from those men again the next night—and got the same retort. But weaker.

And the third night the men uttered the question yet again—with anguish, and absently. This time—and the following night—the wives fidgeted feebly, and tried to say something. But didn't.

And the night after that they found their tongues and responded —longingly:

"Oh, if we *could* only guess!"

Halliday's comments grew daily more and more sparklingly disagreeable and disparaging. He went diligently about, laughing at the town, individually and in mass. But his laugh was the only one left in the village: it fell upon a hollow and mournful vacancy and emptiness. Not even a smile was findable anywhere. Halliday carried a cigar-box around on a tripod, playing that it was a camera, and halted all passers and aimed the thing and said, "Ready!—now look pleasant, please," but not even this capital joke could surprise the dreary faces into any softening.

So three weeks passed—one week was left. It was Saturday evening—after supper. Instead of the aforementioned Saturday-evening flutter and bustle and shopping and larking, the streets were empty and desolate. Richards and his old wife sat apart in their little parlor—miserable and thinking. This was become their evening habit now: the lifelong habit which had preceded it, of reading, knitting, and contented chat, or receiving or paying neighborly calls, was dead and gone and forgotten, ages ago—two or three weeks ago; nobody talked now, nobody read, nobody visited—the whole village sat at home, sighing, worrying, silent. Trying to guess out that remark.

The postman left a letter. Richards glanced listlessly at the superscription and the postmark—unfamiliar, both—and tossed the letter on the table and resumed his might-have-beens and his hopeless dull miseries where he had left them off. Two or three hours later his wife got wearily up and was going away to bed without a good night—custom now—but she stopped near the letter and eyed it awhile with a dead interest, then broke it open, and began to skim it over. Richards, sitting there with his chair tilted back against the wall and his chin between his knees, heard something fall. It was his wife. He sprang to her side, but she cried out:

"Leave me alone, I am too happy. Read the letter—read it!"

He did. He devoured it, his brain reeling. The letter was from a distant state, and it said:

I am a stranger to you, but no matter: I have something to tell. I have just arrived home from Mexico, and learned about that episode. Of course you do not know who made that remark, but I know, and I am the only person living who does know. It was GOODSON. I knew him well, many years ago. I passed through your village that very night, and was his guest till the midnight train came along. I overheard him make that remark to the stranger in the dark—it was in Hale Alley. He and I talked of it the rest of the way home, and while smoking in his house. He mentioned many of your villagers in the course of his talk—most of them in a very uncomplimentary way, but two or three favorably; among these latter yourself. I say "favorably"—nothing stronger. I remember his saying he did not actually LIKE any person in the town—not one; but that you—I THINK he said you—am almost sure—had done him a very great service once, possibly without knowing the full value of it, and he wished he had a fortune, he would leave it to you when he died, and a curse apiece for the rest of the citizens. Now, then, if it was you that did him that service, you are his legitimate heir, and entitled to the sack of gold. I know that I can trust to your honor and honesty, for in a citizen of Hadleyburg these virtues are an unfailing inheritance, and so I am going to reveal to you the remark, well satisfied that if you are not the right man you will seek and find the right one and see that poor Goodson's debt of gratitude for the service referred to is paid. This is the remark: "YOU ARE FAR FROM BEING A BAD MAN: GO, AND REFORM."

HOWARD L. STEPHENSON

"Oh, Edward, the money is ours, and I am so grateful, *oh*, so grateful—kiss me, dear, it's forever since we kissed—and we needed it so—the money—and now you are free of Pinkerton and his bank, and nobody's slave any more; it seems to me I could fly for joy."

It was a happy half-hour that the couple spent there on the settee caressing each other; it was the old days come again—days that had begun with their courtship and lasted without a break till the stranger brought the deadly money. By and by the wife said:

"Oh, Edward, how lucky it was you did him that grand service, poor Goodson! I never liked him, but I love him now. And it was fine and beautiful of you never to mention it or brag about it." Then, with a touch of reproach, "But you ought to have told *me*, Edward, you ought to have told your wife, you know."

"Well, I—er—well, Mary, you see——"

"Now stop hemming and hawing, and tell me about it, Edward. I always loved you, and now I'm proud of you. Everybody believes there was only one good generous soul in this village, and now it turns out that you—Edward, why don't you tell me?"

"Well—er—er— Why, Mary, I can't!"

"You *can't? Why* can't you?"

"You see, he—well, he—he made me promise I wouldn't."

The wife looked him over, and said, very slowly:

"Made—you—promise? Edward, what do you tell me that for?"

"Mary, do you think I would lie?"

She was troubled and silent for a moment, then she laid her hand within his and said:

"No . . . no. We have wandered far enough from our bearings— God spare us that! In all your life you have never uttered a lie. But now—now that the foundations of things seem to be crumbling from under us, we—we—" She lost her voice for a moment, then said, brokenly, "Lead us not into temptation. . . . I think you made the promise, Edward. Let it rest so. Let us keep away from that ground. Now—that is all gone by; let us be happy again; it is no time for clouds."

Edward found it something of an effort to comply, for his mind kept wandering—trying to remember what the service was that he had done Goodson.

The couple lay awake the most of the night, Mary happy and busy, Edward busy but not so happy. Mary was planning what she would do with the money. Edward was trying to recall that service. At first his conscience was sore on account of the lie he had told Mary—if it was a lie. After much reflection—suppose it *was* a lie? What then? Was it such a great matter? Aren't we always *acting* lies? Then why not *tell* them? Look at Mary—look what she had done. While he was hurrying off on his honest errand, what was she doing? Lamenting because the papers hadn't been destroyed and the money kept! Is theft better than lying?

That point lost its sting—the lie dropped into the background and left comfort behind it. The next point came to the front: *Had* he rendered that service? Well, here was Goodson's own evidence as reported in Stephenson's letter; there could be no better evidence than that—it was even *proof* that he had rendered it. Of course.

So that point was settled. . . . No, not quite. He recalled with a wince that this unknown Mr. Stephenson was just a trifle unsure as to whether the performer of it was Richards or some other—and, oh dear, he had put Richards on his honor! He must himself decide whither that money must go—and Mr. Stephenson was not doubting that if he was the wrong man he would go honorably and find the right one. Oh, it was odious to put a man in such a situation—ah, why couldn't Stephenson have left out that doubt! What did he want to intrude that for?

Further reflection. How did it happen that *Richards's* name remained in Stephenson's mind as indicating the right man, and not some other man's name? That looked good. Yes, that looked very good. In fact, it went on looking better and better, straight along—until by and by it grew into positive *proof*. And then Richards put the matter at once out of his mind, for he had a private instinct that a proof once established is better left so.

He was feeling reasonably comfortable now, but there was still one other detail that kept pushing itself on his notice: of course he had done that service—that was settled; but what *was* that service? He must recall it—he would not go to sleep till he had recalled it; it would make his peace of mind perfect. And so he thought and thought. He thought of a dozen things—possible services, even probable services—but none of them seemed adequate, none of them seemed large enough, none of them seemed worth the money—worth the fortune Goodson had wished he could leave in his will. And besides, he couldn't remember having done them, anyway. Now, then—now, then—what *kind* of a service would it be that would make a man so inordinately grateful? Ah—the saving of his soul! That must be it. Yes, he could remember, now, how he once set himself the task of converting Goodson, and labored at it as much as—he was going to say three months; but upon closer examination it shrunk to a month, then to a week, then to a day, then to nothing. Yes, he remembered now, and with unwelcome vividness, that Goodson had told him to go to thunder and mind his own business—*he* wasn't hankering to follow Hadleyburg to heaven!

So that solution was a failure—he hadn't saved Goodson's soul. Richards was discouraged. Then after a little came another idea:

had he saved Goodson's property? No, that wouldn't do—he hadn't any. His life? That is it! Of course. Why, he might have thought of it before. This time he was on the right track, sure. His imagination-mill was hard at work in a minute, now.

Thereafter during a stretch of two exhausting hours he was busy saving Goodson's life. He saved it in all kinds of difficult and perilous ways. In every case he got it saved satisfactorily up to a certain point; then, just as he was beginning to get well persuaded that it had really happened, a troublesome detail would turn up which made the whole thing impossible. As in the matter of drowning, for instance. In that case he had swum out and tugged Goodson ashore in an unconscious state with a great crowd looking on and applauding, but when he had got it all thought out and was just beginning to remember all about it, a whole swarm of disqualifying details arrived on the ground: the town would have known of the circumstance, Mary would have known of it, it would glare like a limelight in his own memory instead of being an inconspicuous service which he had possibly rendered "without knowing its full value." And at this point he remembered that he couldn't swim, anyway.

Ah—*there* was a point which he had been overlooking from the start: it had to be a service which he had rendered "possibly without knowing the full value of it." Why, really, that ought to be an easy hunt—much easier than those others. And sure enough, by and by he found it. Goodson, years and years ago, came near marrying a very sweet and pretty girl, named Nancy Hewitt, but in some way or other the match had been broken off; the girl died, Goodson remained a bachelor, and by and by became a soured one and a frank despiser of the human species. Soon after the girl's death the village found out, or thought it had found out, that she carried a spoonful of Negro blood in her veins. Richards worked at these details a good while, and in the end he thought he remembered things concerning them which must have gotten mislaid in his memory through long neglect. He seemed to dimly remember that it was *he* that found out about the Negro blood; that it was he that told the village; that the village told Goodson where they got it; that he thus saved Goodson from marrying the tainted girl; that he had done him this great service "without knowing the full value of it," in fact without knowing that he *was* doing it; but that Goodson knew the value of it, and what a narrow escape he had had, and so went to his grave grateful to his benefactor and wishing he had a fortune to leave him. It was all clear and simple now, and the more he went over it the more luminous and certain it grew; and at last, when he nestled to sleep satisfied and happy, he remembered the whole thing just as if it had been yesterday. In fact, he dimly remembered Goodson's *telling* him his gratitude once. Meantime Mary had spent six thousand dollars on a new house for herself and a pair of slippers for her pastor, and then had fallen peacefully to rest.

That same Saturday evening the postman had delivered a letter to each of the other principal citizens—nineteen letters in all. No two of the envelopes were alike, and no two of the superscriptions were in the same hand, but the letters inside were just like each other in every detail but one. They were exact copies of the letter received by Richards—handwriting and all—and were all signed by Stephenson, but in place of Richards's name each receiver's own name appeared.

All night long eighteen principal citizens did what their caste-brother Richards was doing at the same time—they put in their energies trying to remember what notable service it was that they had unconsciously done Barclay Goodson. In no case was it a holiday job; still they succeeded.

And while they were at this work, which was difficult, their wives put in the night spending the money, which was easy. During that one night the nineteen wives spent an average of seven thousand dollars each out of the forty thousand in the sack—a hundred and thirty-three thousand altogether.

Next day there was a surprise for Jack Halliday. He noticed that the faces of the nineteen chief citizens and their wives bore that expression of peaceful and holy happiness again. He could not understand it, neither was he able to invent any remarks about it that could damage it or disturb it. And so it was his turn to be dissatisfied with life. His private guesses at the reasons for the happiness failed in all instances, upon examination. When he met Mrs. Wilcox and noticed the placid ecstasy in her face, he said to himself, "Her cat has had kittens"—and went and asked the cook: it was not so; the cook had detected the happiness, but did not know the cause. When Halliday found the duplicate ecstasy in the face of "Shadbelly" Billson (village nickname), he was sure some neighbor of Billson's had broken his leg, but inquiry showed that this had not happened. The subdued ecstasy in Gregory Yates's face could mean but one thing—he was a mother-in-law short: it was another mistake. "And Pinkerton—Pinkerton—he has collected ten cents that he thought he was going to lose." And so on, and so on. In some cases the guesses had to remain in doubt, in the others they proved distinct errors. In the end Halliday said to himself, "Anyway it foots up that there's nineteen Hadleyburg families temporarily in heaven: I don't know how it happened; I only know Providence is off duty to-day."

An architect and builder from the next state had lately ventured to set up a small business in this unpromising village, and his sign had now been hanging out a week. Not a customer yet; he was a discouraged man, and sorry he had come. But his weather changed suddenly now. First one and then another chief citizen's wife said to him privately:

"Come to my house Monday week—but say nothing about it for the present. We are thinking of building."

He got eleven invitations that day. That night he wrote his daughter and broke off her match with her student. He said she could marry a mile higher than that.

Pinkerton the banker and two or three other well-to-do men planned country-seats—but waited. That kind don't count their chickens until they are hatched.

The Wilsons devised a grand new thing—a fancy-dress ball. They made no actual promises, but told all their acquaintanceship in confidence that they were thinking the matter over and thought they should give it—"and if we do, you will be invited, of course." People were surprised, and said, one to another, "Why, they are crazy, those poor Wilsons, they can't afford it." Several among the nineteen said privately to their husbands, "It is a good idea: we will keep still till their cheap thing is over, then *we* will give one that will make it sick."

The days drifted along, and the bill of future squanderings rose higher and higher, wilder and wilder, more and more foolish and reckless. It began to look as if every member of the nineteen would not only spend his whole forty thousand dollars before receiving-day, but be actually in debt by the time he got the money. In some cases light-headed people did not stop with planning to spend, they really spent—on credit. They bought land, mortgages, farms, speculative stocks, fine clothes, horses, and various other things, paid down the bonus, and made themselves liable for the rest—at ten days. Presently the sober second thought came, and Halliday noticed that a ghastly anxiety was beginning to show up in a good many faces. Again he was puzzled, and didn't know what to make of it. "The Wilcox kittens aren't dead, for they weren't born; nobody's broken a leg; there's no shrinkage in mother-in-laws; *nothing* has happened—it is an unsolvable mystery."

There was another puzzled man, too—the Rev. Mr. Burgess. For days, wherever he went, people seemed to follow him or to be watching out for him; and if he ever found himself in a retired spot, a member of the nineteen would be sure to appear, thrust an envelope privately into his hand, whisper "To be opened at the town-hall Friday evening," then vanish away like a guilty thing. He was expecting that there might be one claimant for the sack—doubtful, however, Goodson being dead—but it never occurred to him that all this crowd might be claimants. When the great Friday came at last, he found that he had nineteen envelopes.

III

The town hall had never looked finer. The platform at the end of it was backed by a showy draping of flags; at intervals along the walls there were festoons of flags; the gallery fronts were clothed in flags; the supporting columns were swathed in flags; all this was to impress the stranger, for he would be there in considerable force, and in a large degree he would be connected with the press. The house was full. The 412 fixed seats were occupied; also the 68 extra chairs which had been packed into the aisles; the steps of the platform were occupied; some distinguished strangers were given seats on the platform; at the horseshoe of tables which fenced the front and sides of the platform sat a strong force of special correspondents who had come from everywhere. It was the best-dressed house the town had ever produced. There were some tolerably expensive toilets there, and in several cases the ladies who wore them had the look of being unfamiliar with that kind of clothes. At least the town thought they had that look, but the notion could have arisen from the town's knowledge of the fact that these ladies had never inhabited such clothes before.

The gold-sack stood on a little table at the front of the platform where all the house could see it. The bulk of the house gazed at it with a burning interest, a mouth-watering interest, a wistful and pathetic interest; a minority of nineteen couples gazed at it tenderly, lovingly, proprietarily, and the male half of this minority kept saying over to themselves the moving little impromptu speeches of thankfulness for the audience's applause and congratulations which they were presently going to get up and deliver. Every now and then one of these got a piece of paper out of his vest pocket and privately glanced at it to refresh his memory.

Of course there was a buzz of conversation going on—there always is; but at last when the Rev. Mr. Burgess rose and laid his hand on the sack he could hear his microbes gnaw, the place was so still. He related the curious history of the sack, then went on to speak in warm terms of Hadleyburg's old and well-earned reputation for spotless honesty, and of the town's just pride in this reputation. He said that this reputation was a treasure of priceless value; that under Providence its value had now become inestimably enhanced, for the recent episode had spread this fame far and wide, and thus had focused the eyes of the American world upon this village, and made its name for all time, as he hoped and believed, a synonym for commercial incorruptibility. [*Applause.*] "And who is to be the guardian of this noble treasure—the community as a whole? No! The responsibility is individual, not communal. From this day forth each and every one of you is in his own person its special guardian, and individually responsible that no harm shall come to it. Do you—does each of you—accept this great trust? [*Tumultuous assent.*] Then all is well. Transmit it to your children and to your children's children. To-day your purity is beyond reproach—see to it that it shall remain so. To-day there is not a person in your community who could be beguiled to touch a penny not his own—see to it that you abide in this grace." ["*We will! we will!*"]

This is not the place to make comparisons between ourselves and other communities—some of them ungracious toward us; they have their ways, we have ours; let us be content. [*Applause.*] I am done. Under my hand, my friends, rests a stranger's eloquent recognition of what we are; through him the world will always henceforth know what we are. We do not know who he is, but in your name I utter your gratitude, and ask you to raise your voices in indorsement."

The house rose in a body and made the walls quake with the thunders of its thankfulness for the space of a long minute. Then it sat down, and Mr. Burgess took an envelope out of his pocket. The house held its breath while he slit the envelope open and took from it a slip of paper. He read its contents—slowly and impressively —the audience listening with tranced attention to this magic document, each of whose words stood for an ingot of gold:

"*'The remark which I made to the distressed stranger was this: "You are very far from being a bad man: go, and reform."'*" Then he continued:

"We shall know in a moment now whether the remark here quoted corresponds with the one concealed in the sack; and if that shall prove to be so—and it undoubtedly will—this sack of gold belongs to a fellow-citizen who will henceforth stand before the nation as the symbol of the special virtue which has made our town famous throughout the land—Mr. Billson!"

The house had gotten itself all ready to burst into the proper tornado of applause; but instead of doing it, it seemed stricken with a paralysis; there was a deep hush for a moment or two, then a wave of whispered murmurs swept the place—of about this tenor: "*Billson!* oh, come, this is *too* thin! Twenty dollars to a stranger—or anybody—*Billson!* tell it to the marines!" And now at this point the house caught its breath all of a sudden in a new access of astonishment, for it discovered that whereas in one part of the hall Deacon Billson was standing up with his head meekly bowed, in another part of it Lawyer Wilson was doing the same. There was a wondering silence now for a while.

Everybody was puzzled, and nineteen couples were surprised and indignant.

Billson and Wilson turned and stared at each other. Billson asked, bitingly:

"Why do *you* rise, Mr. Wilson?"

"Because I have a right to. Perhaps you will be good enough to explain to the house why *you* rise?"

"With great pleasure. Because I wrote that paper."

"It is an impudent falsity! I wrote it myself."

It was Burgess's turn to be paralyzed. He stood looking vacantly at first one of the men and then the other, and did not seem to know what to do. The house was stupefied. Lawyer Wilson spoke up, now, and said,

"I ask the Chair to read the name signed to that paper."

That brought the Chair to itself, and it read out the name:

"'John Wharton *Billson*.'"

"There!" shouted Billson, "what have you got to say for yourself, now? And what kind of apology are you going to make to me and to this insulted house for the imposture which you have attempted to play here?"

"No apologies are due, sir; and as for the rest of it, I publicly charge you with pilfering my note from Mr. Burgess and substituting a copy of it signed with your own name. There is no other way by which you could have gotten hold of the test-remark; I alone, of living men, possessed the secret of its wording."

There was likely to be a scandalous state of things if this went on; everybody noticed with distress that the short-hand scribes were scribbling like mad; many people were crying "Chair, Chair! Order! order!" Burgess rapped with his gavel, and said:

"Let us not forget the proprieties due. There has evidently been a mistake somewhere, but surely that is all. If Mr. Wilson gave me an envelope—and I remember now that he did—I still have it."

He took one out of his pocket, opened it, glanced at it, looked surprised and worried, and stood silent a few moments. Then he waved his hand in a wandering and mechanical way, and made an effort or two to say something, then gave it up, despondently. Several voices cried out:

"Read it! read it! What is it?"

So he began in a dazed and sleep-walker fashion:

"'*The remark which I made to the unhappy stranger was this:* "*You are far from being a bad man.* [The house gazed at him, marveling.] *Go, and reform.*" ' [*Murmurs:* "Amazing! what can this mean?"] This one," said the Chair, "is signed Thurlow G. Wilson."

"There!" cried Wilson. "I reckon that settles it! I knew perfectly well my note was purloined."

"Purloined!" retorted Billson. "I'll let you know that neither you nor any man of your kidney must venture to——"

The Chair. "Order, gentlemen, order! Take your seats, both of you, please."

They obeyed, shaking their heads and grumbling angrily. The house was profoundly puzzled; it did not know what to do with this curious emergency. Presently Thompson got up. Thompson was the hatter. He would have liked to be a Nineteener; but such was not for him: his stock of hats was not considerable enough for the position. He said:

"Mr. Chairman, if I may be permitted to make a suggestion, can both of these gentlemen be right? I put it to you, sir, can both have happened to say the very same words to the stranger? It seems to me——"

The tanner got up and interrupted him. The tanner was a disgruntled man; he believed himself entitled to be a Nineteener, but he couldn't get recognition. It made him a little unpleasant in his ways and speech. Said he:

"Sho, *that's* not the point! *That* could happen—twice in a hundred years—but not the other thing. *Neither* of them gave the twenty dollars!"

[*A ripple of applause.*]

Billson. "I did!"

Wilson. "I did!"

Then each accused the other of pilfering.

The Chair. "Order! Sit down, if you please—both of you. Neither of the notes has been out of my possession at any moment."

A Voice. "Good—that settles *that!*"

The Tanner. "Mr. Chairman, one thing is now plain: one of these men has been eavesdropping under the other one's bed, and filching family secrets. If it is not unparliamentary to suggest it, I will remark that both are equal to it. [*The Chair.* "Order! order!"] I withdraw the remark, sir, and will confine myself to suggesting that *if* one of them has overheard the other reveal the test-remark to his wife, we shall catch him now."

A Voice. "How?"

The Tanner. "Easily. The two have not quoted the remark in exactly the same words. You would have noticed that, if there hadn't been a considerable stretch of time and an exciting quarrel inserted between the two readings."

A Voice. "Name the difference."

The Tanner. "The word *very* is in Billson's note, and not in the other."

Many Voices. "That's so—he's right!"

The Tanner. "And so, if the Chair will examine the test-remark in the sack, we shall know which of these two frauds— [*The Chair.* Order!"]—which of these two Adventurers—[*The Chair.* "Order! order!"]—which of these two gentlemen—[*laughter and applause*] —is entitled to wear the belt as being the first dishonest blatherskite ever bred in this town—which he has dishonored, and which will be a sultry place for him from now out!" [*Vigorous applause.*]

Many Voices. "Open it!—open the sack!"

Mr. Burgess made a slit in the sack, slid his hand in and brought out an envelope. In it were a couple of folded notes. He said:

"One of these is marked, 'Not to be examined until all written communications which have been addressed to the Chair—if any— shall have been read.' The other is marked '*The Test.*' Allow me. It is worded—to wit:

" 'I do not require that the first half of the remark which was made to me by my benefactor shall be quoted with exactness, for it was not striking, and could be forgotten; but its closing fifteen words are quite striking, and I think easily rememberable; unless *these* shall be accurately reproduced, let the applicant be regarded as an imposter. My benefactor began by saying he seldom gave advice to any one, but that it always bore the hall-mark of high value when he did give it. Then he said this—and it has never faded from my memory: *"You are far from being a bad man——*" ' "

Fifty Voices. "That settles it—the money's Wilson's! Wilson! Wilson! Speech! Speech!

People jumped up and crowded around Wilson, wringing his

hand and congratulating fervently—meantime the Chair was hammering with the gavel and shouting:

"Order, gentlemen! Order! Order! Let me finish reading, please." When quiet was restored, the reading was resumed—as follows:

" ' "Go, and reform—or, mark my words—some day, for your sins, you will die and go to hell or Hadleyburg—TRY AND MAKE IT THE FORMER." ' "

A ghastly silence followed. First an angry cloud began to settle darkly upon the faces of the citizenship; after a pause the cloud began to rise, and a tickled expression tried to take its place; tried so hard that it was only kept under with great and painful difficulty; the reporters, the Brixtonites, and other strangers bent their heads down and shielded their faces with their hands, and managed to hold in by main strength and heroic courtesy. At this most inopportune time burst upon the stillness the roar of a solitary voice—Jack Halliday's:

"*That's* got the hall-mark on it!"

Then the house let go, strangers and all. Even Mr. Burgess's gravity broke down presently, then the audience considered itself officially absolved from all restraint, and it made the most of its privilege. It was a good long laugh, and a tempestuously wholehearted one, but it ceased at last—long enough for Mr. Burgess to try to resume, and for the people to get their eyes partially wiped; then it broke out again; and afterward yet again; then at last Burgess was able to get out these serious words:

"It is useless to try to disguise the fact—we find ourselves in the presence of a matter of grave import. It involves the honor of your town, it strikes at the town's good name. The difference of a single word between the test-remarks offered by Mr. Wilson and Mr. Billson was itself a serious thing, since it indicated that one or the other of these gentlemen had committed a theft——"

The two men were sitting limp, nerveless, crushed; but at these words both were electrified into movement, and started to get up——

"Sit down!" said the Chair, sharply, and they obeyed. "That, as I have said, was a serious thing. And it was—but for only one of them. But the matter has become graver; for the honor of *both* is now in formidable peril. Shall I go even further, and say in inextricable peril? *Both* left out the crucial fifteen words." He paused. During several moments he allowed the pervading stillness to gather and deepen its impressive effects, then added: "There would seem to be but one way whereby this could happen. I ask these gentlemen —Was there *collusion?—agreement?*"

A low murmur sifted through the house; its import was, "He's got them both."

Billson was not used to emergencies; he sat in a helpless collapse. But Wilson was a lawyer. He struggled to his feet, pale and worried, and said:

"I ask the indulgence of the house while I explain this most painful matter. I am sorry to say what I am about to say, since it must inflict irreparable injury upon Mr. Billson, whom I have always esteemed and respected until now, and in whose invulnerability to temptation I entirely believed—as did you all. But for the preservation of my own honor I must speak—and with frankness. I confess with shame—and I now beseech your pardon for it—that I said to the ruined stranger all of the words contained in the test-remark, including the disparaging fifteen. [*Sensation.*] When the late publication was made I recalled them, and I resolved to claim the sack of coin, for by every right I was entitled to it. Now I will ask you to consider this point, and weigh it well: that stranger's gratitude to me that night knew no bounds; he said himself that he could find no words for it that were adequate, and that if he should ever be able he would repay me a thousand-fold. Now, then, I ask you this: Could I expect—could I believe—could I even remotely imagine—that, feeling as he did, he would do so ungrateful a thing as to add those quite unnecessary fifteen words to his test?—set a trap for me?—expose me as a slanderer of my own town before my own people assembled in a public hall? It was preposterous; it was impossible. His test would contain only the kindly opening clause of my remark. Of that I had no shadow of doubt. You would have thought as I did. You would not have expected a base betrayal from one whom you had befriended and against whom you had committed no offense. And so, with perfect confidence, perfect trust, I wrote on a piece of paper the opening words—ending with 'Go, and reform,' and signed it. When I was about to put it in an envelope I was called into my back office, and without thinking

I left the paper lying open on my desk." He stopped, turned his head slowly toward Billson, waited a moment, then added: "I ask you to note this: when I returned, a little later, Mr. Billson was retiring by my street door." [*Sensation.*]

In a moment Billson was on his feet and shouting:

"It's a lie! It's an infamous lie!"

The Chair. "Be seated, sir! Mr. Wilson has the floor."

Billson's friends pulled him into his seat and quieted him, and Wilson went on:

"Those are the simple facts. My note was now lying in a different place on the table from where I had left it. I noticed that, but attached no importance to it, thinking a draught had blown it there. That Mr. Billson would read a private paper was a thing which could not occur to me; he was an honorable man, and he would be above that. If you will allow me to say it, I think his extra word '*very*' stands explained; it is attributable to a defect of memory. I was the only man in the world who could furnish here any detail of the test-remark—by *honorable* means. I have finished."

There is nothing in the world like a persuasive speech to fuddle the mental apparatus and upset the convictions and debauch the emotions of an audience not practised in the tricks and delusions of oratory. Wilson sat down victorious. The house submerged him in tides of approving applause; friends swarmed to him and shook him by the hand and congratulated him, and Billson was shouted down and not allowed to say a word. The Chair hammered and hammered with its gavel, and kept shouting:

"But let us proceed, gentlemen, let us proceed!"

At last there was a measurable degree of quiet, and the hatter said:

"But what is there to proceed with, sir, but to deliver the money?"

Voices. "That's it! That's it! Come forward, Wilson!"

The Hatter. "I move three cheers for Mr. Wilson, Symbol of the special virtue which——"

The cheers burst forth before he could finish; and in the midst of them—and in the midst of the clamor of the gavel also—some enthusiasts mounted Wilson on a big friend's shoulder and were going to fetch him in triumph to the platform. The Chair's voice now rose above the noise——

"Order! To your places! You forget that there is still a document to be read." When quiet had been restored he took up the document, and was going to read it, but laid it down again, saying, "I forgot; this is not to be read until all written communications received by me have first been read." He took an envelope out of his pocket, removed its inclosure, glanced at it—seemed astonished —held it out and gazed at it—stared at it.

Twenty or thirty voices cried out:

"What is it? Read it! read it!"

And he did—slowly, and wondering:

"'The remark which I made to the stranger—[*Voices.* "Hello! how's this?"]—was this: "You are far from being a bad man. [*Voices.* "Great Scott!"] Go, and reform."' [*Voice.* "Oh, saw my leg off!"] Signed by Mr. Pinkerton, the banker."

The pandemonium of delight which turned itself loose now was of a sort to make the judicious weep. Those whose withers were unwrung laughed till the tears ran down; the reporters, in throes of laughter, set down disordered pot-hooks which would never in the world be decipherable; and a sleeping dog jumped up, scared out of its wits, and barked itself crazy at the turmoil. All manner of cries were scattered through the din: "We're getting rich—*two* Symbols of Incorruptibility!—without counting Billson!" "*Three*—count Shadbelly in—we can't have too many!" "All right—Billson's elected!" "Alas, poor Wilson—victim of *two* thieves!"

A Powerful Voice. "Silence! The Chair's fished up something more out of its pocket."

Voices. "Hurrah! Is it something fresh? Read it! read! read!"

The Chair [*reading*]. "'The remark which I made,' etc.: ' "You are far from being a bad man. Go,"' etc. Signed, 'Gregory Yates.'"

Tornado of Voices. "Four Symbols!" "'Rah for Yates!" "Fish again!"

The house was in a roaring humor now, and ready to get all the fun out of the occasion that might be in it. Several Nineteeners, looking pale and distressed, got up and began to work their way toward the aisles, but a score of shouts went up:

"The doors, the doors—close the doors; no Incorruptible shall leave this place! Sit down, everybody!"

The mandate was obeyed.

"Fish again! Read! read!"

The Chair fished again, and once more the familiar words began to fall from its lips—"'You are far from being a bad man.'"

"Name! name! What's his name?"

"'L. Ingoldsby Sargent.'"

"Five elected! Pile up the Symbols! Go on, go on!"

"'You are far from being a bad—'"

"Name! name!"

"'Nicholas Whitworth.'"

"Hooray! hooray! it's a symbolical day!"

Somebody wailed in, and began to sing this rhyme (leaving out "it's") to the lovely "Mikado" tune of "When a man's afraid, a beautiful maid—"; the audience joined in, with joy; then, just in time, somebody contributed another line——

And don't you this forget——

The house roared it out. A third line was at once furnished——

Corruptibles far from Hadleyburg are——

The house roared that one too. As the last note died, Jack Halliday's voice rose high and clear, freighted with a final line——

But the Symbols are here, you bet!

That was sung, with booming enthusiasm. Then the happy house started in at the beginning and sang the four lines through twice, with immense swing and dash, and finished up with a crashing three-times-three and a tiger for "Hadleyburg the Incorruptible and all Symbols of it which we shall find worthy to receive the hall-mark to-night."

Then the shoutings at the Chair began again, all over the place:

"Go on! go on! Read! read some more! Read all you've got!"

"That's it—go on! We are winning eternal celebrity!"

A dozen men got up now and began to protest. They said that this farce was the work of some abandoned joker, and was an insult to the whole community. Without a doubt these signatures were all forgeries——

"Sit down! sit down! Shut up! You are confessing. We'll find *your* names in the lot."

"Mr. Chairman, how many of those envelopes have you got?"

The Chair counted.

"Together with those that have been already examined, there are nineteen."

A storm of derisive applause broke out.

"Perhaps they all contain the secret. I move that you open them all and read every signature that is attached to a note of that sort—and read also the first eight words of the note."

"Second the motion!"

It was put and carried—uproariously. Then poor old Richards got up, and his wife rose and stood at his side. Her head was bent down, so that none might see that she was crying. Her husband gave her his arm, and so supporting her, he began to speak in a quavering voice:

"My friends, you have known us two—Mary and me—all our lives, and I think you have liked us and respected us——"

The Chair interrupted him:

"Allow me. It is quite true—that which you are saying, Mr. Richards: this town *does* know you two; it *does* like you; it *does* respect you; more—it honors you and *loves* you——"

Halliday's voice rang out:

"That's the hall-mark truth, too! If the Chair is right, let the house speak up and say it. Rise! Now, then—hip! hip! hip!—all together!"

The house rose in mass, faced toward the old couple eagerly, filled the air with a snow-storm of waving handkerchiefs, and delivered the cheers with all its affectionate heart.

The Chair then continued:

"What I was going to say is this: We know your good heart, Mr. Richards, but this is not a time for the exercise of charity toward offenders. [*Shouts of "Right! right!"*] I see your generous purpose in your face, but I cannot allow you to plead for these men——"

"But I was going to——"

"Please take your seat, Mr. Richards. We must examine the rest of these notes—simple fairness to the men who have already been exposed requires this. As soon as that has been done—I give you my word for this—you shall be heard."

Many Voices. "Right!—the Chair is right—no interruption can be permitted at this stage! Go on!—the names! the names!—according to the terms of the motion!"

The old couple sat reluctantly down, and the husband whispered to the wife, "It is pitifully hard to have to wait; the shame will be greater than ever when they find we were only going to plead for *ourselves.*"

Straightway the jollity broke loose again with the reading of the names.

"'You are far from being a bad man—' Signature, 'Robert J. Titmarsh.'

"'You are far from being a bad man—' Signature, 'Eliphalet Weeks.'

"'You are far from being a bad man—' Signature, 'Oscar B. Wilder.'"

At this point the house lit upon the idea of taking the eight words out of the Chairman's hands. He was not unthankful for that. Thenceforward he held up each note in its turn, and waited. The house droned out the eight words in a massed and measured and musical deep volume of sound (with a daringly close resemblance to a well-known church chant)—"'You are f-a-r from being a b-a-a-a-d man.'" Then the Chair said, "Signature, 'Archibald Wilcox.'" And so on, and so on, name after name, and everybody had an increasingly and gloriously good time except the wretched Nineteen. Now and then, when a particularly shining name was called, the house made the Chair wait while it chanted the whole of the test-remark from the beginning to the closing words, "And go to hell or Hadleyburg—try and make it the for-or-m-e-r!" and in these special cases they added a grand and agonized and imposing "A-a-a-a-*men!*"

The list dwindled, dwindled, dwindled, poor old Richards keeping tally of the count, wincing when a name resembling his own was pronounced, and waiting in miserable suspense for the time to come when it would be his humiliating privilege to rise with Mary and finish his plea, which he was intending to word thus: "... for until now we have never done any wrong thing, but have gone our humble way unreproached. We are very poor, we are old, and have no chick nor child to help us; we were sorely tempted, and we fell. It was my purpose when I got up before to make confession and beg that my name might not be read out in this public place, for it seemed to us that we could not bear it; but I was prevented. It was just; it was our place to suffer with the rest. It has been hard for us. It is the first time we have ever heard our name fall from any one's lips—sullied. Be merciful—for the sake of the better days; make our shame as light to bear as in your charity you can." At this point in his revery Mary nudged him, perceiving that his mind was absent. The house was chanting, "You are f-a-r," etc.

"Be ready," Mary whispered. "Your name comes now; he has read eighteen."

The chant ended.

"Next! next! next!" came volleying from all over the house.

Burgess put his hand into his pocket. The old couple, trembling, began to rise. Burgess fumbled a moment, then said,

"I find I have read them all."

Faint with joy and surprise, the couple sank into their seats, and Mary whispered:

"Oh, bless God, we are saved!—he has lost ours—I wouldn't give this for a hundred of those sacks!"

The house burst out with its "Mikado" travesty, and sang it three times with ever-increasing enthusiasm, rising to its feet when it reached for the third time the closing line—

But the Symbols are here, you bet!

and finishing up with cheers and a tiger for "Hadleyburg purity and our eighteen immortal representatives of it."

Then Wingate, the saddler, got up and proposed cheers "for the cleanest man in town, the one solitary important citizen in it who didn't try to steal that money—Edward Richards."

They were given with great and moving heartiness; then somebody proposed that Richards be elected sole guardian and Symbol of the now Sacred Hadleyburg Tradition, with power and right to stand up and look the whole sarcastic world in the face.

Passed, by acclamation; then they sang the "Mikado" again, and ended it with:

And there's ONE Symbol left, you bet!

There was a pause; then——

A Voice. "Now, then, who's to get the sack?"

The Tanner (with bitter sarcasm). "That's easy. The money has to be divided among the eighteen Incorruptibles. They gave the suffering stranger twenty dollars apiece—and that remark—each in his turn—it took twenty-two minutes for the procession to move past. Staked the stranger—total contribution, $360. All they want is just the loan back—and interest—forty thousand dollars altogether."

Many Voices [derisively]. "That's it! Divvy! divvy! Be kind to the poor—don't keep them waiting!"

The Chair. "Order! I now offer the stranger's remaining document. It says 'If no claimant shall appear [*grand chorus of groans*] I desire that you open the sack and count out the money to the principal citizens of your town, they to take it in trust [*cries of "Oh! Oh! Oh!"*], and use it in such ways as to them shall seem best for the propagation and preservation of your community's noble reputation for incorruptible honesty [*more cries*]—a reputation to which their names and their efforts will add a new and far-reaching luster.' [*Enthusiastic outburst of sarcastic applause.*] That seems to be all. No—here is a postscript:

" 'P. S.—CITIZENS OF HADLEYBURG: There *is* no test-remark—nobody made one. [*Great sensation.*] There wasn't any pauper stranger, nor any twenty-dollar contribution, nor any accompanying benediction and compliment—these are all inventions. [*General buzz and hum of astonishment and delight.*] Allow me to tell my story—it will take but a word or two. I passed through your town at a certain time, and received a deep offense which I had not earned. Any other man would have been content to kill one or two of you and call it square, but to me that would have been a trivial revenge, and inadequate; for the dead do not *suffer*. Besides, I could not kill you all—and, anyway, made as I am, even that would not have satisfied me. I wanted to damage every man in the place, and every woman—and not in their bodies or in their estate, but in their vanity—the place where feeble and foolish people are most vulnerable. So I disguised myself and came back and studied you. You were easy game. You had an old and lofty reputation for honesty, and naturally you were proud of it—it was your treasure of treasures, the very apple of your eye. As soon as I found out that you carefully and vigilantly kept yourselves and your children *out of temptation*, I knew how to proceed. Why, you simple creatures, the weakest of all weak things is a virtue which has not been tested in the fire. I laid a plan, and gathered a list of names. My project was to corrupt Hadleyburg the Incorruptible. My idea was to make liars and thieves of nearly half a hundred smirchless men and women who had never in their lives uttered a lie or stolen a penny. I was afraid of Goodson. He was neither born nor reared in Hadleyburg. I was afraid that if I started to operate my scheme by getting my letter laid before you, you would say to yourselves, "Goodson is the only man among us who would give away twenty dollars to a poor devil"—and then you might not bite at my bait. But Heaven took Goodson; then I knew I was safe, and I set my trap and baited it. It may be that I shall not catch all the men to whom I mailed the pretended test secret, but I shall catch the most of them, if I know Hadleyburg nature. [*Voices.* "Right—he got every last one of them."] I believe they will even steal ostensible *gamble*-money, rather than miss, poor, tempted, and mistrained fellows. I am hoping to eternally and everlastingly squelch your vanity and give Hadleyburg a new renown—one that will *stick*—and spread far. If I have succeeded, open the sack and summon the Committee on Propagation and Preservation of the Hadleyburg Reputation.'"

A *Cyclone of Voices.* "Open it! Open it! The Eighteen to the front! Committee on Propagation of the Tradition! Forward—the Incorruptibles!"

The Chair ripped the sack wide, and gathered up a handful of bright, broad, yellow coins, shook them together, then examined them——

"Friends, they are only gilded disks of lead!"

There was a crashing outbreak of delight over this news, and when the noise had subsided, the tanner called out:

"By right of apparent seniority in this business, Mr. Wilson is Chairman of the Committee on Propagation of the Tradition. I suggest that he step forward on behalf of his pals, and receive in trust the money."

A *Hundred Voices.* "Wilson! Wilson! Wilson! Speech! Speech!"

Wilson [*in a voice trembling with anger*]. "You will allow me to say, and without apologies for my language, *damn* the money!"

A Voice. "Oh, and him a Baptist!"

A Voice. "Seventeen Symbols left! Step up, gentlemen, and assume your trust!"

There was a pause—no response.

The Saddler. "Mr. Chairman, we've got *one* clean man left, anyway, out of the late aristocracy; and he needs money, and deserves it. I move that you appoint Jack Halliday to get up there and auction off that sack of gilt twenty-dollar pieces, and give the result to the right man—the man whom Hadleyburg delights to honor—Edward Richards."

This was received with great enthusiasm, the dog taking a hand again; the saddler started the bids at a dollar, the Bixton folk and Barnum's representative fought hard for it, the people cheered every jump that the bids made, the excitement climbed moment by moment higher and higher, the bidders got on their mettle and grew steadily more and more daring, more and more determined, the jumps went from a dollar up to five, then to ten, then to twenty, then fifty, then to a hundred, then——

At the beginning of the auction Richards whispered in distress to his wife: "Oh Mary, can we allow it? It—it—you see, it is an honor-reward, a testimonial to purity of character, and—and—can we allow it? Hadn't I better get up and—O Mary, what ought we to do?—what do you think we—[*Halliday's voice.* "Fifteen I'm bid! —fifteen for the sack!—twenty!—ah, thanks!—thirty—thanks again. Thirty, thirty, thirty!—do I hear forty?—forty it is! Keep the ball rolling, gentlemen, keep it rolling!—fifty! thanks, noble Roman! going at fifty, fifty, fifty!—seventy!—ninety!—splendid!—a hundred! —pile it up, pile it up!—hundred and twenty—forty!—just in time! —hundred and fifty!—TWO hundred!—superb! Do I hear two h— thanks!—two hundred and fifty!—"]

"It is another temptation, Edward—I'm all in a tremble—but, oh, we've escaped *one* temptation, and that ought to warn us to—["*Six* did I hear?—thanks!—six-fifty, six-f—SEVEN hundred!"] And yet, Edward, when you think—nobody susp— ["*Eight hundred dollars!* —hurrah!—make it nine!—Mr. Parsons, did I hear you say—thanks— nine!—this noble sack of virgin lead going at only nine hundred *dollars, gilding and all—come! do I hear—a thousand!—gratefully yours!—did some one say eleven?— sack which is going to be the most celebrated in the whole Uni—*"] O Edward" (beginning to sob), "we are *so* poor!—but—but—do as you think best—do as you think best."

Edward fell—that is, he sat still; sat with a conscience which was not satisfied, but which was overpowered by circumstances.

Meantime a stranger, who looked like an amateur detective gotten up as an impossible English earl, had been watching the evening's proceedings with manifest interest, and with a contented expression in his face; and he had been privately commenting to himself. He was now soliloquizing somewhat like this: "None of the Eighteen are bidding; that is not satisfactory; I must change that—the dramatic unities require it; they must buy the sack they tried to steal; they must pay a heavy price, too—some of them are rich. And another thing, when I make a mistake in Hadleyburg nature the man that puts that error upon me is entitled to a high honorarium, and some one must pay it. This poor old Richards has brought my judgment to shame; he is an honest man:—I don't understand it, but I acknowledge it. Yes, he saw my deuces *and* with a straight flush, and by rights the pot is his. And it shall be a jack-pot, too, if I can manage it. He disappointed me, but let that pass."

He was watching the bidding. At a thousand, the market broke; the prices tumbled swiftly. He waited—and still watched. One competitor dropped out; then another, and another. He put in a bid or two, now. When the bids had sunk to ten dollars, he added a five—some one raised him a three; he waited a moment, then flung in a fifty-dollar jump, and the sack was his—at $1,282. The house broke out in cheers—then stopped; for he was on his feet, and had lifted his hand. He began to speak.

"I desire to say a word, and ask a favor. I am a speculator in rarities, and I have dealings with persons interested in numismatics all over the world. I can make a profit on this purchase, just as it stands; but there is a way, if I can get your approval, whereby I can make every one of these leaden twenty-dollar pieces worth its face in gold, and perhaps more. Grant me that approval, and I will give part of my gains to your Mr. Richards, whose invulnerable probity you have so justly and so cordially recognized to-night; his share shall be ten thousand dollars, and I will hand him the money to-morrow. [*Great applause from the house.* But the "invulnerable probity" made the Richardses blush prettily; however, it went for modesty, and did no harm.] If you will pass my proposition by a good majority—I would like a two-thirds vote—I will regard that as the town's consent, and that is all I ask. Rarities are always helped by any device which will rouse curiosity and compel remark. Now if I may have your permission to stamp upon the faces of each of these ostensible coins the names of the eighteen gentlemen who——"

Nine-tenths of the audience were on their feet in a moment—dog and all—and the proposition was carried with a whirlwind of approving applause and laughter.

They sat down, and all the Symbols except "Dr." Clay Harkness got up, violently protesting against the proposed outrage, and threatening to——

"I beg you not to threaten me," said the stranger, calmly. "I know my legal rights, and am not accustomed to being frightened at bluster." [*Applause.*] He sat down. "Dr." Harkness saw an opportunity here. He was one of the two very rich men of the place, and Pinkerton was the other. Harkness was proprietor of a mint; that is to say, a popular patent medicine. He was running for the legislature on one ticket, and Pinkerton on the other. It was a close race and a hot one, and getting hotter every day. Both had strong appetites for money; each had bought a great tract of land, with a purpose; there was going to be a new railway, and each wanted to be in the legislature and help locate the route to his own advantage; a single vote might make the decision, and with it two or three fortunes. The stake was large, and Harkness was a daring speculator. He was sitting close to the stranger. He leaned over while one or another of the other Symbols was entertaining the house with protests and appeals, and asked, in a whisper,

"What is your price for the sack?"

"Forty thousand dollars."

"I'll give you twenty."

"No."

"Twenty-five."

"No."

"Say thirty."

"The price is forty thousand dollars; not a penny less."

"All right, I'll give it. I will come to the hotel at ten in the morning. I don't want it known: will see you privately."

"Very good." Then the stranger got up and said to the house:

"I find it late. The speeches of these gentlemen are not without merit, not without interest, not without grace; yet if I may be excused I will take my leave. I thank you for the great favor which you have shown me in granting my petition. I ask the Chair to keep the sack for me until to-morrow, and to hand these three five-hundred-dollar notes to Mr. Richards." They were passed up to the Chair. "At nine I will call for the sack, and at eleven will deliver the rest of the ten thousand to Mr. Richards in person, at his home. Good night."

Then he slipped out, and left the audience making a vast noise, which was composed of a mixture of cheers, the "Mikado" song, dog-disapproval, and the chant, "You are f-a-r from being a b-a-a-d man—a-a-a-a-men!"

IV

At home the Richardses had to endure congratulations and compliments until midnight. Then they were left to themselves. They looked a little sad, and they sat silent and thinking. Finally Mary sighed and said,

"Do you think we are to blame, Edward—*much* to blame?" and her eyes wandered to the accusing triplet of big bank-notes lying on the table, where the congratulators had been gloating over them and reverently fingering them. Edward did not answer at once; then he brought out a sigh and said, hesitatingly:

"We—we couldn't help it, Mary. It—well, it was ordered. *All things are.*"

Mary glanced up and looked at him steadily, but he didn't return the look. Presently she said:

"I thought congratulations and praises always tasted good. But —it seems to me, now—Edward?"

"Well?"

"Are you going to stay in the bank?"

"N-no."

"Resign?"

"In the morning—by note."

Underwood and Underwood

"I like the degree well enough, but I'm crazy about the clothes"—Mark Twain poses in the scarlet gown conferred along with the honorary Doctor of Literature degree by the University of Oxford.

Underwood and Underwood

The humorist acquired the habit of working in bed.

"It does seem best."

Richards bowed his head in his hands and muttered:

"Before, I was not afraid to let oceans of people's money pour through my hands, but—Mary, I am so tired, so tired——"

"We will go to bed."

At nine in the morning the stranger called for the sack and took it to the hotel in a cab. At ten Harkness had a talk with him privately. The stranger asked for and got five checks on a metropolitan bank—drawn to "Bearer"—four for $1,500 each, and one for $34,000. He put one of the former in his pocketbook, and the remainder, representing $38,500, he put in an envelope, and with these he added a note, which he wrote after Harkness was gone. At eleven he called at the Richards house and knocked. Mrs. Richards peeped through the shutters, then went and received the envelope, and the stranger disappeared without a word. She came back flushed and a little unsteady on her legs, and gasped out:

"I am sure I recognized him! Last night it seemed to me that maybe I had seen him somewhere before."

"He is the man that brought the sack here?"

"I am almost sure of it."

"Then he is the ostensible Stephenson, too, and sold every important citizen in this town with his bogus secret. Now if he has sent checks instead of money, we are sold, too, after we thought we had escaped. I was beginning to feel fairly comfortable once more, after my night's rest, but the look of that envelope makes me sick. It isn't fat enough; $8,500 in even the largest bank-notes makes more bulk than that."

"Edward, why do you object to checks?"

"Checks signed by Stephenson! I am resigned to take the $8,500 if it could come in bank-notes—for it does seem that it was so ordered, Mary—but I have never had much courage, and I have not the pluck to try to market a check signed with that disastrous name. It would be a trap. That man tried to catch me; we escaped somehow or other; and now he is trying a new way. If it is checks—"

"Oh, Edward, it is *too* bad!" and she held up the checks and began to cry.

"Put them in the fire! quick! We mustn't be tempted. It is a trick to make the world laugh at *us*, along with the rest, and— Give them to *me*, since you can't do it!" He snatched them and tried to hold his grip till he could get to the stove; but he was human, he was a cashier, and he stopped a moment to make sure of the signature. Then he came near to fainting.

"Fan me, Mary, fan me! They are the same as gold!"

"Oh, how lovely, Edward! Why?"

"Signed by Harkness. What can the mystery of that be, Mary?"

"Edward, do you think——"

"Look here—look at this! Fifteen—fifteen—fifteen—thirty-four. Thirty-eight thousand five hundred! Mary, the sack isn't worth twelve dollars, and Harkness, apparently, has paid about par for it."

"And does it all come to us, do you think—instead of the ten thousand?"

"Why, it looks like it. And the checks are made to 'Bearer,' too."

"Is that good, Edward? What is it for?"

"A hint to collect them at some distant bank, I reckon. Perhaps Harkness doesn't want the matter known. What is that—a note?"

"Yes. It was with the checks."

It was in the "Stephenson" handwriting, but there was no signature. It said:

"I am a disappointed man. Your honesty is beyond the reach of temptation. I had a different idea about it, but I wronged you in that, and I beg your pardon, and do it sincerely. I honor you—and that is sincere too. This town is not worthy to kiss the hem of your garment. Dear sir, I made a square bet with myself that there were nineteen debauchable men in your self-righteous community. I have lost. Take the whole pot, you are entitled to it."

Richards drew a deep sigh, and said:

"It seems written with fire—it burns so. Mary—I am miserable again."

"I, too. Ah, dear, I wish——"

"To think, Mary—he *believes* in me."

"Oh, don't, Edward—I can't bear it."

"If those beautiful words were deserved, Mary—and God knows I believed I deserved them once—I think I could give the forty thousand dollars for them. And I would put that paper away, as representing more than gold and jewels, and keep it always. But now— We could not live in the shadow of its accusing presence, Mary."

He put it in the fire.

A messenger arrived and delivered an envelope.

Richards took from it a note and read it; it was from Burgess.

"You saved me, in a difficult time. I saved you last night. It was at cost of a lie, but I made the sacrifice freely, and out of a grateful heart. None in this village knows so well as I know how brave and good and noble you are. At bottom you cannot respect me, knowing as you do of that matter of which I am accused, and by the general voice condemned; but I beg that you will at least believe that I am a grateful man; it will help me to bear my burden.

[Signed]   "BURGESS"

"Saved, once more. And on such terms!" He put the note in the fire. "I—I wish I were dead, Mary, I wish I were out of it all."

"Oh, these are bitter, bitter days, Edward. The stabs, through their very generosity, are so deep—and they come so fast!"

Three days before the election each of two thousand voters suddenly found himself in possession of a prized memento—one of the renowned bogus double-eagles. Around one of its faces was stamped these words: "THE REMARK I MADE TO THE POOR STRANGER WAS—" Around the other face was stamped these: "GO, AND REFORM. [SIGNED] PINKERTON." Thus the entire remaining refuse of the renowned joke was emptied upon a single head, and with calamitous effect. It revived the recent vast laugh and concentrated it upon Pinkerton; and Harkness's election was a walkover.

Within twenty-four hours after the Richardses had received their checks their consciences were quieting down, discouraged; the old couple were learning to reconcile themselves to the sin which they had committed. But they were to learn, now, that a sin takes on new and real terrors when there seems a chance that it is going to be found out. This gives it a fresh and most substantial and important aspect. At church the morning sermon was of the usual pattern; it was the same old things said in the same old way; they had heard them a thousand times and found them innocuous, next to meaningless, and easy to sleep under; but now it was different: the sermon seemed to bristle with accusations; it seemed aimed straight and specially at people who were concealing deadly sins. After church they got away from the mob of congratulators as soon as they could, and hurried homeward, chilled to the bone at they did not know what—vague, shadowy, indefinite fears. And by chance they caught a glimpse of Mr. Burgess as he turned a corner. He paid no attention to their nod of recognition! He hadn't seen it; but they did not know that. What could his conduct mean? It might mean—it might mean—oh, a dozen dreadful things. Was it possible that he knew that Richards could have cleared him of guilt in that bygone time, and had been silently waiting for a chance to even up accounts? At home, in their distress they got to imagining that their servant might have been in the next room listening when Richards revealed the secret to his wife that he knew of Burgess's innocence; next, Richards began to imagine that he had heard the swish of a gown in there at that time; next, he was sure he *had* heard it. They would call Sarah in, on a pretext, and watch her face: if she had been betraying them to Mr. Burgess, it would show in her manner. They asked her some questions—questions which were so random and incoherent and seemingly purposeless that the girl felt sure that the old people's minds had been affected by their sudden good fortune; the sharp and watchful gaze which they bent upon her frightened her, and that completed the business. She blushed, she became nervous and confused, and to the old people these were plain signs of guilt—guilt of some fearful sort or other—without doubt she was a spy and a traitor. When they were alone again they began to piece many unrelated things together and get horrible results out of the combination. When things had got about to the worst, Richards was delivered of a sudden gasp, and his wife asked:

"Oh, what is it?—what is it?"

"The note—Burgess's note! Its language was sarcastic, I see it now." He quoted: " 'At bottom you cannot respect me, *knowing*, as you do, of *that matter* of which I am accused'—oh, it is perfectly plain, now, God help me! He knows that I know! You see the ingenuity of the phrasing. It was a trap—and like a fool, I walked into it. And Mary——?"

"Oh, it is dreadful—I know what you are going to say—he didn't return your transcript of the pretended test-remark."

"No—kept it to destroy us with. Mary, he has exposed us to some already. I know it—I know it well. I saw it in a dozen faces after church. Ah, he wouldn't answer our nod of recognition—*he* knew what he had been doing!"

In the night the doctor was called. The news went around in the morning that the old couple were rather seriously ill—prostrated by the exhausting excitement growing out of their great windfall, the congratulations, and the late hours, the doctor said. The town was sincerely distressed; for these old people were about all it had left to be proud of, now.

Two days later the news was worse. The old couple were delirious, and were doing strange things. By witness of the nurses, Richards had exhibited checks—for $8,500? No—for an amazing sum—$38,500! What could be the explanation of this gigantic piece of luck?

The following day the nurses had more news—and wonderful. They had concluded to hide the checks, lest harm come to them; but when they searched they were gone from under the patient's pillow—vanished away. The patient said:

"Let the pillow alone; what do you want?"

"We thought it best that the checks——"

"You will never see them again—they are destroyed. They came from Satan. I saw the hell-brand on them, and I knew they were sent to betray me to sin." Then he fell to gabbling strange and dreadful things which were not clearly understandable, and which the doctor admonished them to keep to themselves.

Richards was right; the checks were never seen again.

A nurse must have talked in her sleep, for within two days the forbidden gabblings were the property of the town; and they were of a surprising sort. They seemed to indicate that Richards had been a claimant for the sack himself, and that Burgess had concealed that fact and then maliciously betrayed it.

Burgess was taxed with this and stoutly denied it. And he said it was not fair to attach weight to the chatter of a sick old man who was out of his mind. Still, suspicion was in the air, and there was much talk.

After a day or two it was reported that Mrs. Richards's delirious deliveries were getting to be duplicates of her husband's. Suspicion flamed up into conviction, now, and the town's pride in the purity of its one undiscredited important citizen began to dim down and flicker toward extinction.

Six days passed, then came more news. The old couple were dying. Richards's mind cleared in his latest hour, and he sent for Burgess. Burgess said:

"Let the room be cleared. I think he wishes to say something in privacy."

"No!" said Richards: "I want witnesses. I want you all to hear my confession, so that I may die a man, and not a dog. I was clean—artificially—like the rest; and like the rest I fell when temptation came. I signed a lie, and claimed the miserable sack. Mr. Burgess remembered that I had done him a service, and in gratitude (and ignorance) he suppressed my claim and saved me. You know the thing that was charged against Burgess years ago. My testimony, and mine alone, could have cleared him, and I was a coward, and left him to suffer disgrace——"

"No—no—Mr. Richards, you——"

"My servant betrayed my secret to him——"

"No one has betrayed anything to me——"

—"and then he did a natural and justifiable thing, he repented of the saving kindness which he had done me, and he *exposed* me—as I deserved——"

"Never!—I make oath——"

"Out of my heart I forgive him."

Burgess's impassioned protestations fell upon deaf ears; the dying man passed away without knowing that once more he had done poor Burgess a wrong. The old wife died that night.

The last of the sacred Nineteen had fallen a prey to the fiendish sack; the town was stripped of the last rag of its ancient glory. Its mourning was not showy, but it was deep.

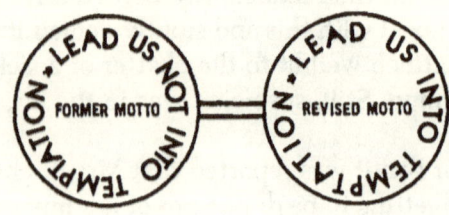

By act of the Legislature—upon prayer and petition—Hadleyburg was allowed to change its name to (never mind what—I will not give it away), and leave one word out of the motto that for many generations had graced the town's official seal.

It is an honest town once more, and the man will have to rise early that catches it napping again. » » »

The reader of Mark Twain who takes up his books in the chronological order of their writing, if he is interested primarily in the writer as artist, suffers a letdown when he turns from *Huckleberry Finn* (1884) to its successor, *A Connecticut Yankee* (1889). What has happened to the chronicler of midwestern boyhood, he asks himself, and to the purveyor of nineteenth-century optimism, between the writing of the two books? If he survives the first jolt and proceeds hopefully into the story, he becomes increasingly bewildered to the end. He finds plenty of laughs, some of them of the old-time heartiness. But here is a different Mark Twain—a more uncertain observer of the human race. Here is the spirit of adventure, it is true, but how different its mood from the picaresque irresponsibility of Huckleberry Finn!

After a fuller study of Mark Twain's life and writings, the reader reaches the conclusion that *A Connecticut Yankee* marks a transition both in the life and in the literary career of its author; it stands between the writings of his prime, what are considered by critics to entitle him most surely to a claim to immortality, and the pieces that show evidence of his decline as a literary artist. He was fifty-four years old when the book was published. Since the publication of *Huckleberry Finn* five years before, he had become embroiled in business. His marriage and his distinguished social and professional success had caused him to throw his lot with the fortunate of the earth, among the people who made much money and spent much money. At the time of his publication of *A Connecticut Yankee*, his resources had become stretched almost to the breaking point.

It was not merely that his family budget made "ghastly" demands upon his resources; he had caught the money-making fever of the Gilded Age, and it was his undoing. The part of Mr. Van

Wyck Brooks's very useful examination into the causes of Mark Twain's dissatisfaction with life that accounts for his business failure cannot be gainsaid. Because of difficulties with Osgood and Company, he enlisted his nephew, Charles Webster, in 1884, in forming a publishing company of their own. The notable success of Webster and Company in putting out the memoirs of President Grant encouraged them to further and greater undertakings. Furthermore, from 1888 to 1894 he was deeply involved in a scheme to make a fortune from the Paige typesetting machine. By the time Mark Twain was fifty years old, he had become so committed to the success of these two enterprises that his writing became a secondary activity. Susie Clemens, in her childish biography of her father, wrote, "Mama and I have been very much troubled of late because papa, since he has been publishing General Grant's books, has seemed to forget his own works entirely." It was because of the constant demand for more capital for the Paige machine that he finally rushed *A Connecticut Yankee,* which he had begun in 1886, through to completion. He felt that it must be an important publication in order to increase his profits.

Much as he enjoyed "old Sir Thomas Malory's enchanting book," the institution of knight-errantry as there dramatized had so affected his imagination that he conceived the irreverent desire to show up its absurdities and, further, to show what could have been done for sixth-century England if modern American democratic standards of living and of government had been introduced by an ingenious Yankee equipped with the know-how. The author's residence in Hartford, Connecticut, with its Colt arms factory, and his zeal for the success of the Paige machine had doubtless contributed to the idea for the extravaganza.[21]

Because it is transitional, more than any other of his works, *A Connecticut Yankee in King Arthur's Court* represents the many-sided Mark Twain—what was contradictory and paradoxical in his mind and character. Here are to be found an optimistic vision of

---

[21] In his *Notebook,* 171, Mark Twain wrote: "Fall of '84—while Cable and I were giving readings, Cable got a Morte d'Arthur and gave it to me to read. I began to make notes in my head, for a book. Nov. 11, 1886, I read the first chapter (all that was then written) at Governors Island, and closed the reading with an outline of the probable contents of the future book. Wrote a book, 'The Yankee at Arthur's Court' in '87 and '88."

good and a pessimistic despair for the human race, burlesque and delicacy, sacrilegious debunking and tender appreciation, boisterous buffoonery and grave social philosophy, trite journalese and colloquial freshness, flippant indulgence in cleverness and literary felicity, crass common sense and poetry, realism and romance, comedy and tragedy.

Only the filtering process of time, a sifting that takes care of itself, can determine which is the true account, Van Wyck Brooks's charge that the Missourian's environment stood in the way of his realizing the best possibilities of his genius or William Dean Howells' conviction that what he actually accomplished is of universal significance in spite of what, to our near view, appear to be crudities.

What, in that sifting, will be the fate of *A Connecticut Yankee* is especially teasing. Will it come to be recognized as an allegory of the collapse of feudalism and, finally, of the Industrial Revolution as well, comparable to *Gulliver's Travels* in its allegorical method?[22] The evidences of Swift's and Cervantes' influence almost from the time Mark Twain began to write have often been pointed out. Will its literary qualities that seem objectionable to us now, come to appear excusably quaint a century from now? And will its lashing out against sham and injustice entitle it to be compared to Cervantes' exposure of the absurdities of the institution of chivalry?[23] If Mark Twain is now adventuring where Captain Stormfield did, he is still concerned, we must believe, that his fate may lie in the lap of other authorities than the critics.

If, then, in the far distant future, *A Connecticut Yankee* is classed

[22] Mark Twain had read *Gulliver's Travels* by 1870. In *Roughing It*, he imagines himself to be Brobdingnag among Lilliputian ants. For a discussion of the social significance of the book, see Jerry Allen's *The Adventures of Mark Twain*, 45-53; also, Gladys Bellamy's *Mark Twain as a Literary Artist*, 312-16.

[23] Concerning the satirical intent of *A Connecticut Yankee*, Vernon L. Parrington says in his *Main Currents in American Thought*, III, 97: "The book has been grossly misunderstood. It is not an attack on chivalry—at least not primarily; it is rather an attack on thirteen centuries heavy with sorrow and misery and frustrated hopes— a meaningless succession of foolish and futile generations, wandering in fogs of their own brewing, hagridden by superstitions, deceived and exploited by priest and noble, with no will to be free." Stephen Leacock, on the other hand, comments in his *Mark Twain*, 10: "People who had tried in vain to rise to the dummy figures and sentimental unreality of Tennyson's *Idylls of the King* got set straight on chivalry and all its works when they read *The Connecticut Yankee at King Arthur's Court*."

with *Gulliver's Travels* as a satirical allegory, representing what came of the Industrial Revolution, its author may be considered to have been a prophet. His bitter experience with the machine age caused him to prefigure the forces of the mysterious universe, of which he made Merlin a symbol, taking over when the machine age backfired. A hundred years from now the comicalities of the Yankee-of-the-Yankees tramping through Arthur's England may have lost their shocking power, and The Boss may be accepted as a mere symbol.

A CONNECTICUT YANKEE IN KING ARTHUR'S COURT[24]

A WORD OF EXPLANATION

« « « It was in Warwick Castle that I came across the curious stranger whom I am going to talk about. He attracted me by three things: his candid simplicity, his marvelous familiarity with ancient armor, and the restfulness of his company—for he did all the talking. We fell together, as modest people will, in the tail of the herd that was being shown through, and he at once began to say things which interested me. As he talked along, softly, pleasantly, flowingly, he seemed to drift away imperceptibly out of this world and time, and into some remote era and old forgotten country; and so he gradually wove such a spell about me that I seemed to move among the specters and shadows and dust and mold of a gray antiquity, holding speech with a relic of it! Exactly as I would speak of my nearest personal friends or enemies, or my most familiar neighbors, he spoke of Sir Bedivere, Sir Bors de Ganis, Sir Launcelot of the Lake, Sir Galahad, and all the other great names of the Table Round—and how old, old, unspeakably old and faded and dry and musty and ancient he came to look as he went on! Presently he turned to me and said, just as one might speak of the weather, or any other common matter—

[24] The book was copyrighted August 7, 1889; copy was filed in Washington, December 5, 1889. The *Century Magazine* for November, 1889, contained "Extracts from 'A Connecticut Yankee' with A Footnote by Mark Twain." The illustrations by Dan Beard added greatly to the author's ideas. An unusual feature of the illustrations was the use of then living industrialists and rulers as "models" for the depicted characters. Mark Twain instructed Beard to "obey his *own* inspiration . . . be it humorous or be it serious. I want his genius to be wholly unhampered" (*Letters*, II, 511).

"You know about transmigration of souls; do you know about transposition of epochs—and bodies?"

I said I had not heard of it. He was so little interested—just as when people speak of the weather—that he did not notice whether I made him any answer or not. There was half a moment of silence, immediately interrupted by the droning voice of the salaried cicerone:

"Ancient hauberk, date of the sixth century, time of King Arthur and the Round Table; said to have belonged to the knight Sir Sagramor le Desirous; observe the round hole through the chain-mail in the left breast; can't be accounted for; supposed to have been done with a bullet since invention of firearms—perhaps maliciously by Cromwell's soldiers."

My acquaintance smiled—not a modern smile, but one that must have gone out of general use many, many centuries ago—and muttered apparently to himself:

"Wit ye well, *I saw it done.*" Then, after a pause, added: "I did it myself."

By the time I had recovered from the electric surprise of this remark, he was gone.

All that evening I sat by my fire at the Warwick Arms, steeped in a dream of the olden time, while the rain beat upon the windows, and the wind roared about the eaves and corners. From time to time I dipped into old Sir Thomas Malory's enchanting book,[25]

---

[25] *Morte D'Arthur* is a collection of prose tales recounting the famous deeds of the Knights of the Round Table. From the historical Arthur, a British chieftain who successfully withstood the invading Saxons, Arthur became the center of a great cycle of legends, as famous on the Continent as in England, about a world-monarch—his birth, marriage, Round Table, conquests, and death, as well as the loves and adventures of his knights, Gawain, Tristam, and Lancelot. To all this became added the Christian legends of the Holy Grail, the cup used by Christ at the last supper. These stories, repeated by word of mouth in many languages in medieval Europe, were as popular as radio and television programs are today. Sir Thomas Malory took this mass of material and by selection and alteration produced a unified version of the whole cycle. Completed by him in 1470, it was published by Caxton when printing was introduced into England in 1485. According to the legend, Arthur was educated by Merlin, the great magician who had made possible the marriage of Arthur's parents, King Uther Pendragon and Igrayne, Duchess of Cornwall. Through Merlin, Arthur received the sword Excalibur from the Lady of the Lake. The clandestine love affair between Queen Guinevere and Lancelot, whom Malory describes as "the gentlest knight that ever ate in hall among ladies, the sternest to his mortal foe that ever put spear at rest," one of the most famous of all love stories, destroyed the Round Table. When finally, according to the Malory

and fed at its rich feast of prodigies and adventures, breathed in the fragrance of its obsolete names, and dreamed again. . . .

As I laid the book down there was a knock at the door, and my stranger came in. I gave him a pipe and a chair, and made him welcome. I also comforted him with a hot Scotch whisky; gave him another one; then still another—hoping always for his story. After a fourth persuader, he drifted into it himself, in a quite simple and natural way:

THE STRANGER'S HISTORY

I am an American. I was born and reared in Hartford, in the state of Connecticut—anyway, just over the river, in the country. So I am a Yankee of the Yankees—and practical; yes, and nearly barren of sentiment, I suppose—or poetry, in other words. My father was a blacksmith, my uncle was a horse-doctor, and I was both, along at first. Then I went over to the great arms factory and learned my real trade; learned all there was to it; learned to make everything: guns, revolvers, cannon, boilers, engines, all sorts of labor-saving machinery. Why, I could make anything a body wanted—anything in the world, it didn't make any difference what; and if there wasn't any quick new-fangled way to make a thing, I could invent one—and do it as easy as rolling off a log. I became head superintendent; had a couple of thousand men under me.

Well, a man like that is a man that is full of fight—that goes without saying. With a couple of thousand rough men under one, one has plenty of that sort of amusement. I had, anyway. At last I met my match, and I got my dose. It was during a misunderstanding conducted with crowbars with a fellow we used to call Hercules. He laid me out with a crusher alongside the head that made everything crack, and seemed to spring every joint in my skull and made it overlap its neighbor. Then the world went out in darkness, and I didn't feel anything more, and didn't know anything at all—at least for a while.

---

version, Arthur was away from England making war on Lancelot, Mordred, Arthur's natural son, whom he had made regent in his absence, raised a rebellion, hoping to seize the crown. In a bloody battle at Dover, Mordred mortally wounded Arthur and was himself slain by the King, who then returned to the Lady of the Lake, who bore him away in a magic barge to the Isle of Avalon. Queen Guinevere died a nun. Lancelot, who left a hermitage to bury her, died soon afterward.

When I came to again, I was sitting under an oak tree, on the grass, with a whole beautiful and broad country landscape all to myself—nearly. Not entirely; for there was a fellow on a horse, looking down at me—a fellow fresh out of a picture-book. He was in old-time iron armor from head to heel, with a helmet on his head the shape of a nail-keg with slits in it; and he had a shield, and a sword, and a prodigious spear; and his horse had armor on, too, and a steel horn projecting from his forehead, and gorgeous red and green silk trappings that hung down all around him like a bedquilt, nearly to the ground.

"Fair sir, will ye just?" said this fellow.

"Will I which?"

"Will ye try a passage of arms for land or lady or for—"

"What are you giving me?" I said. "Get along back to your circus, or I'll report you."

Now what does this man do but fall back a couple of hundred yards and then come rushing at me as hard as he could tear, with his nail-keg bent down nearly to his horse's neck and his long spear pointed straight ahead. I saw he meant business, so I was up the tree when he arrived.

He allowed that I was his property, the captive of his spear. There was argument on his side—and the bulk of the advantage—so I judged it best to humor him. We fixed up an agreement whereby I was to go with him and he was not to hurt me. I came down, and we started away, I walking by the side of his horse. We marched comfortably along, through glades and over brooks which I could not remember to have seen before—which puzzled me and made me wonder—and yet we did not come to any circus or sign of a circus. So I gave up the idea of a circus, and concluded that he was from an asylum. But we never came to an asylum—so I was up a stump, as you may say. I asked him how far we were from Hartford. He said he had never heard of the place; which I took to be a lie, but allowed it to go at that. At the end of an hour we saw a far-away town sleeping in a valley by a winding river; and beyond it on a hill, a vast gray fortress, with towers and turrets, the first I had ever seen out of a picture.

"Bridgport?" said I, pointing.

"Camelot," said he. . . . » » »

The people they met in the village through which they passed bowed low to the Yankee's captor, apparently finding nothing unusual or strange in his old-time iron armor. But when they saw the Yankee in his American clothes, they were "turned to stone," regarding him with mingled astonishment and fear. He thought he must be in an asylum. His captor led him up the height on which the castle stood, through the tall gates, over the drawbridge, and into the great court, where their arrival caused immediate commotion.

Chapter II

KING ARTHUR'S COURT

« « « The moment I got a chance I slipped aside privately and touched an ancient common-looking man on the shoulder and said, in an insinuating confidential way:

"Friend, do me a kindness. Do you belong to the asylum, or are you just here on a visit or something like that?"

"Marry, fair sir, me seemeth—"

"That will do," I said. "I reckon you are a patient."

I moved away, cogitating, and at the same time keeping an eye out for any chance passenger in his right mind that might come along and give me some light. I judged I had found one, presently; so I drew him aside and said in his ear:

"If I could see the head keeper a minute—only just a minute—"

"Prithee do not let me."

"Let you *what?*"

"*Hinder* me, then, if the word please thee better." Then he went on to say he was an under-cook and could not stop to gossip, though he would like it another time; for it would comfort his very liver to know where I got my clothes. As he started away he pointed and said yonder was one who was idle enough for my purpose, and was seeking me besides, no doubt. This was an airy slim boy in shrimp-colored tights that made him look like a forked carrot; the rest of his gear was blue silk and dainty laces and ruffles; and he had long yellow curls, and wore a plumed pink satin cap tilted complacently over his ear. By his look, he was good-natured; by his gait, he was satisfied with himself. He was pretty enough to frame. He arrived, looked me over with a smiling and impudent curiosity; said he had come for me, and informed me that he was a page.

"Go 'long," I said; "you ain't more than a paragraph."

It was pretty severe, but I was nettled. However, it never fazed him; he didn't appear to know he was hurt. He began to talk and laugh, in happy, thoughtless, boyish fashion, as we walked along, and made himself old friends with me at once; asked me all sorts of questions about myself and about my clothes, but never waited for an answer—always chattered straight ahead, as if he didn't know he had asked a question and wasn't expecting any reply, until at last he happened to mention that he was born in the beginning of the year 513.

It made the cold chills creep over me! I stopped, and said, a little faintly:

"Maybe I didn't hear you just right. Say it again—and say it slow. What year was it?"

"513."

"513! You don't look it! Come, my boy, I am a stranger and friendless; be honest and honorable with me. Are you in your right mind?"

He said he was.

"Are these other people in their right minds?"

He said they were.

"And this isn't an asylum? I mean, it isn't a place where they cure crazy people?"

He said it wasn't.

"Well, then," I said, "either I am a lunatic, or something just as awful has happened. Now tell me, honest and true, where am I?"

"In King Arthur's Court."

I waited a minute, to let that idea shudder its way home, and then said:

"And according to your notions, what year is it now?"

"528—nineteenth of June."

I felt a mournful sinking at the heart, and muttered: "I shall never see my friends again—never, never again. They will not be born for more than thirteen hundred years yet."

I seemed to believe the boy, I didn't know why. *Something* in me seemed to believe him—my consciousness, as you may say; but my reason didn't. My reason straightway began to clamor; that was natural. I didn't know how to go about satisfying it, because I knew that the testimony of men wouldn't serve—my reason would say they were lunatics, and throw out their evidence. But all of a sudden I stumbled on the very thing, just by luck. I knew that the only total eclipse of the sun in the first half of the sixth century occurred on the 21st of June, A.D. 528, O.S., and began at 3 minutes after 12 noon. I also knew that no total eclipse of the sun was due in what to *me* was the present year—*i.e.*, 1879. So, if I could keep my anxiety and curiosity from eating the heart out of me for forty-eight hours, I should then find out for certain whether this boy was telling me the truth or not.

Wherefore, being a practical Connecticut man, I now shoved this whole problem clear out of my mind till its appointed day and hour should come, in order that I might turn all my attention to the circumstances of the present moment, and be alert and ready to make the most out of them that could be made. One thing at a time, is my motto—and just play that thing for all it is worth, even if it's only two pair and a jack. I made up my mind to two things: if it was still the nineteenth century and I was among lunatics and couldn't get away, I would presently boss that asylum or know the reason why; and if, on the other hand, it was really the sixth century, all right, I didn't want any softer thing: I would boss the whole country inside of three months; for I judged I would have the start of the best-educated man in the kingdom by a matter of thirteen hundred years and upward.[26] I'm not a man to waste time after my mind's made up and there's work on hand; so I said to the page:

"Now, Clarence, my boy—if that might happen to be your name —I'll get you to post me up a little if you don't mind. What is the name of that apparition that brought me here?"

"My master and thine? That is the good knight and great lord Sir Kay the Seneschal, foster-brother to our liege the king."

"Very good; go on, tell me everything."

---

[26] Mark Twain wrote to Dan Beard: "You know this Yankee of mine has neither refinement or a college education; he is a perfect ignoramus; he is boss of a machine shop; he can build a locomotive or a Colt's revolver, he can put up and run a telegraph line, but he is an ignoramus, nevertheless" (*Notebook*, II, 887–88).

He made a long story of it; but the part that had immediate interest for me was this: He said I was Sir Kay's prisoner, and that in the due course of custom I would be flung into a dungeon and left there on scant commons until my friends ransomed me—unless I chanced to rot, first. I saw that the last chance had the best show, but I didn't waste any bother about that; time was too precious. The page said, further, that dinner was about ended in the great hall by this time, and that as soon as the sociability and the heavy drinking should begin, Sir Kay would have me in and exhibit me before King Arthur and his illustrious knights seated at the Table Round, and would brag about his exploit in capturing me, and would probably exaggerate the facts a little, but it wouldn't be good form for me to correct him, and not over-safe, either; and when I was done being exhibited, then ho for the dungeon; but he, Clarence, would find a way to come and see me every now and then, and cheer me up, and help me get word to my friends.

Get word to my friends! I thanked him; I couldn't do less; and about this time a lackey came to say I was wanted; so Clarence led me in and took me off to one side and sat down by me.

Well, it was a curious kind of spectacle, and interesting. It was an immense place, and rather naked—yes, and full of loud contrasts. It was very, very lofty; so lofty that the banners depending from the arched beams and girders away up there floated in a sort of twilight; there was a stone-railed gallery at each end, high up, with musicians in one, and women, clothed in stunning colors, in the other. The floor was of big stone flags laid in black and white squares, rather battered by age and use, and needing repair. As to ornament, there wasn't any, strictly speaking; though on the walls hung some huge tapestries which were probably taxed as works of art; battle-pieces, they were, with horses shaped like those which children cut out of paper or create in gingerbread; with men on them in scale armor whose scales are represented by round holes—so that the man's coat looks as if it had been done with a biscuit-punch. There was a fireplace big enough to camp in; and its projecting sides and hood, of carved and pillared stonework, had the look of a cathedral door. Along the walls stood men-at-arms, in breastplate and morion, with halberds for their only weapon—rigid as statues; and that is what they looked like.

In the middle of this groined and vaulted public square was an oaken table which they called the Table Round. It was as large as a circus-ring; and around it sat a great company of men dressed in such various and splendid colors that it hurt one's eyes to look at them. They wore their plumed hats, right along, except that whenever one addressed himself directly to the king, he lifted his hat a trifle just as he was beginning his remark.

Mainly they were drinking—from entire ox horns; but a few were still munching bread or gnawing beef bones. . . .

As a rule, the speech and behavior of these people were gracious and courtly; and I noticed that they were good and serious listeners when anybody was telling anything—I mean in a dog-fightless interval. And plainly, too, they were a childlike and innocent lot; telling lies of the stateliest pattern with a most gentle and winning naïveté, and ready and willing to listen to anybody else's lie, and believe it, too. It was hard to associate them with anything cruel or dreadful; and yet they dealt in tales of blood and suffering with a guileless relish that made me almost forget to shudder.

I was not the only prisoner present. There were twenty or more. Poor devils, many of them were maimed, hacked, carved, in a frightful way; and their hair, their faces, their clothing, were caked with black and stiffened drenchings of blood. They were suffering sharp physical pain, of course; and weariness, and hunger and thirst, no doubt; and at least none had given them the comfort of a wash, or even the poor charity of a lotion for their wounds; yet you never heard them utter a moan or a groan, or saw them show any sign of restlessness, or any disposition to complain. The thought was forced upon me: "The rascals—*they* have served other people so in their day; it being their own turn, now, they were not expecting any better treatment than this; so their philosophical bearing is not an outcome of mental training, intellectual fortitude, reasoning; it is mere animal training; they are white Indians." » » »

Clarence came to visit the Yankee in his dungeon, bringing the terrifying news that the captive was to be burned alive on the morrow. Merlin, Clarence told him, had woven a spell around him. The Yankee met this first test of his resourcefulness by assuring the boy that he was a greater magician than Merlin—so great that he could "smother the whole world in the dead blackness of midnight." Knowing that there was to be a total eclipse of the sun on June 21, A.D. 528, he sent a message to the King to the effect that he would blot out the sun if he were not released.

Chapter VI

THE ECLIPSE

« « « . . . In the stillness and the darkness, the knowledge that I was in deadly danger took to itself deeper and deeper meaning all the time; a something which was realization crept inch by inch through my veins and turned me cold.

But it is a blessed provision of nature that at times like these, as soon as a man's mercury has got down to a certain point there comes a revulsion, and he rallies. Hope springs up, and cheerfulness along with it, and then he is in good shape to do something for himself, if anything can be done. When my rally came, it came with a bound. I said to myself that my eclipse would be sure to save me, and make me the greatest man in the kingdom besides. . . .

The door opened, and some men-at-arms appeared. The leader said:

"The stake is ready. Come!"

The stake! The strength went out of me, and I almost fell down. It is hard to get one's breath at such a time, such lumps come into one's throat, and such gaspings; but as soon as I could speak, I said:

"But this is a mistake—the execution is tomorrow."

"Order changed; been set forward a day. Haste thee!"

I was lost. There was no help for me. I was dazed, stupefied; I had no command over myself; I only wandered purposelessly about, like one out of his mind; so the soldiers took hold of me, and pulled me along with them, out of the cell and along the maze of underground corridors, and finally into the fierce glare of daylight and the upper world. As we stepped into the vast inclosed court of the castle I got a shock; for the first thing I saw was the stake, standing in the center, and near it the piled fagots and a monk. On all four sides of the court the seated multitudes rose rank above rank, forming sloping terraces that were rich with color. The king and the queen sat in their thrones, the most conspicuous figures there, of course.

To note all this, occupied but a second. The next second Clarence had slipped from some place of concealment and was pouring news into my ear, his eyes beaming with triumph and gladness. He said:

"'Tis through *me* the change was wrought! And main hard have I worked to do it, too. But when I revealed to them the calamity in store, and saw how mighty was the terror it did engender, then saw I also that this was the time to strike! Wherefore I diligently pretended, unto this and that and the other one, that your power against the sun could not reach its full until the morrow; and so if any would save the sun and the world, you must be slain to-day, while your enchantments are but in the weaving and lack potency. . . .

You will not need to do the sun a *real* hurt—ah, forget not that, on your soul forget it not! Only make a little darkness—only the littlest little darkness, mind, and cease with that. It will be sufficient. They will see that I spoke falsely—being ignorant, as they will fancy—and with the falling of the first shadow of that darkness you shall see them go mad with fear; and they will set you free and make you great! Go to thy triumph, now! But remember—ah, good friend, I implore thee remember my supplication, and do the blessed sun no hurt. For *my* sake, thy true friend." . . .

As the soldiers assisted me across the court the stillness was so profound that if I had been blindfold I should have supposed I was in a solitude instead of walled in by four thousand people. There was not a movement perceptible in those masses of humanity; they were as rigid as stone images, and as pale; and dread sat upon every countenance. This hush continued while I was being chained to the stake; it still continued while the fagots were carefully and tediously piled about my ankles, my knees, my thighs, my body. Then there was a pause, and a deeper hush, if possible, and a man knelt down at my feet with a blazing torch; the multitude strained forward, gazing, and parting slightly from their seats without knowing it; the monk raised his hands above my head, and his eyes toward the blue sky, and began some words in Latin;

in this attitude he droned on and on, a little while, and then stopped. I waited two or three moments; then looked up; he was standing there petrified. With a common impulse the multitude rose slowly up and stared into the sky. I followed their eyes; as sure as guns, there was my eclipse beginning! The life went boiling through my veins; I was a new man! The rim of black spread slowly into the sun's disk, my heart beat higher and higher, and still the assemblage and the priest stared into the sky, motionless. I knew that this gaze would be turned upon me, next. When it was, I was ready. I was in one of the most grand attitudes I ever struck, with my arm stretched up pointing to the sun. It was a noble effect. You could *see* the shudder sweep the mass like a wave. Two shouts rang out, one close upon the heels of the other:

"Apply the torch!"

"I forbid it!"

The one was from Merlin, the other from the king. Merlin started from his place—to apply the torch himself, I judged. I said:

"Stay where you are. If any man moves—even the king—before I give him leave, I will blast him with thunder, I will consume him with lightnings!"

The multitude sank meekly into their seats, and I was just expecting they would. Merlin hesitated a moment or two, and I was on pins and needles during that little while. Then he sat down, and I took a good breath; for I knew I was master of the situation now. The king said:

"Be merciful, fair sir, and essay no further in this perilous matter, lest disaster follow. It was reported to us that your powers could not attain unto their full strength until the morrow; but—"

"Your Majesty thinks the report may have been a lie? It *was* a lie."

That made an immense effect; up went appealing hands everywhere, and the king was assailed with a storm of supplications that I might be bought off at any price, and the calamity stayed. The king was eager to comply. He said:

"Name any terms, reverend sir, even to the halving of my kingdom; but banish this calamity, spare the sun!"

My fortune was made, I would have taken him up in a minute, but *I* couldn't stop an eclipse; the thing was out of the question. So I asked time to consider. The king said:

"How long—ah, how long, good sir? Be merciful; look, it groweth darker, moment by moment. Prithee how long?"

"Not long. Half an hour—maybe an hour."

There were a thousand pathetic protests, but I couldn't shorten up any, for I couldn't remember how long a total eclipse lasts. I was in a puzzled condition, anyway, and wanted to think. Something was wrong about that eclipse, and the fact was very unsettling. If this wasn't the one I was after, how was I to tell whether this was the sixth century, or nothing but a dream? Dear me, if I could only prove it was the latter! Here was a glad new hope. If the boy was right about the date, and this was surely the 20th, it *wasn't* the sixth century. I reached for the monk's sleeve, in considerable excitement, and asked him what day of the month it was.

Hang him, he said it was the *twenty-first!* It made me turn cold to hear him. I begged him not to make any mistake about it; but he was sure; he knew it was the 21st. So, that feather-headed boy had botched things again; the time of the day was right for the eclipse; I had seen that for myself, in the beginning, by the dial that was near by. Yes, I *was* in King Arthur's court, and I might as well make the most of it I could.

The darkness was steadily growing, the people becoming more and more distressed. I now said:

"I have reflected, Sir King. For a lesson, I will let this darkness proceed, and spread night in the world; but whether I blot out the sun for good, or restore it shall rest with you. These are the terms, to wit: You shall remain king over all your dominions, and receive all the glories and honors that belong to the kingship; but you shall appoint me your perpetual minister and executive, and give me for my services one per cent. of such actual increase of revenue over and above its present amount as I may succeed in creating for the state. If I can't live on that, I sha'n't ask anybody to give me a lift. Is it satisfactory?

There was a prodigious roar of applause, and out of the midst of it the king's voice rose, saying:

"Away with his bonds, and set him free! and do him homage, high and low, rich and poor, for he is become the king's right hand, is clothed with power and authority, and his seat is upon the highest step of the throne! Now sweep away this creeping night, and bring the light and cheer again, that all the world may bless thee."

But I said:

"That a common man should be shamed before the world, is nothing; but it were dishonor to the *king* if any that saw his minister naked should not also see him delivered from his shame. If I might ask that my clothes be brought again—"

"They are not meet," the king broke in. "Fetch raiment of another sort; clothe him like a prince!"

My idea worked. I wanted to keep things as they were till the eclipse was total, otherwise they would be trying again to get me to dismiss the darkness, and of course I couldn't do it. Sending for the clothes gained some delay, but not enough. So I had to make another excuse. I said it would be but natural if the king should change his mind and repent to some extent of what he had done under excitement; therefore I would let the darkness grow awhile, and if at the end of a reasonable time the king had kept his mind the same, the darkness should be dismissed. Neither the king nor anybody else was satisfied with that arrangement, but I had to stick to my point.

It grew darker and darker and blacker and blacker, while I struggled with those awkward sixth-century clothes. It got to be pitch-dark, at last, and the multitude groaned with horror to feel the cold uncanny night breezes fan through the place and see the stars come out and twinkle in the sky. At last the eclipse was total, and I was very glad of it, but everybody else was in misery; which was quite natural. I said:

"The king, by his silence, still stands to the terms." Then I lifted up my hand—stood just so a moment—then I said, with the most awful solemnity: "Let the enchantment dissolve and pass harmless away!"

There was no response, for a moment, in that deep darkness and that graveyard hush. But when the silver rim of the sun pushed itself out, a moment or two later, the assemblage broke loose with a vast shout and came pouring down like a deluge to smother me with blessings and gratitude; and Clarence was not the last of the wash, to be sure. » » »

The Yankee set out upon his adventure of reconditioning sixth-century England according to nineteenth-century American standards.[27] He made Clarence his head executive, and the two worked as inconspicuously as possible—sometimes, from fear of antagonizing the Church, secretly at night. In four years he had established a system of schools, including Sunday schools; a "teacher factory"; a bicycle factory; an arms factory; telephone and telegraph lines; and fire, life, and accident insurance businesses. One of his deepest secrets was his "West Point." All the time he had "confidential agents trickling through the country" studying how to "undermine Knighthood by imperceptible degrees and to gnaw at this and that and the other superstition and so prepare the way gradually for a better order of things."

The King had been insisting that The Boss should start out to seek adventures and "get up a reputation of a size to break a lance with Sir Sagramor." That knight, before starting in search of the Holy Grail, had, because of a fancied insult, challenged the Yankee to joust with him in the tournament on his return. When the chance came, the King appointed The Boss to champion the cause of the Demoiselle Alisande la Carteloise (The Boss called her Sandy), a fair maiden who had come up to Camelot to petition aid for her mistress, who was "a captive in a vast and gloomy castle, along with forty-four other young and beautiful maidens, pretty much all of them princesses; they had been languishing in that cruel captivity for twenty-six years; the masters of the castle were three stupendous brothers, each with four arms and one eye in the center of the forehead." The severest test of the Yankee's ability to fill the part of a knight lay in his difficulty in becoming conditioned to traveling in armor.

[27] In his travels about the kingdom, the Yankee observes so much social injustice, which he attributes to the rigid caste system with its rich and all-powerful aristocracy imposed on the mass of the people, that in Chapter XIII he makes the caustic comment: "So to speak, I was become a stockholder in a corporation where nine hundred and ninety-four of the members furnished all the money and did all the work, and the other six elected themselves a permanent board of direction and took all the dividends. It seemed to me that what the nine hundred and ninety-four dupes needed was a new deal." The late President Franklin D. Roosevelt said that he borrowed the term "New Deal" from *A Connecticut Yankee* (*Saturday Review of Literature*, December 16, 1933, "Mark Twain's New Deal").

A CONNECTICUT YANKEE IN KING ARTHUR'S COURT

Chapter XI

THE YANKEE IN SEARCH OF ADVENTURE

« « « . . . I was to have an early breakfast, and start at dawn, for that was the usual way; but I had the demon's own time with my armor,[28] and this delayed me a little. It is troublesome to get into, and there is so much detail. First you wrap a layer or two of blanket around your body, for a sort of cushion and to keep off the cold iron; then you put on your sleeves and shirt of chain mail —these are made of small steel links woven together, and they form a fabric so flexible that if you toss your shirt onto the floor, it slumps into a pile like a peck of wet fish-net; it is very heavy and is nearly the uncomfortablest material in the world for a nightshirt, yet plenty used it for that—tax-collectors, and reformers, and one-horse kings with a defective title, and those sorts of people; then you put on your shoes—flat-boats roofed over with interleaving bands of steel—and screw your clumsy spurs into the heels. Next you buckle your greaves on your legs, and your cuisses on your thighs; then come your back-plate and your breast-plate, and you begin to feel crowded; then you hitch onto the breast-plate the half-petticoat of broad overlapping bands of steel which hangs down in front but is scolloped out behind so you can sit down, and isn't any real improvement on an inverted coal-scuttle, either for looks or for wear, or to wipe your hands on; next you belt on your sword; then you put your stove-pipe joints onto your arms, your iron gauntlets onto your hands, your iron rat-trap onto your head, with a rag of steel web hitched onto it to hang over the back of your neck—and there you are, snug as a candle in a candle-mold. This is no time to dance. Well, a man that is packed away like that is a nut that isn't worth the cracking, there is so little of the meat, when you get down to it, by comparison with the shell.

The boys helped me, or I never could have got in. Just as we

---

[28] An entry in the *Notebook*, 171, reads: "Dream of being a knight-errant in armor in the Middle Ages. Have the notions and thoughts of the present day mixed with the necessities of that. No pockets in the armor. Can't scratch. Cold in the head —can't blow—can't get a handkerchief, can't use iron sleeve. Iron gets redhot in the sun—leaks in the rain, gets white with frost and freezes me solid in winter. Makes disagreeable clatter when I enter church. Can't dress or undress myself. Always getting struck by lightning. Fall down and can't get up."

finished, Sir Bedivere happened in, and I saw that as like as not I hadn't chosen the most convenient outfit for a long trip. How stately he looked; and tall and broad and grand. He had on his head a conical steel casque that only came down to his ears, and for visor had only a narrow steel bar that extended down to his upper lip and protected his nose; and all the rest of him, from neck to heel, was flexible chain mail, trousers and all. But pretty much all of him was hidden under his outside garment, which of course was of chain mail, as I said, and hung straight from his shoulders to his ankles; and from his middle to the bottom, both before and behind, was divided, so that he could ride and let the skirts hang down on each side. He was going grailing, and it was just the outfit for it, too. I would have given a good deal for that ulster, but it was too late now to be fooling around. The sun was just up, the king and the court were all on hand to see me off and wish me luck; so it wouldn't be etiquette for me to tarry. You don't get on your horse yourself; no, if you tried it you would get disappointed. They carry you out, just as they carry a sunstruck man to the drug store, and put you on, and help get you to rights, and fix your feet in the stirrups; and all the while you do feel so strange and stuffy and like somebody else—like somebody that has been married on a sudden, or struck by lightning, or something like that, and hasn't quite fetched around yet, and is sort of numb, and can't just get his bearings. Then they stood up the mast they called a spear, in its socket by my left foot, and I gripped it with my hand; lastly they hung my shield around my neck, and I was all complete and ready to up anchor and get to sea. Everybody was as good to me as they could be, and a maid of honor gave me the stirrup-cup her own self. There was nothing more to do now, but for that damsel to get up behind me on a pillion, which she did, and put an arm or so around me to hold on. . . . » » »

After a series of highly ridiculous adventures (intended by the author to satirize the absurdities of knight-errantry and such "faded nonsense") the Yankee and Sandy came to the castle of Morgan le Fay.

Chapter XVI

MORGAN LE FAY

« « « If knights errant were to be believed, not all castles were desirable places to seek hospitality in. ... So I was pleased when I saw in the distance a horseman making the bottom turn of the road that wound down from this castle.

As we approached each other, I saw that he wore a plumed helmet, and seemed to be otherwise clothed in steel, but bore a curious addition also—a stiff square garment like a herald's tabard. However, I had to smile at my own forgetfulness when I got nearer and read this sign on his tabard:

"*Persimmons's Soap—All the Prime-Donne Use It.*"

That was a little idea of my own, and had several wholesome purposes in view toward the civilizing and uplifting of this nation....

In due time we were challenged by the warders, from the castle walls, and after a parley admitted. I have nothing pleasant to tell about the visit. But it was not a disappointment, for I knew Mrs. le Fay by reputation, and was not expecting anything pleasant. She was held in awe by the whole realm, for she had made everybody believe she was a great sorceress. All her ways were wicked, all her instincts devilish. She was loaded to the eyelids with cold malice. All her history was black with crime; and among her crimes murder was common. I was most curious to see her; as curious as I could have been to see Satan. To my surprise she was beautiful; black thoughts had failed to make her expression repulsive, age had failed to wrinkle her satin skin or mar its bloomy freshness. She could have passed for old Uriens' granddaughter, she could have been mistaken for sister to her own son. . . .

She caused us to be seated, and then she began, with all manner of pretty graces and graciousnesses, to ask me questions. Dear me, it was like a bird or a flute, or something, talking. I felt persuaded that this woman must have been misrepresented, lied about. She trilled along, and trilled along, and presently a handsome young page, clothed like the rainbow, and as easy and undulatory of movement as a wave came with something on a golden salver, and, kneeling to present it to her, overdid his graces and lost his balance, and so fell lightly against her knee. She slipped a dirk into him in as matter-of-course a way as another person would have harpooned a rat!

Poor child! he slumped to the floor, twisted his silken limbs in one great straining contortion of pain, and was dead. . . . Sir Uwaine, at a sign from his mother, went to the anteroom and called upon some servants, and meanwhile madame went rippling sweetly along with her talk. . . .

Marvelous woman. And what a glance she had: when it fell in reproof upon those servants, they shrunk and quailed as timid people do when the lightning flashes out of a cloud. I could have got the habit myself. . . .

In the midst of the talk I let drop a complimentary word about King Arthur, forgetting for the moment how this woman hated her brother. That one little compliment was enough. She clouded up like a storm; she called for her guards, and said:

"Hale me these varlets to the dungeons."

That struck cold on my ears, for her dungeons had a reputation. Nothing occurred to me to say—or do. But not so with Sandy. As the guard laid a hand upon me, she piped up with the tranquilest confidence, and said:

"God's wownds, dost thou covet destruction, thou maniac? It is The Boss!"

Now what a happy idea that was!—and so simple; yet it would never have occurred to me. I was born modest; not all over, but in spots; and this was one of the spots.

The effect upon madame was electrical. It cleared her countenance and brought back her smiles and all her persuasive graces and blandishments; but nevertheless she was not able to entirely cover up with them the fact that she was in a ghastly fright. She said:

"La, but do list to thine handmaid! as if one gifted with powers like to mine might say the thing which I have said unto one who has vanquished Merlin, and not be jesting. By mine enchantments I foresaw your coming, and by them I knew you when you entered here. I did but play this little jest with hope to surprise you into some display of your art, as not doubting you would blast the guards with occult fires, consuming them to ashes on the spot, a marvel much beyond mine own ability, yet one which I have long been childishly curious to see."

The guards were less curious, and got out as soon as they got permission. » » »

They finally escaped from the realm of Morgan le Fay, rode on to the castle of the three ogres, and delivered the lady and the forty-four maidens who had been the objects of their search. They then joined a procession of pilgrims journeying to the Valley of Holiness "for to be blessed of the godly hermits and drink of the miraculous waters and be cleansed from sin."

Chapter XXI

THE PILGRIMS

« « « . . . It was not going our way, but we joined it, nevertheless; for it was hourly being borne in upon me now, that if I would govern this country wisely, I must be posted in the details of its life, and not at second hand, but by personal observation and scrutiny.

This company of pilgrims resembled Chaucer's in this: that it had in it a sample of about all the upper occupations and professions the country could show, and a corresponding variety of costume. There were young men and old men, young women and old women, lively folk and grave folk. . . .

Early in the afternoon we overtook another procession of pilgrims; but in this one was no merriment, no jokes, no laughter, no playful ways, nor any happy giddiness, whether of youth or age. Yet both were here, both age and youth; gray old men and women, strong men and women of middle age, young husbands, young wives, little boys and girls, and three babies at the breast. Even the children were smileless; there was not a face among all these half a hundred people but was cast down, and bore that set expression of hopelessness which is bred of long and hard trials and old acquaintance with despair. They were slaves. Chains led from their fettered feet and their manacled hands to a soleleather belt about their waists; and all except the children were also linked together in a file, six feet apart, by a single chain which led from collar to collar all down the line. They were on foot, and had tramped three hundred miles in eighteen days, upon the cheapest odds and ends of food, and stingy rations of that. They had slept in these chains every night, bundled together like swine. They had upon their bodies some poor rags, but they could not be said to be clothed. Their irons had chafed the skin from their ankles and made sores which were ulcerated and wormy. Their naked feet were torn, and none walked without a limp. Originally there had been a hundred of these unfortunates, but about half had been sold on the trip. The trader in charge of them rode a horse and carried a whip with a short handle and a long heavy lash divided into several knotted tails at the end. With this whip he cut the shoulders of any that tottered from weariness and pain, and straightened them up. He did not speak; the whip conveyed his desire without that. None of these poor creatures looked up as we rode along by; they showed no consciousness of our presence. And they made no sound but one; that was the dull and awful clank of their chains from end to end of the long file, as forty-three burdened feet rose and fell in unison. The file moved in a cloud of its own making.

All these faces were gray with a coating of dust. One has seen the like of this coating upon furniture in unoccupied houses, and has written his idle thought in it with his finger. I was reminded of this when I noticed the faces of some of those women, young mothers carrying babes that were near to death and freedom, how a something in their hearts was written in the dust upon their faces, plain to see, and lord, how plain to read! for it was the track of tears. One of these young mothers was but a girl, and it hurt me to the heart to read that writing, and reflect that it was come up out of the breast of such a child, a breast that ought not to know trouble yet, but only the gladness of the morning of life; and no doubt—

She reeled just then, giddy with fatigue, and down came the lash and flicked a flake of skin from her naked shoulder. It stung me as if I had been hit instead. The master halted the file and jumped from his horse. He stormed and swore at this girl, and said she had made annoyance enough with her laziness, and as this was the last chance he should have, he would settle the account now. She dropped on her knees and put up her hands and began to beg, and cry, and implore, in a passion of terror, but the master gave no attention. He snatched the child from her, and then made the men-slaves who were chained before and behind her throw her on the ground and hold her there and expose her body; and then he laid on with his lash like a madman till her back was flayed, she shrieking and struggling the while piteously. One of the men who was holding her turned away his face, and for this humanity he was reviled and flogged.

All our pilgrims looked on and commented—on the expert way in which the whip was handled. They were too much hardened by lifelong every-day familiarity with slavery to notice that there was anything else in the exhibition that invited comment. This was what slavery could do, in the way of ossifying what one may call the superior lobe of human feeling; for these pilgrims were kind-hearted people, and they would not have allowed that man to treat a horse like that.

I wanted to stop the whole thing and set the slaves free, but that would not do. I must not interfere too much and get myself a name for riding over the country's laws and the citizen's rights rough-shod. If I lived and prospered I would be the death of slavery, that I was resolved upon; but I would try to fix it so that when I became its executioner it should be by command of the nation.

Just here was the wayside shop of a smith; and now arrived a landed proprietor who had bought this girl a few miles back, deliverable here where her irons could be taken off. They were removed; then there was a squabble between the gentleman and the dealer as to which should pay the blacksmith. The moment the girl was delivered from her irons, she flung herself, all tears and frantic sobbings, into the arms of the slave who had turned away his face when she was whipped. He strained her to his breast, and smothered her face and the child's with kisses, and washed them with the rain of his tears. I suspected. I inquired. Yes, I was right; it was husband and wife. They had to be torn apart by force; the girl had to be dragged away, and she struggled and fought and shrieked like one gone mad till a turn of the road hid her from sight; and even after that, we could still make out the fading plaint of those receding shrieks. And the husband and father, with his wife and child gone, never to be seen by him again in life?—well, the look of him one might not bear at all, and so I turned away; but I knew I should never get his picture out of my mind again, and there it is to this day, to wring my heart-strings whenever I think of it. . . . » » »

As the procession neared the Valley of Holiness, the travelers met a knight who bore "parlous news." Nine days before, the miraculous fountain, the object of their pilgrimage, had ceased to flow. The popular belief was that it was divine disapproval of the baths indulged in by the monks living there that caused the water to dry up. The abbot sent for The Boss to try magic and enchantment, but when the Yankee could not be found, he had a messenger bring Merlin, who for three days worked his magic unavailingly. When the Yankee arrived, he discovered that the water for the fountain had been supplied from a well. By means of a windlass and chain, the monks had been accustomed to pour the water into troughs which carried it to stone reservoirs outside the chapel. Though none but monks had been allowed to enter the well chamber, The Boss went in and, by exercising his authority, was let down into the well and discovered that it had sprung a leak. He sent by secret messenger to ask Clarence to forward to him as soon as possible everything needed for the restoration.

Chapter XXIII

RESTORATION OF THE FOUNTAIN

« « « . . . My two experts arrived in the evening, and pretty well fagged, for they had traveled double tides. They had pack-mules along, and had brought everything I needed—tools, pump, lead pipe, Greek fire, sheaves of big rockets, roman candles, colored fire sprays, electric apparatus, and a lot of sundries—everything necessary for the stateliest kind of a miracle. They got their supper and a nap, and about midnight we sallied out through a solitude so wholly vacant and complete that it quite overpassed the required conditions. We took possession of the well and its surroundings. My boys were experts in all sorts of things, from the stoning-up of a well to the constructing of a mathematical instrument. An hour before sunrise we had that leak mended in shipshape fashion, and the water began to rise. Then we stowed our fireworks in the chapel, locked up the place, and went home to bed.

Before the noon mass was over, we were at the well again; for there was a deal to do yet, and I was determined to spring the miracle before midnight, for business reasons; for whereas a miracle worked for the Church on a week-day is worth a good deal, it is worth six times as much if you get it in on a Sunday. In nine hours the water had risen to its customary level; that is to say, it was within twenty-three feet of the top. We put in a little iron pump, one of the first turned out by my works near the capital; we bored into a stone reservoir which stood against the outer wall of the well-chamber and inserted a section of lead pipe that was long enough to reach to the door of the chapel and project beyond the threshold, where the gushing water would be visible to the two hundred and fifty acres of people I was intending should be present on the flat plain in front of this little holy hillock at the proper time.

We knocked the head out of an empty hogshead and hoisted this hogshead to the flat roof of the chapel, where we clamped it down fast, poured in gunpowder till it lay loosely an inch deep on the bottom, then we stood up rockets in the hogshead as thick as they could loosely stand, all the different breeds of rockets there are; and they made a portly and imposing sheaf, I can tell you. We grounded the wire of a pocket electrical battery in that powder, we placed a whole magazine of Greek fire on each corner of the roof—blue on one corner, green on another, red on another, and purple on the last—and grounded a wire in each.

About two hundred yards off, in the flat, we built a pen of scantlings, about four feet high, and laid planks on it, and so made a platform. We covered it with swell tapestries borrowed for the occasion, and topped it off with the abbot's own throne. When you are going to do a miracle for an ignorant race, you want to get in every detail that will count; you want to make all the properties impressive to the public eye; you want to make matters comfortable for your head guest; then you can turn yourself loose and play your effects for all they are worth. I know the value of these things, for I know human nature. You can't throw too much style into a miracle. It costs trouble, and work, and sometimes money; but it pays in the end. Well, we brought the wires to the ground at the chapel, and then brought them under the ground to the platform, and hid the batteries there. We put a rope fence a hundred feet square around the platform to keep off the common multitude, and that finished the work. My idea was, doors open at ten-thirty, performance to begin at eleven-twenty-five sharp. I wished I could charge admission, but of course that wouldn't answer. I instructed my boys to be in the chapel as early as ten, before anybody was around, and be ready to man the pumps at the proper time, and make the fur fly. Then we went home to supper.

The news of the disaster to the well had traveled far by this time; and now for two or three days a steady avalanche of people had been pouring into the valley. The lower end of the valley was become one huge camp; we should have a good house, no question about that. Criers went the rounds early in the evening and announced the coming attempt, which put every pulse up to fever-heat. They gave notice that the abbot and his official suite would move in state and occupy the platform at ten-thirty, up to which time all the region which was under my ban must be clear; the bells would then cease from tolling, and this sign should be permission to the multitudes to close in and take their places.

I was at the platform and all ready to do the honors when the abbot's solemn procession hove in sight—which it did not do till it was nearly to the rope fence, because it was a starless black night and no torches permitted. With it came Merlin, and took a front seat on the platform; he was as good as his word for once. One could not see the multitudes banked together beyond the ban, but they were there, just the same. The moment the bells stopped, those banked masses broke and poured over the line like a vast black wave, and for as much as a half-hour it continued to flow, and then it solidified itself, and you could have walked upon a pavement of human heads to—well, miles.

We had a solemn stage-wait, now, for about twenty minutes—a thing I had counted on for effect; it is always good to let your audience have a chance to work up its expectancy. At length, out of the silence a noble Latin chant—men's voices—broke and swelled up and rolled away into the night, a majestic tide of melody. I had put that up, too, and it was one of the best effects I ever invented. When it was finished I stood up on the platform and extended my hands abroad, for two minutes, with my face uplifted—that always produces a dead hush—and then slowly pronounced this ghastly word with a kind of awfulness which caused hundreds to tremble, and many women to faint:

"Constantinopolitanischerdudelsackspfeifenmachersgesellschafft!"

Just as I was moaning out the closing hunks of that word, I touched off one of my electric connections, and all that murky world of people stood revealed in a hideous blue glare! It was immense—that effect! Lots of people shrieked, women curled up and quit in every direction, foundlings collapsed by platoons. The abbot and the monks crossed themselves nimbly and their lips fluttered with agitated prayers. Merlin held his grip, but he was astonished clear down to his corns; he had never seen anything to begin with that, before. Now was the time to pile in the effects. I lifted my hands and groaned out this word—as it were in agony:

"Nihilistendynamittheaterkaestchenssprengungsattentaetsversuchungen!"

—and turned on the red fire! You should have heard that Atlantic of people moan and howl when that crimson hell joined the blue! After sixty seconds I shouted:

"Transvaaltruppentropentransporttrampelthiertreibertrauungsthraentragoedie!"

—and lit up the green fire! After waiting only forty seconds this time, I spread my arms abroad and thundered out the devastating syllables of this word of words:

"Mekkamuselmannenmassenmenchenmoerdermohrenmuttermarmormonumentenmacher!"

—and whirled on the purple glare! There they were, all going at once, red, blue, green, purple!—four furious volcanoes pouring vast clouds of radiant smoke aloft, and spreading a blinding rainbowed noonday to the furthest confines of that valley. In the distance one could see that fellow on the pillar standing rigid against the background of sky, his seesaw stopped for the first time in twenty years. I knew the boys were at the pump now and ready. So I said to the abbot:

"The time is come, Father. I am about to pronounce the dread name and command the spell to dissolve. You want to brace up, and take hold of something." Then I shouted to the people, "Behold, in another minute the spell will be broken, or no mortal can break it. If it break, all will know it, for you will see the sacred water gush from the chapel door!"

I stood a few moments, to let the hearers have a chance to spread my announcement to those who couldn't hear, and so convey it to the furthest ranks, then I made a grand exhibition of extra posturing and gesturing and shouted:

"Lo, I command the fell spirit that possesses the holy fountain to now disgorge into the skies all the infernal fires that still remain in him, and straightway dissolve his spell and flee hence to the pit, there to lie bound a thousand years. By his own dread name I command it—BGWJJILLIGKKK!"

Then I touched off the hogshead of rockets, and a vast fountain of dazzling lances of fire vomited itself toward the zenith with a hissing rush, and burst in mid-sky into a storm of flashing jewels! One mighty groan of terror started up from the massed people—then suddenly broke into a wild hosannah of joy—for there, fair and plain in the uncanny glare, they saw the freed water leaping forth! The old abbot could not speak a word, for tears and the chokings in his throat; without utterance of any sort, he folded me in his arms and mashed me. It was more eloquent than speech. And harder to get over, too, in a country where there were really no doctors that were worth a damaged nickel.

You should have seen those acres of people throw themselves down in that water and kiss it; kiss it, and pet it, and fondle it, and talk to it as if it were alive, and welcome it back with the dear names they gave their darlings, just as if it had been a friend who was long gone away and lost, and was come home again. . . . » » »

After having restored the fountain, The Boss reconditioned the bath for the monks in spite of their superstitious fear that it might cause the fountain to stop flowing again. When he had finished his work and left Sandy in a nunnery, he resolved to disguise himself as a peasant and travel on foot through the country to satisfy himself about living conditions and about how the laws were executed. Then he learned through a secret telephone that the King had set out with part of the court to see for himself the miracle of the restored fountain. Shortly after his arrival the Yankee disclosed to him his plan for visiting the country in disguise. The King was so much interested that he proposed to join in the adventure. Accordingly, after disposing of various matters of business, such as touching for the king's evil, and after being coached by the Yankee in the manners of the lowly, the King assumed the same disguise as his prime minister, and the two started forth. Their chief difficulty as they proceeded lay in the King's forgetting his disguise and exciting suspicion. One of their most distressing adventures was at an apparently abandoned hut.

Chapter XXIX

THE SMALLPOX HUT

« « « . . . No animal was around anywhere, no living thing in sight. The stillness was awful, it was like the stillness of death. The cabin was a one-story one, whose thatch was black with age, and ragged from lack of repair.

The door stood a trifle ajar. We approached it stealthily—on tiptoe and at half-breath—for that is the way one's feeling makes him do, at such a time. The king knocked. We waited. No answer. Knocked again. No answer. I pushed the door softly open and looked in. I made out some dim forms, and a woman started up from the ground and stared at me, as one does who is wakened from sleep. Presently she found her voice:

"Have mercy!" she pleaded. "All is taken, nothing is left."

"I have not come to take anything, poor woman."

"You are not a priest?"

"No."

"Nor come not from the lord of the manor?"

"No, I am a stranger."

"Oh, then, for the fear of God, who visits with misery and death such as be harmless, tarry not here, but fly! This place is under his curse—and his Church's."

"Let me come in and help you—you are sick and in trouble."

I was better used to the dim light now. I could see her hollow eyes fixed upon me. I could see how emaciated she was.

"I tell you the place is under the Church's ban. Save yourself—and go, before some straggler see thee here, and report it."

"Give yourself no trouble about me; I don't care anything for the Church's curse. Let me help you."

"Now all good spirits—if there be any such—bless thee for that word. Would God I had a sup of water!—but hold, hold, forget I said it, and fly; for there is that here that even he that feareth not the Church must fear: this disease whereof we die. Leave us, thou brave, good stranger, and take with thee such whole and sincere blessing as them that be accursed can give."

But before this I had picked up a wooden bowl and was rushing past the king on my way to the brook. It was ten yards away. When I got back and entered, the king was within, and was opening the shutter that closed the window-hole, to let in air and light. The place was full of a foul stench. I put the bowl to the woman's lips, and as she gripped it with her eager talons the shutter came open and a strong light flooded her face. Smallpox!

I sprang to the king, and said in his ear:

"Out of the door on the instant, sire! the woman is dying of that disease that wasted the skirts of Camelot two years ago."

He did not budge.

"Of a truth I shall remain—and likewise help."

I whispered again:

"King, it must not be. You must go."

"Ye mean well, and ye speak not unwisely. But it were shame that a king should know fear, and shame that belted knight should withhold his hand where be such as need succor. Peace, I will not go. It is you who must go. The Church's ban is not upon me, but it forbiddeth you to be here, and she will deal with you with a heavy hand an word come to her of your trespass."

It was a desperate place for him to be in, and might cost him his life, but it was no use to argue with him. If he considered his knightly honor at stake here, that was the end of argument; he would stay, and nothing could prevent it; I was aware of that. And so I dropped the subject. The woman spoke:

"Fair sir, of your kindness will ye climb the ladder there, and bring me news of what ye find? Be not afraid to report, for times can come when even a mother's heart is past breaking—being already broke."

"Abide," said the king, "and give the woman to eat. I will go." And he put down the knapsack.

I turned to start, but the king had already started. He halted, and looked down upon a man who lay in a dim light, and had not noticed us thus far, or spoken.

"Is it your husband?" the king asked.

"Yes."

"Is he asleep?"

"God be thanked for that one charity, yes—these three hours. Where shall I pay to the full, my gratitude! for my heart is bursting with it for that sleep he sleepeth now."

I said:

"We will be careful. We will not wake him."

"Ah, no, that ye will not, for he is dead."

"Dead?"

"Yes, what triumph it is to know it! None can harm him, none insult him more. He is in heaven now, and happy; or if not there, he bides in hell and is content; for in that place he will find neither abbot nor yet bishop. We were boy and girl together; we were man and wife these five-and-twenty years, and never separated till this day. Think how long that is to love and suffer together. This morning was he out of his mind, and in his fancy we were boy and girl again and wandering in the happy fields; and so in that innocent glad converse wandered he far and farther, still lightly gossiping, and entered into those other fields we know not of, and was shut away from mortal sight. And so there was no parting, for in his fancy I went with him; he knew not but I went with him, my hand in his—my young soft hand, not this withered claw. Ah, yes, to go, and know it not; to separate and know it not; how could one go peacefuler than that? It was his reward for a cruel life patiently borne."

There was a slight noise from the direction of the dim corner where the ladder was. It was the king descending. I could see that he was bearing something in one arm, and assisting himself with the other. He came forward into the light; upon his breast lay a slender girl of fifteen. She was but half conscious; she was dying of smallpox. Here was heroism at its last and loftiest possibility, its utmost summit; this was challenging death in the open field unarmed, with all the odds against the challenger, no reward set upon the contest, and no admiring world in silks and cloth-of-gold to gaze and applaud; and yet the king's bearing was as serenely brave as it had always been in those cheaper contests where knight meets knight in equal fight and clothed in protecting steel. He was great now; sublimely great. . . .

He laid the girl down by her mother, who poured out endearments and caresses from an overflowing heart, and one could detect a flickering faint light of response in the child's eyes, but that was all. The mother hung over her, kissing her, petting her, and imploring her to speak, but the lips only moved and no sound came. I snatched my liquor flask from my knapsack, but the woman forbade me, and said:

"No—she does not suffer; it is better so. It might bring her back to life. None that be so good and kind as ye are would do her that cruel hurt. For look you—what is left to live for? Her brothers are gone, her father is gone, her mother goeth, the Church's curse is upon her, and none may shelter or befriend her even though she lay perishing in the road. She is desolate. I have not asked you, good heart, if her sister be still on live, here overhead; I had no need; ye had gone back, else, and not left the poor thing forsaken—"

"She lieth at peace," interrupted the king, in a subdued voice.

"I would not change it. How rich is this day in happiness! Ah, my Annis, thou shalt join thy sister soon—thou'rt on thy way, and these be merciful friends that will not hinder."

And so she fell to murmuring and cooing over the girl again, and softly stroking her face and hair, and kissing her and calling her by endearing names; but there was scarcely sign of response now in the glazing eyes. I saw tears well from the king's eyes, and trickle down his face. The woman noticed them, too, and said:

"Ah, I know that sign: thou'st a wife at home, poor soul, and you and she have gone hungry to bed, many's the time, that the little ones might have your crust; you know what poverty is, and the daily insults of your betters, and the heavy hand of the Church and the king."

The king winced under this accidental home-shot, but kept still; he was learning his part; and he was playing it well, too, for a pretty dull beginner. I struck up a diversion. I offered the woman food and liquor, but she refused both. She would allow nothing to come between her and the release of death. Then I slipped away and brought the dead child from aloft, and laid it by her. This broke her down again, and there was another scene that was full of heartbreak. By and by I made another diversion, and beguiled her to sketch her story.

"Ye know it well yourselves, having suffered it—for truly none of our condition in Britain escape it. It is the old, weary tale. We fought and struggled and succeeded; meaning by success, that we lived and did not die; more than that is not to be claimed. No troubles came that we could not outlive, till this year brought them; then came they all at once, as one might say, and overwhelmed us. Years ago the lord of the manor planted certain fruit-trees on our farm; in the best part of it, too—a grievous wrong and shame—"

"But it was his right," interrupted the king.

"None denieth that, indeed; an the law mean anything, what is the lord's is his, and what is mine is his also. Our farm was ours by lease, therefore 'twas likewise his, to do with it as he would. Some little time ago, three of those trees were found hewn down. Our three grown sons ran frightened to report the crime. Well, in his lordship's dungeon there they lie, who saith there shall they lie and rot till they confess. They have naught to confess, being innocent, wherefore there will they remain until they die. Ye know that right well, I ween. Think how this left us; a man, a woman, and two children, to gather a crop that was planted by so much greater force, yes, and protect it night and day from pigeons and prowling animals that be sacred and must not be hurt by any of our sort. When my lord's crop was nearly ready for the harvest, so also was ours; when his bell rang to call us to his fields to harvest his crop for nothing, he would not allow that I and my two girls should count for our three captive sons, but for only two of them; so, for the lacking one were we daily fined. All this time our own crop was perishing through neglect; and so both the priest and his lordship fined us because their shares of it were suffering through damage. In the end the fines ate up our crop—and they took it all; they took it all and made us harvest it for them, without pay or food, and we starving. Then the worst came when I, being out of my mind with hunger and loss of my boys, and grief to see my husband and my little maids in rags and misery and despair, uttered a deep blasphemy—oh! a thousand of them!—against the Church and the Church's ways. It was ten days ago. I had fallen sick with this disease, and it was to the priest I said the words, for he was come to chide me for lack of due humility under the chastening hand of God. He carried my trespass to his betters; I was stubborn; wherefore, presently upon my head and upon all heads that were dear to me, fell the curse of Rome.

"Since that day we are avoided, shunned with horror. None has come near this hut to know whether we live or not. The rest of us were taken down. Then I roused me and got up, as wife and mother will. It was little they could have eaten in any case; it was less than little they had to eat. But there was water, and I gave them that. How they craved it! and how they blessed it! But the end came yesterday; my strength broke down. Yesterday was the last time I ever saw my husband and this youngest child alive.

I have lain here all these hours—these ages, ye may say—listening, listening for any sound up there that—"

She gave a sharp quick glance at her eldest daughter, then cried out, "Oh, my darling!" and feebly gathered the stiffening form to her sheltering arms. She had recognized the death-rattle.

Chapter XXX

THE TRAGEDY OF THE MANOR-HOUSE

At midnight all was over, and we sat in the presence of four corpses. We covered them with such rags as we could find, and started away, fastening the door behind us. Their home must be these people's grave, for they could not have Christian burial, or be admitted to consecrated ground. They were as dogs, wild beasts, lepers, and no soul that valued its hope of eternal life would throw it away by meddling in any sort with these rebuked and smitten outcasts. . . . » » »

When they heard the four sons return to inform their parents of their escape, the wanderers proceeded on their way rather than hear the sons' lament at what met their eyes inside. The King had a struggle with his conscience when it occurred to him that he should properly give the escaped prisoners over to their lord, but the Yankee managed to turn his attention to another matter, and the two continued on their educational journey. A few days later, the King, when he attempted to talk to a group of peasants about agricultural methods, displayed such ignorance that they thought God had smitten his mind; the King was a madman and the Yankee a spy. The wanderers escaped only to be seized by the retinue of a passing lord and sold at auction to a dealer taking a chain gang of slaves to London.

Chapter XXXV

A PITIFUL INCIDENT

« « « . . . We had adventures all along. One day we ran into a procession. And such a procession! All the riffraff of the kingdom seemed to be comprehended in it; and all drunk at that. In the van was a cart with a coffin in it, and on the coffin sat a comely young girl of about eighteen suckling a baby, which she squeezed to her breast in a passion of love every little while, and every little while wiped from its face the tears which her eyes rained down upon it; and always the foolish little thing smiled up at her, happy and content, kneading her breast with its dimpled fat hand, which she patted and fondled right over her breaking heart.

Men and women, boys and girls, trotted along beside or after the cart, hooting, shouting profane and ribald remarks, singing snatches of foul song, skipping, dancing—a very holiday of hellions, a sickening sight. We had struck a suburb of London, outside the walls, and this was a sample of one sort of London society. Our master secured a good place for us near the gallows. A priest was in attendance, and he helped the girl climb up, and said comforting words to her, and made the under-sheriff provide a stool for her. Then he stood there by her on the gallows, and for a moment looked down upon the mass of upturned faces at his feet, then out over the solid pavement of heads that stretched away on every side occupying the vacancies far and near, and then began to tell the story of the case. And there was pity in his voice—how seldom a sound that was in that ignorant and savage land! I remember every detail of what he said, except the words he said it in; and so I change it into my own words:

"Law is intended to mete out justice. Sometimes it fails. This cannot be helped. We can only grieve, and be resigned, and pray for the soul of him who falls unfairly by the arm of the law, and that his fellows may be few. A law sends this poor young thing to death—and it is right. But another law had placed her where she must commit her crime or starve with her child—and before God that law is responsible for both her crime and her ignominious death!

"A little while ago this young thing, this child of eighteen years, was as happy a wife and mother as any in England; and her lips were blithe with song, which is the native speech of glad and innocent hearts. Her young husband was as happy as she; for he was doing his whole duty, he worked early and late at his handicraft, his bread was honest bread well and fairly earned, he was prospering, he was furnishing shelter and sustenance to his family, he was adding his mite to the wealth of the nation. By consent of a treacherous law, instant destruction fell upon this holy home and swept it away! That young husband was waylaid and impressed, and sent to sea. The wife knew nothing of it. She sought him everywhere, she moved the hardest hearts with the supplications of her tears, the broken eloquence of her despair. Weeks dragged by, she watching, waiting, hoping, her mind going slowly to wreck under the burden of her misery. Little by little all her small possessions went for food. When she could no longer pay her rent, they turned her out of doors. She begged, while she had strength; when she was starving at last, and her milk failing, she stole a piece of linen cloth of the value of a fourth part of a cent, thinking to sell it and save her child. But she was seen by the owner of the cloth. She was put in jail and brought to trial. The man testified to the facts. A plea was made for her, and her sorrowful story was told in her behalf. She spoke, too, by permission, and said she did steal the cloth, but that her mind was so disordered of late by trouble that when she was overborne with hunger all acts, criminal or other, swam meaningless through her brain and she knew nothing rightly, except that she was *so* hungry! For a moment all were touched, and there was disposition to deal mercifully with her, seeing that she was so young and friendless, and her case so piteous, and the law that robbed her of her support to blame as being the first and only cause of her transgression; but the prosecuting officer replied that whereas these things were all true, and most pitiful as well, still there was much small theft in these days, and mistimed mercy here would be a danger to property—oh, my God, is there no property in ruined homes, and orphaned babes, and broken hearts that British law holds precious! —and so he must require sentence.

"When the judge put on his black cap, the owner of the stolen linen rose trembling up, his lip quivering, his face as gray as ashes; and when the awful words came, he cried out, 'Oh, poor child, poor child, I did not know it was death!' and fell as a tree falls. When they lifted him up his reason was gone; before the sun was set, he had taken his own life. A kindly man; a man whose heart was right, at bottom; add his murder to this that is to be now done here; and charge them both where they belong—to the rulers and the bitter laws of Britain. The time is come, my child; let me pray over thee—not *for* thee, dear abused poor heart and innocent, but for them that be guilty of thy ruin and death, who need it more."

After his prayer they put the noose around the young girl's neck, and they had great trouble to adjust the knot under her ear, because she was devouring the baby all the time, wildly kissing it, and snatching it to her face and her breast, and drenching it with tears, and half moaning, half shrieking all the while, and the baby crowing, and laughing, and kicking its feet with delight over what it took for romp and play. Even the hangman couldn't stand it, but turned away. When all was ready the priest gently pulled and tugged and forced the child out of the mother's arms, and stepped quickly out of her reach; but she clasped her hands, and made a wild spring toward him, with a shriek; but the rope—and the under-sheriff—held her short. Then she went on her knees and stretched out her hands and cried:

"One more kiss—oh, my God, one more, one more—it is the dying that begs it!"

She got it; she almost smothered the little thing. And when they got it away again, she cried out:

"Oh, my child, my darling, it will die! It has no home, it has no father, no friend, no mother—"

"It has them all!" said that good priest. "All these will I be to it till I die." . . . » » »

In London the Yankee managed to pick the locks of their manacles, and the two wanderers escaped into the crowd; but, in the scuffle that ensued when their escape was discovered, the slave driver was killed, and the two were finally arrested and condemned to be hanged as murderers. In the meantime, however, The Boss managed to telephone to ask Clarence to send a band of knights to their rescue.

Chapter XXXVIII

SIR LAUNCELOT AND KNIGHTS TO THE RESCUE

« « « Nearing four in the afternoon. The scene was just outside the walls of London. A cool, comfortable, superb day, with a brilliant sun; the kind of day to make one want to live, not die. The multitude was prodigious and far-reaching; and yet we fifteen poor devils hadn't a friend in it. There was something painful in that thought, look at it how you might. There we sat, on our tall scaffold, the butt of the hate and mockery of all those enemies. We were being made a holiday spectacle. They had built a sort of grand-stand for the nobility and gentry, and these were there in full force, with their ladies. We recognized a good many of them.

The crowd got a brief and unexpected dash of diversion out of the king. The moment we were freed of our bonds he sprang up, in his fantastic rags, with face bruised out of all recognition, and proclaimed himself Arthur, King of Britain, and denounced the awful penalties of treason upon every soul there present if hair of his sacred head were touched. It startled and surprised him to hear them break into a vast roar of laughter. It wounded his dignity, and he locked himself up in silence, then, although the crowd begged him to go on, and tried to provoke him to it by catcalls, jeers, and shouts of:

"Let him speak! The king! The king! his humble subjects hunger and thirst for words of wisdom out of the mouth of their master his Serene and Sacred Raggedness!"

But it went for nothing. He put on all his majesty and sat under this rain of contempt and insult unmoved. He certainly was great in his way. Absently, I had taken off my white bandage and wound it about my right arm. When the crowd noticed this, they began upon me. They said:

"Doubtless this sailor-man is his minister—observe his costly badge of office!"

I let them go on until they got tired, and then I said:

"Yes, I am his minister, The Boss; and to-morrow you will hear that from Camelot which—"

I got no further. They drowned me out with joyous derision. But presently there was silence; for the sheriffs of London, in their official robes, with their subordinates, began to make a stir which indicated that business was about to begin. In the hush which followed, our crime was recited, the death-warrant read, then everybody uncovered while a priest uttered a prayer.

Then a slave was blindfolded; the hangman unslung his rope.

There lay the smooth road below us, we upon one side of it, the banked multitude walling its other side—a good clear road, and kept free by the police—how good it would be to see my five hundred horsemen come tearing down it! But no, it was out of the possibilities. I followed its receding thread out into the distance—not a horseman on it, or sign of one.

There was a jerk, and the slave hung dangling; dangling and hideously squirming, for his limbs were not tied.

A second rope was unslung, in a moment another slave was dangling.

In a minute a third slave was struggling in the air. It was dreadful. I turned away my head a moment, and when I turned back I missed the king! They were blindfolding him! I was paralyzed; I couldn't move, I was choking, my tongue was petrified. They finished blindfolding him, they led him under the rope. I couldn't shake off that clinging impotence. But when I saw them put the noose around his neck, then everything let go in me and I made a spring to the rescue—and as I made it I shot one more glance abroad—by George! here they came, a-tilting!—five hundred mailed and belted knights on bicycles!

The grandest sight that ever was seen. Lord, how the plumes streamed, how the sun flamed and flashed from the endless procession of webby wheels!

I waved my right arm as Launcelot swept in—he recognized my rag—I tore away noose and bandage, and shouted:

"On your knees, every rascal of you, and salute the king! Who fails shall sup in hell to-night!"

I always use that high style when I'm climaxing an effect. Well, it was noble to see Launcelot and the boys swarm up onto that scaffold and heave sheriffs and such overboard. And it was fine to see that astonished multitude go down on their knees and beg their lives of the king they had just been deriding and insulting. And as he stood apart there, receiving this homage in rags, I thought to myself, well, really there *is* something peculiarly grand about the gait and bearing of a king, after all.

I was immensely satisfied. Take the whole situation all around, it was one of the gaudiest effects I ever instigated.

And presently up comes Clarence, his own self! and winks, and says, very modernly:

"Good deal of a surprise, wasn't it? I knew you'd like it. I've had the boys practising this long time, privately; and just hungry for a chance to show off." » » »

When the King and The Boss arrived in Camelot, the latter found that Sir Sagramor had returned from his quest of the Holy Grail and had published a notice that he would meet "Hank Morgan, the which is surnamed The Boss" in the lists; each combatant might use any kind of weapon he preferred. All Camelot knew that Sir Sagramor was to be protected by the enchantment of Merlin; the combat would be a measuring of Merlin's magic against the Yankee's. But The Boss regarded the struggle as something more important than that. He considered himself "the champion of hard unsentimental common sense and reason" against the falderal of knight-errantry. "I was entering the lists to either destroy knight-errantry or be its victim." On the appointed day all the aristocracy of England had places on the grand stand draped with streamers and rich tapestry.

Chapter XXXIX

THE YANKEE'S FIGHT WITH THE KNIGHTS

« « « . . . At the appointed hour the king made a sign, and the heralds, in their tabards, appeared and made proclamation, naming the combatants and stating the cause of quarrel. There was a pause, then a ringing bugle-blast, which was the signal for us to come forth. All the multitude caught their breath, and an eager curiosity flashed into every face.

Out from his tent rode great Sir Sagramor, an imposing tower of iron, stately and rigid, his huge spear standing upright in its socket and grasped in his strong hand, his grand horse's face and breast cased in steel, his body clothed in rich trappings that almost dragged the ground—oh, a most noble picture. A great shout went up, of welcome and admiration.

And then out I came. But I didn't get any shout. There was a wondering and eloquent silence for a moment, then a great wave of laughter began to sweep along that human sea, but a warning bugle-blast cut its career short. I was in the simplest and comfortablest of gymnast costumes—flesh-colored tights from neck to heel, with blue silk puffings about my loins, and bareheaded. My horse was not above medium size, but he was alert, slender-limbed, muscled with watch-springs, and just a greyhound to go. He was a beauty, glossy as silk, and naked as he was when he was born, except for bridle and ranger-saddle.

The iron tower and the gorgeous bed-quilt came cumbrously but gracefully pirouetting down the lists, and we tripped lightly up to meet them. We halted; the tower saluted, I responded; then we wheeled and rode side by side to the grand-stand and faced our king and queen, to whom we made obeisance. The queen exclaimed:

"Alack, Sir Boss, wilt fight naked, and without lance or sword or—"

But the king checked her and made her understand, with a polite phrase or two, that this was none of her business. The bugles rang again; and we separated and rode to the ends of the lists, and took position. Now old Merlin stepped into view and cast a dainty web of gossamer threads over Sir Sagramor which turned him into Hamlet's ghost; the king made a sign, the bugles blew, Sir Sagramor laid his great lance in rest, and the next moment here he came thundering down the course with his veil flying out behind, and I went whistling through the air like an arrow to meet him—cocking my ear the while, as if noting the invisible knight's position and progress by hearing, not sight. A chorus of encouraging shouts burst out for him, and one brave voice flung out a heartening word for me—said:

"Go it, slim Jim!"

It was an even bet that Clarence had procured that favor for me—and furnished the language, too. When that formidable lance-point was within a yard and a half of my breast I twitched my horse aside without an effort, and the big knight swept by, scoring a blank. I got plenty of applause that time. We turned, braced up, and down we came again. Another blank for the knight, a roar of applause for me. This same thing was repeated once more; and it fetched such a whirlwind of applause that Sir Sagramor lost his temper, and at once changed his tactics and set himself the task of chasing me down. Why, he hadn't any show in the world at that; it was a game of tag, with all the advantage on my side; I whirled out of his path with ease whenever I chose, and once, I slapped him on the back as I went to the rear. Finally I took the chase into my own hands; and after that, turn, or twist, or do what he would, he was never able to get behind me again; he found himself always in front at the end of his manoeuver. So he gave up that business and retired to his end of the lists. His temper was clear gone now, and he forgot himself and flung an insult at me which disposed of mine. I slipped my lasso from the horn of my saddle, and grasped the coil in my right hand. This time you should have seen him come!—it was a business trip, sure; by his gait there was blood in his eye. I was sitting my horse at ease, and swinging the great loop of my lasso in wide circles about my head; the moment he was under way, I started for him; when the space between us had narrowed to forty feet, I sent the snaky spirals of the rope a-cleaving through the air, then darted aside and faced about and brought my trained animal to a halt with all his feet braced under him for a surge. The next moment the rope sprang taut and yanked Sir Sagramor out of the saddle! Great Scott, but there was a sensation!

Unquestionably, the popular thing in this world is novelty. These people had never seen anything of that cowboy business before, and it carried them clear off their feet with delight. From all around and everywhere, the shout went up:

"Encore! encore!" . . .

The moment my lasso was released and Sir Sagramor had been assisted to his tent, I hauled in the slack, took my station and began to swing my loop around my head again. I was sure to have use for it as soon as they could elect a successor for Sir Sagramor, and that couldn't take long where there were so many hungry candidates. Indeed, they elected one straight off—Sir Hervis de Revel.

Bzz! Here he came, like a house afire! I dodged: he passed like a flash, with my horse-hair coils settling around his neck; a second or so later, *fst!* his saddle was empty.

I got another encore; and another, and another, and still another. When I had snaked five men out, things began to look serious to the ironclads, and they stopped and consulted together. As a result, they decided that it was time a waive etiquette and send their greatest and best against me. To the astonishment of that little world, I lassoed Sir Lamorak de Galis, and after him Sir Galahad. So you see there was simply nothing to be done now, but play their right bower—bring out the superbest of the superb, the mightiest of the mighty, the great Sir Launcelot himself!

A proud moment for me? I should think so. Yonder was Arthur, King of Britain; yonder was Guinever; yes, and whole tribes of little provincial kings and kinglets; and in the tented camp yonder, renowned knights from many lands; and likewise the selectest body known to chivalry, the Knights of the Table Round, the most illustrious in Christendom; and biggest fact of all, the very sun of their shining system was yonder couching his lance, the focal point of forty thousand adoring eyes; and all by myself, here was I laying for him. Across my mind flitted the dear image of a certain hello-girl of West Hartford, and I wished she could see me now. In that moment, down came the Invincible, with the rush of a whirlwind—the courtly world rose to its feet and bent forward—the fateful coils went circling through the air, and before you could wink I was towing Sir Launcelot across the field on his back, and kissing my hand to the storm of waving kerchiefs and the thunder-crash of applause that greeted me!

Said I to myself, as I coiled my lariat and hung it on my saddle-horn, and sat there drunk with glory, "The victory is perfect—no other will venture against me—knight-errantry is dead." Now imagine my astonishment—and everybody else's, too—to hear the peculiar bugle-call which announces that another competitor is about to enter the lists! There was a mystery here; I couldn't account for this thing. Next, I noticed Merlin gliding away from me; and then I noticed that my lasso was gone! The old sleight-of-hand expert had stolen it, sure, and slipped it under his robe.

The bugle blew again. I looked, and down came Sagramor riding again, with his dust brushed off and his veil nicely rearranged. I trotted up to meet him, and pretended to find him by the sound of his horse's hoofs. He said:

"Thou'rt quick of ear, but it will not save thee from this!" and he touched the hilt of his great sword. "An ye are not able to see it, because of the influence of the veil, know that it is no cumbrous lance, but a sword—and I ween ye will not be able to avoid it."

His visor was up; there was death in his smile. I should never be able to dodge his sword, that was plain. Somebody was going to die this time. If he got the drop on me, I could name the corpse. We rode forward together, and saluted the royalties. This time the king was disturbed. He said:

"Where is thy strange weapon?"

"It is stolen, sire."

"Hast another at hand?"

"No, sire, I brought only the one."

Then Merlin mixed in:

"He brought but the one because there was but the one to bring. There exists none other but that one. It belongeth to the king of the Demons of the Sea. This man is a pretender, and ignorant; else he had known that that weapon can be used in but eight bouts only, and then it vanisheth away to its home under the sea."

"Then is he weaponless," said the king. "Sir Sagramor, ye will grant him leave to borrow."

"And I will lend!" said Sir Launcelot, limping up. "He is as brave a knight of his hands as any that be on live, and he shall have mine."

He put his hand on his sword to draw it, but Sir Sagramor said:

"Stay, it may not be. He shall fight with his own weapons; it was his privilege to choose them and bring them. If he has erred, on his head be it."

"Knight!" said the king. "Thou'rt overwrought with passion; it disorders thy mind. Wouldst kill a naked man?"

"An he do it, he shall answer it to me," said Sir Launcelot.

"I will answer it to any he that desireth!" retorted Sir Sagramor hotly.

Merlin broke in, rubbing his hands and smiling his low-downest smile of malicious gratification:

"'Tis well said, right well said! And 'tis enough of parleying, let my lord the king deliver the battle signal."

The king had to yield. The bugle made proclamation, and we

turned apart and rode to our stations. There we stood, a hundred yards apart, facing each other, rigid and motionless, like horsed statues. And so we remained, in a soundless hush, as much as a full minute, everybody gazing, nobody stirring. It seemed as if the king could not take heart to give the signal. But at last he lifted his hand, the clear note of a bugle followed, Sir Sagramor's long blade described a flashing curve in the air, and it was superb to see him come. I sat still. On he came. I did not move. People got so excited that they shouted to me:

"Fly, fly! Save thyself! This is murther!"

I never budged so much as an inch till that thundering apparition had got within fifteen paces of me; then I snatched a dragoon revolver out of my holster, there was a flash and a roar, and the revolver was back in the holster before anybody could tell what had happened.

Here was a riderless horse plunging by, and yonder lay Sir Sagramor, stone dead.

The people that ran to him were stricken dumb to find that the life was actually gone out of the man and no reason for it visible, no hurt upon his body, nothing like a wound. There was a hole through the breast of his chain-mail, but they attached no importance to a little thing like that; and as a bullet-wound there produces but little blood, none came in sight because of the clothing and swaddlings under the armor. The body was dragged over to let the king and the swells look down upon it. They were stupefied with astonishment naturally. I was requested to come and explain the miracle. But I remained in my tracks, like a statue, and said:

"If it is a command, I will come, but my lord the king knows that I am where the laws of combat require me to remain while any desire to come against me."

I waited. Nobody challenged. Then I said:

"If there are any who doubt that this field is well and fairly won, I do not wait for them to challenge me, I challenge them."

"It is a gallant offer," said the king, "and well beseems you. Whom will you name first?"

"I name none, I challenge all! Here I stand, and dare the chivalry of England to come against me—not by individuals, but in mass!"

"What!" shouted a score of knights.

"You have heard the challenge. Take it, or I proclaim you recreant knights and vanquished every one!"

It was a "bluff" you know. At such a time it is sound judgment to put on a bold face and play your hand for a hundred times what it is worth; forty-nine times out of fifty nobody dares to "call," and you rake in the chips. But just this once—well, things looked squally! In just no time, five hundred knights were scrambling into their saddles, and before you could wink a widely scattering drove were under way and clattering down upon me. I snatched both revolvers from the holsters and began to measure distances and calculate chances.

Bang! One saddle empty. Bang! another one. Bang—Bang, and I bagged two. Well, it was nip and tuck with us, and I knew it. If I spent the eleventh shot without convincing these people, the twelfth man would kill me, sure. And so I never did feel so happy as I did when my ninth downed its man and I detected the wavering in the crowd which is premonitory of panic. An instant lost now could knock out my last chance. But I didn't lose it. I raised both revolvers and pointed them—the halted host stood their ground just about one good square moment, then broke and fled.

The day was mine. Knight-errantry was a doomed institution. The march of civilization was begun. How did I feel? Ah, you never could imagine it. . . . » » »

Three years after the victory of The Boss in the tournament, he had such reason to feel satisfied with the transformation of the country that he opened for inspection his mines and "vast system of clandestine factories and workshops."

And then the turn came. Doctors decreed that he must take Sandy and their child, who was having difficulty recuperating from a serious illness, cruising around the coast of France for sea air. He set out with a train of 250 attendants and for some months had little thought for anything else but whether Hello Central could return to health.

Chapter XLI

THE INTERDICT

« « « However, my attention was suddenly snatched from such matters; our child began to lose ground again, and we had to go to sitting up with her, her case became so serious. We couldn't bear to allow anybody to help in this service, so we two stood watch-and-watch, day in and day out. Ah, Sandy, what a right heart she had, how simple, and genuine, and good she was! She was a flawless wife and mother; and yet I had married her for no other particular reasons, except that by the customs of chivalry she was my property until some knight should win her from me in the field. She had hunted Britain over for me; had found me at the hanging-bout outside of London, and had straightway resumed her old place at my side in the placidest way and as of right. I was a New-Englander, and in my opinion this sort of partnership would compromise her, sooner or later. She couldn't see how, but I cut argument short and we had a wedding.

Now I didn't know I was drawing a prize, yet that was what I did draw. Within the twelvemonth I became her worshiper; and ours was the dearest and perfectest comradeship that ever was. People talk about beautiful friendships between two persons of the same sex. What is the best of that sort, as compared with the friendship of man and wife, where the best impulses and highest ideals of both are the same? There is no place for comparison between the two friendships; the one is earthly, the other divine.[29]

. . .

Well, during two weeks and a half we watched by the crib, and in our deep solicitude we were unconscious of any world outside of that sick-room. Then our reward came: the center of the universe turned the corner and began to mend. Grateful? It isn't the term. There *isn't* any term for it. You know that yourself, if you've watched your child through the Valley of the Shadow and seen it come back to life and sweep night out of the earth with one all-illuminating smile that you could cover with your hand.

Why, we were back in this world in one instant! Then we looked

---

[29] In an entry of 1893, Mark Twain writes in his *Notebook*, 235, "Love seems the swiftest but is the slowest of all growth. No man and woman really know what perfect love is until they have been married a quarter of a century."

the same startled thought into each other's eyes at the same moment; more than two weeks gone, and that ship not back yet! . . . » » »

When the crisis in the illness of his child had passed and The Boss once more joined his train of attendants, he discovered that they were greatly troubled by indications that all might not be going well in Britain. He left at once in disguise for that country to discover the cause. What he found there was something worse than he with all his resourcefulness knew how to cope with. His fear of the Church had not been unfounded; although it had from the first looked upon his activities with the greatest disapproval, as he had suspected, it had bided its time. He later discovered that, by instructing the doctors to make an alarming diagnosis of the child's illness, the Church had been instrumental in getting him out of the kingdom. Then it placed an interdict upon all Britain.

« « « . . . I approached England the next morning, with the wide highway of salt-water all to myself. There were ships in the harbor, at Dover, but they were naked as to sails, and there was no sign of life about them. It was Sunday; yet at Canterbury the streets were empty; strangest of all, there was not even a priest in sight, and no stroke of a bell fell upon my ear. The mournfulness of death was everywhere. I couldn't understand it. At last, in the further edge of that town I saw a small funeral procession—just a family and a few friends following a coffin—no priest; a funeral without bell, book, or candle; there was a church there close at hand, but they passed it by weeping, and did not enter it; I glanced up at the belfry, and there hung the bell, shrouded in black, and its tongue tied back. Now I knew! Now I understood the stupendous calamity that had overtaken England. Invasion? Invasion is a triviality to it. It was the INTERDICT!

I asked no questions; I didn't need to ask any. The Church had struck; the thing for me to do was to get into a disguise, and go warily. One of my servants gave me a suit of clothes, and when we were safe beyond the town I put them on, and from that time I traveled alone; I could not risk the embarrassment of company.

A miserable journey. A desolate silence everywhere. Even in London itself. Traffic had ceased; men did not talk or laugh, or go in groups, or even in couples; they moved aimlessly about, each man by himself, with his head down, and woe and terror at his heart. The Tower showed recent war-scars. Verily, much had been happening.

Of course, I meant to take the train for Camelot. Train! Why, the station was as vacant as a cavern. I moved on. The journey to Camelot was a repetition of what I had already seen. The Monday and the Tuesday differed in no way from the Sunday. I arrived far in the night. From being the best electric-lighted town in the kingdom and the most like a recumbent sun of anything you ever saw, it was become simply a blot—a blot upon darkness—that is to say, it was darker and solider than the rest of the darkness, and so you could see it a little better; it made me feel as if maybe it was symbolical—a sort of sign that the Church was going to *keep* the upper hand now, and snuff out all my beautiful civilization just like that. I found no life stirring in the somber streets. I groped my way with a heavy heart. The vast castle loomed black upon the hilltop, not a spark visible about it. The drawbridge was down, the great gate stood wide, I entered without challenge, my own heels making the only sound I heard—and it was sepulchral enough, in those huge vacant courts. » » »

Clarence, having recognized The Boss through his disguise, told him about all that had happened in his absence. The immediate provocation of the displeasure of the Church was not the Yankee's reforms. After years of blindness, the King was finally apprised of the grievous wrong done him by Launcelot and the Queen. A civil war ensued. The King, leaving Mordred to rule the kingdom until the Yankee should return, collected the knights who were loyal to him and attacked the forces of Launcelot in his stronghold at Guienne in France. In the King's absence, Mordred attempted to force the Queen to marry him, whereupon the Church visited the interdict upon both Mordred and The Boss, to be in force as long as they lived.

In the great conflict the King met death at the hands of Mordred, whom he had mortally wounded. The Queen went into the nunnery at Almsbury, and Launcelot took refuge in a hermitage.

"Smart as you are, the Church was smarter," Clarence told The Boss. From now on the conflict was to be between the Church, which had gathered under its banner all the knights that were still alive, and the Yankee, who had only Clarence and a loyal band of fifty-two youths whom Clarence had trained in technical skills. Only they, Clarence reasoned, could be trusted to resist the power of the Church. The railway, telephone, and telegraph services ceased, and the Church laid a ban on electric lights.

Clarence and his work squad made a stronghold of Merlin's cave with a circle one hundred yards in diameter fenced around it with charged wires and such other defenses as could be manipulated from inside the cave. Electric wires from dynamos they had moved into the cave connected with all the factories and other installations constructed by the Yankee's ingenuity. If the worst came, they planned to "blow up their civilization."

The Yankee's first move upon his return was to proclaim a republic.

Chapter XLII

WAR!

PROCLAMATION

« « « "BE IT KNOWN UNTO ALL. Whereas the king having died and left no heir, it becomes my duty to continue the executive authority vested in me, until a government shall have been created and set in motion. The monarchy has lapsed, it no longer exists. By consequence, all political power has reverted to its original source, the people of the nation. With the monarchy, its several adjuncts died also; wherefore there is no longer a nobility, no longer a privileged class, no longer an Established Church; all men are become exactly equal; they are upon one common level, and religion is free. *A Republic is hereby proclaimed,* as being the natural estate of a nation when other authority has ceased. It is the duty of the British people to meet together immediately, and by their votes elect representatives and deliver into their hands the government." » » »

His band of helpers, strong as an army, waited a week within their defenses. Their spies brought in reports that knights and priests from all England were collecting for an attack. While at first the masses of the Republic shouted for joy, as soon as the Church, the nobility, and the gentry frowned in disapproval, they became sheep crying, "Down with the Republic!"

Chapter XLIII

THE BATTLE OF THE SAND-BELT

« « « . . . The big day arrived on time. At dawn the sentry on watch in the corral came into the cave and reported a moving black mass under the horizon, and a faint sound which he thought to be military music. Breakfast was just ready; we sat down and ate it.

This over, I made the boys a little speech, and then sent out a detail to man the battery, with Clarence in command of it.

The sun rose presently and sent its unobstructed splendors over the land, and we saw a prodigious host moving slowly toward us, with the steady drift and aligned front of a wave of the sea. Nearer and nearer it came, and more and more sublimely imposing became its aspect; yes, all England was there, apparently. Soon we could see the innumerable banners fluttering, and then the sun struck the sea of armor and set it all aflash. Yes, it was a fine sight; I hadn't ever seen anything to beat it.

At last we could make out details. All the front ranks, no telling how many acres deep, were horsemen—plumed knights in armor. Suddenly we heard the blare of trumpets; the slow walk burst into a gallop, and then—well, it was wonderful to see! Down swept that vast horse-shoe wave—it approached the sand-belt—my breath stood still; nearer, nearer—the strip of green turf beyond the yellow belt grew narrower—narrower still—became a mere ribbon in front of the horses—then disappeared under their hoofs. Great Scott! Why, the whole front of that host shot into the sky with a thunder-crash, and became a whirling tempest of rags and fragments; and along the ground lay a thick wall of smoke that hid what was left of the multitude from our sight.

Time for the second step in the plan of campaign! I touched

a button, and shook the bones of England loose from her spine!

In that explosion all our noble civilization-factories went up in the air and disappeared from the earth. It was a pity, but it was necessary. We could not afford to let the enemy turn our own weapon against us.

Now ensued one of the dullest quarter-hours I had ever endured. We waited in a silent solitude inclosed by our circles of wire, and by a circle of heavy smoke outside of these. We couldn't see over the wall of smoke, and we couldn't see through it. But at last it began to shred away lazily, and by the end of another quarter-hour the land was clear and our curiosity was enabled to satisfy itself. No living creature was in sight! We now perceived that additions had been made to our defenses. The dynamite had dug a ditch more than a hundred feet wide, all around us, and cast up an embankment some twenty-five feet high on both borders of it. As to destruction of life, it was amazing. Moreover, it was beyond estimate. Of course, we could not *count* the dead, because they did not exist as individuals, but merely as homogeneous protoplasm, with alloys of iron and buttons.

No life was in sight, but necessarily there must have been some wounded in the rear ranks, who were carried off the field under cover of the wall of smoke; there would be sickness among the others—there always is, after an episode like that. But there would be no reinforcements; this was the last stand of the chivalry of England; it was all that was left of the order, after the recent annihilating wars. So I felt quite safe in believing that the utmost force that could for the future be brought against us would be but small; that is, of knights. I therefore issued a congratulatory proclamation to my army in these words:

> SOLDIERS, CHAMPIONS OF HUMAN LIBERTY AND EQUALITY: Your General congratulates you! In the pride of his strength and the vanity of his renown, an arrogant enemy came against you. You were ready. The conflict was brief; on your side, glorious. This mighty victory, having been achieved utterly without loss, stands without example in history. So long as the planets shall continue to move in their orbits, the BATTLE OF THE SAND-BELT will not perish out of the memories of men.
>
> THE BOSS.

I read it well, and the applause I got was very gratifying to me. I then wound up with these remarks:

"The war with the English nation, as a nation, is at an end. The nation has retired from the field and the war. Before it can be persuaded to return, war will have ceased. This campaign is the only one that is going to be fought. It will be brief—the briefest in history. Also the most destructive to life, considered from the standpoint of proportion of casualties to numbers engaged. We are done with the nation; henceforth we deal only with the knights. English knights can be killed, but they cannot be conquered. We know what is before us. While one of these men remains alive, our task is not finished, the war is not ended. We will kill them all." [Loud and long-continued applause.]

I picketed the great embankments thrown up around our lines by the dynamite explosion—merely a lookout of a couple of boys to announce the enemy when he should appear again.

Next, I sent an engineer and forty men to a point just beyond our lines on the south, to turn a mountain brook that was there, and bring it within our lines and under our command, arranging it in such a way that I could make instant use of it in an emergency. The forty men were divided into two shifts of twenty each, and were to relieve each other every two hours. In ten hours the work was accomplished.

It was nightfall now, and I withdrew my pickets. The one who had had the northern outlook reported a camp in sight, but visible with the glass only. He also reported that a few knights had been feeling their way toward us, and had driven some cattle across our lines, but that the knights themselves had not come very near. That was what I had been expecting. They were feeling us, you see; they wanted to know if we were going to play that red terror on them again. They would grow bolder in the night, perhaps. I believed I knew what project they would attempt, because it was plainly the thing I would attempt myself if I were in their places and as ignorant as they were. I mentioned it to Clarence.

"I think you are right," said he; "it is the obvious thing for them to try."

"Well, then," I said, "if they do it they are doomed."

"Certainly."

"They won't have the slightest show in the world."

"Of course they won't."

"It's dreadful, Clarence. It seems an awful pity."

The thing disturbed me so that I couldn't get any peace of mind for thinking of it and worrying over it. So, at last, to quiet my conscience, I framed this message to the knights:

To the Honorable the Commander of the Insurgent Chivalry of England: You fight in vain. We know your strength—if one may call it by that name. We know that at the utmost you cannot bring against us above five-and-twenty thousand knights. Therefore, you have no chance—none whatever. Reflect: we are well equipped, well fortified, we number 54. Fifty-four what? Men? No, *minds*—the capablest in the world; a force against which mere animal might may no more hope to prevail than may the idle waves of the sea hope to prevail against the granite barriers of England. Be advised. We offer you your lives; for the sake of your families, do not reject the gift. We offer you this chance, and it is the last: throw down your arms; surrender unconditionally to the Republic, and all will be forgiven.

(Signed)   The Boss.

I read it to Clarence, and said I proposed to send it by a flag of truce. He laughed the sarcastic laugh he was born with, and said:

"Somehow it seems impossible for you to ever fully realize what these nobilities are. Now let us save a little time and trouble. Consider me the commander of the knights yonder. Now, then, you are the flag of truce; approach and deliver me your message, and I will give you your answer."

I humored the idea. I came forward under an imaginary guard of the enemy's soldiers, produced my paper, and read it through. For answer, Clarence struck the paper out of my hand, pursed up a scornful lip and said with lofty disdain:

"Dismember me this animal, and return him in a basket to the base-born knave who sent him; other answer have I none!"

How empty is theory in presence of fact! And this was just fact, and nothing else. It was the thing that would have happened, there was no getting around that. I tore up the paper and granted my mistimed sentimentalities a permanent rest.

Then, to business. I tested the electric signals from the Gatling platform to the cave, and made sure that they were all right; I tested and retested those which commanded the fences—these were signals whereby I could break and renew the electric current in each fence independently of the others at will. I placed the brook-connection under the guard and authority of three of my best boys, who would alternate in two-hour watches all night and promptly obey my signal, if I should have occasion to give it—three revolver-shots in quick succession. Sentry duty was discarded for the night, and the corral left empty of life; I ordered that quiet be maintained in the cave, and the electric lights turned down to a glimmer.

As soon as it was good and dark, I shut off the current from all the fences, and then groped my way out to the embankment bordering our side of the great dynamite ditch. I crept to the top of it and lay there on the slant of the muck to watch. But it was too dark to see anything. As for sounds, there were none. The stillness was deathlike. True, there were the usual night sounds of the country—the whir of night birds, the buzzing of insects, the barking of distant dogs, the mellow lowing of far-off kine—but these didn't seem to break the stillness, they only intensified it, and added a gruesome melancholy to it into the bargain.

I presently gave up looking, the night shut down so black, but I kept my ears strained to catch the least suspicious sound, for I judged I had only to wait, and I shouldn't be disappointed. However, I had to wait a long time. At last I caught what you may call indistinct glimpses of sound—dulled metallic sound. I pricked up my ears, then, and held my breath, for this was the sort of thing I had been waiting for. This sound thickened, and approached—from toward the north. Presently, I heard it at my own level—the ridge-top of the opposite embankment, a hundred feet or more away. Then I seemed to see a row of black dots appear along that ridge—human heads? I couldn't tell; it mightn't be anything at all; you can't depend on your eyes when your imagination is out of focus. However, the question was soon settled. I heard that metallic noise descending into the great ditch. It augmented fast, it spread all along, and it unmistakably furnished me this fact: an armed host was taking up its quarters in the ditch. Yes, these people were arranging a little surprise party for us. We could expect entertainment about dawn, possibly earlier.

I groped my way back to the corral now; I had seen enough. I went to the platform and signaled to turn the current on to the two inner fences. Then I went into the cave, and found everything satisfactory there—nobody awake but the working-watch. I woke Clarence and told him the great ditch was filling up with men, and that I believed all the knights were coming for us in a body. It was my notion that as soon as dawn approached we could expect the ditch's ambuscaded thousands to swarm up over the embankment and make an assault, and be followed immediately by the rest of their army.

Clarence said:

"They will be wanting to send a scout or two in the dark to make preliminary observations. Why not take the lightning off the outer fences, and give them a chance?"

"I've already done it, Clarence. Did you ever know me to be inhospitable?"

"No, you are a good heart. I want to go and—"

"Be a reception committee? I will go, too."

We crossed the corral and lay down together between the two inside fences. Even the dim light of the cave had disordered our sight somewhat, but the focus straightway began to regulate itself and soon it was adjusted for present circumstances. We had had to feel our way before, but we could make out to see the fence-posts now. We started a whispered conversation, but suddenly Clarence broke off and said:

"What is that?"

"What is what?"

"That thing yonder."

"What thing—where?"

"There beyond you a little piece—a dark something—a dull shape of some kind—against the second fence."

I gazed and he gazed. I said:

"Could it be a man, Clarence?"

"No, I think not. If you notice, it looks a lit— why, it *is* a man!—leaning on the fence."

"I certainly believe it is; let us go and see."

We crept along on our hands and knees until we were pretty close, and then looked up. Yes, it was a man—a dim great figure in armor, standing erect, with both hands on the upper wire—and, of course, there was a smell of burning flesh. Poor fellow, dead as a door-nail, and never knew what hurt him. He stood there like a statue—no motion about him, except that his plumes swished about a little in the night wind. We rose up and looked in through the bars of his visor, but couldn't make out whether we knew him or not— features too dim and shadowed.

We heard muffled sounds approaching, and we sank down to the ground where we were. We made out another knight vaguely; he was coming very stealthily, and feeling his way. He was near enough now for us to see him put out a hand, find an upper wire, then bend and step under it and over the lower one. Now he arrived at the first knight—and started slightly when he discovered him. He stood a moment—no doubt wondering why the other one didn't move on; then he said, in a low voice, "Why dreamest thou here, good Sir Mar—" then he laid his hand on the corpse's shoulder —and just uttered a little soft moan and sunk down dead. Killed by a dead man, you see—killed by a dead friend, in fact. There was something awful about it.

These early birds came scattering along after each other, about one every five minutes in our vicinity, during half an hour. They brought no armor of offense but their swords; as a rule, they carried the sword ready in the hand, and put it forward and found the wires with it. We would now and then see a blue spark when the knight that caused it was so far away as to be invisible to us; but we knew what had happened, all the same; poor fellow, he had touched a charged wire with his sword and been elected. We had brief intervals of grim stillness, interrupted with piteous regularity by the clash made by the falling of an ironclad; and this sort of thing was going on, right along, and was very creepy there in the dark and lonesomeness.

We concluded to make a tour between the inner fences. We elected to walk upright, for convenience' sake; we argued that if discerned, we should be taken for friends rather than enemies, and in any case we should be out of reach of swords, and these gentry did not seem to have any spears along. Well, it was a curious trip. Everywhere dead men were lying outside the second fence, not plainly visible, but still visible; and we counted fifteen of those pathetic statues—dead knights standing with their hands on the upper wire.

One thing seemed to be sufficiently demonstrated: our current was so tremendous that it killed before the victim could cry out. Pretty soon we detected a muffled and heavy sound, and next moment we guessed what it was. It was a surprise in force coming! I whispered to Clarence to go and wake the army, and notify it to wait in silence in the cave for further orders. He was soon back, and we stood by the inner fence and watched the silent lightning do its awful work upon that swarming host. One could make out but little of detail; but he could note that a black mass was piling itself up beyond the second fence. That swelling bulk was dead men! Our camp was inclosed with a solid wall of the dead—a bulwark, a breastwork, of corpses, you may say. One terrible thing about this thing was the absence of human voices; there were no cheers, no war-cries; being intent upon a surprise, these men moved as noiselessly as they could; and always when the front rank was near enough to their goal to make it proper for them to begin to to get a shout ready, of course they struck the fatal line and went down without testifying.

I sent a current through the third fence now; and almost immediately through the fourth and fifth, so quickly were the gaps filled up. I believed the time was come now for my climax; I believed that that whole army was in our trap. Anyway, it was high time to find out. So I touched a button and set fifty electric suns aflame on the top of our precipice.

Land, what a sight! We were inclosed in three walls of dead men! All the other fences were pretty nearly filled with the living, who were stealthily working their way forward through the wires. The sudden glare paralyzed this host, petrified them, you may say, with astonishment; there was just one instant for me to utilize their immobility in, and I didn't lose the chance. You see, in another instant they would have recovered their faculties, then they'd have burst into a cheer and made a rush, and my wires would have gone down before it; but that lost instant lost them their opportunity forever; while even that slight fragment of time was still unspent, I shot the current through all the fences and struck the whole host dead in their tracks! *There* was a groan you could *hear!* It voiced the death-pang of eleven thousand men. It swelled out on the night with awful pathos.

A glance showed that the rest of the enemy—perhaps ten thousand strong—were between us and the encircling ditch, and pressing forward to the assault. Consequently we had them *all!* and had them past help. Time for the last act of the tragedy. I fired the three appointed revolver-shots—which meant:

"Turn on the water!"

There was a sudden rush and roar, and in a minute the mountain brook was raging through the big ditch and creating a river a hundred feet wide and twenty-five deep.

"Stand to your guns, men! Open fire!"

The thirteen Gatlings began to vomit death into the fated ten thousand. They halted, they stood their ground a moment against that withering deluge of fire, then they broke, faced about and swept toward the ditch like chaff before a gale. A full fourth part of their force never reached the top of the lofty embankment; the three-fourths reached it and plunged over—to death by drowning.

Within ten short minutes after we had opened fire, armed resistance was totally annihilated, the campaign was ended, we fifty-four were masters of England! Twenty-five thousand men lay dead around us.

But how treacherous is fortune! In a little while—say an hour—happened a thing, by my own fault, which—but I have no heart to write that. Let the record end here.

Chapter XLIV

A POSTSCRIPT BY CLARENCE

I, Clarence, must write it for him. He proposed that we two go out and see if any help could be accorded the wounded. I was strenuous against the project. I said that if there were many, we could do but little for them; and it would not be wise for us to trust ourselves among them, anyway. But he could seldom be turned from a purpose once formed; so we shut off the electric current from the fences, took an escort along, climbed over the inclosing ramparts of dead knights, and moved out upon the field. The first wounded man who appealed for help was sitting with his back against a dead comrade. When The Boss bent over him and spoke to him, the man recognized him and stabbed him. That knight was Sir Meliagraunce, as I found out by tearing off his helmet. He will not ask for help any more.

We carried The Boss to the cave and gave his wound, which was not very serious, the best care we could. In this service we had the help of Merlin, though we did not know it. He was disguised as a woman, and appeared to be a simple old peasant goodwife. In this disguise, with brown-stained face and smooth-shaven, he had appeared a few days after The Boss was hurt, and offered to cook for us, saying her people had gone off to join certain new camps which the enemy were forming, and that she was starving. The Boss had been getting along very well, and had amused himself with finishing up his record.

We were glad to have this woman, for we were short-handed. We were in a trap, you see—a trap of our own making. If we stayed where we were, our dead would kill us; if we moved out of our defenses, we should no longer be invincible. We had conquered; in turn we were conquered. The Boss recognized this; we all recognized it. If we could go to one of those new camps and patch up some kind of terms with the enemy—yes, but The Boss could not go, and neither could I, for I was among the first that were made sick by the poisonous air bred by those dead thousands. Others were taken down, and still others. To-morrow—

To-morrow. It is here. And with it the end. About midnight I awoke, and saw that hag making curious passes in the air about The Boss's head and face, and wondered what it meant. Everybody but the dynamo-watch lay steeped in sleep; there was no sound. The woman ceased from her mysterious foolery, and started tiptoeing toward the door. I called out:

"Stop! What have you been doing?"

She halted, and said with an accent of malicious satisfaction:

"Ye were conquerors; ye are conquered! These others are perishing—you also. Ye shall all die in this place—every one—except *him.* He sleepeth now—and shall sleep thirteen centuries. I am Merlin!"

Then such delirium of silly laughter overtook him that he reeled about like a drunken man, and presently fetched up against one of our wires. His mouth is spread open yet; apparently he is still laughing. I suppose the face will retain that petrified laugh until the corpse turns to dust.

The Boss has never stirred—sleeps like a stone. If he does not wake to-day we shall understand what kind of a sleep it is, and his body will then be borne to a place in one of the remote recesses of the cave where none will ever find it to desecrate it. As for the rest of us—well, it is agreed that if any one of us ever escapes alive from this place, he will write the fact here, and loyally hide this Manuscript with The Boss, our dear good chief, whose property it is, be he alive or dead. » » »

In "The Mysterious Stranger" the humorist is all but lost, although this story contains Mark Twain's firmest defense of humor —of its power in the cause of reform. In this sardonic tale of the nephew of Satan disporting himself among the simple villagers of Eseldorf, Mark Twain does to the limit what he had done more guardedly in "The Man That Corrupted Hadleyburg."[30] He exposes the cruelty and helplessness of the race of man. The pity of it arouses our compassion more than our condemnation. The inconsistency of representing creatures at the mercy of their Creator and yet responsible for their misdeeds seems not to have disturbed the author. There are compensations for this discrepancy, however, much as we deplore the fact that he never reached the stage of maturity at which he could accept man's situation, vouchsafed, as he is, the gift of life, but in a universe whose meaning he is not capable of discerning. Mark Twain could not feel the necessity for faith, but we are richer for his having recorded his adventure in living and for his disillusion so frankly and fully expressed. The paradoxes of life challenged and irritated him. He flung out his arms,

---

[30] An entry of 1895 in Mark Twain's *Notebook*, 256, reads: "It is the strangest thing that the world is not full of books that scoff at the pitiful world, and the useless universe, and violent, contemptible human race—books that laugh at the whole paltry scheme and deride it. Curious, for millions of men die every year with these feelings in their hearts. Why don't I write such a book? Because I have a family. There is no other reason."

shaking his fists in protest at man and the universe and its Maker, finally finding escape in his dream philosophy.

THE MYSTERIOUS STRANGER[31]

Once upon a time there lived in the village of Eseldorf in Medieval Austria three boys who, one day when they were idling on a wooded hill beyond the village, had a strange visitant. A glamorous youth came amongst them out of nowhere, who told them that his real name was Satan. He was a nephew, they found, of the Satan whom the village feared. But he asked them to call him Philip Traum. He knew their names without their telling him: Theodor Fischer (who tells the story for us), Nikolaus Bauman, and Seppi Wohlmeyer. The stranger was a good entertainer; he made birds out of clay and set them free, so that they flew away singing. Then he created a miniature castle and five hundred tiny villagers and workmen, whom he destroyed when they displeased him.

« « « . . . You know that kind of quiver that trembles around through you when you are seeing something so strange and enchanting and wonderful that it is just a fearful joy to be alive and look at it; and you know how you gaze, and your lips turn dry and your breath comes short, but you wouldn't be anywhere but there, not for the world. I was bursting to ask one question—I had it on my tongue's end and could hardly hold it back—but I was ashamed to ask it; it might be a rudeness. Satan set an ox down that he had been making, and smiled up at me and said:

---

[31] An entry in Mark Twain's *Notebook* in September, 1898, reads: "Story of little Satan, Jr., who came to Hannibal, went to school, was popular and greatly liked by those who knew his secret. The others were jealous and the girls didn't like him because he smelled of brimstone. He was always doing miracles—his pals knew they were miracles, the others thought they were mysteries." On May 12, 1899, Mark Twain wrote to William Dean Howells: "What I have been wanting is a chance to write a book without reserves—a book which should take account of no one's feelings, and no one's prejudices, opinions, beliefs, hopes, illusions, delusions; a book which should say my say, right out of my heart, in the plainest language and without a limitation of any sort. . . . It is under way now. . . . I believe I can make it say what I think of Man. . . . I let the madam into the secret day before yesterday, and locked the doors and read to her the opening chapters. She said—'It is perfectly horrible—and perfectly beautiful!'" (*Letters*, II, 681). The closing chapter was not found until after Mark Twain's death in 1910. Six years later "The Mysterious Stranger" was published serially in *Harper's Magazine* in seven installments, May to November, 1916.

"It wouldn't be a rudeness, and I should forgive it if it was. Have I seen him? Millions of times. From the time that I was a little child a thousand years old I was his second favorite among the nursery angels of our blood and lineage—to use a human phrase—yes, from that time until the Fall, eight thousand years, measured as you count time."

"Eight—thousand!"

"Yes." He turned to Seppi, and went on as if answering something that was in Seppi's mind: "Why, naturally I look like a boy, for that is what I am. With us what you call time is a spacious thing; it takes a long stretch of it to grow an angel to full age." There was a question in my mind, and he turned to me and answered it, "I am sixteen thousand years old—counting as you count." Then he turned to Nikolaus and said: "No, the Fall did not affect me nor the rest of the relationship. It was only he that I was named for who ate of the fruit of the tree and then beguiled the man and the woman with it. We others are still ignorant of sin; we are not able to commit it; we are without blemish, and shall abide in that estate always. We——" Two of the little workmen were quarreling, and in buzzing little bumblebee voices they were cursing and swearing at each other; now came blows and blood; then they locked themselves together in a life-and-death struggle. Satan reached out his hand and crushed the life out of them with his fingers, threw them away, wiped the red from his fingers on his handkerchief, and went on talking where he had left off: "We cannot do wrong; neither have we any disposition to do it, for we do not know what it is."

It seemed a strange speech, in the circumstances, but we barely noticed that, we were so shocked and grieved at the wanton murder he had committed—for murder it was, that was its true name, and it was without palliation or excuse, for the men had not wronged him in any way. It made us miserable, for we loved him, and had thought him so noble and so beautiful and gracious, and had honestly believed he was an angel; and to have him do this cruel thing—ah, it lowered him so, and we had had such pride in him. He went right on talking, just as if nothing had happened, telling about his travels, and the interesting things he had seen in the big worlds of our solar systems and of other solar systems far away in the remoteness of space, and about the customs of the immortals that inhabit them, somehow fascinating us, enchanting us, charming us in spite of the pitiful scene that was now under our eyes, for the wives of the little dead men had found the crushed and shapeless bodies and were crying over them, and sobbing and lamenting, and a priest was kneeling there with his hands crossed upon his breast, praying; and crowds and crowds of pitying friends were massed about them, reverently uncovered, with their bare heads bowed, and many with the tears running down—a scene which Satan paid no attention to until the small noise of the weeping and praying began to annoy him, then he reached out and took the heavy board seat out of our swing and brought it down and mashed all those people into the earth just as if they had been flies, and went on talking just the same.

An angel, and kill a priest! An angel who did not know how to do wrong, and yet destroys in cold blood hundreds of helpless poor men and women who had never done him any harm! It made us sick to see that awful deed, and to think that none of those poor creatures was prepared except the priest, for none of them had ever heard a mass or seen a church. And we were witnesses; we had seen these murders done and it was our duty to tell, and let the law take its course.

But he went on talking right along, and worked his enchantments upon us again with that fatal music of his voice. He made us forget everything; we could only listen to him, and love him, and be his slaves, to do with us as he would. He made us drunk with the joy of being with him, and of looking into the heaven of his eyes, and of feeling the ecstasy that thrilled along our veins from the touch of his hand.

The stranger had seen everything, he had been everywhere, he knew everything, and he forgot nothing. What another must study, he learned at a glance; there were no difficulties for him. And he made things live before you when he told about them. He saw the world made; he saw Adam created; he saw Samson surge against the pillars and bring the temple down in ruins about him; he saw Caesar's death; he told of the daily life in heaven; he had seen the damned writhing in the red waves of hell; and he made us see all these things, and it was as if we were on the spot and looking at them with our own eyes. And we felt them, too, but there was no sign that they were anything to him beyond mere entertainments. Those visions of hell, those poor babes and women and girls and lads and men shrieking and supplicating in anguish—why, we could hardly bear it, but he was as bland about it as if it had been so many imitation rats in an artificial fire.

And always when he was talking about men and women here on the earth and their doings—even their grandest and sublimest—we were secretly ashamed, for his manner showed that to him they and their doings were of paltry poor consequence; often you would think he was talking about flies, if you didn't know. Once he even said, in so many words, that our people down here were quite interesting to him, notwithstanding they were so dull and ignorant and trivial and conceited, and so diseased and rickety, and such a shabby, poor, worthless lot all around. He said it in a quite matter-of-course way and without bitterness, just as a person might talk about bricks or manure or any other thing that was of no consequence and hadn't feelings. I could see he meant no offense, but in my thoughts I set it down as not very good manners.

"Manners!" he said. "Why, it is merely the truth, and truth is good manners; manners are a fiction. The castle is done. Do you like it?"

Any one would have been obliged to like it. It was lovely to look at, it was so shapely and fine, and so cunningly perfect in all its particulars, even to the little flags waving from the turrets. . . .

A small storm-cloud began to settle down black over the castle, and the miniature lightning and thunder began to play, and the ground to quiver, and the wind to pipe and wheeze, and the rain to fall, and all the people flocked into the castle for shelter. The cloud settled down blacker and blacker, and one could see the castle only dimly through it; the lightning blazed out flash upon flash and pierced the castle and set it on fire, and the flames shone out red and fierce through the cloud, and the people came flying out, shrieking, but Satan brushed them back, paying no attention to our begging and crying and imploring; and in the midst of the howling of the wind and volleying of the thunder the magazine blew up, the earthquake rent the ground wide, and the castle's wreck and ruin tumbled into the chasm, which swallowed it from sight, and closed upon it, with all that innocent life, not one of the five hundred poor creatures escaping. Our hearts were broken; we could not keep from crying.

"Don't cry," Satan said; "they were of no value."

"But they are gone to hell!"

"Oh, it is no matter; we can make plenty more."

It was of no use to try to move him; evidently he was wholly without feeling, and could not understand. He was full of bubbling spirits, and as gay as if this were a wedding instead of a fiendish massacre. And he was bent on making us feel as he did, and of course his magic accomplished his desire. It was no trouble to him; he did whatever he pleased with us. In a little while we were dancing on that grave, and he was playing to us on a strange, sweet instrument which he took out of his pocket; and the music—but there is no music like that, unless perhaps in heaven, and that was where he brought it from, he said. It made one mad, for pleasure; and we could not take our eyes from him, and the looks that went out of our eyes came from our hearts, and their dumb speech was worship. He brought the dance from heaven, too, and the bliss of paradise was in it.

Presently he said he must go away on an errand. But we could not bear the thought of it, and clung to him, and pleaded with him to stay; and that pleased him, and he said so, and said he would not go yet, but would wait a little while and we would sit down and talk a few minutes longer; and he told us Satan was only his real name, and he was to be known by it to us alone, but he had chosen another one to be called by in the presence of others; just a common one, such as people have—Philip Traum.

It sounded so odd and mean for such a being! But it was his decision, and we said nothing; his decision was sufficient.

We had seen wonders this day; and my thoughts began to run on the pleasure it would be to tell them when I got home, but he noticed those thoughts, and said:

"No, all these matters are a secret among us four. I do not mind your trying to tell them, if you like, but I will protect your tongues, and nothing of the secret will escape from them."

It was a disappointment, but it couldn't be helped, and it cost us a sigh or two. We talked pleasantly along, and he was always reading our thoughts and responding to them, and it seemed to me that this was the most wonderful of all the things he did, but he interrupted my musings and said:

"No, it would be wonderful for you, but it is not wonderful for me. I am not limited like you. I am not subject to human conditions. I can measure and understand your human weaknesses, for I have studied them; but I have none of them. My flesh is not real, although it would seem firm to your touch; my clothes are not real; I am a spirit. . . . » » »

In Eseldorf were two priests, Father Adolf and Father Peter. Father Adolf had met the Devil face to face and had no fear of him. It made people shudder to hear him tell of his encounters with the Devil; they crossed themselves lest something fearful should happen. But they loved Father Peter; he taught them that God was all goodness and mercy. He drew down upon himself the displeasure of the Bishop by declaring that all poor human beings would be saved. And he was hated by the astrologer, whom he denounced as a charlatan. The Bishop dismissed him from his church and put Father Adolf in his place. His niece Marget, a classmate of the boys, suffered because of his disgrace; her music pupils left her and all her friends dropped away except Willhelm Meidling, the young lawyer who loved her. She and Father Peter were about to be turned out of their home penniless.

Just as Satan vanished from the boys' sight on the woody hilltop, they saw Father Peter wandering along the path from the village with his head bent down searching the ground. When he looked up and saw them, he said:

« « « . . . "How long have you been here, boys?"

"A little while, Father."

"Then it is since I came by, and maybe you can help me. Did you come up by the path?"

"Yes, Father."

"That is good. I came the same way. I have lost my wallet. There wasn't much in it, but a very little is much to me, for it was all I had. I suppose you haven't seen anything of it?"

"No, Father, but we will help you hunt."

"It is what I was going to ask you. Why, here it is!"

We hadn't noticed it; yet there it lay, right where Satan stood when he began to melt—if he did melt and it wasn't a delusion. Father Peter picked it up and looked very much surprised.

"It is mine," he said, "but not the contents. This is fat; mine was flat; mine was light; this is heavy." He opened it; it was stuffed as full as it could hold with gold coins. He let us gaze our fill; and of course we did gaze, for we had never seen so much money at one time before. All our mouths came open to say "Satan did it!" but nothing came out. There it was, you see—we couldn't tell what Satan didn't want told; he had said so himself.

"Boys, did you do this?"

It made us laugh. And it made him laugh, too, as soon as he thought what a foolish question it was.

"Who has been here?"

Our mouths came open to answer, but stood so for a moment, because we couldn't say "Nobody," for it wouldn't be true, and the right word didn't seem to come; then I thought of the right one, and said it:

"Not a human being."

"That is so," said the others, and let their mouths go shut.

"It is not so," said Father Peter, and looked at us very severely. "I came by here a while ago, and there was no one here, but that is nothing; some one has been here since. I don't mean to say that the person didn't pass here before you came, and I don't mean to say you saw him, but some one did pass, that I know. On your honor—you saw no one?"

"Not a human being."

"That is sufficient; I know you are telling me the truth."

He began to count the money on the path, we on our knees eagerly helping to stack it in little piles.

"It's eleven hundred ducats odd!" he said. "Oh, dear! if it were only mine—and I need it so!" and his voice broke and his lips quivered.

"It is yours, sir!" we all cried out at once, "every heller!"

"No—it isn't mine. Only four ducats are mine; the rest . . .!" He fell to dreaming, poor old soul, and caressing some of the coins in his hands, and forgot where he was, sitting there on his heels with his old gray head bare; it was pitiful to see. "No," he said waking up, "it isn't mine. I can't account for it. I think some enemy . . . it must be a trap!"

Nikolaus said: "Father Peter, with the exception of the astrologer you haven't a real enemy in the village—nor Marget, either. And not even a half-enemy that's rich enough to chance eleven hundred ducats to do you a mean turn. I'll ask you if that's so or not?"

He couldn't get around that argument, and it cheered him up. "But it isn't mine, you see—it isn't mine, in any case."

He said it in a wistful way, like a person that wouldn't be sorry, but glad, if anybody would contradict him.

"It is yours, Father Peter, and we are witness to it. Aren't we, boys?"

"Yes, we are—and we'll stand by it, too."

"Bless your hearts, you do almost persuade me; you do, indeed. If I had only a hundred-odd ducats of it! The house is mortgaged for it, and we've no home for our heads if we don't pay to-morrow. And that four ducats is all we've got in the——"

"It's yours, every bit of it, and you've got to take it—we are bail that it's all right. Aren't we, Theodor? Aren't we, Seppi?"

We two said Yes, and Nikolaus stuffed the money back into the shabby old wallet and made the owner take it. So he said he would use two hundred of it, for his house was good enough security for that, and would put the rest at interest till the rightful owner came for it; and on our side we must sign a paper showing how he got the money—a paper to show to the villagers as proof that he had not got out of his troubles dishonestly. . . . » » »

Father Peter paid his rent, and the attitude of the village became friendly once more. Marget's music pupils came back, and their household had returned to its normal life when the astrologer appeared in the village and heard of the priest's good fortune. He quizzed the boys and then declared that Father Peter had stolen the money from him and dropped it in his path so as to make them his witnesses that he had come by it honestly. After much excitement throughout the village Father Peter was thrust into prison and the money sealed up and placed in the hands of officers of the law. Marget's fortunes were again at the lowest ebb. Old Ursula, her nurse, took in washing, and her friends dropped away again. Public opinion so turned against Father Peter and her that though the boys wanted to go to comfort her their parents forbade them to go near the house. They were humiliated because their sons would be the only witnesses for Father Peter in his impending trial. Wilhelm Meidling would be his lawyer.

« « « ... I was walking along the path, feeling very down-hearted, when a most cheery and tingling freshening-up sensation went rippling through me, and I was too glad for any words, for I knew by that sign that Satan was by. I had noticed it before. Next moment he was alongside of me and I was telling him all my trouble and what had been happening to Marget and her uncle. While we were talking we turned a curve and saw old Ursula resting in the shade of a tree, and she had a lean stray kitten in her lap and was petting it. I asked her where she got it, and she said it came out of the woods and followed her; and she said it probably hadn't any mother or any friends and she was going to take it home and take care of it. Satan said:

"I understand you are very poor. Why do you want to add another mouth to feed? Why don't you give it to some rich person?"

Ursula bridled at this and said: "Perhaps you would like to have it. You must be rich, with your fine clothes and quality airs." Then she sniffed and said: "Give it to the rich—the idea! The rich don't care for anybody but themselves; it's only the poor that have feeling for the poor, and help them. The poor and God. God will provide for this kitten."

"What makes you think so?"

Ursula's eyes snapped with anger. "Because I know it!" she said. "Not a sparrow falls to the ground without His seeing it."

"But it falls, just the same. What good is seeing it fall?"

Old Ursula's jaws worked, but she could not get any word out for the moment, she was so horrified. When she got her tongue she stormed out, "Go about your business, you puppy, or I will take a stick to you!"

I could not speak, I was so scared. I knew that with his notions about the human race Satan would consider it a matter of no consequence to strike her dead, there being "plenty more"; but my tongue stood still, I could give her no warning. But nothing happened; Satan remained tranquil—tranquil and indifferent. I suppose he could not be insulted by Ursula any more than the king could be insulted by a tumble-bug. The old woman jumped to her feet when she made her remark, and did it as briskly as a young girl. It had been many years since she had done the like of that. That was Satan's influence; he was a fresh breeze to the weak and the sick, wherever he came. His presence affected even the lean kitten, and it skipped to the ground and began to chase a leaf. This surprised Ursula, and she stood looking at the creature and nodding her head wonderingly, her anger quite forgotten.

"What's come over it?" she said. "Awhile ago it could hardly walk."

"You have not seen a kitten of that breed before," said Satan.

Ursula was not proposing to be friendly with the mocking stranger, and she gave him an ungentle look and retorted: "Who asked you to come here and pester me, I'd like to know? And what do you know about what I've seen and what I haven't seen?"

"You haven't seen a kitten with the hair-spines on its tongue pointing to the front, have you?"

"No—nor you, either."

"Well, examine this one and see."

Ursula was become pretty spry, but the kitten was spryer, and she could not catch it, and had to give it up. Then Satan said:

"Give it a name, and maybe it will come."

Ursula tried several names, but the kitten was not interested.

"Call it Agnes. Try that."

The creature answered to the name and came. Ursula examined its tongue. "Upon my word, it's true!" she said. "I have not seen this kind of a cat before. Is it yours?"

"No."

"Then how did you know its name so pat?"

"Because all cats of that breed are named Agnes; they will not answer to any other."

Ursula was impressed. "It is the most wonderful thing!" Then a shadow of trouble came into her face, for her superstitions were aroused, and she reluctantly put the creature down, saying: "I suppose I must let it go; I am not afraid—no, not exactly that, though the priest—well, I've heard people—indeed, many people . . . And, besides, it is quite well now and can take care of itself." She sighed, and turned to go, murmuring: "It is such a pretty one, too, and would be such company—and the house is so sad and lonesome these troubled days . . . Miss Marget so mournful and just a shadow, and the old master shut up in jail."

"It seems a pity not to keep it," said Satan.

Ursula turned quickly—just as if she were hoping some one would encourage her.

"Why?" she asked, wistfully.

"Because this breed brings luck."

"Does it? Is it true? Young man, do you know it to be true? How does it bring luck?"

"Well, it brings money, anyway."

Ursula looked disappointed. "Money? A cat bring money? The idea! You could never sell it here; people do not buy cats here; one can't even give them away." She turned to go.

"I don't mean sell it. I mean have an income from it. This kind is called the Lucky Cat. Its owner finds four silver groschen in his pocket every morning."

I saw the indignation rising in the old woman's face. She was insulted. This boy was making fun of her. That was her thought. She thrust her hands into her pockets and straightened up to give him a piece of her mind. Her temper was all up, and hot. Her mouth came open and let out three words of a bitter sentence, . . . then it fell silent, and the anger in her face turned to surprise or wonder or fear, or something, and she slowly brought out her hands from her pockets and opened them and held them so. In one was my piece of money, in the other lay four silver groschen. She gazed a little while, perhaps to see if the groschen would vanish away; then she said, fervently:

"It's true—it's true—and I'm ashamed and beg forgiveness, O dear master and benefactor!" And she ran to Satan and kissed his hand, over and over again, according to the Austrian custom.

In her heart she probably believed it was a witch-cat and an agent of the Devil; but no matter, it was all the more certain to be able to keep its contract and furnish a daily good living for the family, for in matters of finance even the piousest of our peasants would have more confidence in an arrangement with the Devil than with an archangel. Ursula started homeward, with Agnes in her arms, and I said I wished I had her privilege of seeing Marget.

Then I caught my breath, for we were there. There in the parlor, and Marget standing looking at us, astonished. She was feeble and pale, but I knew that those conditions would not last in Satan's atmosphere, and it turned out so. I introduced Satan—that is, Philip Traum—and we sat down and talked. There was no constraint. We were simple folk, in our village, and when a stranger was a pleasant person we were soon friends. Marget wondered how we got in without her hearing us. Traum said the door was open, and we walked in and waited until she should turn around and greet us. This was not true; no door was open; we entered through the walls or the roof or down the chimney, or somehow; but no matter, what Satan wished a person to believe, the person was sure to believe, and so Marget was quite satisfied with that explanation. And then the main part of her mind was on Traum, anyway; she couldn't keep her eyes off him, he was so beautiful. That gratified me, and made me proud. I hoped he would show off some, but he didn't. He seemed only interested in being friendly and telling lies. He said he was an orphan. That made Marget pity him. The water came into her eyes. He said he had never known his mamma; she passed away while he was a young thing; and said his papa was in shattered health, and had no property to speak of—in fact, none of any earthly value—but he had an uncle in business down in the tropics, and he was very well off and had a monopoly, and it was from this uncle that he drew his support. The very mention of a kind uncle was enough to remind Marget of her own, and her eyes filled again. She said she hoped their two uncles would meet, some day. It made me shudder. Philip said he hoped so, too; and that made me shudder again.

"Maybe they will," said Marget. "Does your uncle travel much?"

"Oh yes, he goes all about; he has business everywhere."

And so they went on chatting, and poor Marget forgot her sorrow for one little while, anyway. It was probably the only really bright and cheery hour she had known lately. I saw she liked Philip, and I knew she would. And when he told her he was studying for the ministry I could see that she liked him better than ever. And then, when he promised to get her admitted to the jail so that she could see her uncle, that was the capstone. He said he would give the guards a little present, and she must always go in the evening after dark, and say nothing, "but just show this paper and pass in, and show it again when you come out"—and he scribbled some queer marks on the paper and gave it to her, and she was ever so thankful, and right away was in a fever for the sun to go down; for in that old, cruel time prisoners were not allowed to see their friends, and sometimes they spent years in the jails without ever seeing a friendly face. I judged that the marks on the paper were an enchantment, and that the guards would not know what they were doing, nor have any memory of it afterward; and that was indeed the way of it. Ursula put her head in at the door now and said:

"Supper's ready, miss." Then she saw us and looked frightened, and motioned me to come to her, which I did, and she asked if we had told about the cat. I said no, and she was relieved, and said please don't; for if Miss Marget knew, she would think it was an unholy cat and would send for a priest and have its gifts all purified out of it, and then there wouldn't be any more dividends. So I said we wouldn't tell, and she was satisfied. Then I was beginning to say good-by to Marget, but Satan interrupted and said, ever so politely—well, I don't remember just the words, but anyway he as good as invited himself to supper, and me, too. Of course Marget was miserably embarrassed, for she had not reason to suppose there would be half enough for a sick bird. Ursula heard him, and she came straight into the room, not a bit pleased. At first she was astonished to see Marget looking so fresh and rosy, and said so; then she spoke up in her native tongue, which was Bohemian, and said—as I learned afterward—"Send him away, Miss Marget; there's not victuals enough."

Before Marget could speak, Satan had the word, and was talking back to Ursula in her own language—which was a surprise to her, and for her mistress, too. He said, "Didn't I see you down the road awhile ago?"

"Yes, sir."

"Ah, that pleases me; I see you remember me." He stepped to her and whispered: "I told you it is a Lucky Cat. Don't be troubled; it will provide."

That sponged the slate of Ursula's feelings clean of its anxieties, and a deep, financial joy shone in her eyes. The cat's value was augmenting. It was getting full time for Marget to take some sort of notice of Satan's invitation, and she did it in the best way, the honest way that was natural to her. She said she had little to offer, but that we were welcome if we would share it with her.

We had supper in the kitchen, and Ursula waited at table. A small fish was in the frying-pan, crisp and brown and tempting, and one could see that Marget was not expecting such respectable food as this. Ursula brought it, and Marget divided it between Satan and me, declining to take any of it herself; and was beginning to say she did not care for fish to-day, but she did not finish the remark. It was because she noticed that another fish had appeared in the pan. She looked surprised, but did not say anything. She probably meant to inquire of Ursula about this later. There were other surprises: flesh and game and wines and fruits—things which had been strangers in that house lately; but Marget made no explanations, and now even looked unsurprised, which was Satan's influence, of course. Satan talked right along, and was entertaining, and made the time pass pleasantly and cheerfully; and although he told a good many lies, it was no harm in him, for he was only an angel and did not know any better. They do not know right from wrong; I knew this, because I remembered what he had said about it. He got on the good side of Ursula. He praised her to Marget, confidentially, but speaking just loud enough for Ursula to hear. He said she was a fine woman, and he hoped some day to bring her and his uncle together. Very soon Ursula was mincing and simpering around in a ridiculous girly way, and smoothing out her gown and prinking at herself like a foolish old hen, and all the time pretending she was not hearing what Satan was saying. I was ashamed, for it showed us to be what Satan considered us, a silly race and trivial. Satan said his uncle entertained a great deal, and to have a clever woman presiding over the festivities would double the attractions of the place.

"But your uncle is a gentleman, isn't he?" asked Marget.

"Yes," said Satan indifferently; "some even call him a Prince, out of compliment, but he is not bigoted; to him personal merit is everything, rank nothing."

My hand was hanging down by my chair; Agnes came along and licked it; by this act a secret was revealed. I started to say, "It is all a mistake; this is just a common, ordinary cat; the hair-needles on her tongue point inward, not outward." But the words did not come, because they couldn't. Satan smiled upon me, and I understood.

When it was dark Marget took food and wine and fruit, in a basket, and hurried away to the jail, and Satan and I walked toward my home. I was thinking to myself that I should like to see what the inside of the jail was like; Satan overheard the thought, and the next moment we were in the jail. We were in the torture-chamber, Satan said. The rack was there, and the other instruments, and there was a smoky lantern or two hanging on the walls and helping to make the place look dim and dreadful. There were people there—and executioners—but as they took no notice of us, it meant that we were invisible. A young man lay bound, and Satan said he was suspected of being a heretic, and the executioners were about to inquire into it. They asked the man to confess to the charge, and he said he could not, for it was not true. Then they drove splinter after splinter under his nails, and he shrieked with the pain. Satan was not disturbed, but I could not endure it, and had to be whisked out of there. I was faint and sick, but the fresh air revived me, and we walked toward my home. I said it was a brutal thing.

"No, it was a human thing. You should not insult the brutes by such a misuse of that word; they have not deserved it," and he went on talking like that. "It is like your paltry race—always lying, always claiming virtues which it hasn't got, always denying them to the higher animals, which alone possess them. No brute ever does a cruel thing—that is the monopoly of those with the Moral Sense." . . .

So all went well with Marget. She took food to Father Peter at the jail and reassured him in every way she could. Then old Ursula made the mistake of hiring Gottfried Narr to help her in and around the house. His grandmother had been burned as a witch. She had been guilty of curing bad headaches by kneading a person's head and neck with her fingers and, when accused, of confessing that her power came from the Devil. When Gottfried Narr was questioned about how Marget could afford to employ him, he revealed that she had plenty of money. People began to watch to find the source of her prosperity. Ursula had not confided to her that the cat had supernatural financial powers. While Marget at times had misgivings about their sudden prosperity, she was satisfied when Ursula assured her that Providence was caring for them. She entertained lavishly all friends who came, "proud as a princess." It was whispered about that witchcraft was at the bottom of her prosperity. When it was finally discovered, through the astrologer's quizzing Gottfried Narr, that the wines and food for a party she gave were not brought in from the outside, Father Adolf was convinced that they were produced by a new kind of witchcraft, and when the astrologer filled a four-quart bowl of wine from a pint bottle, Father Adolf declared the house bewitched and accursed. The boys were not brave enough to defend Marget or tell what they knew about the strange youth who had appeared at the party and imparted this strange power to the astrologer. And some weeks later when, in fear of what might be reported about them, they joined in stoning the woman accused of witchcraft, Satan accused them of cowardly acquiescence.

« « « That made him laugh again, and he said, "Yes, I was laughing at you, because, in fear of what others might report about you, you stoned the woman when your heart revolted at the act—but I was laughing at the others, too."

"Why?"

"Because their case was yours."

"How is that?"

"Well, there were sixty-eight people there, and sixty-two of them had no more desire to throw a stone than you had."

"Satan!"

"Oh, it's true. I know your race. It is made up of sheep. It is governed by minorities, seldom or never by majorities. It suppresses its feelings and its beliefs and follows the handful that makes the most noise. Sometimes the noisy handful is right, sometimes wrong; but no matter, the crowd follows it. The vast majority of the race, whether savage or civilized, are secretly kind-hearted and shrink from inflicting pain, but in the presence of the aggressive and pitiless minority they don't dare to assert themselves. Think of it! One kind-hearted creature spies upon another, and sees to it that he loyally helps in iniquities which revolt both of them. Speaking as an expert, I know that ninety-nine out of a hundred of your race were strongly against the killing of witches when that foolishness was first agitated by a handful of pious lunatics in the long ago. And I know that even to-day, after ages of transmitted prejudice and silly teaching, only one person in twenty puts any real heart into the harrying of a witch. And yet apparently everybody hates witches and wants them killed. Some day a handful will rise up on the other side and make the most noise—perhaps even a single daring man with a big voice and a determined front will do it—and in a week all the sheep will wheel and follow him, and witch-hunting will come to a sudden end.

Monarchies, aristocracies, and religions are all based upon that large defect in your race—the individual's distrust of his neighbor, and his desire, for safety's or comfort's sake, to stand well in his neighbor's eye. These institutions will always remain, and always flourish, and always oppress you, affront you, and degrade you, because you will always be and remain slaves of minorities. There was never a country where the majority of the people were in their secret hearts loyal to any of these institutions."

I did not like to hear our race called sheep, and said I did not think they were.

"Still, it is true, lamb," said Satan. "Look at you in war—what mutton you are, and how ridiculous!"

"In war? How?"

"There has never been a just one, never an honorable one—on the part of the instigator of the war.[32] I can see a million years ahead,

---

[32] Probably the most sardonic protest that Mark Twain ever wrote against man's inhumanity to man was his "War Prayer" (see A. B. Paine's *Mark Twain: A Bi-*

and this rule will never change in so many as half a dozen instances. The loud little handful—as usual—will shout for the war. The pulpit will—warily and cautiously—object—at first; the great, big, dull bulk of the nation will rub its sleepy eyes and try to make out why there should be a war, and will say, earnestly and indignantly, 'It is unjust and dishonorable, and there is no necessity for it.' Then the handful will shout louder. A few fair men on the other side will argue and reason against the war with speech and pen, and at first will have a hearing and be applauded; but it will not last long; those others will outshout them, and presently the anti-war audiences will thin out and lose populaity. Before long you will see this curious thing: the speakers stoned from the platform, and free speech strangled by hordes of furious men who in their secret hearts are still at one with those stoned speakers—as earlier—but do not dare to say so. And now the whole nation—pulpit and all—will take up the war-cry, and shout itself hoarse, and mob any honest man who ventures to open his mouth; and presently such mouths will cease to open. Next the statesmen will invent cheap lies, putting the blame upon the nation that is attacked, and every man will be glad of those conscience-soothing falsities, and will diligently study them, and refuse to examine any refutations of them; and thus he will by and by convince himself that the war is just, and will thank God for the better sleep he enjoys after this process of grotesque self-deception."[33] . . . » » »

---

ography, III, 1232-36): "O Lord our Father, our young patriots, idols of our hearts, go forth to battle—be Thou near them! With them—in spirit—we also go from the sweet peace of our beloved firesides to smite the foe.

"O Lord our God, help us to tear their soldiers to bloody shreds with our shells; help us to cover their smiling fields with the pale forms of their patriot dead; help us to drown the thunder of the guns with the shrieks of their wounded, writhing in pain; help us to lay waste their humble homes with a hurricane of fire; help us to wring the hearts of their unoffending widows with unavailing grief; help us to turn them out roofless with their little children to wander unfriended the wastes of their desolated land in rags and hunger and thirst, sports of the sun-flames of summer and the icy winds of winter, broken in spirit, worn with travail, imploring Thee for the refuge of the grave and denied it—for our sakes, who adore Thee, Lord, blast their hopes, blight their lives, protract their bitter pilgrimage, make heavy their steps, water their way with their tears, stain the white snow with the blood of their wounded feet! We ask of one who is the Spirit of love and who is the ever-faithful refuge and friend of all that are sore beset, and seek His aid with humble and contrite hearts. Grant our prayer, O Lord, and Thine shall be the praise and honor and glory now and forever, Amen."

[33] In the concluding chapter of his *Mark Twain: The Man and His Work*, 259,

Satan took Theodor on journeys to far places, to show him how absurdly the human race behaved the world over. He merely set him down wherever he wished to show these "wonders." Time and distance, he said, were mere human "artificialities." When they returned from China, he revealed to Theodor that he was about to take a hand in the fortunes of some of the boys' friends in the village. Father Peter would be acquitted when his case came up for trial, and his good name restored. The astrologer would be removed so that he could cause no more trouble. Also, he revealed that Nikolaus would be drowned while attempting to save little Lisa Brandt from drowning. These things turned out as he had foretold. He defended his interference in each case as more human than the normal life of the village would have been. He said that our race was mistaking good fortune for bad. Nikolaus and Lisa Brandt he had saved from years of anxiety and suffering. When Father Peter lost his reason, as a part of Satan's plan for him, and imagined himself an emperor, Theodor reproached Satan. Satan replied:

« « « . . . "Ah, you mistake; it was the truth. I said he would be happy the rest of his days, and he will, for he will always think he is the Emperor, and his pride in it and his joy in it will endure to the end. He is now, and will remain, the one utterly happy person in this empire."

"But the method of it, Satan, the method! Couldn't you have done it without depriving him of his reason?"

265, Edward Wagenknecht says: "It was under the influence of his hatred of imperialism that Mark Twain came, then, to write the caustic commentaries that make it possible for us to claim him today, at his best, as a prophet of the modern peace movement. 'All Christendom is a soldier camp,' he cried, 'the poor have been taxed in some nations to the starvation point to support the giant armaments which Christian governments have built up, each to protect itself from the rest of the Christian brotherhood, and incidentally to snatch any scrap of real estate left exposed by a wealthy owner.' . . . From this point of view also he wrote his magnificent 'Greeting from the Nineteenth Century to the Twentieth Century': 'I bring you the stately nation named Christendom, returning, bedraggled, besmirched, and dishonored from pirate raids in Kiao-Chow, Manchuria, South Africa, and the Philippines, with her soul full of meanness, her pockets full of boodle, and her mouth full of pious hypocrisies. Give her soap and a towel, but hide the looking-glass.' Because we are too lethargic to intrust the operation of our political and economic machinery to those who have brains and conscience . . . this very moment . . . we face the imminent possibility, indeed, of a return to chaos, which would undo everything that all the builders have achieved since life crawled out of the primeval slime. . . . If the day ever comes when we have a warless world, then, at last, the boy from Hannibal will take his place among the prophets."

It was difficult to irritate Satan, but that accomplished it.

"What an ass you are!" he said. "Are you so unobservant as not to have found out that sanity and happiness are an impossible combination? No sane man can be happy, for to him life is real, and he sees what a fearful thing it is. Only the mad can be happy, and not many of those. The few that imagine themselves kings or gods are happy, the rest are no happier than the sane. Of course, no man is entirely in his right mind at any time, but I have been referring to the extreme cases. I have taken from this man that trumpery thing which the race regards as a Mind; I have replaced his tin life with a silver-gilt fiction; you see the result—and you criticize! I said I would make him permanently happy, and I have done it. I have made him happy by the only means possible to his race—and you are not satisfied!" He heaved a discouraged sigh, and said, "It seems to me that this race is hard to please."

There it was, you see. He didn't seem to know any way to do a person a favor except by killing him or making a lunatic out of him. I apologized, as well as I could; but privately I did not think much of his processes—at that time.

Satan was accustomed to say that our race lived a life of continuous and uninterrupted self-deception. It duped itself from cradle to grave with shams and delusions which it mistook for realities, and this made its entire life a sham. Of the score of fine qualities which it imagined it had and was vain of, it really possessed hardly one. It regarded itself as gold, and was only brass. One day when he was in this vein he mentioned a detail—the sense of humor. I cheered up then, and took issue. I said we possessed it.

"There spoke the race!" he said; "always ready to claim what it hasn't got, and mistake its ounce of brass filings for a ton of gold-dust. You have a mongrel perception of humor, nothing more; a multitude of you possess that. This multitude see the comic side of a thousand low-grade and trivial things—broad incongruities, mainly; grotesqueries, absurdities, evokers of the horse-laugh. The ten thousand high-grade comicalities which exist in the world are sealed from their dull vision. Will a day come when the race will detect the funniness of these juvenilities and laugh at them—and by laughing at them destroy them? For your race, in its poverty, has unquestionably one really effective weapon—laughter. Power, money, persuasion, supplication, persecution—these can lift at a colossal humbug—push it a little—weaken it a little, century by century; but only laughter can blow it to rags and atoms at a blast. Against the assault of laughter nothing can stand. You are always fussing and fighting with your other weapons. Do you ever use that one? No; you leave it lying rusting. As a race, do you ever use it at all? No; you lack sense and the courage." . . . » » »

Finally Satan came to bid Theodor good-by, for the last time.

« « « "And you are going away, and will not come back any more?"

"Yes," he said. "We have comraded long together, and it has been pleasant—pleasant for both; but I must go now, and we shall not see each other any more."

"In this life, Satan, but in another? We shall meet in another, surely?"

Then, all tranquilly and soberly, he made the strange answer, "*There is no other.*" . . .

"*Life itself is only a vision, a dream.*"

It was electrical. By God! I had had that very thought a thousand times in my musings!

"*Nothing* exists; all is a dream. God—man—the world—the sun, the moon, the wilderness of stars—a dream, all a dream; they have no existence. *Nothing exists save empty space—and you!*"

"I!"

"And you are not you—you have no body, no blood, no bones, you are but a *thought*. I myself have no existence; I am but a dream—your dream, creature of your imagination. In a moment you will have realized this, then you will banish me from your visions and I shall dissolve into the nothingness out of which you made me. . . .

"I am perishing already—I am failing—I am passing away. In a little while you will be alone in shoreless space, to wander its limitless solitudes without friend or comrade forever—for you will remain a *thought*, the only existent thought, and by your nature inextinguishable, indestructible. But I, your poor servant, have revealed you to yourself and set you free. Dream other dreams, and better!

"Strange! that you should not have suspected years ago—centuries, ages, eons, ago! — for you have existed, companionless, through all the eternities. Strange, indeed, that you should not have suspected that your universe and its contents were only dreams, visions, fiction! Strange, because they are so frankly and hysterically insane—like all dreams: a God who could make good children as easily as bad, yet preferred to make bad ones; who could have made every one of them happy, yet never made a single happy one; who made them prize their bitter life, yet stingily cut it short; who gave his angels eternal happiness unearned, yet required his other children to earn it; who gave his angels painless lives, yet cursed his other children with biting miseries and maladies of mind and body; who mouths justice and invented hell—mouths mercy and invented hell—mouths Golden Rules, and forgiveness multiplied by seventy times seven, and invented hell; who mouths morals to other people and has none himself; who frowns upon crimes, yet commits them all; who created man without invitation, then tries to shuffle the responsibility for man's acts upon man, instead of honorably placing it where it belongs, upon himself; and finally, with altogether divine obtuseness, invites this poor, abused slave to worship him! . . .

"You perceive, *now*, that these things are all impossible except in a dream. You perceive that they are pure and puerile insanities, the silly creations of an imagination that is not conscious of its freaks—in a word, that they are a dream, and you the maker of it. The dream-marks are all present; you should have recognized them earlier.

"It is true, that which I have revealed to you; there is no God, no universe, no human race, no earthly life, no heaven, no hell. It is all a dream—a grotesque and foolish dream. Nothing exists but you. And you are but a *thought*—a vagrant thought, a useless thought, a homeless thought, wandering forlorn among the empty eternities!"

He vanished, and left me appalled; for I knew, and realized, that all he had said was true.[34] » » »

[34] In his *Notebook*, 360-63, Mark Twain wrote in 1898: "The being who to

3. The American Prometheus

IN SPITE OF Bernard De Voto's insistence that "Clemens's earliest impulses led to the production of humor" and that "nothing whatever suggests any literary impulse or desire of any other kind," there is some evidence that from the first Samuel L. Clemens visioned himself as a writer in the literary rather than the subliterary tradition. This desire paralleled his ambition to become a cultured gentleman. One recalls him standing with his sister, opera glass in hand, before Frederick Church's "Heart of the Andes" (*Letters*, I, 46 [1860]) in St. Louis between assignments on the river and then doing a writing exercise about the painting for his brother Orion in Keokuk. He has seen the dramatic landscape "several times." His brain *"gasps and strains"* in the effort to take in the full wonder of it. Apparently the later advice of Anson Burlingame in Hawaii only served to bring to the surface this latent ambition to become cultured.

In a way Mark Twain's attitude toward the early American humorists can be compared with that of Conrad's Lord Jim toward his ship's crew: apparently he felt almost from the first that he didn't have to be like them. In his youthful experiments while as-

me is the real God is the One who created the majestic universe and rules it. He is the only Originator . . . of thoughts. . . . This is indeed a God! He is not jealous, trivial, ignorant, revengeful—it is impossible. He has personal dignity—dignity answerable to this grandeur, this greatness, his might, his sublimity. He cares nothing for men's flatteries. . . . [His real Bible] the Bible of Nature tells us no word about any future life." Many of Mark Twain's most valued friends were clergymen. Joseph Twichell, a devout Christian minister in Hartford, was one of the Clemenses' neighbors with whom he most often exchanged ideas. In a letter written in Nevada in 1864 (*Letters*, I, 96), in which he accepted an invitation to speak at a church benefit, Mark Twain wrote: "Although I am not a very duty Christian, I take an absorbing interest in church affairs." It remains for someone thoroughly conversant with existentialism to show how nearly Mark Twain came to that philosophy in his last writings. He would have agreed with Kierkegaard in his distrust of institutions and in his pessimism. And many doctrines of recent theologians would have interested him. He would have agreed to Reinhold Niebuhr's doctrine of original sin and would have sought to understand Paul Tillich's doctrine of individualization, of conscience, and of justice.

sisting his brother with the *Hannibal Journal*, he wrote feature stories in the conventional English he had used for "The Dandy Frightening the Squatter." The success of Dickens' *Pickwick Papers*, which his brother enjoyed, may have excited his youthful fancy. His declaration to Ed Brownell that he would some day write a better book than the book of humor he was reading; his dissatisfaction in California with being known internationally as the author of "The Jumping Frog"; his simple-hearted satisfaction in Elmira with Livy's more literary taste when they were reading the proof sheets of *Innocents Abroad;* his giving up the *Buffalo Express* to move to Hartford to a conventional literary atmosphere; his giving up the lecture platform to devote himself to "literature"; his abortive experiment with an accepted model, *The Gilded Age;* his taking time out to write a conventional historical romance, *The Prince and the Pauper*, at the same time that he was taking his friend Howells' advice to work out the mine nearest home; and his final great creative attempt in the satire of *A Connecticut Yankee*—all indicate that from the first he felt himself to be pursuing a literary, not a subliterary career. That Mark Twain, like William Faulkner, as Lionel Trilling points out, "reinforces the colloquial tradition with the literary tradition" seems to have fulfilled a resolve that started him on a writing career.

With his forward-looking mind and his rare sensitivity Mark Twain related himself to twentieth-century writers beyond the date of his death, 1910. His commentators have found many instances of his foresight:

He was ahead of his time in condemning race discrimination. In San Francisco as a reporter he fearlessly lashed out against the treatment of the Chinese in the city. At the turn of the century he rebuked his native state for having "joined the lynchers." He was so sympathetic with Negroes, in fact, that his wife suggested to him the motto: "Treat every man as if he were colored until he is proved white."

His "Carnival of Crime" has for its theme a split personality.

He was a pioneer among semanticists with his insistence that writers first get their facts firm.

He was one of the first writers to use fingerprints in the solution of a mystery story.

He appreciated Thomas Paine long before Paine enthusiasts reprinted his writings.

He discovered the resort possibilities of Hawaii and Lake Tahoe in the 1860's.

Tom Sawyer, who ushered in air travel across the Atlantic in 1894, in *Tom Sawyer Abroad,* speaks of himself as an "erronort."

He anticipated James Gould Cozzens in his interest in courts of justice. As Gladys Bellamy says (*Mark Twain as a Literary Artist,* 359n.): "Mark Twain's fiction reflects his interest in legal procedure. Besides the trial of Father Peter, we have the trial scene which is, naturally, the high point of *Joan of Arc;* murder trials appear in *The Gilded Age, Tom Sawyer, Pudd'nhead Wilson,* and *Tom Sawyer, Detective.*"

He anticipated the vogue of Negro spirituals.

Albert Bigelow Paine points out in *Mark Twain's Note-Book* that he recorded an idea for something like radio and that he predicted movies and television.

He was ahead of the historians in his appraisal of the Gilded Age. None of them has revealed more effectively than he, in his novel with that title, the greed, acquisitiveness, and get-ahead-at-any-cost spirit of the period of expansion following the Civil War.

What has not been so generally noted is that in *A Connecticut Yankee* he previsioned the destruction of our scientific civilization through its own backfiring.

How fundamental his foresight was is realized when it is seen that in one way or another Mark Twain anticipated Sinclair Lewis, Theodore Dreiser, Edgar Lee Masters, and other twentieth-century naturalists. Gladys Bellamy, in her chapter entitled "Revolt From the Village" (*Mark Twain as a Literary Artist),* makes it clear that Sinclair Lewis' strictures on the "village virus" are to be found in embryo in *The Gilded Age* and *The Man That Corrupted Hadleyburg.* And the nineteenth-century Clemens's conviction that a man's life is determined by heredity and circumstance closely parallels the twentieth-century Dreiser's idea that environment and the combination of chemisms in a man's body determine his fate. Not only is Edgar Lee Masters' satire on obituary verse anticipated, in comic vein, in *Huckleberry Finn,* but the two men present much the same pessimistic view of the human race. And such naturalists as Hemingway acknowledge Mark Twain influence. They, as Lionel Trilling says of Huck, are possessed of "profound and bitter knowledge of human depravity"—though some of them cannot, with him, give man credit, also, for shining virtues.

Almost half a century before C. S. Lewis, a modern British Moralist, published *The Screwtape Letters* to expose the way in which the Devil insinuates himself among unsuspecting men, Mark Twain wrote an allegory to show how the Devil conducted himself among a gang of boys and their families. And the humorist was one of the first modern debunkers; among his more nearly serious writings his strictures upon James Fenimore Cooper and Sir Walter Scott were intended to prick popular bubbles, as Van Wyck Brooks later attempted to do in *The Ordeal of Mark Twain*. President Franklin D. Roosevelt found the term "New Deal" in *A Connecticut Yankee*, and while Mark Twain is not responsible for the "forgotten man," in *The American Claimant* he hailed America as the home of the common man. His Englishman exclaims, "What a civilization it is!—brought about almost wholly by the common man; not by Oxford-trained aristocrats, but by men who stand shoulder to shoulder in the ranks of life and earn the bread they eat." And it may be said that not even President Roosevelt was a more consistent pleader for the four freedoms than the Missouri humorist fifty years his senior—for freedom from want and fear, by implication, in *The Mysterious Stranger;* for freedom of worship, by implication, in *Captain Stormfield's Visit to Heaven;* for freedom of thought and its expression in the defense of the American press against Matthew Arnold's charge of irreverence in *The American Claimant*.

The last writings of Mark Twain forced his readers to recognize that his railing at man and man's fate, which they had earlier taken as coming from a half-serious, more or less transitory mood of dissatisfaction with man and God, was in reality a fixed conviction. Satan in *The Mysterious Stranger* laughs at the shams and cruelties of the human race—"shabby, poor, worthless vermin." This discovery forced upon the humorist's admirers an unwelcome reappraisal of "the delegate at large for the human race." The dispenser of American optimism, who "fired the national joke heard round the world," was a bitter pessimist. Many of them felt that he had betrayed his American heritage.

If, while he sojourned in India, Mark Twain could have caught the spirit of Oriental religions and their submission to the Order of the Universe with its paradoxes and its cycles of light and dark; or if he could have understood the Christian necessity for humility and atonement—of leaving to Caesar the things that are Caesar's—and centered his faith in the love and mercy that his heart craved for the world, Mark Twain's conclusion about human values might have been different. His tragedy was that he had spiritually to flounder through life. His blind struggle against man's fate was more humiliating and galling than the ordinary man's because his sensibilities were more acute than the ordinary man's. His case history might have served to illustrate the central theme of the great Mexican painter Orozco. Man's fate, as this muralist represents it, is not only to struggle against the evil of the world, against conflicting instincts and impulses within himself, but to take part in the war between the values which his mental endowment tells him are good and the conflicting values which other men's endowments tell them are good. In his mural at Pomona College in California, Orozco represents Prometheus attempting to change the universe. *Mark Twain in Eruption* makes clear the extent of this last type of struggle in Mark Twain. He was indeed something of a Prometheus.

To say, as Van Wyck Brooks did, that the humorist suffered from megalomania is not to say that he was different from most other human beings—at least from others who have contributed to the making of Western civilization. When Nature made man a self-conscious creature, the business of living, which in the animals is pursued unconsciously, became to man of prime concern. This preoccupation brought him a satisfaction that developed into pride equal to that by which the angels fell. Man's "occupational disease" is megalomania. From being, in his own eyes, the greatest of all God's creatures, he comes to feel, when he is an individual of rare endowment, sensitive to all his possibilities and that his conception of the world and how it should be run is the valid one. His effectiveness as an individual depends largely upon this conviction. Because his heart was larger and because all the reports that his senses brought in to him were more sharply clear than those of the general run of men, Mark Twain was more concerned than most men are about his world and the people that inhabited it. His reactions were more painful than those of the ordinary run of men, and his resentment at what he and others of his race had to suffer was more intense—so intense that only an irrational power, from his point of view, could be responsible for such a world.

Through the various controversies that have grown out of the attempt to account for Mark Twain's pessimism has come the conception of an American who was fifty years and more ahead of his country in his struggle for understanding. William Dean Howells, who knew him better than most men did, testified to "the intensity with which Mark Twain pierced to the heart of life, and the breadth of vision with which he compassed the whole world, and tried for the reason of things, and then left trying."

PART III

Mark Twain, Epigrammatist

MARK TWAIN, EPIGRAMMATIST

Not all of Mark Twain's humor was in the form of anecdotes, tall tales, satire, or burlesque. Much of his humor emerged from his philosophizing, in the form of quips and epigrams. His many disappointments in financial affairs, his disillusionments from his travels, his study of history and its darker records of civilization, his personal bereavements of wife and children, his ultimate despair over "the damned human race"—all developed in his writing a vein of irony that revealed itself best in witty, pungent, and often sardonic remarks. These bits of philosophical humor, usually loaded with serious implications unsuspected by the casual reader when he encounters them in their context, are scattered all through his writings. Since their full impact cannot be felt when they are scattered and diffused among other passages of such varying tone, a representative collection of these epigrams is brought together and offered to the reader here so that he can better appreciate this other facet of the Mark Twain personality:

> [Speaking of missionaries] How sad it is to think of the multitudes who have gone to their graves in this beautiful island [of Hawaii] and never knew there was a hell.
>
> *(Roughing It)*

> Negroes are deemed as good as white people, in Venice, and so this man feels no desire to go back to his native land. His judgment is correct.
>
> *(The Innocents Abroad)*

> If all the poetry and nonsense that have been discharged upon the

fountains and the bland scenery of this region [Palestine] were collected in a book, it would make a most valuable volume to burn.
(*Ibid.*)

I can *understand* German as well as the maniac that invented it, but I *talk* it best through an interpreter.
(*A Tramp Abroad*)

Training is everything. The peach was once a bitter almond; cauliflower is nothing but cabbage with a college education.
(*Pudd'nhead Wilson's Calendar*)

One of the most striking differences between a cat and a lie is that a cat has only nine lives.
(*Ibid.*)

When I reflect upon the number of disagreeable people who I know have gone to a better world, I am moved to lead a different life.
(*Ibid.*)

Nothing so needs reforming as other people's habits.
(*Ibid.*)

Behold, the fool saith, "Put not all thine eggs in the one basket"—which is but a manner of saying, "Scatter your money and your attention"; but the wise man saith, "Put all your eggs in the one basket and—WATCH THAT BASKET."
(*Ibid.*)

If you pick up a starving dog and make him prosperous, he will not bite you. This is the principal difference between a dog and a man.
(*Ibid.*)

Few things are harder to put up with than the annoyance of a good example.
(*Ibid.*)

April 1. This is the day upon which we are reminded of what we are on the other three hundred and sixty-four.
(*Ibid.*)

The chief function of an English journal is that of all other journals the world over: it must keep the public eye fixed admiringly upon certain things, and keep it diligently diverted from certain others.
(The American Claimant)

... the traveling Briton's everlasting disposition [is] to generalize whole mountain ranges from single sample-grains of sand. ...
(Ibid.)

... I asked Tom if countries always apologized when they had done wrong, and he says: "Yes; the little ones does."
(Tom Sawyer Abroad)

Only sixty years ago [the Fiji Islanders] were sunk in darkness; now they have the bicycle.
(Following the Equator)

There are many humorous things in the world; among them the white man's notion that he is less savage than the other savages.
(Ibid.)

I admire [Cecil Rhodes], I frankly confess it; and when his day comes I shall buy a piece of the rope for a keepsake.
(Ibid.)

It is more trouble to make a maxim than it is to do right.
(Pudd'nhead Wilson's New Calendar)

In statesmanship get the formalities right, never mind about the moralities.
(Ibid.)

When in doubt, tell the truth.
(Ibid.)

Truth is the most valuable thing we have. Let us economize it.
(Ibid.)

We should be careful to get out of an experience only the wisdom that is in it—and stop there; lest we be like the cat that sits down on a hot stove-lid. She will never sit down on a hot stove-lid again; but also she will never sit down on a cold one any more.

(Ibid.)

There are those who scoff at the school-boy, calling him frivolous and shallow. Yet it was the school-boy who said, "Faith is believing what you know ain't so."

(Ibid.)

We can secure other people's approval, if we do right and try hard; but our own is worth a hundred of it, and no way has been found out of securing that.

(Ibid.)

There is a Moral Sense, and there is an Immoral Sense. History shows us that the Moral Sense enables us to perceive morality and how to avoid it, and that the Immoral Sense enables us to perceive immorality and how to enjoy it.

(Ibid.)

The English are mentioned in the Bible: Blessed are the meek, for they shall inherit the earth.

(Ibid.)

It is easier to stay out than get out.

(Ibid.)

It is by the goodness of God that in our country we have those three unspeakably precious things: freedom of speech, freedom of conscience, and the prudence never to practice either of them.

(Ibid.)

Man will do many things to get himself loved, he will do all things to get himself envied.

(Ibid.)

Nothing is so ignorant as a man's left hand, except a lady's watch.

(Ibid.)

Be careless in your dress if you must, but keep a tidy soul.

(Ibid.)

"*Classic.*" A book which people praise and don't read.

(Ibid.)

Man is the Only Animal that Blushes. Or needs to.

(Ibid.)

The man with a new idea is a Crank until the idea succeeds.

(Ibid.)

Prosperity is the best protector of principle.

(Ibid.)

Few of us can stand prosperity. Another man's, I mean.

(Ibid.)

Each person is born to one possession which outvalues all his others —his last breath.

(Ibid.)

It takes your enemy and your friend, working together, to hurt you to the heart; the one to slander you and the other to get the news to you.

(Ibid.)

Grief can take care of itself; but to get the full value of a joy you must have somebody to divide it with.

(Ibid.)

Let me make the superstitions of a nation and I care not who makes its laws or its songs either.

(Ibid.)

Wrinkles should merely indicate where smiles have been.

(Ibid.)

True irreverence is disrespect for another man's god.

(Ibid.)

There are two times in a man's life when he should not speculate: when he can't afford it, and when he can.

(Ibid.)

Every one is a moon, and has a dark side which he never shows to anybody.

(Ibid.)

The very ink with which all history is written is merely fluid prejudice.

(Ibid.)

There isn't a Parallel of Latitude but thinks it would have been the Equator if it had had its rights.

(Ibid.)

In a country where they have ranks and castes, a man isn't ever a man, he is only part of a man, he can't ever get his full growth.

(A Connecticut Yankee)

Whereas principle is a great and noble protection against showy and degrading vanities and vices, poverty is worth six of it.

(The $30,000 Bequest)

A man who cannot learn stands in his own light.

("An Entertaining Article")

We all love to get some of the drippings of Conspicuousness, and we will put up with a single, humble drip, if we can't get any more.

("Does the Race of Man Love A Lord?")

Monday.—I believe I see what the week is for: it is to give time to rest up from the weariness of Sunday.

(Adam's Diary)

Principles have no real force except when one is well fed.

(Ibid.)

A loving good heart is riches, and riches enough, and . . . without it intellect is poverty.

(Eve's Diary)

To have nothing the matter with you and no habits is pretty tame, pretty colorless. It is just the way a saint feels, I reckon; it is at least the way he looks.

(Europe and Elsewhere)

Germanic people are just mad for views—they never get enough of a view—if they owned Mont Blanc, they would build a tower on top of it.

(Ibid.)

Later I took a twilight tramp along the high banks of a moist ditch called the Guires River. If it was my river I wouldn't leave it outdoors nights, in this careless way, where any dog can come along and lap it up. It is a tributary of the Rhone when it is in better health.

(Ibid.)

It was twenty-eight miles to Marseilles, and we should have been obliged to row. That would not have been pleasure; it would have meant work for the sailor, and I do not like work even when another person does it.

(Ibid.)

The Moral Sense teaches us what is right, and how to avoid it—when unpopular.

(Ibid.)

Half of the results of a good intention are evil; half the results of an evil intention are good. No man can command the results, nor allot them.

(Ibid.)

The Offensive Stranger: Take yet one more instance. With the best intentions the missionary has been laboring in China for eighty years.
The Dervish: The evil result is—
The Offensive Stranger: That nearly a hundred thousand Chinamen have acquired our Civilization.
The Dervish: And the good result is—
The Offensive Stranger: That by the compassion of God four hundred millions have escaped it.

(Ibid.)

It is our nature to conform; it is a force which not many can successfully resist.

(Ibid.)

We are creatures of outside influences; as a rule we do not think, we only imitate.

(Ibid.)

Hardly a man in the world has an opinion upon morals, politics, or religion which he got otherwise than through his associations and sympathies. Broadly speaking, there are none but corn-pone opinions. And broadly speaking, corn-pone stands for self-approval. Self-approval is acquired mainly from the approval of other people. The result is conformity.

(Ibid.)

We all do no end of feeling, and we mistake it for thinking. And out of it we get an aggregation which we consider a boon. Its name is Public Opinion. It is held in reverence. It settles everything. Some think it the Voice of God.

(Ibid.)

I said it was like being in heaven. The Reverend rebukingly and rather pointedly advised me to make the most of it, then.

(Atlantic Monthly Papers, December 1877)

I do not admire the human being—as an intellectual marvel—as much as I did when I was young, and got him out of books, and did not know him personally.

(What Is Man and Other Essays)

The watch doesn't wind itself and doesn't regulate itself—these things are done exteriorly. Outside influences, outside circumstances, wind the *man* and regulate him.

(Ibid.)

And there was poor Columbus. He elaborated a deep plan to find a new route to an old country. Circumstances revised his plan for him, and he found a new *world*. And *he* gets the credit of it to this day. He hadn't anything to do with it.

(Ibid.)

The *temperament* is the man; the thing tricked out with clothes and named Man is merely its shadow, nothing more.

(Ibid.)

Who review the books? People who never wrote one.
(Sketches New and Old)

The less a man knows the bigger noise he makes and the higher salary he commands.
(Ibid.)

"Well, the fact is, there warn't any interest in a murder trial then, because the fellow was always brought in 'not guilty,' the jury expecting him to do as much for them some time...."
(Ibid.)

Barring that natural expression of villainy which we all have, the man looked honest enough.
(Ibid.)

"My experience of men had long ago taught me that one of the surest ways of begetting an enemy was to do some stranger an act of kindness which should lay upon him the irritating sense of an obligation."
(Autobiography)

It is good to begin life poor; it is good to begin life rich—these are wholesome; but to begin it poor and *prospectively* rich! The man who has not experienced it cannot imagine the curse of it.
(Ibid.)

When I was younger I could remember anything, whether it had happened or not; but my faculties are decaying now, and soon I shall be so that I cannot remember any but the things that never happened.
(Ibid.)

A Chronology of Mark Twain's Life and Literary Career

1835	Born November 30 at Florida, Missouri, fifth child of John Clemens and Jane Lampton Clemens.
1839–53 (age 4–18)	Boyhood at Hannibal, Missouri. Apprentice printer (age 14–18). Wrote local items for the Hannibal *Journal* (age 16–18).
1852 (age 16)	Published "The Dandy Frightening the Squatter" in the May 1 issue of the Boston *Carpet-Bag*.
1853–57 (age 18–22)	Itinerant printer in Philadelphia, New York City, and Muscatine and Keokuk, Iowa. Job printer in Cincinnati.
1857–61 (age 22–26)	Mississippi river-boat pilot. Apprentice: April, 1857–September, 1858. Licensed pilot: September, 1858–April, 1861.
1861 (age 26)	Two weeks' campaigning with Missouri Confederate rangers.
1861 (age 26)	Appointed personal secretary to the Secretary of Nevada Territory. Nineteen-day trip on the Overland Stage to Carson City, July–August. First impressions of the West. Silver prospecting experiences, later recorded in *Roughing It*.
1862–64 (age 27–28)	Reporter for the Virginia City *Territorial Enterprise*. First use of pen name "Mark Twain" in issue of February 2, 1863.
1864 (age 28)	Reporter for the San Francisco *Morning Call* and the Sacramento *Union*. Wrote articles and sketches for the *Golden Era*, the *Californian*, and the *Territorial Enter-*

	prise. Fraternized with Bret Harte, Artemus Ward, Orpheus C. Kerr, and Joaquin Miller.
1865 (age 29)	Published "Jim Smiley and His Jumping Frog" in November 18 issue of *The New York Saturday Press*. Continued writing for the western newspapers.
1866 (age 30)	Voyage to the Hawaiian Islands, March–August. First public lecture in San Francisco on October 2.
1867 (age 31)	Trip to New York City via the sea and Panama. Published "Jim Wolfe and the Tom-Cats" in the July 14 issue of the New York *Sunday Mercury*. Published first book, *The Celebrated Jumping Frog*, in May. Excursion to Southern Europe and the Holy Land on the ship "Quaker City," June–November. Travel letters to the *Alta California* and the New York *Tribune*.
1868 (age 32)	Letters to the New York *Tribune, Herald, Citizen*, and other newspapers. Lectures in California and Nevada on "The Holy Land." Began lifelong friendship with Rev. Joseph H. Twitchell and William Dean Howells.
1869 (age 32–33)	Published *The Innocents Abroad* in July. Edited, and wrote editorials for, the Buffalo *Express*. Wrote sketches for *Packard's Monthly*, *Wood's Magazine*, and other periodicals. Lecture tour during the winter season.
1870 (age 34)	Married Olivia Langdon, January 2. Contributions to the Buffalo *Express* and *Galaxy Magazine*. Began his sporadic "Autobiography" (not published in full until 1924).
1871 (age 35)	Edited the "Memoranda" for the *Galaxy Magazine*. Published his burlesque *Autobiography and First Romance* (booklet) in February. Lecture tour during the winter season.
1872 (age 36)	Published *Roughing It* in February. Settled in Hartford, Connecticut. Son Langdon died (age 2). First trip to England, on business, August–November: first impressions of England and introduction to English celebrities and fashionable life of London. First met Edwin Booth, Robert Browning, Lewis Carroll, Charles Kingsley, Ivan Turgenieff, and other writers. Visit to Dr. John Brown at Edinburgh.

1873 (age 37–38)	Letters to the New York *Tribune* on the Sandwich Islands. Second trip to England in May. First London lectures, on "Our Fellow Savages of the Sandwich Islands," October and December–January. Published *The Gilded Age* with Charles Dudley Warner in December.
1874 (age 38)	Wrote "Colonel Sellers," a play.
1875 (age 39)	Published "Old Times on the Mississippi" serially in the *Atlantic Monthly,* January–June, 1875. Published *Sketches New and Old* in July. Began crusade for international copyright.
1876 (age 40)	Published "The Recent Carnival of Crime" in the June issue of the *Atlantic Monthly.* Privately printed *1601.* Published *The Adventures of Tom Sawyer* in December.
1877 (age 41)	Holiday trip to Bermuda with Rev. Joseph H. Twichell in May. Whittier birthday speech in Boston, December 17.
1878 (age 42)	Visited Germany, Switzerland, Italy, and France: April, 1878–July, 1879.
1879 (age 43)	Third visit to London, July–August. Speech on "The Babies" at the General Grant dinner in Chicago, November 13. Met Darwin, Whistler, and Henry James.
1880 (age 44)	Published *A Tramp Abroad* in March.
1881 (age 45)	Published *The Prince and the Pauper* in December.
1882 (age 46)	Revisited the Mississippi and scenes of his boyhood and piloting days in April. Published *The Stolen White Elephant and Other Stories* in June.
1883 (age 47)	Published *Life on the Mississippi* in May. Wrote "The American Claimant," a play, with William Dean Howells. Called on Ralph Waldo Emerson. Met Matthew Arnold.
1884 (age 48)	Published *The Adventures of Huckleberry Finn* in December. Platform readings with George Washington Cable during the winter season.

1885 (age 50)   Began the publishing firm of Charles L. Webster and Company with his nephew and published General Grant's *Memoirs*. Saved Grant and his widow from insolvency. Published "A Campaign That Failed" in December issue of *Century*.

1887 (age 51)   Met Robert Louis Stevenson.

1888 (age 52)   Wrote "Meisterschaft," a play. Awarded an honorary Master of Arts degree by Yale University in June.

1889 (age 53)   Met Rudyard Kipling, a lifelong admirer. Published *A Connecticut Yankee in King Arthur's Court* in December.

1890 (age 54)   Began promotion of the Paige typesetting machine.

1891 (age 55)   Began several years' sojourn on the Continent with visits and residences in Paris, Geneva, Germany, Switzerland, France, and Italy with long stays in Berlin and Florence.

1891 (age 55)   Dined with Emperor William II, February 20.

1892 (age 56)   Published *The American Claimant* in May. Met the Prince of Wales.

1893 (age 57)   Published "£1,000,000 Bank-Note" in January issue of *Century*. Published "Tom Sawyer Abroad" serially in *St. Nicholas*, November, 1893–April, 1894. Published "Pudd'nhead Wilson" serially in *Century*, December, 1893–June, 1894. Celebrated back in America as "The Belle of New York."

1894 (age 58)   Failure of Charles L. Webster and Company in April and refusal of Mark Twain to accept bankruptcy ($70,000 personal indebtedness paid off during the next two and one half years). Published *Tom Sawyer Abroad* in April and *Pudd'nhead Wilson* in November.

1895–96 (age 59–60)   Published "Personal Recollections of Joan of Arc" serially in *Harper's Magazine*, April, 1895–April, 1896. Lecture trip around the world, July, 1895–July, 1896.

1896 (age 60)   Death of his daughter Susan (age 25) on August 18. Published *Joan of Arc* in May and *Tom Sawyer, Detec-*

	tive and Other Stories in November. Fourth London residence, August, 1896–July, 1897.
1897 (age 62)	Published *How To Tell a Story and Other Essays* in March. Elected to the London Savage Club in May. Published *Following the Equator* in November.
1897–99 (age 61–62)	European residences: Switzerland, Vienna, Germany.
1899–1900 (age 63–64)	Fifth London residence, June, 1899–October, 1900.
1899 (age 63)	Audience with Emperor Franz Joseph in Vienna. Visit to Sweden, July–October. Published "The Man That Corrupted Hadleyburg" in December issue of *Harper's Magazine*. First publication of uniform editions of Mark Twain's works: Author's National Edition, De Luxe Edition, Autograph Edition (1899–1907).
1900 (age 64)	Met the King of Sweden and Winston Churchill in England. Appealed to the House of Lords for a perpetual copyright law. Many speeches in London and New York. Returned to America and a national welcome, October 15. Popularly called "Ambassador-at-Large of the U.S.A."
1901 (age 65)	Published "To the Person Sitting in Darkness" in the February issue of the *North American Review*. Was awarded an honorary Doctor of Letters degree by Yale University. Hillcrest Edition and Underwood Edition of Mark Twain's works published.
1902 (age 66)	Published "A Double-Barrelled Detective Story" in January–February *Harper's Magazine*. Awarded an honorary Doctor of Laws degree by the University of Missouri in June. Revisited Hannibal, Missouri, boyhood home.
1903–1904 (age 67–68)	Returned to Florence, Italy, for seven months' residence, in November.
1904 (age 68)	Published portions of his autobiography in *Harper's Weekly* and the *North American Review*. Published *Extracts from Adam's Diary* in April. Death of Mrs. Clemens in Italy, June 5.

CHRONOLOGY OF MARK TWAIN'S LIFE AND LITERARY CAREER

1905 (age 69)   Wrote "The War Prayer." Published *King Leopold's Soliloquy* in September. Published "Eve's Diary" in December *Harper's Magazine*. Honored at his seventieth birthday celebration, December 5.

1906–1908 (age 70–72)   Dictated remainder of his autobiography to Albert Bigelow Paine and published portions in the *North American Review*, September, 1906–December, 1907.

1906 (age 70)   Privately printed *What Is Man?* in August. Published *The $30,000 Bequest and Other Stories*.

1907 (age 71)   Published *Christian Science* in February. Sixth and last visit to England, June–July. Tremendous ovation. Met George Bernard Shaw. Presented to the King and Queen at Buckingham Palace. Awarded an honorary Doctor of Letters degree by Oxford University, June 26. Published "Extract from Captain Stormfield's Visit to Heaven" in *Harper's Magazine*, December, 1907–January, 1908.

1908 (age 72)   Last Lotos Club speech in New York, January 11.

1908–1910 (age 72–74)   Spent last years in residence at "Stormfield," Redding, Connecticut.

1909 (age 73)   Published *Is Shakespeare Dead?* in April. Death of his daughter Jean (age 24) on December 24.

1910 (age 74)   Death of Mark Twain, April 21. Buried at Elmira, New York.

POSTHUMOUS PUBLICATIONS

1910   *Mark Twain's Speeches.*
1916   *The Mysterious Stranger: A Romance.*
1917   *What Is Man? and Other Essays.*
     Mark Twain's Letters, edited by Albert Bigelow Paine.
1919   *The Curious Republic of Gondour and Other Whimsical Sketches.*
1922   *The Mysterious Stranger and Other Stories.*
1923   *Mark Twain's Speeches*, edited by Albert Bigelow Paine.
     Europe and Elsewhere.
     Definitive Edition of Mark Twain's works.

1924 *Mark Twain's Autobiography*, edited by Albert Bigelow Paine.
1925 *Conversation, as It Was by the Social Fireside, in the Time of the Tudors.*
1926 *Sketches of the Sixties, by Bret Harte and Mark Twain*, edited by John Howell.
1928 *The Adventures of Thomas Jefferson Snodgrass*, edited by Charles Honce.
1929 *Mark Twain's Works.* Stormfield Edition. 37 vols.
1935 *Mark Twain's Notebook*, edited by Albert Bigelow Paine. *Slovenly Peter (Der Struwwelpeter). Translated into English Jingles from the Original German of Dr. Heinrich Hoffman by Mark Twain.*
1938 *Mark Twain's Letters from the Sandwich Islands Written for the "Sacramento Union,"* edited by G. Ezra Dane.
The Washoe Giant in San Francisco, edited by Franklin Walker and G. Ezra Dane.
1939 *Letters from Honolulu, Written for the "Sacramento Union" by Mark Twain*, edited by John W. Vandercook.
1940 *Mark Twain in Eruption. Hitherto Unpublished Pages about Men and Events, by Mark Twain*, edited by Bernard De Voto.
1941 *Mark Twain's Letters to Will Bowen*, edited by Theodore Hornberger.
Republican Letters, edited by Cyril Clemens.
1942 *Mark Twain's Letters in the Muscatine Journal*, edited by Edgar M. Branch.
1943 *Washington in 1868*, edited by Cyril Clemens.
1946 *The Letters of Quintus Curtius Snodgrass*, edited by Ernest E. Leisy.
1949 *The Letters of Mark Twain to Mrs. Fairbanks*, edited by Dixon Wecter.
The Love Letters of Mark Twain, edited by Dixon Wecter.
1952 *Report from Paradise* (including the complete *Captain Stormfield's Visit to Heaven*), edited by Dixon Wecter.
1957 *The Complete Short Stories of Mark Twain* (collected here for the first time), edited by Charles Neider.
Mark Twain of the Enterprise: Newspaper Arts and Other Documents, 1862–64, edited by Henry Nash Smith with the assistance of Frederick Anderson.
1958 *Traveling with the Innocents Abroad; Mark Twain's Original Reports from Europe and the Holy Land*, edited by Daniel M. McKeithan.

Selected Bibliography

A WEALTH OF biographical study, critical commentary, and bibliographical investigation is available to both the general reader and the specialized student, on many aspects of Mark Twain. For useful general bibliographies the reader is referred to Minnie M. Brashear, Bernard De Voto, Archibald Henderson, Fred Pattee, and Edward Wagenknecht, whose works are listed in the bibliography. More extensive bibliographies can be found in the following:

Cambridge History of American Literature (ed. by W. P. Trent and others). New York, G. P. Putnam's Sons, 1922.
Hartwick, Harry. "Bibliographies" in Walter F. Taylor, *A History of American Letters*. New York, American Book Company, 1936.
Literary History of the United States (ed. by Robert E. Spiller and others). New York, The Macmillan Company, 1948.
The Literature of the American People (ed. by Arthur H. Quinn). New York, Appleton-Century-Crofts, 1951.

Lists of articles appearing in American periodicals are available in the following sources:

"American Bibliography," published annually since 1922 in *Publications of the Modern Language Association*.
Leary, Lewis (comp.). *Articles on American Literature Appearing in Current Periodicals, 1900–1950*. Durham, N. C., Duke University Press, 1954.
——— (comp.). "Doctoral Dissertations in American Literature," *American Literature*, Vol. XX (May, 1948), 175 (kept up to date by quarterly announcements in "Research in Progress" in *American Literature* and annually in April supplements of *Publications of the Modern Language Association*).

Leisy, Ernest E., and Jay B. Hubbell (comps.). "Doctoral Dissertations in American Literature," *American Literature*, Vol. IV (January, 1933), 438.

Information about first appearances and first editions of Mark Twain's writings is provided in the following:
Johnson, Merle C. *A Bibliography of the Works of Mark Twain, Samuel Langhorne Clemens*. Revised edition. New York, Harper & Brothers, 1935.
Paine, Albert Bigelow. *Mark Twain, A Biography*. New York, Harper & Brothers, 1912.

Although the bulk of Mark Twain criticism appeared during the 1930's, many appreciative studies of this writer had already appeared early in the century, a direct outgrowth of Mark Twain's personality and literary career and of the Mark Twain legends that had accumulated ever since H. R. Haweis first launched the humorist into literary controversy in 1882. Scholarly interest has continued steadily during the past two decades. Critical as well as popular interest seems to be increasing, as evidenced by the appearance, during the past nine years, of ten major studies of Mark Twain and by the attention given to him by two leading critics, T. S. Eliot and Lionel Trilling. The publication of fourteen volumes of previously unpublished Mark Twain writings since the 1935 centennial is further testimony to his continued popularity with modern readers (see the Chronology on page 410 of this book).

The following is a selected list of these many biographies, critiques, scholarly investigations, and special studies. Among these items the reader will find books and articles that deal with Mark Twain's American background, his western experiences, his travels abroad, his humor, influences upon him, his literary reputation and significance, his personality and popularity, his social attitudes and critical ideas, his personal and philosophical problems, and many other facets of the man and his time.

Allen, Jerry. *The Adventures of Mark Twain*. Boston, Little Brown & Company, 1954.
Andrews, Kenneth R. *Nook Farm: Mark Twain's Hartford Circle*. Cambridge, Harvard University Press, 1950.
Armstrong, C. J. "Mark Twain's Early Writings Discovered," *Missouri Historical Review*, Vol. XXIV (July, 1930), 485–501.
Asselineau, Roger. *The Literary Reputation of Mark Twain from 1910 to 1950; A Critical Essay and Bibliography*. Paris, M. Didier, 1954.

Bellamy, Gladys C. *Mark Twain as a Literary Artist*. Norman, University of Oklahoma Press, 1950.
Benson, Ivan. *Mark Twain's Western Years, Together with Hitherto Unprinted Clemens Western Items*. Stanford, California, Stanford University Press, 1938.
Blair, Walter. *Native American Humor: 1800–1900*. New York, American Book Company, 1937.
Branch, Edgar M. *The Literary Apprenticeship of Mark Twain, with Selections from His Apprentice Writing*. Urbana, University of Illinois Press, 1950.
Brashear, M. M. "Formative Influences in the Mind and Writings of Mark Twain." University of North Carolina Ph. D. dissertation, 1930.
———. "Mark Twain in Perspective," *Virginia Quarterly Review*, Vol. XII (January, 1936), 127–30.
———. "Mark Twain Juvenilia," *American Literature*, Vol. II (1930), 25–53.
———. *Mark Twain, Son of Missouri*, Chapel Hill, University of North Carolina Press, 1934.
———. "The Washoe Giant in San Francisco," *The Mississippi Valley Historical Review*, Vol. XXVI (June, 1939), 111–12.
Brooks, Van Wyck. *The Ordeal of Mark Twain*. New York, E. P. Dutton and Company, 1920; revised edition, 1933.
Canby, Henry S. *Turn West, Turn East: Mark Twain and Henry James*. Boston, Houghton Mifflin Company, 1951.
Cardwell, Guy A. *Twins of Genius*. East Lansing, Michigan State College Press, 1953.
Carter, Paul J. "The Social and Political Ideas of Mark Twain." University of Cincinnati Ph. D. dissertation, 1939.
Clemens, Clara. *My Father, Mark Twain*. New York, Harper & Brothers, 1931.
Clemens, Cyril. *Mark Twain, the Letter Writer*. Boston, Meador Publishing Company, 1932.
———. *My Cousin, Mark Twain*. Emmaus, Pennsylvania, Rodale Press, 1939.
Clemens, Will M. *Mark Twain: His Life and Works, a Biographical Sketch*. N.p., The Clemens Publishing Company, 1892, 1894.
Compton, Charles H. "Who Reads Mark Twain?," *American Mercury*, Vol. XXXI (April, 1934), 465–71.
Davidson, William Earl. "Mark Twain and Conscience." University of Missouri M. A. thesis, 1940.
De Voto, Bernard. *Mark Twain's America*. Boston, Little, Brown & Company, 1932.

———— (ed.). *Mark Twain in Eruption.* New York, Harper & Brothers, 1940.

————. *Mark Twain at Work.* Cambridge, Harvard University Press, 1942.

Dreiser, Theodore. "Mark the Double Twain," *English Journal,* Vol. XXIV (1935), 615-27.

Eastman, Max. "Mark Twain's Elmira," *Harper's Magazine,* Vol. CLXXVI (May, 1938), 620-32.

Ferguson, DeLancey. *Mark Twain: Man and Legend.* Indianapolis, Bobbs-Merrill Company, 1943.

Fisher, Henry W. *Abroad with Mark Twain and Eugene Field: Tales They Told to a Fellow Correspondent.* New York, Nicholas L. Brown, 1922.

Foner, Philip S. *Mark Twain: Social Critic.* New York, International Publishers, 1958.

Frear, Walter F. *Mark Twain and Hawaii.* Chicago, The Lakeside Press, 1947.

Gillis, W. R. *Gold Rush Days with Mark Twain.* New York, Albert and Charles Boni, 1930.

Goodpasture, A. V. "Mark Twain, Southerner," *Tennessee Historical Magazine,* Series II, Vol. I (July, 1931), 253-60.

Gould, Edgar H. "Mark Twain on the Writing of Fiction," *American Literature,* Vol. XXVI, No. 2 (May, 1954), 141-53.

Haweis, H. R. *American Humorists.* New York, J. B. Alden, 1885.

Hemminghaus, Edgar H. *Mark Twain in Germany.* New York, Columbia University Press, 1939.

Henderson, Archibald. *Mark Twain.* New York, Duckworth and Company, 1912.

————. "The International Fame of Mark Twain," *North American Review,* Vol. CXCII (1910), 805-15.

Howells, William Dean. *My Mark Twain: Reminiscences and Criticisms.* New York, Harper & Brothers, 1910.

Kipling, Rudyard. "An Interview with Mark Twain," in *From Sea to Sea: Letters of Travel.* Part II, Vol. XVI of *The Writings in Prose and Verse of Rudyard Kipling.* New York, Charles Scribner's Sons, 1899.

Lawton, Mary. *A Lifetime with Mark Twain: The Memories of Katie Leary,* for Thirty Years His Faithful and Devoted Servant. New York, Harcourt, Brace & Company, 1925.

Leacock, Stephen. *Mark Twain.* New York, D. Appleton & Company, 1933.

Lorch, Fred W. "Mark Twain in Iowa," *Iowa Journal of History and Politics,* Vol. XXVII (1929), 408-56, and Vol. XXVIII (1930), 268-76.

McGuire, Edna E. Schupp. "Mark Twain as a Historical Novelist." University of Missouri M. A. thesis, 1944.

McHarg, Cynthia Wilkes. "An Investigation of Mark Twain's Views on War as Found in His Writings." University of Missouri M. A. thesis, 1942.

Mack, Effie M. *Mark Twain in Nevada.* New York, Charles Scribner's Sons, 1947.

Martin, Alma. *A Vocabulary Study of "The Gilded Age."* Webster Groves, Missouri, Mark Twain Society, 1930.

Matthews, Brander. "Mark Twain and the Art of Writing," *Harper's Magazine,* Vol. CXLI (October, 1910), 635-43.

———. "Memories of Mark Twain" in *The Tocsin of Revolt and Other Essays.* New York, Charles Scribner's Sons, 1922.

Meine, Franklin J. (ed.). *Tall Tales of the Southwest: An Anthology of Southern and Southwestern Humor, 1830–1860.* (American Deserta Series.) New York, Alfred A. Knopf, 1930.

Moore, Olin Harris. "Mark Twain and Don Quixote," *Publications of the Modern Language Association,* Vol. XXXVII (1922), 324-46.

Paine, Albert Bigelow. *Mark Twain: A Biography.* The Personal and Literary Life of Samuel Langhorne Clemens. 3 vols. New York, Harper & Brothers, 1912.

———. *The Boys' Life of Mark Twain.* New York, Harper & Brothers, 1916.

———. *A Short Life of Mark Twain.* New York, Harper & Brothers, 1920.

Parrington, Vernon L. *The Beginnings of Critical Realism in America, 1860–1900,* Vol. III of *Main Currents in American Thought.* ("The Backwash of the Frontier—Mark Twain") New York, Harcourt, Brace & Company, 1927.

Pattee, Fred Lewis. *A History of American Literature Since 1870.* New York, The Century Company, 1915.

Pellowe, W. E. S. *Mark Twain: Pilgrim from Hannibal.* New York, Hobson Book Press, 1945.

Pochmann, Henry A. "The Mind of Mark Twain." University of Texas M. A. thesis, 1924.

Ramsay, Robert L., and Frances G. Emberson. *A Mark Twain Lexicon* (*The University of Missouri Studies,* Vol. XIII, No. 1). Columbia, 1938.

Read, Opie P. *Mark Twain and I.* Chicago, Reilly and Lee, 1940.

Rodney, Robert M. "Mark Twain in England: A Study of the English Criticism of and Attitude Toward Mark Twain, 1867-1940." University of Wisconsin Ph. D. dissertation, 1945.

Rourke, Constance M. *American Humor: A Study of National Character.* New York, Harcourt, Brace & Company, 1931.

Schönemann, Friedrich. *Mark Twain als literarische Persönlichkeit.* Jena, Verlag der Frommanschen Buchhandlung, Walter Biedermann, 1925.

Scott, Arthur L. (ed.). *Mark Twain: Selected Criticism.* Dallas, Southern Methodist University Press, 1955.

Scott, Harold P. "Mark Twain's Theory of Humor: An Analysis of the Laughable in Literature." University of Michigan Ph. D. dissertation, n.d.

Sherman, Stuart P. *Our Contemporary Literature.* New York, Henry Holt and Company, 1917.

———. "Mark Twain," *The Cambridge History of American Literature,* III. New York, G. P. Putnam's Sons, 1921.

———. "Mark Twain's Last Phase," *The Main Stream.* New York, Charles Scribner's Sons, 1927.

Sosey, Frank H. "Palmyra and Its Historical Environment," *Missouri Historical Review,* Vol. XXIII (1929), 361–79.

Suddath, Jennie K. "Mark Twain and Henry Adams in Account with the Gilded Age." University of Missouri M.A. thesis, 1942.

Swann, William R. "An Investigation of the Career of Mark Twain as a Journalist." University of Missouri M.A. thesis, 1941.

Taylor, Coley B. *Mark Twain's Margins on Thackeray's Swift.* New York, Gotham House, 1935.

Trilling, Lionel. *The Liberal Imagination: Essays on Literature and Society.* New York, The Viking Press, 1950.

Twain, Mark. *The Adventures of Huckleberry Finn.* New York, Chanticleer Press, 1950.

———. *Traveling with the Innocents Abroad* (ed. by Daniel M. McKeithan). Norman, University of Oklahoma Press, 1958.

———. *The Complete Short Stories of Mark Twain* (ed. by Charles Neider). Long Island, New York, Garden City, 1957.

———. *The Portable Mark Twain* (ed. by Bernard De Voto). New York, Viking Press, 1946.

———. *The Favorite Works of Mark Twain* (ed. by Owen Wister). Long Island, New York, Garden City, 1939.

Underwood, John C. *Literature and Insurgency.* New York, M. Kennerly, 1914.

Van Doren, Carl. "Mark Twain," *Dictionary of American Biography.* New York, Charles Scribner's Sons, 1928.

———. *The American Novel: 1789–1939*. New York, The Macmillan Company, 1921.
Wagenknecht, Edward. *Mark Twain: The Man and His Work*. New Haven, Yale University Press, 1935.
Walker, Franklin. *San Francisco's Literary Frontier*. New York, Alfred A. Knopf, 1930.
Wallace, Elizabeth. *Mark Twain and the Happy Island*. Chicago, A. C. McClurg and Company, 1913.
Webster, Samuel C. *Mark Twain, Business Man*. Boston, Little, Brown and Company, 1946.
Wecter, Dixon. *Sam Clemens of Hannibal*. Boston, Houghton Mifflin Company, 1952. (A meticulous scholar, Dixon Wecter planned a two-volume life of Mark Twain. Only *Sam Clemens of Hannibal*, the first section, was finished before Wecter's untimely death at the age of forty-four.)
West, Victor R. *Folklore in the Works of Mark Twain* (*University of Nebraska Studies in Language, Literature, and Criticism*, No. 10). Lincoln, 1930.
Wister, Owen. "In Homage to Mark Twain," *Harper's Magazine*, Vol. CLXXI (1935), 547–56.

Index

"Adam's Diary": 400
Addison, Joseph: 182
American Claimant, The: 390, 397
Animal descriptions: 82, 83, 83n.
Arnold, Matthew: 390
"Atlantic Monthly Papers": 402
"Autobiography and First Romance": 9n.

"Baker's Bluejay Yarn": 105–109
Barlow, Joel: 9n.
Beard, Dan: 304n., 310n.
Bellamy, Gladys: 6n., 389
Bixby, Horace: 57n., 60, 64
Bradford, Gamaliel: 197
Branch, Edgar: 6n.
Brashear, Minnie M.: 7n.
Brooks, Van Wyck: 301, 390, 391
Browne, Charles Farrar: *see* Ward, Artemus
Brownell, Ed: 388
Bryant, William Cullen: 136n.
Burlingame, Anson: 387

Cable, George Washington: 15n.
Captain Stormfield's Visit to Heaven: 390
"Celebrated Jumping Frog of Calaveras County, The": 105, 185, 187, 196, 197–203
Cervantes, Miguel de: 115, 303
Clemens, Jane: 12n.
Clemens, Livy: 9n., 388
Clemens, Orion: 78, 79n.

Clemens, Susie: 302
Connecticut Yankee in King Arthur's Court, A: 116, 135, 168, 189, 190, 301, 302, 303, 304-64, 388, 389, 390, 400
Conrad, Joseph: 387
Cooper, James Fenimore: 9n., 16n., 136n., 390
Cozzens, James Gould: 389

Dana, Richard Henry: 192
"Dandy Frightening the Squatter, The": 186, 193, 194-96, 388
"Dan Murphy": 187
DeVoto, Bernard: 6n., 17n., 186, 387
Dickens, Charles: 9n., 388
Disney, Walt: 83
"Does the Race of Man Love a Lord?": 400
"Double-Barreled Detective Story, A": 191
Dreiser, Theodore: 389
"Dutch Nick Massacre": 187

Edward VII: 130n.
Eliot, T. S.: 6n.
Emerson, Ralph Waldo: 136n.
"Entertaining Article, An": 400
Europe and Elsewhere: 111-13, 113-14, 115, 169, 169-70, 400
"Eve's Diary": 187, 400

"Facts Concerning the Recent Carnival of Crime in Connecticut, The": 188, 229, 230-45, 388
Faulkner, William: 388
Field, Joseph M.: 183, 184
Field, Matthew C.: 183, 184
Fink, Mike: 181, 183, 184
Following the Equator: 35-36, 111, 151-52, 169, 177, 397
Frontier boasters: 52n.

Garland, Hamlin: 11n.
Gilded Age, The: 6n., 9n., 188, 388, 389
Grant, General Ulysses S.: 207n., 210n.
Griswold, Rufus W.: 185

Hale, Edward Everett: 253
Harris, Joel Chandler: 15n.

Harte, Bret: 79, 98n., 99
Hawthorne, Nathaniel: 136n., 246
Hemingway, Ernest: 390
Henderson, Archibald: 206, 253n.
Hobbes, Thomas: 182
Holy Land: 139n.
Howells, William Dean: 136n., 207n., 229, 254, 365n., 392
Hubbard, Elbert: 253
Huckleberry Finn, The Adventures of: 5, 6n., 9n., 17n., 27–29, 30–34, 37–38, 49–52, 52n., 68–69, 69–71, 71–75, 75–77, 115, 186, 188, 210, 301, 389
Hume, David: 127n.

Innocents Abroad, The: 92, 138–39, 140–43, 143–46, 146–48, 149, 150, 154–55, 155, 156–57, 168, 187, 388, 395
Irving, Washington: 9n., 136n.

James, Henry: 136n.
Joan of Arc: 116, 190, 389
Jones, Betsy: 186
"Journalism in Tennessee": 187

Keemle, Charles: 183, 184
Kierkegaard: 387n.
Kinney, John D.: 92n.

"Last Lotos Club Speech": 187, 192–93
Lecky, W. E. H.: 115, 169n.
Lewis, C. S.: 390
Lewis, Sinclair: 389
Life on the Mississippi: 5, 6n., 9n., 47–49, 56–57, 58–60, 60–64, 64–67
Longfellow, Henry Wadsworth: 136n.
Lowell, James Russell: 136n., 197
Ludlow, Noah M.: 183, 184

Malory, Sir Thomas: 302n., 305n.
"Man That Corrupted Hadleyburg, The": 16n., 186, 191, 254–301, 364, 389
Mark Twain's Autobiography: 403
Mark Twain's contempt for conformity: 71n.
Mark Twain's "duel": 158n.

421

Mark Twain in Eruption: 39, 42–45
Mark Twain's Letters: 116n., 117n.
Masters, Edgar Lee: 389
Meine, J. Franklin: 183
Miller, Joaquin: 79
Murrell, John: 181
"My First Literary Venture": 194n.
Mysterious Stranger, The: 16n., 168, 192, 364, 365–86, 390

Niebuhr, Reinhold: 387n.

"Oddities and Eccentricities of the English, The": 110n.
"Old Times on the Mississippi": 52–56
Orozco, José: 391

Paine, Albert Bigelow: 9n., 389
Paine, Thomas: 389
Parrington, Vernon L.: 303n.
Pattee, Fred Lewis: 6n.
Pessimism: 254n.
"Petrified Man, The": 191
Prince and the Pauper, The: 116, 117n., 117–19, 119–20, 121–22, 122–25, 125–27, 127–29, 130, 130–31, 131–34, 135, 189, 388
"Private History of a Campaign That Failed, The": 186, 189, 210, 211–29
Porter, William T.: 183
Problem of evil: 25n.
Pudd'nhead Wilson: 11n., 190, 389, 396, 397

Quarles, John: 8, 9n., 12n., 197
Quarles, Patsy: 12n.
"Queen Victoria's Jubilee": 110

Robb, John S.: 183, 185, 186
Rodney, Robert M.: 7n.
Roosevelt, Franklin D.: 318n., 390
Roughing It: 79–82, 82–83, 83–85, 86–88, 88–90, 90–91, 93–97, 97–98, 99–105, 171–72, 187, 395

Scott, Sir Walter: 390
"Scrap of Curious History, A": 246–53
Sketches New and Old: 11n., 403

Slade, J. A.: 98n.
Smith, Solomon: 184
"Speech on the Babies": 188, 207-10
Swift, Jonathan: 303

"$30,000 Bequest, The": 400
Thoreau, Henry David: 172n.
Tillich, Paul: 387n.
Tom Sawyer, The Adventures of: 6n., 9n., 12n., 17n., 18-23, 24-27, 115, 188, 210, 389
Tom Sawyer Abroad: 17n., 389, 397
Tom Sawyer, Detective: 17n., 17-18, 389
"To Raise Poultry": 187, 188, 203, 204-206
Tramp Abroad, A: 38-42, 105-109, 153, 154, 157-58, 159-68, 172-76, 396
Trilling, Lionel: 6n., 206, 388, 390
"True Story, A": 11n.
Twichell, Joseph: 38n.
Tyler, Royall: 193

Voltaire, François: 177

Wagenknecht, Edward: 196, 383n.
Ward, Artemus: 187, 194n.
Warner, Charles Dudley: 188
"War Prayer": 381n.
Webster, Charles: 302
Wecter, Dixon: 7n.
Wetmore, Alphonso: 183
"What Is Man?": 16n., 168, 192, 402
Whittier, John Greenleaf: 11n.
Wilhelm II, emperor of Germany: 130n.
"William Dean Howells": 192
Wister, Owen: 99

Yonge, Charlotte: 117n.

www.ingramcontent.com/pod-product-compliance
Lightning Source LLC
Chambersburg PA
CBHW020939230426
43666CB00005B/85